The American Ideas

13 American Originals to Know, Love, and Defend

By an American

AMERICAN BOOKS

BOSTON • KANSAS CITY

Designed in America by Truxaw Creative

Typesetting completed in America on July 4, 2011

Printed In The United States of America on American paper

ISBN 978-0-9823161-1-5

For More About The American Ideas, Visit www.theamericanideas.com

The Publisher May Be Contacted At:

> Telephone (U.S.): (888)-580-4650

> Email: contact@theamericanideas.com

Please visit us at www.TheAmericanIdeas.com for additional resources:

- References and citations
- Index of terms
- Dynamic detail on the Action Points from each of the 13 Ideas

We hope you will join the discussion.

*To all Americans – those past, those present,
and those yet to be born and arrive*

Contents

THE AMERICAN IDEAS

INTRODUCTION

The Enduring Power of American Ideas

America. At its core, it really isn't a place.

It is – and always has been – a splendid set of Ideas.

And what Ideas! America was a hope for something better – better than all ancient civilizations, better than Greece, better than Rome, even better than the Renaissance of Greece and Rome. People felt it in their bones: *There must be a better way to live. There has to be a shining city on a hill.*

And those Ideas came to life in people's hearts and minds long before they found a geographical home. These ideas involved many new pieces. They put the individual human being at the center rather than kings and queens, dictators, and nation-states.

These Ideas suggested, in an ever-clearer voice, that those individuals had immense value. They should be allowed to fully possess and enjoy the freedom, justice, dignity, and opportunity that God had seen fit to give them all. In a wonderful paradox, everyone was created both different and yet somehow equal. Everyone had a responsibility not only to provide for themselves and their own, but also to be generous with others.

Religion would be respected by all and have great influence but would control no person or government. Society would be a place of nurturing and mutual support, not manipulation and crippling fear. Government would be "of the people, by the people, for the people,"[1] not of, by, and for the privileged few. Political and military alliances would give way to shared discoveries and mutually beneficial trade. There would be fewer wars, less violence, diminished terror – and a lot more peace.

As years went by, none of this seemed like it should be that hard to see, to have, and to hold. Although the old notions clung tenaciously – at times ferociously – to the throats of suffering, longing millions, they finally gave way to the Ideas.

These new Ideas stirred souls – first brave souls, then many souls. The first brave souls were called heretics, troublemakers, rebels. But they wouldn't give up the Ideas. They knew that these Ideas were more important than kings, more important than power, more important than "the tread of mighty armies."[2] The Ideas won – not everywhere, not even today - but they won in enough hearts and in enough places to be the Ideas that will not go away.

And then these Ideas found themselves welcome and growing in a New World.

America.

The word has extraordinary magic. For four hundred years, that word has been the best drawing card in the history of the planet. The Ideas were more important than the name, but the name – America – somehow, some way, became shorthand for the Ideas.

Few nations, governments, or cultures have enjoyed the longevity of the concept called "America." Immense empires have collapsed, mighty governments have fallen, churning nations have been reborn again and again, but through it all the concept of America has flourished.

America has offered hope, relief, safety, opportunity, liberty – hope of a better life, relief from never-ending subjugation, safety from endless violence, opportunity to create and build and prosper, and liberty to own your own life at last.

And for four hundred years, people have responded to that concept of America. The Old World, whose kings and wars drove so many to the New World, slowly learned from that New World the stupendous lesson that it could do without kings. Even if those European "Americans" couldn't or didn't come to America, they took the concept of America back into Europe and threw the rascals out.

Many millions who had a glimpse of the Ideas decided to go to a place where they hoped these Ideas might be real and enveloping – the place called "America." They came with inexplicable faith, sure of what they hoped for and certain of what they hadn't yet seen.

And they came with fire in their hearts. They came to experience the Ideas for themselves – no filtering, no nobles, no classes, no artificial breakdowns of the human race into "superiors" and "inferiors." And the fire in their hearts helped set the Ideas aflame in America.

The concept of America – and the dreams and hopes behind it – isn't owned by the American government or culture. It's owned by everyone. People can be Americans in spirit even if they aren't or can't be Americans in citizenship. Many have been, many are, and many more will be Americans.

So, first and foremost, America is a set of Ideas. It is a set of Ideas before it is anything else – a society or a government or a nation or a place outlined on a map of the world.

It was a set of Ideas in its childhood in the 17th century, its youth in the 18th, and its adolescence in the 19th. It was still a set of Ideas as it came of age in the 20th century and is no less so as it explores its youthful maturity in the 21st.

It was a set of Ideas when it was ruled by a king who was the law and is still a set of Ideas when ruled by a law which is the king.

It was a set of Ideas before nation-states, against nation-states, and as a nation-state.

It was a set of Ideas when a few colonies clung to the European ocean-umbilical, when the Louisiana Purchase doubled its size, and now as it rests comfortably "from sea to shining sea."[3]

The world has always needed the Ideas and a place – a laboratory, a home – where those Ideas could be defined and lived. The concept of America as an embodiment of the great Ideas is universal – universally desired, and universally needed.

America the Concept and America the Place

America's existence is irrefutable proof that everyone is indeed created to be free and equal, that no tyrant has ever had the right to put a saddle on the backs of the many and drive them with whips and spurs. America the place broke away from an empire, but America the Ideas broke away from an old way of thinking and a deadly way of living. America is a new thing in history, an invention that is – even with its flaws – a great city on a high hill.

America the Ideas took root strongly and grew mightily in America the place. It existed in people's minds for a thousand years or more, sometimes clearly, sometimes fragmentarily, always looking for clarification and affirmation. At long last, there it was, a place – America the Beautiful. Beautiful for its natural splendor, but even more so for the stunning Ideas that were planted there.

America the place gave America the Ideas a home, and those Ideas have lived comfortably in this inviting place for centuries. American citizens are the beneficiaries of a long, slow climb out of the unrelenting curses of humankind – tyranny of the soul, oppression of the mind, thwarting of the will, and battering of the body. It was always ugly everywhere else, or about to be so. But in America, there were better Ideas, different Ideas, the *American* Ideas.

And American citizens themselves have had diverse opinions representing in a million different ways the American Ideas. Sometimes Americans don't realize how rare these Ideas are, how different they are, how much they stray from the historical norm. It's only normal to appreciate less what you already have and even to take it for granted. But the American Ideas are worth savoring. Taking them for granted could mean watching them fade away.

So the Ideas found a home in the New World, just to the north of the Spanish and Portuguese conquistadores. It's been a very good home. The Ideas have thrived in these safe and nurturing surroundings.

But it's good for us to remember that the Ideas didn't start here. They began in the hearts and minds of human beings, people who were willing to think in new ways about the 13 Ideas in this book, bright souls who were eager to put those Ideas into action wherever and whenever and however they could. These 13 grand Ideas are humanity's treasure, represented but not owned by America.

Long before there were American citizens, there were Americans – people who believed that life could be better, should be better, and would be better given enough hope and faith, character and commitment, hard work and persistence, a measure of wisdom and a whole lot of common sense.

And even today, there are Americans who are not American citizens. They are those men and women who trace their own thinking back through the Enlightenment and Renaissance and spiritual wakenings to the Greco-Roman dawn of Western Civilization. If they share the American Ideas, they're Americans – even if they can't describe the origins of their thinking, even if they've been born into a non-Western culture.

This was the true driver of the huge influx of people into the place called "America" – they were Americans in spirit before they were Americans in name.

America, the home of Ideas. There has never been anything quite like it, anytime or anywhere. These American Ideas have great and enduring power. They have many homes, but for now – and we hope, forever – they've had their principal residence in a place called "America." But the Ideas made the place, not the other way around.

The Ideas Find a Home

Irish musician and philanthropist Bono said, "America is more than just a country; it's an idea."[4] He saw clearly what so many have seen or felt – that there are two Americas: the America of mountains and rivers and plains inhabited by flesh-and-blood, living beings, and the America of the mind that inhabits flesh-and-blood human beings.

These 13 Ideas took firm root in the place that is America. The great discovery that ended the Dark Ages wasn't the printing press or medicine. It was liberty, first sighted in 1215 when the English Magna Carta put the first cracks in the supposed "divine right of kings" to run roughshod over everyone else. Liberty sputtered and struggled in Europe for centuries until it finally found its home in the American Idea of Freedom.

Was it mere coincidence that as the knowledge of freedom grew, a new place was discovered where this knowledge could be lived? That as our ancestors sought religious and political and economic freedom, a new world provided a safe haven to escape the always-raging storm of Old-World tyranny?

America the place became the embodiment of an American Idea of Freedom.

America the place is where people can be dragged in as slaves and have descendants who own businesses and lead governments. Where the Irish can escape 800 long years of oppression and build transcontinental railroads and become president. Where Jews can choose any career and are truly safe for the first time since Solomon. Where Latinos leave families and swim rivers and negotiate with monsters to get to the land of opportunity.

America is the craziest, wildest, most impossible-to-explain place on the face of the planet – even more, in the history of the planet. People with nothing – no money, no pedigree, no name, no connections – can live in peace and freedom like kings. And there are no kings. We have some good leaders and some bad leaders and many mediocre leaders, and we possess the right and means to be rid of them all.

There's bounty – good bounty, not in the main taken from others, but built instead out of nothing with creativity and hard work. We can (mostly) read, think, believe, and say what we want. We can go where we want, live where we want, work where we want. We have an overtaxed and overburdened but ferociously productive economic system, which anyone can enter to create new wealth. And we have the Rule of Law – a gift hard to get, hard to keep, easy to lose, but for now, still ours.

In America, we individual people – each one of us – have rights, granted by a gracious God and now surrounded by powerfully defined and hard-won concepts:

- Natural rights, inherited from nature's God;

- Human rights, inherited from the Renaissance, Reformation, and long battles with kings and nobles and collectives;

- Political rights, inherited from Britain;

- Civil rights, inherited from freedom fighters and marchers and suffragettes; and

- Enumerated rights, inherited from the Enlightenment and the Great Awakening and the mind of Jefferson.

Immigrants know this. In a world where 90% of its people live within 100 miles of their birthplace, people come to America in droves. Some come from vast distances and against incomprehensible odds. They come for more – more food, more freedom, more peace. They're self-chosen Americans, who share an unbreakable bond with those who have come before them including the ancestors of us all.

They know – or will soon know– America's problems, but when they come, they only know its promise. They love America – the Idea and the place. They see clearly what wondrous Ideas these are and what a good place this is to try them on for size.

America the place has not always represented the American Ideas well. Individuals with even the best of principles or values often fall short of living up to them, as do societies and governments. Sometimes America the place has totally misplaced the American Ideas. But the amazing thing – the thing that actually best illustrates the enduring power of the Ideas – is that they simply will not go away.

America the Ideas is more important than, and higher than, America the place. For America to mean the most for people's lives, it has to first take them to the Ideas and only second to the place. We never want the Ideas to be spoiled by the human failings of the place.

Instead, we should want the place to mirror the Ideas as closely as possible so people will have a living picture of the Ideas, so they will know that the Ideas are real, and so the Ideas will never be allowed to fade away.

The American Ideas and Rights

The American Ideas are strongly rooted in the concept of rights. But more: They're strongly rooted in the concept of individual rights.

Throughout history, all sorts of people have claimed to have rights – monarchs, dictators, tyrants, aristocrats and elitists – often claiming to speak for the "nation" or "society" or "the people," but usually speaking for themselves. Their "rights" always included the right to steal the rights of everyone else. The few at the top had rights, while everyone else had duties.

The American Ideas shredded that crippling and treacherously dishonest notion that rights belonged to the few, whether claiming it in the name of God or the people (or out of the barrel of a gun, as Mao Zedong asserted). In an amazing upside-down formulation, rights belonged to the individual, who could choose to grant some duties to the governing few for a time – and take them away, if properly annoyed.

In this new formulation, it is each individual – unique, complex, full of thoughts and plans and dreams, bustling with eccentricities – that strides the earth like a colossus. The community is still important, but it isn't primary – and it's only important so long as it serves and edifies the individuals who make it up.

Rights are crucial, and – in the American formulation – only you and I have them.

So we will be addressing some essential rights among these American Ideas: Justice and Dignity (the right to life), Freedom and Diversity (the right to liberty), Equality, Opportunity, Responsibility, and Generosity (the right to pursue happiness). All of these Ideas are about individuals. And all of these rights belong to individuals.

The American Ideas strip religion, society, government, politics, military, and organizations of the notion that they have any "rights." It doesn't take their rights away. It simply says that they have no rights. There's nothing to take away but pretense. These entities have duties and responsibilities, but in America, they most certainly have no rights.

And the Ideas clear up any misconception about the source of those individual rights as expressed so clearly in the American Declaration of Independence in 1776:

We hold these truths to be self-evident, that all men are created equal; that they are endowed by their Creator with certain unalienable rights....[5]

Rights don't come from humanistic impulses, remarkable aberrations from natural selection, kind leaders, or good governments. They come from God. The source of everyone and everything is also the source of rights. Some people believe that governments give us our rights – this ghastly idea has shown up in textbooks in elementary schools – but they don't. And even if they did, that would be very bad news: It would mean that they could also take those rights away.

When God grants rights, they stay granted. When God grants them, governments do well when they protect them and poorly if they try to take them away. When governments claim to grant rights, those rights are fleeting. When God grants them, they are unalienable. As President John F. Kennedy said,

The same revolutionary beliefs for which our forebears fought are still at issue around the globe – the belief that the rights of man come not from the generosity of the state, but from the hand of God.[6]

Either the Declaration got this right – that human beings are gifted by God with rights that cannot be taken away – or there are no rights, except the Darwinian right of "survival of the fittest." And we know where that "jungle right" leads – to the "rights" of the few who are strong, and the oppression of the many who are weak. When governments confuse their power with higher power, they always start chipping away at unalienable rights. And they conjure up new "rights" that are all too often a perversion of the American Ideas.

The concept of America has always been bound up with the certainty that there is a right-granting God, a God who hard-wired these rights into nature and humanity. Thomas Jefferson, the embodiment of the Enlightenment, made this clear when he asked,

Can the liberties of a nation be thought secure when we have removed their only firm basis, a conviction in the minds of the people that these liberties are the gift of God? That they are not to be violated but with His wrath?[7]

The answer isn't that hard. If we remove God, rights have no foundation – and violating them has no sure punishment. Jefferson concluded the Declaration of Independence by "appealing to the Supreme Judge of the world for the rectitude of our intentions...with a firm reliance on the protection of Divine Providence...."[8]

Only God grants and ultimately protects rights. Government can guard them or steal them, but it cannot grant them. And what God has joined together – in this case, human beings and unalienable rights – let no one have the audacity to put asunder.

The Concept of America Is More than Rights

In America, there has always been a recognition that there are things that can't be done by individuals. Individuals come together – have to come together – from need or desire to do those things.

But the concept of America presents a very different perspective on those "comings together." It teaches us that those collective efforts involve no collective rights, but only many collective responsibilities. Until very recently, the notion of group rights – that this or that group has some sort of special claim to justice or opportunity or government assistance – was alien and unwelcome.

What are those rights-less collective efforts?

> • Religion has the responsibility to guide us, to bring solace and understanding to each of us as we deal with the ups and downs of life, to provide a place where our spiritual needs can be met.

> • Society has the responsibility to bless us, to bring the possibility of happiness to each of us as we interrelate and care and serve, to provide a place where our emotional and relational and psychological needs can be met.

> • Government has the responsibility to protect us, to bring security and safety to us as we deal with the threats and evils always present in a flawed world, to provide a place where our physical needs can be met.

All three – Religion, Society, and Government – have the responsibility to keep us collectively Independent and at Peace.

So the concept of America, at its core, is about rights for the individual and responsibilities for the collective. This is the great inversion from the historical norm, of rights for the collective and responsibilities for the individual.

There is nothing quite like this concept of America. It elevates everyone, by elevating every one.

There are American Ideas, but There Is No Single "American Idea"

Even though America represents 13 Ideas, there isn't one "American Idea."

There isn't a lone definition of what "America" is or means. No singular description of "America" could be constructed or would mean anything if it were.

America isn't a brand that needs a slogan – a crisp distillation of its essence into a handy catchphrase. "It has often been said that any idea is dangerous if it is a person's only idea," noted Pulitzer Prize winner George F. Will. "Talk about 'the' American idea is dangerous because it often is a precursor to, and an excuse for, the missionary impulse…. After all, if the essence of America can be distilled to a single idea, it must be supremely important, and there might be a moral imperative to export it."[9]

America may be the city on a hill. Perhaps it is the "last, best hope of mankind."[10] If so, it's not because it can be condensed into one powerful idea, a secret sauce that meets all human needs, a silver bullet that eliminates all wolves trying to devour humanity. If America is a North Star, it's because it can't be condensed. It's too big, too rich, too far-reaching with its light.

America makes for an outstanding home for Ideas. But trying to condense America into a single idea? That would be a fool's errand.

Although There Is No "American Idea," There Are American Ideas

Writer Victor Hugo said, "Greater than the tread of mighty armies is an idea whose time has come."[11] With America, 13 Ideas found their time. Even though there is no single "American Idea," there is a wonderful array of American Ideas.

There are not only American Ideas, but a mutually reinforcing and self-correcting set of American Ideas. America is a very big concept made up of a collection of immensely rich Ideas. Psychologist James Hillman, in Kinds of Power, said,

> *Of all the little and big forces that subordinate our actions to superior powers, it is ideas that hold the most direct and immediate sway.*[12]

The American Revolution was atypical of revolutions because it was a revolution of ideas. The revolution occurred first as an idea and only then became a physical reality. Most revolutions have been about throwing off oppression, with the revolutionaries often becoming even nastier oppressors than the ones they replaced. There's a simplistic notion: Throw out the tyrants, and replace them with us. The American Revolution had a complex concept: Throw out the bad ideas and replace them with many better ones.

This book focuses on 13 original American Ideas. The topics themselves – cherished words like freedom, equality, justice, opportunity, religion, and peace – aren't unique to America. These topics are, in fact, universal, thought about and fought about in all ages and places. It's the principles behind those topics and the way those topics are defined that make them American Ideas.

The American interpretation of these topics was a radical departure from both the past and the rest. It didn't "split the difference" on past definitions or strike a compromise between competing theories. It didn't seek the middle ground, but rather the higher ground. It drew its wisdom from a wide range of earlier sources but is different from all of them.

This doesn't mean that these Ideas have always been fully understood or generally accepted or consistently applied in the place called "America." They have not. But with each of them, there has always been a seed, always been a strand, always been something there calling out to us, "There is a better way to live."

In one sense, that's the theme of this book: Here's what's really right with America.

The American Ideas and Reality

The American Ideas work, but they aren't preferable to the alternatives just because they work.

Anti-American ideas can also "work." They've been very effective in creating massive and long-lasting wars, propping up despicable tyrants, and squeezing the economic life out of faceless multitudes. They have chopped freedom to pieces, chopped justice to pieces, and chopped people to pieces. Hitler's ovens, Stalin's gulag, and Zedong's Great Leap Forward all worked. They worked because they were aligned with one aspect of human nature, a truth that all people have "bad" bottled up inside and sometimes only stumble into being good.

These American Ideas do work. They've been just as effective as the bad ideas but with a different focus: creating massive and long-lasting prosperity, propping up frail individuals into great leadership, and squeezing the fear out of people yearning to breathe free. They make freedom and justice real and lift people out of the miry clay that trapped them from forever. Washington's constitutional government, Jefferson's republican government, and Jackson's democratic government all worked. They too worked because they were aligned with the reality of human nature, but it was a different one – the truth that all people have "good" bottle up inside and often only stumble into being bad.

The American Ideas were a dream for far too long. Way too many people had good reason to wonder if they could be made a living reality in the midst of the often harsh reality of life.

But the Ideas made it. They aren't automatically anyone's reality, but they can be. They're the better reality, the much better way to live. Settling for ugliness because "it is what it is" is settling for something that's undeniably real when a better reality – now, in America, a proven reality – waits at our fingertips.

America has always represented a wonderful blend of optimism and pragmatism. Americans have very big dreams and very little tolerance for theories that don't work. Somehow, from the beginning, it was clear that America means both innocent and street-smart.

Americans give people the benefit of the doubt. We assume that they intend to do us well until they prove that they intend to do us ill. We trust government to protect us and defend our freedom.

And Americans know that people can do great evil, even while claiming to love us or protect us or be our friend. We know the value of skepticism and checks and balances and term limits and a free and rowdy press and shredders of illusions and of having a safe place for dangerous truths.

We know that governments are prone to steal our freedom under the guise of defending it. Americans value security and order but remember that people who trade freedom for safety will lose both, and deserve neither.

This new being, this American, is an idealist with common sense.

The American-American

I haven't told you who I am because in a very real sense, I am you. I am an American-American, an American both by birth and by sentiment.

But maybe it's more than nature and nurture. Maybe it's the American nature (America the concept) and American nurture (the 13 American Ideas). Maybe, like you, I am in part – perhaps in large part – a son or daughter of America. I love America, both the Ideas and the place that they call home. I see that the American Ideas call us to something higher than our cultural or ethnic or racial heritage without asking us to reject them.

In one sense, calling myself an American-American is my way of asking Americans who live in America the place to stop being hyphenated Americans and simply be Americans.

Who are these Americans? Americans who believe in the concept of America, who love the American Ideas, and who work hard to practice them without hesitation or hypocrisy in a place they also love? These aren't Irish-Americans or German-Americans or African-Americans or Mexican-Americans or Chinese-Americans or Native Americans – they are simply, beautifully, and powerfully *Americans*.

There is a place for hyphenated Americans – Americans who agree with the American Ideas and want to see them come alive but who happen to live somewhere other than America the place.

There were many such Americans in Eastern Europe as the American Ideas of Freedom, Dignity, and Justice battered one of history's many bad ideas – the Soviet Union – and consigned it to the "ash heap of history."[13] We can bow with great respect to those Polish-Americans, Czech-Americans, Hungarian-Americans, and so many others who somehow found their way to the American Ideas.

Maybe they aren't even hyphenated Americans. Maybe they, too, are simply Americans.

Americans. If we define that well, there should be enough goodness and glory in that title for anyone. And everyone.

America as a concept has durability and gives people a dream and a hope. The American Ideas have great power to make that dream and hope come alive. This is in part why 80 percent of Americans "say they believe the country has a unique character and unrivaled standing."[14]

These Ideas have power because they resonate with the best of what it means to be human. Though developed in fits and starts by a wild and flawed group of people, they've become something commandeering, rich, even elegant. These Ideas – working themselves out over four centuries – aren't just old principles to be revered. They're dynamic principles to be revived.

America the place has struggled in recent decades to keep its footing, in great part because it's lost some of its connection to the American Ideas. But the problems can be addressed by coming back to our deep roots. "What is required," one author recently wrote, "is that we dig deep down into our history to find the countervailing insights and rediscover the enduring ideas that can set us right."[15] In this book, you will find 13 of those enduring Ideas.

How important are these Ideas? "In an increasingly empowered and democratized world, in the long run, the battle of ideas is close to everything," Fareed Zakaria wrote in *The Post-American World.*[16] He may or may not be right when he says that the balance of power is changing with "the rise of the rest," that the role of America the place is shifting and will continue to adjust to a changing world order. The American political system and economy may indeed need to continually modify themselves in a world that never stands still.

But not so with the American Ideas. A world that is Post-American Ideas would be a sorry place. We've seen that world before, through long ages of degradation and slaughter. We've seen it so recently in Hitler's Germany, Stalin's Russia, Zedong's China, Pol Pot's Cambodia, and Idi Amin's Uganda. We've seen it in Armenia and Bosnia and Rwanda and the Middle East. And we still see it today, in Burma and Darfur, and far too often in far too many places.

There's a lot of talk about change today. But that's not new - there has always been such talk in America. Americans, always progressive and forward-looking, want change. But they're wise and practical and only want it to be change for the better. They want to change toward something good and right, and not just away from this or that problem. They want change to line up with the American Ideas. If it doesn't, it's just experimentation likely to lead to the very evils the Ideas were established to obliterate.

Americans want to soar, but they want a tether that connects them to four centuries of truly first-rate Ideas. They sense in their souls that all change has to be connected to the core Ideas that give them their identity. They know that when we're sure of who we are at the center of our individual and collective being, we're better able to dialogue and discuss and disagree about how to change the details without threatening our character or existence.

If the battle for ideas is everything, let's win that battle with the best ideas available, the best that have grown deep in the concept of America – 13 powerful, breathtaking, historically radical Ideas that have endured in concrete form for four hundred years, yet which may just be coming into their prime. *The American Ideas.*

In the end, the promise of the American Ideas is simple. If enough Americans are willing to understand them, believe in them, be passionate about them, and fight for them, if enough Americans are honest enough to see the problems in keeping them and keeping them strong, if enough Americans cannot only accept but rejoice in the uniqueness of these classic yet cutting-edge concepts, these Ideas can shower us and our descendents with their blessings for a hundred thousand years.

★ ★ ★ ★ ★ ★ ★ ★ ★ ★ ★ ★ ★

One of the outstanding and uniquely American responses to opportunities and challenges is to ask "What can *I* do?" Near the end of each of the 13 Idea chapters, in a section called "America at It's Best," is the answer to that most meaningful of questions.

The "call to action" points were designed, in the great American tradition, to be principled and pragmatic - and quite often, provocative. There should be at least one point in each chapter where your passion for America and its grand Ideas can find a home.

"The strongest force shaping politics is not blood or money but ideas."

★ The Economist

"The revolution was effected before the war commenced. The revolution was in the minds and hearts of the people."

★ American Founder and President John Adams

"Liberty ought to be the direct end of your government."

★ American Founder and Statesman Patrick Henry

"We are called as a people to give testimony in the sight of the world to our faith that the future shall belong to the free."

★ American President Dwight D. Eisenhower

"Keep ancient lands, your storied pomp! Give me your tired, your poor, your huddled masses yearning to breathe free....I lift my lamp beside the golden door."

★ American Poet Emma Lazarus, for the Statue of Liberty

"We should be borne back ceaselessly into the American past: It is impossible for the young to know but never too late to learn: America is truly something – perhaps the only thing – commensurate with our capacity for wonder."

★ American Writer George Will

"If the spirit of America were killed...the America we know would have perished."

★ American President Franklin Roosevelt

"We will find out what is not working right and we will fix it, and then maybe it will work right. That's been our star...."

★ American Historian David McCullough

CHAPTER 1

The American Idea of Freedom

"Freedom!"

That wonderful word, shouted by a dying William Wallace (as portrayed in the best-picture-winning film *Braveheart*), resonated with audiences in our day, just as it did with freedom-loving Scots in his day so long ago.

Standing on the step in the old section of the British Parliament, on the very spot where Wallace stood to be condemned for claiming freedom as a birthright, is an overpowering experience. You can almost sense him standing there, nearly see his ghost, and definitely feel his defiance.

After life itself, freedom is the indescribable gift. "Life without liberty is like a body without spirit," wrote poet Kahlil Gibran.[1]

"There is no one thing which mankind are more passionately fond of, which they fight with more zeal for, which they possess with more...fear of losing, than liberty," noted American revolutionary Samuel Adams[2] ("truly the Man of the Revolution" according to Thomas Jefferson[3]). People love being free. They fight to get and keep freedom, and, with an intense passion, they hate losing it.

But what *is* "freedom?"

The dictionary defines it as "the condition of being free or unrestricted...personal or civic liberty; absence of slave status...the power of self-determination; the quality of not being controlled by fate or necessity...the state of being free to act."[4] This is a very good start indeed – liberty to be and to do, liberty from restrictions and control.

The American Idea of Freedom has always wanted all of this and more. It fleshes out this definition and adds a beating heart.

Freedom

All people are created free – to believe and think, speak and disagree, relate and seek, choose what is right and act as they see fit.

Real freedom isn't granted by society or government but is owned by every human being as an unassailable gift from God and as a natural right.

But freedom is a paradox – the gift we have to earn if we want to keep it. Freedom is full and rich, a human right that involves freedom from so much and freedom to do even more.

We will sustain freedom if we meet certain conditions and destroy it if we don't.

Society and government are worthy when they protect freedom but intolerable when they take it away.

True freedom is a priceless treasure, always worth our best effort to preserve it.

And so we see, first, that we're created to be free.

All People Are Created Free – to Believe and Think, Speak and Disagree, Relate and Seek, Choose Right and Act as They See Fit

It is one of the most powerful truths of life: We don't acquire freedom by talent, education, hard work, public service, or anything else. We start out with it. We're made that way, with a rock-solid core of freedom and a yearning to live it out loud.

"To hell with being controlled," a hardworking American once said to me. Life comes with enough built-in limitations. People don't need anyone to add a long list of artificial rules to those usual barriers of time and space, money and health, injustice and inequality.

We need freedom in our public lives. In a culture founded on freedom, everything should be moving us toward civic liberty. Freedom should be the first order of business. It shouldn't be an afterthought, as it is too often in religion, society, and government. And nothing should be moving us toward being controlled, needlessly restricted, or limited without very good reason in our choices and actions.

We also need freedom in our personal lives. We need it to determine who we are and who we want to be. And we need it to have the maximum opportunity to act on those determinations. We need freedom from the whims and wishes of others, be they government know-it-alls or communal do-gooders.

And freedom is even more. It means that I mostly get to do what I want to do. I have a right to be let alone, respected fully by all in my colossal individuality. No one but me can pick out a life for me – education, career, relationships, religion. I can pursue my own happiness and the happiness of others if that suits me. I can own things, starting with my own life and including all sorts of property. I can spend or invest or give away my money and possessions the way I choose to use them. And I can spend my life as I decide – wisely or foolishly, energetically or slothfully, for others or just myself.

This is the richness of this grand American Idea. It isn't just a civil liberty, like voting in an ancient democracy in Athens or serving as a senator from the noble class in Rome. In fact, it doesn't start out as a public or civil liberty at all. The American Idea of Freedom begins with the individual. The smallest unit of society – you or me – is also its greatest.

One of the great defenders of liberty, F. A. Hayek, talked about the

> civilization which modern man had built up from the age of the Renaissance and which was, above all, an individualist civilization...individualism which, from elements provided by Christianity and the philosophy of

classical antiquity, was first fully developed during the Renaissance and has since grown and spread into what we know as Western Civilization – [these elements] are the respect for the individual...that is, the recognition of his own views and tastes as supreme in his own sphere...and the belief that it is desirable that men should develop their own individual gifts and bents.[5]

Perhaps the greatest contribution of the Western tradition was this: you count. Esteem of the individual as an individual doesn't exist anywhere else and never has. People are normally treated as subjects, as members of the community, as very small cogs in a very large machine, often as dispensable resources, and not infrequently as cannon fodder. But only in the Western/Christian tradition have people been treated as unique and valuable, one soul at a time.

Hayek went on to say that "freedom for the individual is the only truly progressive policy."[6] It is an abuse of language to call yourself a progressive while maximizing government and the community at the expense of the solitary human being. This is so even if you claim good intentions or a desire to serve the People or a wish to find the greater good. You simply aren't a progressive. You're a regressive – promoting a destructive idealism, taking freedom out of the equation, moving people back into the gloomy night.

And in fact, true progressives know that freedom is more than a progressive policy. It's a fundamental human right – and an unalienable one at that, the second one listed in the Declaration of American Independence. According to that magnificent document, no one is authorized to take it away.

But freedom is even more than all of this, even more than an unalienable right. Freedom is a state of being. The marvelous invitation at the American Statue of Liberty asks those tyrants and controllers who believe in oppression more than in freedom to "give us...your huddled masses, yearning to breathe free."[7] Freedom to human beings is like oxygen, the stuff of life.

Freedom is somehow wired into our DNA. We can see it, hear it, taste it, smell it, touch it. We know if we have it, and can only be fooled for so long by those who want to limit or steal it. It doesn't matter how far down into the mud the bully pushes us; as with William Wallace, that stirring word still rises from our lips.

Freedom! It's our inheritance. Don't try to take it away, because we know that

Freedom Isn't Granted By Society or Government, but Is Owned by Every Human Being as an Unassailable Gift from God and as a Natural Right

What is the origin of freedom? The assurance that we'll keep freedom? A brilliant man, thoroughly versed in all things secular, asked this sobering rhetorical question:

How can people retain their liberties, if they forget those liberties are a gift from God?[8]

Thomas Jefferson, son of the Enlightenment and writer of the American Declaration of Independence (a fairly decent document on the subject of freedom) tells us clearly that freedom comes from God.

And this is very good news indeed. If freedom comes from a higher power, this means that every living human being has started out with a soul, a mind, a heart, a body – and freedom. You're born into slavery? A war-torn disaster area? A death camp?[9] It doesn't matter. God made you free. Your life has value, has meaning, has significance, and you deserve to live it in freedom. President Franklin Roosevelt said,

> *We all understand what it is – the spirit – the faith of America. It is the product of centuries. It was born in the multitudes of those who came from many lands – some of high-degree, but mostly plain people, who sought here, early and late, to find freedom more freely.... In America the impact has been irresistible.*[10]

God is aligned with liberty, not slavery: "Where the Spirit of the Lord is, there is freedom,"[11] we're told. Whatever else we know about spiritual life, we know from this statement that if there's no freedom, the Spirit of God is absent. A higher power is in the business of freeing people, one person at a time. Revolutionary founders frequently compared their ancestors' journey from the ugliness of the Old World to the beauty of the New World with the exodus of the Jews from Egypt to the Promised Land.

If freedom comes from the highest authority, in principle it is safe from assault. Who would dare to set themselves up against the highest authority? What finite, flawed creature would presume to own and control and squeeze the life out of multitudes whom God made free? What kind of person thinks they have a better idea than God – a better idea than freedom?

Coming from that higher authority, freedom should be as safe in practice as it is in principle. It isn't, of course. Millions have been taken into slavery – blacks from Africa to the New World, whites from Europe to Africa,[12] Asians from Korea to Japan, endless violations of this fundamental human right. Many more millions have lived in cruel and oppressive cultures. They've ranged from "benign" dictatorships and "benevolent" monarchies to the rigid whole-life control of Soviet Russia, Communist China, and the Islamic autocracies.

But no matter. These leaders, ranging from misguided to evil, set themselves against an inborn gift of freedom that will not die. They're always shocked when the people finally say enough, finally cry "freedom!", finally take to the streets. These false leaders set themselves up for condemnation from here to eternity because they try to strip away a vital piece of humanity that comes from a higher place.

If we claim that freedom comes from anywhere else, we're in big trouble. Various candidates have been offered as freedom-granters through the centuries. Two of the biggest:

- *Government.* In more recent years, elementary school textbooks, even in America, have taught children that government gives us our rights. That notion may appear to be so, especially in nations that are heavily controlled by a stifling ruling class. But government can't give what it does not own, has not earned, did not create, could not fathom – and too often has exhibited an inclination to destroy.

Rights are God-given, but government is always a human fabrication. Many (if not most) of the governments in history were created initially by treachery and force – one powerful person kills another and then masks the violence with crowns and ceremonies and armies. Some governments were put together by a ruling elite. A few were fashioned by people hammering out compromises on constitutions and laws. But all of them had a start, and precious few had freedom in the equation early or at all.

We shouldn't be thankful when government says, "You can have a little more latitude there." We should tell it, "We're the ones who'll decide this latitude business, about government and ourselves. We want our whole birthright of freedom, and we don't want you ever taking it away, even if the ends seem desirable to you – or to your courtiers and lobbyists and groupies."

• *Society*. People are free in a "state of nature," claimed French philosopher Rousseau.[13] When they come together, so the thinking goes, they voluntarily give up some of their freedom so that they can have the benefits of community. But we can't "give up" something that's an irrevocable gift from God.

Society has no claim on our freedom. Society is merely a combination of people, all of whom were born free. Society can be very fickle and decide that the society is more important than its members (as in China), or that religion is more important than its people (as in Islamic theocracies), or that one group is "more equal"[14] than others (whether the special ones are called "nobility," a "higher caste," a "ruling party," "supreme," or some other term of superiority).

And what kind of society asks us to give up our freedom, anyway? It might ask us to give up killing and raping and pillaging others – but is that really giving up true *freedom*?

We do have freedom as a natural right. But we have to be careful what we mean by this powerful term. Some who want to leave God out of the freedom equation argue for natural rights. But they mean that somehow our freedom just sort of oozes up out of the primeval slime. We have it because we're the highest thing on the food chain. But they've lost connection with this wonderful concept.

When John Locke, Baron de Montesquieu, Patrick Henry, and many other early champions of freedom spoke about natural rights, they meant the rights that God had designed into nature and humanity. Nature was simply another way for them to talk about creation and God. People could use reason and conscience to discern the natural law that was built into life, but reason and conscience are no substitute for that natural law.

If we listen to dogmatic Atheists, the only thing that nature gives us is a jungle. You have the right to scrap and claw and fight. You can kill off the weaker ones around you so you can have more for yourself. John Locke's nature is a very different concept than Charles Darwin's. Locke's version of nature tells us to tear out the stairs and build handicapped ramps. Darwin's version of "nature" tells us to tear out the handicapped.

Freedom is the crown jewel of human life – it's an elegant diamond from God. Try as we might, we can't escape the notion that freedom is granted to us by someone or something else. Much of Europe is currently trying to get by on a God-less freedom, even as they face a growing religious minority that does not believe in personal liberty. Good luck to them with that approach.

The American Declaration of Independence makes the connection between God and freedom very clear. It isn't a declaration of independence from God. It's a declaration of independence from people who try to take God's place. It is, in fact, a remarkable statement of our dependence upon God, since people "are endowed by their Creator with certain unalienable rights...."[15]

And here's a related fact of life: While God is higher than spirituality or religion, the expansion of freedom can't be separated from religion except by a willful ignorance of history and a tortured use of logic. Christianity as practiced has not always been right and at times, in application, has been very wrong. But its core message is one of freedom – from destruction, from folly, from oppression, from ourselves.[16] President Jimmy Carter said,

> *Ours is the first society to define itself in terms of both spirituality and of human liberty.*[17]

Freedom has been a theme of Western Civilization, in up-and-down but ever-growing measure, for two thousand years. It isn't just coincidence that this matches up with the birth of Christianity. And freedom – individual freedom – has exploded as a theme since the Protestant Reformation and Catholic Counter-Reformation.

Historian Paul Johnson observed that "The Great Awakening was...The formative moment in American history, preceding the political drive for independence and making it possible."[18] The majority of Christians of all stripes recognize that freedom – to be, to do, not to be, not to do – is a gift from God. But freedom isn't a simple gift:

Freedom Is a Paradox – the Gift We Have to Earn If We Want to Keep It

Is freedom a gift, or is it an achievement?

Absolutely.

Even while recognizing that freedom is a gift, we can also see that it is one of the matchless yearnings of the human heart. It can take hold of whole communities of people. And people have been willing to work their souls out to get it and keep it.

Its preservation is one of the great themes of Western Civilization, which undergirded freedom with the rule of law (the law is king rather than the king is law), and with human and civil rights. And as we've seen, it underscored the dignity and supreme value of the individual (rather than some defined collective).

The yearning to be free drove people to incredible striving and sacrifice. It led to an effort to carve human freedom out of a history that didn't even recognize freedom as a valid topic for discussion. South African freedom fighter and President Nelson Mandela said,

Let freedom reign. The sun never set on so glorious a human achievement.[19]

This achievement was first given actionable form when a group of people came together in Philadelphia in 1776. They put forth the growing but still-radical proposition that the individual is more important than...anything else. The Declaration of Independence is certainly about truths and rights, but it is foremost about something else: the astonishing concept that each person is so very important that they can't rightly – under any circumstances – be oppressed or violated by another human being.

Only a person – not a city or a county or a state or a nation – has an inextinguishable life, an immortal spirit, and a reason for being. This individual is all too often surrounded by impersonal forces of oppression and control, the forces that the freedom-framers recognized and tried to shackle with their Declaration.

The Declaration itself was the product of a long line of actions toward freedom. It began in 1215 with the English Magna Carta in the realm of politics and governance and at about the same time with John Wycliffe in the realm of freedom of conscience and the right of individuals to relate directly to their God (yes, he was killed for his efforts). Five centuries later, the signers of the American Declaration made clarity about freedom an achievement – a milestone that is impossible-to-ignore. And a human pinnacle.

The great discovery that ended the darkness in the West between Rome and the Renaissance wasn't the medicine to conquer the Black Death or the printing press to defeat the Deep Ignorance. The great discovery was individual Freedom.

Freedom is an achievement that every society has to take on for itself. There are no shortcuts. You have to work for it. It can't be secured at the point of a gun. It can't even be secured by the introduction of good supporting mechanisms like democracy.

Because democracy isn't the thing – freedom is the thing. We only serve to minimize freedom when we confuse it with democracy or use democracy as a cheap substitute for freedom: "Let's help them be free – we'll introduce democracy and give them the right to vote." This has too often been a fatal illusion, as elected tyrants have ground people into powder.

U. S. President Woodrow Wilson wanted to make the world "safe for democracy."[20] Within a few years, Adolf Hitler was elected German Chancellor in a democratic process and then used democracy to make his world safe for lunatics. Wilson needed to worry about making the world safe for freedom, not democracy.

We aren't free because we can vote. In fact, voting can lead to the loss of freedom. We can find ourselves in unwilling servitude to a voting majority, which can be just as obnoxious as other forms of domination. A 51% tyranny is still tyranny. French observer Alexis de Tocqueville warned us about this in his brilliant mid-1800s work Democracy in America:

They console themselves for being in tutelage by the reflection that they have chosen their own guardians. Every man allows himself to be put in leading-strings, because he sees that it is not a person or a class of persons, but the people at large who hold the end of his chain. By this system the people shake off their state of dependence just long enough to select their master and then relapse into it again…. This does not satisfy me: the nature of him I am to obey signifies less to me than the fact of extorted obedience.[21]

Even polling can become a detriment to freedom. We can get caught up with what "the people" think. But who cares if a majority thinks something if the majority is wrong? Again, de Tocqueville:

Every citizen is lost in the crowd, and nothing stands conspicuous but the great and imposing image of the people at large. This naturally gives the men of democratic periods a lofty opinion of the privileges of society and a very humble notion of the rights of individuals.[22]

So we have two forces, individualism and democracy, that can sometimes be at odds with each other. If we aren't careful, the very idea of democracy that sounds so oriented toward the individual (one person = one vote) can lead to the people (the society) becoming more important than the one person who has the vote. Democracy can be one of the best political arrangements available – but only if it's founded solidly on individual freedom.

In the same way that democracy isn't the thing, capitalism isn't the thing. We've been told by political and business leaders, for instance, that there isn't much to worry about regarding China attacking Taiwan because of their economic connections and the folly of destroying Taiwan's economy.

But capitalism isn't a substitute for freedom, and economics isn't always rational. Capitalism is small potatoes when faced with the insanity of power-hungry, repressive, freedom-loathing governments. The same arguments about economic rationality were made about European monarchies and imperial powers in the early 20th century. It was a time of globalized travel and trade, the "beautiful era" – right up to the moment in 1914 that those powers began destroying their nations and economies in two deranged world wars.

Capitalism can even make big mistakes. Instead of enhancing freedom, it can cost people (among other things) freedom of choice, freedom of movement, and financial freedom. We're told that somehow it's all right to mortgage the freedom of future generations to avoid any financial anxiety or discomfort now, all so we can "secure" the capitalist system. But what about securing the future of freedom?

Democratic capitalism, if used for good ends, can be a very good system to support freedom. But it's just a system. It isn't freedom. It isn't even like freedom. It's merely a set of mechanisms that can allow free people to express their freedom. People can be free and not have a vote, and people can be free and not be part of a capitalist system. This was true for the thousands of pioneers who moved into a government-free, capitalism-free – but very free – journey across a new land.

Democracy and capitalism are just tools. They're very good tools, the very best we have. They can be used to protect and expand freedom. But they can be very bad tools, as well. If they're misused, overused, or abused, they can erode and destroy freedom. The only way to ensure their effective use – to make them a hammer to build lives rather than to crush skulls – is to tie them closely to the American Ideas, starting with Freedom.

It's hard to imagine that a good God would bless a bad people with freedom. It's simply too elegant and priceless a gift. The gift and the achievement have to work together if we want sustainable freedom. A free people who are a bad people aren't good candidates to hold onto their freedom.

On the other hand, it's hard to imagine that a good God wouldn't want to bless a good people with freedom. They have to want it as well – to work hard for it, stay focused on it, pay the price for it. But if they stay focused and stay good, freedom will be credited to their account. They'll be able to experience the truth that

Freedom Is Full and Rich, a Human Right that Involves Freedom from So Much and Freedom to Do Even More

There is a fullness and richness to this right to liberty.

As I write this, I'm on the westbound California Zephyr in Colorado, west of the continental divide, with a perspective of mountains and canyons that can only be had from a train. It's expansive and exquisite, open and free, and entirely and most assuredly not the product of human hands. I made this journey, from the Midwest to California and back, to get a sense of what's been given to us in America the place.

The land is remarkable and speaks of freedom. Indeed, people talk about a free land. Even though the land is beautiful, the land isn't free. It has no choice. Only the people who live in it can be free and choose to live freely.

What does this freedom look like? The American Idea of Freedom is made up of at least 7 indispensable and interrelated elements. We could call them the 7 Spirits of Freedom:

1. *Freedom from oppression.* A good portion of history is the story of oppression – rulers oppressing their subjects, upper classes oppressing lower classes, majorities oppressing minorities, owners and managers oppressing workers. It may take us a while – a long while – to eliminate it, as native peoples and blacks and Jews and Asians and the Irish and many others can attest, but, sooner or later, oppression in whatever form – laws, rules, injustices, taboos, bigotry, taxes, war – has to go.

2. *Freedom from control.* And then there's control, the unhealthy notion that the world would be a better place if a select few have power over the rest of us. Thomas Jefferson had the answer: "Sometimes it is said that man cannot be trusted with the government of himself. Can he, then, be trusted with the government of others?"[23] There has always been an underlying and healthy American mistrust of government. It's a belief (borne out by history) that government is, at its best, only a necessary evil – and is at its best only when it's doing as little as absolutely necessary.

3. *Freedom from fear.* From its beginning there has been an American sense of the Rule of Law. People should be free from arbitrariness – arbitrary

searches and seizures and threats from government. And they should be free from violence and crime and abuse and from the warped souls of those who perversely define freedom as "doing whatever I want, regardless." I once asked an Ethiopian immigrant what he loved best about America. "That I can go to bed," he answered without hesitation, "and know that no one will come and take me away in the middle of the night." Historian Richard Rhodes said, "Before it is science and career, before it is livelihood, before even it is family or love, freedom is sound sleep and safety to notice the play of the morning sun."[24]

4. *Freedom to count.* This comes from seeing the divine spark in an actual person, not in the mass of "the people." Each American is free to live a life based on her or his own criteria because there's nothing higher on the entire planet than that person. Americans may bow to each other as individuals but never to kings, queens, dictators, tyrants, or the community. It isn't that the community is devalued. Instead, its value is measured by how well it nurtures and protects and elevates the individuals who make it up. It's the sequel to René Descartes' famous statement, "I think, therefore I am."[25] In the American Idea of Freedom, it's "I am, therefore I matter."

5. *Freedom to achieve.* The American Idea relishes big concepts and goals, including one of the most dizzying of goals, "the pursuit of happiness."[26] Americans instinctively accept the dictum, "It is better to aim high and miss it, than to aim low and achieve it."[27] On its better days, the boundaries and limitations of class, social order, heritage, and current economic condition have never meant much in America. We have an aristocracy of merit, observed American essayist Ralph Waldo Emerson.[28] John Wesley, the founder of Methodism, urged people to, "earn all you can, gain all you can, and [to our next point] give all you can."[29] Freedom is about opportunity – the opportunity to lead a self-determined, satisfying, self-controlled, and responsible life.

6. *Freedom to share.* Sometimes stronger, sometimes weaker, there has always been an American undercurrent of what Jimmy Stewart's character in the classic movie Mr. Smith goes to Washington calls "a little looking out for the other fella."[30] Revolutionary Tom Paine wrote, "Give to every other human being every right that you claim for yourself – that is my doctrine."[31] In most of history and most of the world today, people would think you were insane if you talked about giving your money to church or to a cause or to someone who isn't your relative. Isn't that the government's job? Well, not in the American Idea. We Americans want to give away our own money – and by God, we do it.

7. *Freedom to come back.* "The real glory," noted sports legend Vince Lombardi, "is being knocked to your knees and then coming back."[32] In part this is a freedom to fail – to try, to risk, to make mistakes, and still have the chance for redemption, even resurrection. "The people I want to hear about," declared American poet Robert Frost, "are the people who take risks."[33] There is no last chance in the American Idea – only the next chance. Spanish novelist Miguel de Cervantes gave us the glorious encouragement, "Fortune may yet have a better success for you, and those who lose today may win tomorrow."[34] Americans believe it heart and soul.

The 7 Spirits – 3 freedoms from, 4 freedoms to. Any place where these 7 can be found is a good place for freedom and a very good place for human beings.

Freedom is the greatest asset of any nation. But there are things we have to do to keep freedom – and things we have to fight hard against to keep from losing it. We have to be constantly aware that

We Will Sustain Freedom If We Meet Certain Conditions, and Destroy It If We Don't

Freedom, for many people, is magic. It appeared somewhere out of the mist, and now it's a done deal. It just is. And that's one of the strongest reasons why it's possible for freedom to fade away.

Freedom in practice is rarer than gold. It hardly makes a dent in the long, miserable human history of tyranny and oppression. Freedom is the anomaly. Despotism is the rule. There's no requirement that freedom flourish in any age or country. The Dark Ages (which continue in various ways in parts of the Middle East, Africa, Asia and South America) are ample evidence that life in reduced form can go on for centuries – even millennia – without the magnificent exercise of freedom.

The Declaration calls liberty an unalienable right, and it is. We have it. But we want to experience it. We need freedom, want freedom, crave freedom. But we can only enjoy it and hold onto it if we agree to its demanding terms.

Experiencing freedom is never a given. It can be won, it can be kept, it can be lost, and – if we aren't paying attention – it can be stolen. If we want to possess it, we have to have the 12 conditions of freedom, each of which represents one of the other American Ideas:

1. *An Acceptance of Messiness.* Strong leaders, powerful governments, and most communities favor stability and order. They might not like the status quo, but they do like status quo. Instability leads to tension and volatility, while disorder leads to anxiety and the unknown. A free society tosses all of that into the back seat. Free people have – have to have – an acceptance of a certain amount of disorder and chaos. Freedom is cool, but it isn't neat. Freedom welcomes Diversity, and diversity – racial, ethnic, gender, age, experience, interests, beliefs, thoughts – is guaranteed to bring messiness.

2. *Awareness of the Fundamental Origin of Freedom and Rights.* If I'm sane, I want to know that what I have in my hands is secured by more than the good wishes of my countrymen or a "benevolent" government. There's no guarantee of freedom without the shared conviction that human beings have rights because they're human beings endowed by a Creator. We have many inherent rights including the right to liberty. Justice demands that we be treated with respect as the inheritors of those rights.

3. *A Freedom-Oriented Definition of Equality.* Freedom comes with an insistence on Equality of rights, worth, justice and opportunity. But it also comes with an acceptance of the inequality of results. This is because freedom and equality of results are fundamentally at odds – unless all people are exactly the same in tenacity and talent, which is never the case. This means having a culture that's protective of equality of opportunity for all, even as it recognizes that all people aren't the same and that they will always be at different levels of success and failure.

4. *The Preeminence of the Individual.* It's not even logical when you look at it on the surface. How can one person be more valuable than a hundred million? But that's what freedom requires: a conviction that the individual is more valuable than the group or the nation. Starting anywhere else is a formula for disaster. It doesn't take very much worrying about the rights and needs and wants of "the people" before the individual disappears. Free people know that the way to secure the best for the group is to secure the best for the one. They say to him or her, "You, all by yourself, have splendid Dignity." "All liberty is individual," noted President Calvin Coolidge.[35]

5. *An Evenhanded View of Prosperity.* Free people enjoy freedom not only for its own sake, but also because it's the way to prosperity since everyone in a free place is given real Opportunity. Freedom of choice generally tends to put the best people and resources on the best opportunities. But we also have to understand that this very prosperity can become a threat to freedom. Freedom can evaporate as people fling away their rights to preserve their money and property or as gaps are perceived to be too wide between rich and poor and government intervenes to level out the results, or as the majority who have less demand that the state play Robin Hood with the minority who have more.

6. *Personal Responsibility.* There are really only two ways to have stability in a city, state, or nation: Either a powerful ruler or ruling party exercises top-down control over a subjugated people, or a free people exercise inside-out control over themselves. If free people won't exercise personal Responsibility, real freedom can't survive. This requires personal and collective discipline. We have to resist the temptation to try to prevent people from making brainless decisions or to rescue them after they've made them. Millions of choices are made in every community every day, and many of them are misinformed or "just plain dumb and stupid."[36] If we want freedom of choice, we have to be willing to accept the results of those choices.

7. *A Cultural Safety Net.* A society can't remain fully free if a substantial number of its people are falling off the edge. Everyone has to be given a real chance to participate and compete. Freedom is secured by a pervasive spirit of Generosity. This includes a commitment to a free market with constructive but not destructive competition so that no one's face is driven into the ground. It means free people should have a willing and continual focus on volunteer work and charitable giving. It means a free society should provide cultural safety nets so that no one hits the ground except by their own choice. But as few of these as possible should be run by the government because they quickly get taken over by politics, power, favoritism, redistribution, and bureaucracy that misuse, waste, or eat up the resources.

8. *Truth.* "Work is Freedom,"[37] said the lie posted at the entrance to the

Nazi death camp. Ultimately, freedom can't be secured by lies, half-truths, deceptions, or fact-empty analysis. These have led the United States into many problems, including more than a few wars. Truth is the path to freedom. A commitment of people and their government to truth as the foundation of freedom will go a long way toward securing it. With its claims as a holder of truth, Religion can and should be a truth-telling and truth-demanding component of a free culture. It can and should hold people, society, and government accountable and should continually expose destructive falsehoods.

9. *A Culture that Nurtures Freedom.* Culture, including the families and relationships that make it up, creates the context in which the expansion of freedom either flourishes or dies. It's up to any Society to determine whether it will make it easy or hard for people to exercise the freedom with which they were created. Societies can lead young people to overflow with love of liberty and a willingness to fight for it – even against the bad notions of that free society. But too many societies train young people to submit, to just follow orders, to think only what their leaders tell them to think.

10. *Government of the People, by the People, and for the People.* Freedom can be enhanced by Government, but only if it meets these three non-optional conditions carved in stone at the Lincoln Memorial. It has to be of the people – its authority has to come from the people who own it. "The earth belongs to the living," wrote Thomas Jefferson.[38] All legitimate power derives from the consent of the governed who are alive right now. Government has to be by the people – its structure and processes have to be established by the agreement of the people who live under it. There has to be a commitment to full and open participation of all people in the makeup of their government, and there must be mechanisms to throw out incompetents and miscreants. And government has to be for the people – its purpose has to be to protect the lives, liberty, and property of its individual citizens, not the titles and privileges and nonstop ambition of its leaders.

Freedom also requires eternal vigilance. Free people who gloss over the dual nature of Government are unlikely to be free for very long. There has to be a deep understanding of the two potentials of government – that it's one of the greatest potential protectors of God-given rights and that it's one of the greatest potential violators of those rights. We have to maintain its focus on freedom-protection and distract it from freedom-destruction. It's not a question of whether or not the government can be effective or efficient in growing ever larger and taking on more and more. It's a question of whether freedom can survive if it does. Through long, hard experience, many wise people have learned through the ages the vital truth of the dictum, "that government is best which governs least."[39] If people are going to retain all of their hard-earned freedoms, they need a government with all sorts of limits. Checks, balances, and boundaries are crucial to keeping corrupting power under control. Free people see slow government as good and gridlock as a frequent friend of freedom.

11. *Distance From Foreign Affairs.* In dealing with other nations, limited government means that the government maintains a steadfast Independence from foreign entanglements, commitments, and treaties. Free people re-

member that all of these can overgrow the government and drag us into quarrels not our own. They know that America is exceptional because it minds its own business and avoids intervention – whether driven political, economic, or humanitarian reasons.

12. *War-Ready Pacifism.* Limited government means that we have to doggedly box government in when it sees war as a viable option and is willing to hurl Peace overboard. Few things are as well designed as war to curtail freedom and grow government. "Other factors equal, internal liberty varies inversely as external danger," noted famed historians Will and Ariel Durant.[40] At the same time, government has to be ready to fight because old and new monsters are always on the prowl and eager to devour freedom.

We can have freedom, and we can keep it, and we can keep it strong. But we can only do this if we regularly check all that we're doing, both as individuals and as a government, against this fundamental list of must haves.

This means we need to be aware and ready to act on the concept that

Society and Government Are Worthy When They Protect Freedom, but Intolerable When They Take It Away

British Lord Acton, who famously said "Power corrupts, and absolute power corrupts absolutely,"[41] said that liberty

> *Is not a means to a higher political end. It is itself the highest political end. It is not for the sake of good public administration that it is required, but for the security in the pursuit of the highest objects of civil society, and of private life.*[42]

Many people – perhaps most – have longed for freedom and hungered for it, and not a few have fought for it and died for it. Others have resisted it, hated it, fought against it, and killed others to kill it. From petty tyrants to monstrous dictators, they've rightly seen freedom as their greatest foe.

Freedom is a tree that thrives in the strangest of places and often grows back after it has been cut down. Some of its worst opponents have tried to dig it up by the roots, while others – often well intentioned, not even seeing themselves as freedom's enemies – strip it branch by branch.

We need our institutions – social, religious, political – to be protectors of this precious but fragile freedom.

Government is the "ringer" in the way freedom is played out and in the way the exercise of freedom grows stronger or fades away. We need just enough government to defend our God-given freedom and not enough to take it away. British philosopher John Stuart Mill said,

The aim, therefore, of patriots was to set limits to the power which the ruler should be suffered to exercise over the community; and this limitation was what they meant by liberty.... All that makes existence valuable to any one, depends on the enforcement of restraints upon the actions of other people.[43]

We need enough government to protect us from enemies foreign and domestic. There is evil, and there are evil people, and sometimes they manage to take over nations and parties and tribes and gangs and run them for their evil ends. If not checked by our own government, these evil forces will try to oppress and control and terrify us. They'll work to reduce our value to zero – perhaps to less than nothing – and will make a mockery of our freedoms to achieve and share and come back.

Without a viable government, people are at the mercy of the violent and power-mad who are always lurking in the shadows. In a place without good government, everyone eventually trembles, and many eventually die.

But throughout history, people's freedom has been most often abused and destroyed by their own government. Once a government has the power of the "purse and the sword"[44] (as the American founders called taxation and physical force), it can turn those powers against its own people. It can use a thousand ever-growing taxes, runaway debt and inflation, and wars and rumors of wars to do to us the very things which it still pretends to keep away.

This assault on freedom by a people's own government has often been justified by the perceived threat to freedom from other nations. We can be terrorized into giving up our liberties. New structures and rules can be put into place to restrict and obstruct freedom. F. A. Hayek warned that "even a strong tradition of political liberty is no safeguard if the danger is precisely that new institutions and policies will gradually undermine and destroy that spirit."[45] Our government's cure can be worse than their government's disease.

We want to be realistic about danger, but we don't want to operate from the fear that so many people peddle (the worst of these fear-peddlers often being people who preach loudly against fear-peddling). No society operates as well under fear as it does under hope, and freedom is certainly a hopeful thing. Those who conjure up dreadful tales of woe and horrible predictions to scare us are, in the end, more likely to encourage us to give up our liberty than to preserve it.

There's also a recurring fantasy that government can do for us what we can't do for ourselves – and that it will happily do this without exacting a heavy price. The people in positions of power begin to negotiate with us: "Health care is a problem? Education? Need a house? A bigger house? Company not doing well? We can help!" The unspoken part? What we have to give up to get these things. "The people," noted British statesman Edmund Burke, "never give up their liberties but under some delusion."[46] And delusions are usually cooked up by somebody with an agenda.

Revolutionary hero Patrick Henry, of "Give me liberty or give me death"[47] fame, said:

You are not to inquire how your trade may be increased, nor how you are to become a great and powerful people, but how your liberties can be secured; for liberty ought to be the direct end of your government.[48]

But government isn't alone. Religion and society can be tremendous protectors of freedom. They can keep us connected to the best of what it means to be human.

They can protect us when we're vulnerable and weak and broken. They can hold up hopes and standards that can make life shine.

And they can blot out freedom. They can use rules, regulations, requirements, taboos, shame, guilt, judgment, and gossip to strip people of their freedom, even their humanity. They can even take it away in the name of god or of all that's good or of patriotism. At their worst, throughout history, they've allied with government to seal the deal.

So, we need these three institutions – government, religion, and society. But before that, undergirding the whole structure, we need a mindset and a heartset – a mindset that freedom's the first thing and a heartset that it's the main thing.

Knowing that freedom's enemies are always active, if we want freedom to grow, we have to remember that

True Freedom Is a Priceless Treasure, Always Worth Our Best Effort to Preserve It

The American Idea of Freedom has always included the concept that freedom is worth fighting and dying for. There aren't many things worth this kind of sacrifice, but freedom is right up there with faith and family and friends.

Why should we fight for freedom?

Because it's the right thing for human beings. It's the perfect fit. People were designed for it. It's the greatest expression of their humanity, of the best of who they are and can be. British philosopher John Stuart Mill wrote,

> *The only freedom which deserves the name, is that of pursuing our own good in our own way, so long as we do not attempt to deprive others of theirs....*[49]

But more, much more. Freedom has real and unique advantages. For the individual, these include self-fulfillment, achievement, enjoyment, and meaning. For the community, these include creativity, productivity, and prosperity. And leaders in a free society have to rely on wisdom and persuasion rather than force and violence.

The benefits of freedom aren't the main reason to treasure it. But collectively, these benefits are another powerful argument for liberty.

The alternative to fighting for freedom? To work and play, spend and laugh, learn and love – and wake up on a distant morning in chains. "Freedom is a delicate and subtle gift, easily perverted and often squandered," noted theologian Eugene Peterson.[50]

No group of people, no nation, has ever kept freedom by accident. The forces arrayed against it are too many and too rapacious. Only people who are aware of the value of freedom and alert to its enemies – both crude and subtle – can keep this breathtaking treasure. Freedom is a precious commodity, but it is extremely vulnerable to both direct assault and – perhaps even worse – to slow, insidious annihilation.

People will usually be on their guard against a sudden restriction of freedom. But freedom is seldom snatched away in one sweeping movement. It's the long, slow, gradual loss of liberty that catches them unaware. Through the ages and the histories of nations, it has simply seeped away so that the people couldn't even remember exactly when or how they lost this most exquisite possession.

It's sad but true that some are always ready to impose their will, even if their vision is wrong-headedly unrealistic. Freedom can be a bulwark against this unreality. When people are free to think and speak and act, utopian fantasies lack the stuff to confuse them. People can still be deluded by conniving politicians and appeals to phony patriotism, but sooner or later the reality will break through – if people use their freedom to reflect and take action and thoughtfully change and restore, and not just to focus on what they still are "allowed" to do.

Free people need leaders who will fight on their side for freedom – leaders who are both strong and self-restrained. They have to be secure in who they are, not needing the satisfaction of domination, the approval of the crowds, or kudos from other nations. We need limited government but not weak leaders. It's weak leaders who cater to bad ideas and who end up bellowing and roaring and leading nations into disaster.

People won't fight or die for something they don't understand or value. But if they know the true meaning and value of freedom, no sacrifice is too great.

America At Its Best

TheAmericanIdeas.com

After life itself, freedom is the greatest of gifts and the most valuable of rights. We can preserve and expand it if we'll:

Take Action

Insist on freedom's preeminence as a God-given gift.

★

Remember that freedom is only owned by individual human beings.

★

Be aware and unembarrassed about the Western, Christian foundation of freedom.

★

Make freedom the first criterion in public discussion.

★

Know that freedom dies in the absence of watchfulness.

★

Resist confusing democracy & capitalism with freedom.

★

Check politicians and their platforms against the 12 conditions of freedom.

★

Weigh government on the freedom scale.

★

Weigh society on its ability to enhance true freedom.

To see detail on these Action Points and
to add your voice visit www.theamericanideas.com

We might think that freedom will just hang around because it's been here so long. That would be a very sad and very fatal illusion.

American patriot Patrick Henry put the American Idea of Freedom on the highest plane:

> *Liberty, the greatest of all earthly blessings – give us that precious jewel and you may take everything else…. Suspect everyone who approaches that jewel.*[51]

The first time I visited the Statue of Liberty, I walked around her and fell in love with her. She is actually striding forward on powerful legs, thrusting the flame of freedom into the welcoming harbor. I was struck deeply by her shining defiance, as if she were saying, "Come! I'll hold the door open. If you have the courage, I have the freedom!"

Until America, real freedom was an undiscovered country. The longings of countless souls were perhaps met on the inside – not a small victory – but had little or no chance of being met in some ways on the outside, in the life shared with others. But the New World came along and took its pilgrims' breath away, and it was the freedom more than anything else that did it.

The American Idea of Freedom changed all that, perhaps forever. We can still lose it, and if we do, there is nowhere else where freedom is secure. But we don't have to let it go. We can feel its fire anew and etch it deeply in our hearts. We should, we can, and we must. Why?

Because we're Americans. We were born to be free.

CHAPTER 2

The American Idea of Diversity

French observer and writer Hector St. John de Crevecoeur described with astonishment

> *This American, this new man...here individuals of all nations are melted into a new race of men.*[1]

He found a powerful way to capture the American Idea of Diversity. He saw that there were people – individual human beings – from everywhere with diversity so great that it couldn't even really be measured. A wild and focused, motley and brilliant people.

And then he saw them come together, willingly and freely and fully. He observed that they were "melted" together to form something brand new – a new race, the American race.

There's a dance in this American Idea, a choreographed movement between individuality and community, between diversity and unity, between the many and the one. And this dance produces a whole new race – people who aren't German-American or English-American or Japanese-American, but rather Americans with a German or English or Japanese twist.

This Idea has always driven diversity onto common, constructive ground. Americans might complain about and resist the newest versions of diversity for a while, and it can take a long time for bigotry to die. But in spite of this flaw in human nature, America eventually absorbs the diversity and the best that this diversity has to offer.

Those who come to America freely choose to become Americans. Those who are already Americans come to accept the new-comers at last. And all of them together, in some profound way, become one. *E Pluribus Unum* has been the American way for centuries: Out of the many, one.

No one, certainly not on a large scale, had ever done this before. *Or even tried.*

That's why it's the American Idea.

And so we see, first, that we're created to be free. Americans know that:

Diversity

Diversity is an exceptional strength, but only as long as there is a unified, shared core.

We know that diversity can be valuable or destructive, depending on the way it's used.

We highly value the great diversity, diversity of thought.

We believe that an American is defined by what he or she believes and wants and fights for, not by an accident of birth.

If you think like an American, you are an American, and you are welcome here.

And more: If you're yearning to breathe free, you aren't leaving your home to come to America – you're coming home.

In the end, we refuse to judge a book by its cover because even though everyone is different on the outside, we all bleed the same color.

Diversity Is An Exceptional Strength, But Only As Long As There Is a Unified, Shared Core

America means unity and diversity.

It means unity around core ideas and values – on the things that really count and have counted for Americans for four hundred years. And it means diversity about how to apply those ideas and values. President Bill Clinton said that America was

> *Ennobled by the faith that our nation can summon from its myriad diversity, the deepest measure of unity.*[2]

Every truly great culture, community, or organization needs to have a continuing balance of unity and diversity. We need strong individuals and strong communities. We need a strong, integrated core of shared Ideas so that our wildly wonderful diversity will be anchored to something. We need common ground so our diversity won't tear us apart.

On the Ideas that count, Americans drop their hyphens and believe and act as one. What does that look like? We believe, among other things, that

• All people are, in truth, created free, have immense value, are equal before the law and in opportunity, and should be both responsible about their own needs and generous about the needs of others.

• We were in fact endowed by our Creator with rights like life and liberty and the pursuit of our dreams, rights that can never be rightfully taken away, all exercised in a civilized community of free and decent human beings.

• Evil should forever be resisted and firmly opposed by each of us and by our government and within our government.

• We should have an independent culture and nation and the commitment to live in peace with all others, as far as that depends on us.

With that settled core, our diversity is free to roam. One of the wonderful outcomes of having a strong, shared core is that it frees us to disagree about everything else. Differences then are between Americans, not between enemies.

With that core, the same disagreement that can so easily destroy now has a context. Instead of screaming, "You and I aren't the same," and, "You sound so un-American," we can now say, "It's okay. I know we don't see eye-to-eye on this, but I know in my heart that it isn't rooted in widely different principles." The core creates a safe place to discuss even very big differences and very dangerous truth.

But without that core, every disagreement on every topic feels like disconnection, misunderstanding, even betrayal. And in a very real sense, it is. If I think the right to life is superseded by the right to choose and you don't, if I think it's your job to take care of your needs and you think that's my job, if I think government's a force for good and you think it's good for force, if you think foreign entanglements are disastrous and I think they should extend to nation-building and preemptive wars – we have a huge problem.

It's more. It's an insurmountable problem, because we don't share the American Ideas – in the preceding examples, the Ideas of Dignity, Responsibility, Government, and Independence. Debating particulars, even agreeing on particulars around the edges, will never move us away from that sense of alienation. If we continue the disagreement without agreeing on the Ideas, we'll only enlarge that feeling of estrangement.

America has struggled more than most with the question of what to do with diversity, but not because it is more bigoted than other nations or cultures. In America, the question of how to create unity without losing diversity has always been open, and it has taken a lot of work and warfare to get to an incredibly rich solution.

In most nations and cultures, the question has never been open, at least not for very long. The long history of humanity is one of destructive diversity, with a ruling group singling out and oppressing all others. The norm is tribe over tribe, ideology (communism, socialism, fascism, Great Leap Forward) over the masses, Christians over Muslims and Jews, Muslims over Christians and Jews, Muslims over Hindus, Hindus over Muslims, upper class over lower class, educated urban over ignorant rural. Second-class citizens abound – along with third-class citizens and zero-class citizens.

But the American Idea of Diversity says, "No more." It values diversity without glorifying it. It protects diversity without giving it unfair advantage. It acknowledges the size of the differences but refuses to let them become the main thing. It says, "Let's take what could destroy us and hammer out a way to make us strong." Historian Jacques Barzun wrote that, "The melting pot had not eliminated all diversity; it had created a common core."[3]

In a very special way, America has cracked the code. From the beginning, there were shared Ideas that bound together individuals who were at the same time more diverse than people anywhere else on earth. Unity and diversity are both enshrined in our founding documents. We really do have a shared core, one that can make us even greater as new generations shed the last old baggage of bigotry on their way to loving the differences.

In fact, the shared core gives us a way to make sense of the differences. This is so important, because

We know that Diversity Can Be Valuable or Destructive, Depending on the Way It's Used

Some say, "Diversity is our great strength." But this isn't always or even often true. Diversity, for many cultures, is actually their great weakness. Only when diversity and unity are bound *together* are they a great strength.

Diversity is a sword that can cut both ways. Its value, or lack of value, depends on how we treat it and use it.

Diversity is valuable if we remember the better angels of what makes us – or whatever groupings to which we belong – different. And America has always had a plethora of diverse groups, with many better angels.

There are things that different groups do very well, perhaps better than other groups – valuing hard work, being thrifty, caring for the downtrodden, honoring the aged, protecting the helpless, fighting for the underdog, actively resisting oppression, being resilient, treasuring the spiritual. Even as you read the last sentence, you might be able to put a group's name with each of these good things – or not, since they've become so much a part of the definition of "American."

That's what the American Idea pushes us to absorb: the good things. There has never been an American belief in cultural equivalence, the notion that all cultures have ideas that, although different, are equally valuable. There's always been an understanding that most cultures have really bad ideas and some have truly horrendous ideas and that we don't want any of those in the mix.

The American Idea has always sought the best that those cultures have to offer and blended them into something greater than any of them. America is a greatest hits album with countless artists singing unique music, but all with a common theme.

Not everything about those diverse groups was good, of course, and not all of it should be carried forward. Arrogance, bigotry, mistreatment of others, anger, resentment, disrespect for life – much of that collective memory is ugly and should be allowed to die.

Many came to America to shed those ugly parts of their heritage. But there was a problem – as people, we too easily carry things in our hearts that we know in our heads to be ugly. We can run from ugliness and still bring it with us. Americans have had to learn how to kill the ugliness in their culture. To do that, they've first had to learn how to kill the ugliness inside themselves. They've used the sword of diversity to cut away the bad ideas and the ugliness.

That sword has another side to its blade though, a destructive one. Diversity is our great problem if we have nothing at the center to hold us together, no shared values, no pervasive Ideas. This detached diversity has been a primary driver of war around the world for millennia. It's a diversity that's perfectly designed to tear us apart.

In fact, this kind of diversity is really more accurately described as divisiveness. There's a huge difference between an enhancing diversity and a crippling division. Diversity says, "We bring something to the table that will make everything that's America better." Division says, "We bring everything that's important to the table, and it's better than America."

This divisive twisting of diversity is kept alive to the detriment of America and all Americans. The European-American, Latino-American, Asian-American, African-American, and other splits serve to temporarily advance one group of Americans at the expense of all others, to create artificial "group rights" at the expense of individual, unalienable rights.

It can produce some short-term gains. Eventually, however, it harms everyone, including the promoting group – by culturally marginalizing them, producing resentment all around them, and driving other groups to fixate on and puff up their own identity as better.

A healthy cultural appreciation can turn into a sick cultural pride that separates, segregates, and diminishes. Those cultural distinctives can only maintain their beauty and power if they become a force for enriched unity, not a force for ugly separation. One American writer, part of the Latino minority, said

> *I believe in assimilation. I think that assimilation is the only model that works in a society as diverse as ours, that if each and every group keeps its primary attachment to the ethnic group or the racial group or the religious group that it's divisive. Having said that, though, one of the unique characteristics about American assimilation is that we do feel that we have some connection to the past. I mean, we eat different foods; we have different kinds of traditions in our homes and celebrations. I think that so long as the ethnic part is private, so long as public funds are not being used to promote it that there's nothing wrong with it and it, in fact, can make a richer nation and make a richer life. It's when…we begin expending public money to promote attachment to ethnicity or race that I have a problem.[4]*

Another writer, part of the even smaller minority from India, said that becoming an American does not "require surrendering one's cultural heritage…. I can wear Gandhi hats and eat curry, even while adopting the assimilation strategy pioneered by American immigrants since the nation's earliest days."[5] Immigration isn't a problem, but immigration without assimilation is tragedy in the making.

What we mean by assimilation is very important. To assimilate is to "absorb (people) into a larger group…make like; cause to resemble."[6] It doesn't mean making everyone exactly alike along the lines of the Borg in *Star Trek*. That isn't possible with human beings, in any case. We're designed to be different. We have to choose to be one.

Assimilation in America is absorbing people into American culture, making them look like Americans, causing them to resemble others who have lived the American life for four centuries. It means, at bottom, having some workable concept of the American Ideas, a commitment to those Ideas, and a respect for how they've taken form in American culture.

And of course it includes a common language – not so we can sound "American" (even with the same language we sound so very different), but because it provides the only way we have to talk about those Ideas and to find common ground.

President Theodore Roosevelt addressed this need for unity when he said that citizenship should be dependent on the immigrant's "becoming in very fact an American, and nothing but an American. There can be no divided allegiance here.... We have room for but one language here, and that is the English language."[7] Appreciation of the many, allegiance to the one – and an easy, shared way to talk about what this means.

In America, it's not a unity devoid of diversity – it's a unity born of diversity. So here's the question: "Is diversity our great strength, or is unity our great strength?"

The unique, American answer? *Absolutely.*

This answer is so rich, so unusual, so powerful that it frees us to honestly say that

We Highly Value the Great Diversity, Diversity of Thought

Polls taken before the second Iraq war showed that a solid majority of Americans supported it. As time went on, the support dwindled and then withered away.

Does this mean that Americans are stupid? Either to support it or not support it? In some cases, surely. But it means so much more. Americans are dependent on their leaders to inform them, and too often, those leaders misinform. In a free, democratic republic, it's incumbent upon leaders to give people all of the information on a situation, even the information that differs from the leaders' conclusions and decisions. But often they don't. So Americans, short of facts, give faulty or erroneous opinions.

But Americans keep thinking and evaluating. They get more information and allow it to influence their opinions. Often, they come to recognize that it's a sow's ear and not a silk purse. And when they do, they have the intellectual honesty to change their minds.

This is, for example, unlike the general view on war that's given mankind such gems as the Thirty Years' War and its big brother, the Hundred Years' War, and a World War in the last century that lasted off and on from 1914 to 1945. Did America lose in Korea and Vietnam? Or rather, did Americans rethink whether the goal was worth all of the blood and treasure? We might be deceived – but not forever. President Abraham Lincoln saw this American trait when he noted that

> You may fool all the people some of the time; you can even fool some of the people all of the time; but you can't fool all of the people all of the time.[8]

The American Idea of Diversity elevates diversity of thought. It's this diversity that prevents Americans from following bad ideas or bad leaders forever, a common occurrence in so much of the Old World. Americans don't just believe what they're told. They often resent those who try to tell them, who try to force their views down

44

an unwilling mind.

Diversity of thought is like good science, which values and digs into the lone idea that disagrees with the theory more than it does into the hundred ideas that support it. There are ten good reasons to pass this legislation or raise these taxes or spend this money or make this treaty or start this war? Well, what about this one good reason that says we shouldn't?

The American Idea of Diversity belittles conformity and refuses to teach the next generation to lead conformist lives. It sees danger in everyone thinking the same way. It worries about cheap or too-early consensus. Mistakes get written in stone. Directions are maintained to the disastrous end. More time is spent doing post-mortems than saving lives. There's a rebellious undercurrent, tracing its roots back to America's earliest arrivals and ultimately enshrined in the Declaration of Independence.

This undercurrent prizes a willingness to question everything. It promotes healthy and not-easily-swayed skepticism. It relies on common sense and rejects the pronouncements of the "experts" about whom it's been said they can see "something happen in practice and [wonder] if it would work in theory."[9]

It worries about too much bipartisanship and gets a little queasy when people reach across the aisle and finds itself asking what that will cost in freedom and money. It loses sleep when it hears that "all scientists agree" or that "the debate is over." It has great misgivings when someone in authority says, "mission accomplished," "it's not my fault," or, "we're not giving into the special interests." And it doesn't quickly dismiss "rancorous debate" or nay-saying or gridlock as people with power often do.

Not that all thoughts are valued equally. Far from it. Different can be stupid or un-helpful just as easily as it can be brilliant and beneficial. But Americans are generally open. They usually don't throw out options before they hear them out. By listening to all of the voices, they know at best that their decisions and actions will be better, and at the least, that those voices won't give up speaking because of a failure to be heard.

When living the American Ideas, Americans treasure their dissenting voices and worry when there are none. They understand with chilling certainty that the scarcest diversity in human history is diversity of thought.

Americans know that unity is a glorious thing and that unity is a dangerous thing. They define loyalty not as "my country right or wrong," but as, "I love my country too much to let it miss the right and commit the wrong." They look around the world and see diversity run amok (like sub-Saharan Africa), but they also look around the world and see unity run amok (like China and Saudi Arabia).

Aren't some ideas destructive? Of course. But Thomas Jefferson reminded us that

> We are not afraid to follow truth wherever it may lead, nor to tolerate any error so long as reason is left free to combat it.[10]

Americans recognize that some heretics are evil, but not all of them are. Everyone who believed in the American Idea of Freedom would have been burned at the stake as a heretic if they'd been born at the wrong time or in another place.

The only diversity Americans can't sanction is a notion that freedom means "we have the right to do what we want, even if it harms others," or that freedom is bad and must be obliterated. Freedom can't be used as a cover-up for evil, and it can't be used to destroy itself. But other than that? Think away.

It's no coincidence that America always leads the surveys of the "most innovative nations/cultures."[11] Why? Because to innovate, you first have to think freely, to think for yourself, to be comfortable in your own individual skin. And, "The country that scores highest on the individualism end of [the individualism-collectivism] scale is the United States."[12] Americans are free, individual people thinking freely, creating constantly.

We're so committed to thinking freely,

We Believe that an American Is Defined By What He or She Believes and Wants and Fights For, Not By an Accident of Birth

Possibly other than Native Americans – and even they probably didn't start here – everyone traces their ancestry to people born somewhere else.

So what made America? Americans. People who thought differently and who wanted a different kind of life to go with that different way of looking at life.

So that's why no one can define an American in the same way they might define Arab, Indian, Chinese, or Japanese people. One only has to look at the parade that opens the Olympic Games to see that Americans are just so...different. It's not where they were born or the way they look that makes them Americans, but things much deeper than that – what they believe, what they care about, what they want, and what they'll fight and die for.

This is wholly different than the requirements for a badge of citizenship virtually everywhere else in world history. Jews weren't accepted as full members of society in Europe even though they had been some of the most productive and valuable citizens there for hundreds of years. Muslims are outsiders in much of Europe, as are Turks in Germany, Germans in Turkey, Christians in the Middle East, everyone not Chinese or Japanese in China or Japan, or those who can't speak "perfect" French in France.

One observer noted that "European societies do not seem able to take in and assimilate people from strange and unfamiliar cultures [and] Asian countries have as much trouble with immigrants as European ones." But America? "America, on the other hand, is creating the first universal nation.... America has succeeded not because of the ingenuity of its government programs but because of the vigor of its society."[13]

When people in those societies look at these outside criteria to determine who the outsiders are, there's an infinite number of things that divide and nothing that unites.

Not so with the American Idea. You're an American – first and foremost – on the inside. To paraphrase Dr. Martin Luther King, you're an American not because of the color of your skin, but because of the content of your character. Character is the building. The rest is just architectural details.

If we find ourselves concerned about nations who will allow – or send – their supposed "riff-raff" to our shores, we should take a pause. From the beginning, those who came were seldom of the highest class because most of those who had it made had no reason to come. It was the poor from the debtors' prisons, the religious dissenters, the political outcasts, the "rabble" searching for freedom and opportunity and respect – this was the stuff out of which a new nation "conceived in liberty"[14] was founded. And we should pause a second time because most of us are descended from that riff-raff.

This humility, this understanding, this revolutionary concept about origins should allow us to say to everyone who lives anywhere,

> *If You Think Like an American, You Are an American, and You Are Welcome Here*

Here's a great American truth: If you want a life of freedom and dignity and opportunity, if you share the American ideas, you are already an American – you're coming home.

America was restrictive on immigration at first and kept coming up with more restrictions through the years – there was always some new group of "undesirable" Americans (including my ancestors) that "established" Americans didn't want to come in. As always, there are new demands for restriction today, the most current being focused on Latino-Americans.

But America just can't help itself. It can't because of the American Idea of Diversity, because of the undeniable common heritage of coming from somewhere else. The Idea keeps saying to the world, in majestically resonant tones, that America is

> *Not like the brazen giant of Greek fame, with conquering limbs astride from land to land; here at our sea-washed, sunset gates shall stand a mighty woman with a torch, whose flame is the imprisoned lightning, and her name Mother of Exiles.... From her beacon-hand glows world-wide welcome. "Keep ancient lands, your storied pomp!" cries she with silent lips. "Give me your tired, your poor, your huddled masses yearning to breathe free, the wretched refuse of your teeming shore. Send these, the homeless, tempest-tost to me, I lift my lamp beside the golden door!"*[15]

It thrilled me the first time I read this, emblazoned on the Statue of Liberty in New York harbor. And still it thrills. At Ellis Island, the great American entry point, I remember seeing the picture of an old Irish woman. As a young teenager in starving Ireland, she was told by her parents that she would have to marry a very, very old

47

butcher. Her response? "So I said 'goodbye,' and went to America."[16]

She was tired and poor, at that time as wretched as any refuse on earth. *And she knew where to go.*

There's been nothing new on this score for four centuries. It seems at times that everyone who wants freedom wants to come here. Many who are already here don't want them to come, but they come anyway because it's America. Welcoming strangers is a big idea, a key component of the American Idea of Diversity. How big? Well, America accepts "more legal immigrants as permanent residents than the rest of the world combined."[17] That's how big.

And this Idea implies more. It says that all who love the concept of America can come. This is hard for some to hear, so they conjure up the same list of plausible and implausible reasons to deny entry that was used against their own ancestors 50 or 100 or 150 years ago.

But new Americans keep coming anyway. The only way to prevent them from coming is to become the anti-America, to treat "outsiders" like they do in immigration-free China or Saudi Arabia. As President Ronald Reagan said in his farewell address, America is

> *The shining city upon a hill...teeming with people of all kinds living in harmony and peace....And if there had to be city walls, the walls had doors and the doors were open to anyone with the will and the heart to get here.... [America is] still a beacon, still a magnet for all who must have freedom, for all the pilgrims from all the lost places who are hurtling through the darkness, toward home.*[18]

Yes, the Idea says that all who hate the idea of America can leave. But this isn't "America, love it or leave it." There are times when America is hard to love, most especially when it's violating its own Ideas. But that's different from hating America and what it stands for, from loathing the rich heritage of the American Ideas. If someone wants to find an anti-America to live in, we don't want to convert them. We want them to go there – if those anti-Americas will even let them in.

America, overall, has been righteously upside-down in its heart toward immigrating Americans. Other nations only took people's land, like Stalin did in the Ukraine, while America gave it away for free through the land grants, the Homestead Act, the Oklahoma land rush. And we keep making it easier for everyone to live as a full-fledged American – from community welcome parties to the Civil Rights Act, from universal male suffrage to universal female suffrage, from eliminating the eugenics of a Margaret Sanger to lifting up the lives of the most severely disabled.

People can see it – this continual reinvention, all driven by the American Idea of Diversity. And when they see it and see it clearly, they want to come to America. They're just waiting for an invitation.

But when you or I receive an invitation to a party or event, certain concepts come into play:

   • First, the inviter gets to set the ground rules – the date, the time, the dress code, whether you may bring others, how long the event will last.

   • Second, we have to play by those ground rules – we can't expect to show up a day early or with our entire family, if we were limited to one guest, and be let in.

• Third, we can expect all guests to be treated the same way.

• And fourth, if our behavior is out of bounds – if we're caught handing out drugs or stealing the silverware or taking food from the kitchen – we can expect to be asked to leave by the host (or their staff or security).

And so it is with the invitation, "You're welcome in America." You're an invited guest, and we get to set the ground rules. You have to play by those ground rules. You can expect to be treated fairly. And you can't expect to stay in America if you hurt people or otherwise break the law.

This means that these ground rules have to be clear and applied equally to all guests. We won't make some people wait in a 5-year line while others come into the party after a decision they made that morning. You can't come in uninvited, illegally. You can't bring others along who weren't invited. And you can't come to bring down our culture or economy – selling drugs, stealing, living off welfare.

But if you come as a gracious guest who wants to add to the life of the party, you're welcome, very welcome, in America.

This is so ingrained in American culture we are able to say

If You're Yearning to Breathe Free, You Aren't Leaving Your Home to Come to America – You're Coming Home

Think of what it took to come to America in the 1600s, 1700s, and 1800s. Why did they do it? Many were simply people who had had enough (of nothing) for too long, had been oppressed for too long, and had been treated like scum and beaten and tortured for too long. They may not have known what they wanted in specific terms, but they knew it had to be something different – something like freedom and opportunity.

In one sense, they took great risks because they had nothing to lose. But there was more. They knew that there might not be a pot of gold at the end of the rainbow, but they knew that there was a rainbow.

Think of what it takes to come to America, even today. You have to take risks. You have to leave home with its familiarity, its basic comfort. You have to make your way to a strange land, full of odd languages and customs. And you mostly have to come with nothing – except an unconquerable spirit.

Coming to America is a grand concept: "I am a human being and I have value. I count. But I don't count where I am – politically, socially, economically, maybe even in my basic right to life. It will be hard, but I will leave. I will go to where I count. I will go to America." You have to be very different inside to even want to come to this very different place that still feels somehow like...home.

Other countries may have more history or better wine or choicer food or cleaner streets. But they're missing a really big thing, a conviction, the strangely non-Darwinian idea that *we will make room for you.*

Latinos – not all Latinos, but those with that concept – want to come? We'll find a spot for you. We'll give you a chance, like someone did with our ancestors – perhaps with doubt and fear and reluctance. We might even remember, if we're feeling especially gracious, that some of your ancestors may have been here first.

If they don't have that concept, if they aren't yearning to breathe free, American air, we can still let them come legally as guest workers – if handled properly, a win-win for them and for America. What could be better than having a dream home like America and inviting some of your neighbors over for help...and for dinner?

But if they have that unshakeable concept of wanting to count in a place where they can be counted – or they come around to having it in spite of themselves – they belong to us. They are Americans.

And we can say to each other and to them that

We Refuse to Judge a Book By Its Cover, Because Even Though Everyone Is Different on the Outside, We All Bleed the Same Color

President Ronald Reagan said that "though our heritage is one of blood lines from every corner of the Earth, we are all Americans pledged to carry on this last, best hope of man on Earth."[19]

I once watched as a Vietnamese-born American (a former commando in the South Vietnamese army), many years after the war, picked shrapnel out of his arm with an unsterilized pen knife. I grimaced, but he looked at me and smiled. "Sir, you see?" he said. "You don't have to go down very far at all to find that we're all the same color!"

The world largely goes way beyond judging a book by its cover to condemning the book because of its cover. There will be bigotry and racism as long as there are human beings. These have thrived in America in the past. But no more. There are still racists in America – including a few who make their living off keeping it alive – but not one who really counts.

Americans who understand this Idea of Diversity can say to those who don't, "Maybe your ancestors have been in America for centuries and have always opposed the newcomers. Those of us whose ancestors came later are glad you didn't win. We're glad that the Idea won't let you win. We're glad that the rest of us got in despite your opposition. We're thrilled that the Idea is bigger than your small notion of national purity. In some way, you're an American citizen who isn't an American. You're living off anger and fear while putting down other people's courage and willingness to find a better life."

We're free people, and we should freely grant that freedom to others. People who aren't free or who don't feel free or who want to control others are unlikely to grant freedom to anyone else. That's because they don't understand it, don't want it, and don't have the sense of acceptance that freedom can produce.

But over time, freedom can breed a spirit of acceptance, the ability to respect rather than fear both difference and those who are different. We can learn to be free from the chains of bigotry and can come to see how little outside differences between groups really mean. "People who bang on about innate differences should remember that variation within subgroups in the population is usually bigger than the variation between subgroups.... Judging people as individuals rather than as representatives of groups is...morally right."[20]

We can search history to find examples of where unfree people or tyrants have been welcoming toward others, and we'll mostly come up empty. But America is the shining example of where free people have learned – slowly, haltingly, imperfectly, but more and more – to offer acceptance. We're the first large-scale society to be a churning melting pot rather than a semi-peaceful mosaic. We're multi-cultural – with an attitude.

In fact, the only overarching problem we have with tolerance – the only one that threatens freedom – is that we're confused. As a society, we're fuzzy about the distinction between being tolerant of difference and being tolerant of evil. We can even be fuzzy about whether the last sentence is a matter of critical importance or a matter of opinion or semantics. We'll see which in the chapter on the American Idea of Society.

Are there evil people who will never be true Americans? Of course. Should we work hard to keep them out? Of course. But we can't let the 5% who are bad eggs cause us to keep the 95% out who want to come in, the 95% who are true Americans in spirit.

It's true that other nations might have large minorities which aren't being perse-cuted. But this isn't so much being tolerant as being separatist. They have an "Arab population" or a "Turkish population" or an "Asian population." But in America – again, very imperfectly – we have an American population.

When you go into an ethnic neighborhood, you find Americans. People talk about being hyphenated Americans, but the cultural core is still resonant everywhere, and they can't help being just Americans. "In the eyes of the government we are just one race here," observed Supreme Court Justice Antonin Scalia. "It is American."[21]

Who, by and large, really comes to America? People who will fuel American en-ergy and freshness and innovation and productivity and that wonderful diversity of thought. People who will help us avoid the European problem of watching its core population dwindle away even while newcomers are treated badly, of carrying its many humanistic pretensions but its even longer history of not welcoming strangers.

The American Idea of Diversity reminds us that people are generally coming to *experience* the Idea, not to destroy it. They don't want to change the Idea that they came for, except to make it bigger.

America is at its best when it makes room, when it watches out for the newcomers. At the end of one of the very best episodes of the television show *The West Wing*, a question was posed by one of the White House staff: What can you say about a country that even protects the rights of those who are trying to destroy it?[22] The answer?

God bless America.

America At Its Best

We can reclaim and rebuild a culture of unified diversity, diversified unity. We can:

Take Action

We can reclaim and rebuild a culture of unified diversity, diversified unity. We can:

★

Agree on the core that makes America exceptional.

★

Keep diversity and unity in equilibrium.

★

Keep in mind that diversity can be destructive.

★

Refuse to let individualism destroy American culture.

★

Refuse to let tribalism destroy American culture.

★

Eliminate the destructiveness of sub-group hyphenation.

★

Cherish diversity of thought.

★

Stay clear on the difference between tolerating difference and tolerating evil.

★

Eliminate tracking of Americans by race and ethnicity.

★

Make a common language a special way to bond.

★

Eliminate dual citizenship.

★

Remember where we came from.

★

Welcome everyone into America who is already an American.

★

Refuse to see immigration and safe borders as mutually exclusive ideas.

★

Take the burden of immigration control off of businesses.

★

See assimilation and cultural identity as compatible.

To see detail on these Action Points and
to add your voice visit www.theamericanideas.com

Diversity and the American Idea

At their best, America and Americans value both diversity and unity.

To say it a bit differently, if Americans were asked whether they value individuality or community, their answer would be a resounding "Yes!" Americans want what most other people would say is an impossibility – blending a ferocious, hard-headed individualism with a caring, soft-hearted communitarianism.

But where do you start? With individuality or community?

If you start with community – by far the common case – the individual becomes a cipher, as is true and has always been true in China. The community is all, greater than any of its parts and even the sum of its parts. The rights of an individual are nothing compared with the rights of the community. If sacrifices must be made, the individual is expected to make – or be – that sacrifice. Community first can create a monolith where those who are different will not be welcome – and may not survive.

But the American approach was to start with the individual and to let him or her build his or her own communities. Individualism can create a thousand communities and does just that. Tocqueville was amazed at the countless associations that Americans formed or joined. In America, communities aren't forced by rule or tradition, but driven by passions and interests. This keeps those communities strong and dynamic and prevents the encrustation and even tyranny of community norms.

In recent times in America, we've moved away from this honoring of the individual in several critical ways. One is to lift up the tribe – race, ethnicity, class. A second is to create group "rights" that can destroy the rights of individuals not in that group. A third is to make America itself the community, to have our own version of the "China syndrome." All of this is at the expense of the individual and severely damages the American Idea of Diversity.

Loving diversity is one of the strongest identifying marks of an American. We can have a big tent of diversity, bustling with energy and grand Ideas, as long as we have a pillar of unity at the center to hold it up.

Unified diversity is the best of who we are. We want it and need it. And with enough wisdom, we can have it.

CHAPTER 3

The American Idea of Justice

The American Idea of Justice isn't first or foremost about law or courts, crime or punishment, rights or retribution. This American Idea is about getting what you deserve.

Getting what you deserve means correlation – society and government working hard to closely connect actions with consequences, inputs with outputs, and effort with reward.

This Idea pushes into the background things that have been primary drivers in most cultures in most of history. This includes privileges based on birth, class, wealth, political power, race, ethnicity, tribe, titles, and credentials.

The Idea says that you shouldn't be able to get more than you deserve by using your name or money, genetic inheritance or position, prefix or degree. It also goes the other way. It objects to using newer drivers like lower social status or poverty, voter collusion or lobbying, media pressure or political action committees to get more than what you deserve.

There has always been a vigorous discussion about what "deserve" means. When the conversation has stayed close to the American Idea, it's brought about human and civil rights – in a fabulous, omni-cultural, multi-ethnic, poly-racial society – that had never before been imagined, much less achieved. When it's strayed from the Idea, justice for some can become injustice for everyone else.

In the American Idea, justice comes in different forms – legal, social, and economic. America hasn't always offered justice in these areas and has at times been a dealer in injustice, but its basic concept of justice – The American Idea – is that we will work through the injustices and drive back the unjust until right next to "let freedom ring," we can write "let justice prevail."

"I think the first duty of society is justice," observed founder Alexander Hamilton.[1]

Justice

Justice means getting what you deserve, as determined by an objective, consistent, and enduring standard.

Legal justice includes securing the freedom and well-being of the blameless, in part by curbing the freedom and well-being of the bad people who harm them.

It makes room for mercy, but only if there is a true willingness to change and to make restitution.

Social justice includes ensuring respect and consideration for every individual, family, and group in that society.

It can't be coerced by government, but can only be brought to life by people of courage and character.

Economic justice includes keeping what you've earned and getting what is due you based on merit and should be related to effort, determination, and ingenuity.

It should not be subject to anyone's arbitrary definition of fairness or to the selfish demands of the rich or poor, the powerful or vulnerable.

Let's explore this rich American Idea. It says first that

Justice Means Getting What You Deserve, as Determined By an Objective, Consistent, and Enduring Standard

All too frequently, people in other parts of the world have been divided unjustly into two groups.

The first group has gotten way more than they deserve based on their poor character, effort, and performance. They've gotten this excess – this injustice – due to a variety of means such as conquest, theft, coercion, collusion, corruption, and circumstances of birth. They deserve X, but somehow they've received 10X or 100X – or, in some brutal cases, all of the Xs.

The second group has gotten way less than they deserve, often in spite of their good character, effort, and performance. They've gotten this reduction – this injustice – based on a variety of means, such as through conquest, theft, coercion, collusion, corruption, and circumstances of birth. They deserve X, but somehow they've received 0.1X or 0.01X – or all too often, no Xs at all.

The American Idea of Justice is diametrically opposed to these historically "normal" outcomes. It acknowledges that not all of these injustices can be corrected – for example, a person of low character may inherit a great estate – but works to correct the correctible. If something was gotten or lost through wrong means, justice says those situations should be corrected.

This is much different from saying, "Everyone should get the same," or, "No one should have more than anyone else," or, "We should override agreements and contracts willingly entered into in order to balance the outcomes." The goal of justice isn't – can't be, shouldn't be – equality of circumstance or redistribution of that which was fairly and justly earned or worrying more about the rights of criminals than the rights of their victims.

The goal of justice the American way is supporting the correlation of

- actions with consequences (legal justice)

- inputs with outputs (social justice), and

- effort with reward (economic justice)

The standards of justice have to be agreed on. And they have to be standards that hold for everyone in the society. They have to be objective, consistent, and enduring:

• *Objective.* It's very easy in life to feel that we've been treated unjustly. But those feelings can't be reasonably translated into intelligent action by a society or government. We have to agree together that this specific act is a crime or is inappropriate in a social setting or is unacceptable in a financial transaction, all based on well-established principles, analysis, and facts. As soon as these and other attempts at justice become random or arbitrary, they no longer deserve to be called justice.

• *Consistent.* If the same crime is given a life sentence here (perhaps on a three-strikes policy) and probation there (perhaps on a good-family policy), if one group is allowed to protest freely on an issue and another group is treated as a racketeering conspiracy on the same issue, if one person is able to keep all of what they've earned and another only gets to keep a half or two thirds – whatever else we have, we don't have justice. If discrimination against one race is disallowed, discrimination against all races should be disallowed. If it's good for the majority, it should be good for the minority – and vice versa. Different standards for different people doing the same thing is a nearly perfect definition of injustice.

• *Enduring.* Justice that varies with time, circumstance, and place is a fragile justice indeed and may not be justice at all. If Japanese-American citizens shouldn't be arrested and relocated in the 1920s or 1960s, then they shouldn't be treated so in the 1940s. If it isn't alright to mistreat blacks in the South, then it isn't all right to mistreat them in the North. If it isn't appropriate to allow insider trading and kickbacks in the 20th century, it's no more appropriate in the 21st. We may grow in our understanding of what "right" and "wrong" are, but that doesn't make right things any more right or wrong things any less wrong than they always were. Ultimately, the application of justice can't be separated from time and circumstance and place – but justice itself must stand like an immovable mountain.

It isn't the government's job alone to secure justice. It has a role, but given it's penchant for political distortion, compromise, and corruption, that role itself has to be kept in check. It can easily become the biggest dealer in injustice. Real justice depends on the character of the people. Founder James Madison said,

> To suppose that any form of government will secure liberty or happiness without any virtue in the people, is a chimerical idea.[2]

The American Idea is radical here. It suggests that all of us have the responsibility to secure justice for all of us. Based on the American definition, the vast majority of human beings throughout history have been dealt with unjustly, but that shall not be so here, not in America where Jefferson said, "The most sacred of the duties of a government [is] to do equal and impartial justice to all its citizens."[3]

Very few societies or governments have ever been just, but we can have that kind of society and government. That's the American Idea. It starts with legal justice and tells us that

Legal Justice Includes Securing the Freedom and Well-Being of the Blameless, in Part by Curbing the Freedom and Well-Being of the Bad People Who Harm Them

There's a difference between "legal" and "just," and sometimes the difference is huge. A thing can be legal and unjust – like segregation – or just and illegal – like hiding runaway slaves. Laws don't make an unjust thing just, or a just thing unjust.

Laws that do these things should be disrespected, an action-oriented concept with a grand American heritage. "Any fool can make a rule," wrote American philosopher and writer Henry David Thoreau, "and every fool will mind it."[4]

So legal justice requires us first and foremost to define what is legal in a moral way. Who cares if it's legal if it's also immoral? We don't want to find ourselves saying (as we so often have to do these days) that "this may be legal, but it sure isn't moral."

All law has a moral – or immoral – base. The further the law gets from a moral base, the less likely the law is to protect the innocent and the more likely it is to become an agent of injustice. Henry David Thoreau, on this, as on so many other things, is uncompromising:

> Most legislators, politicians, lawyers...and office holders, serve the state chiefly with their heads; and as they rarely make any moral distinctions, they are as likely to serve the devil, without intending it, as God.[5]

Americans have always grown weary of leaders who avoid making moral distinctions. We like pragmatic people, but only if their pragmatism comes from a moral center. We have, in the main, wanted just laws. We want laws that take positive action on behalf of the blameless and negative action against the wicked.

Part of the problem – a big part – with legal justice systems is that too often they focus first on the perpetrators of crime. These systems spend their energy and resources on the 5% who break the law rather than the 95% who don't. So much of the current legal justice system concerns itself primarily with the rights of the accused and guilty – that's the wrong place to start.

In the American Idea, the place to begin is with the un-accused and the innocent and the great majority of people who don't deliberately try to hurt someone else, who don't transgress, who don't place themselves or their interests above the law or the rights of others.

Who speaks for the injured and the dead? For the assaulted and violated? For the cheated and deceived? What happened to them? What about their rights? In the American Idea, that's the place for the justice system to begin its work.

In any field, it's too easy to concern ourselves with the 5% who are more bad than good, rather than with the 95% who are more good than bad. This is true both for those who prosecute and for those who defend in the legal justice system.

Even our language here betrays us. Both sides are concerned with the perpetrators, one to prosecute them and the other to defend them. There's no one in this kind of a system to defend the victims. They might be mentioned in a closing statement to generate sympathy from the jury – like a sort of living stage prop – but they're merely bystanders in a big drama.

We talk about perpetrators of crimes paying their "debt to society," which is nebulous and without effect, rather than their debt to the victim, which begins to get at a critical component of justice: restitution.

Crimes aren't committed against society, except by out-of-control governments. Crimes are committed against individuals, people who had a right to life and liberty and the pursuit of happiness and had the use of them stripped away. An individual or family may be forever changed by the crime, while the society only follows the story until it gets bored. Perpetrators are often treated lightly, in part because they're thought to only have dented the society, when what they've really done is crush the individual or family.

How did this happen? How did bad guys often end up with more rights than good guys? It's sad but understandable. Arbitrary laws, false accusations, and unreasonable judgments have been the norm of history. Innocent people have regularly been imprisoned and killed and impoverished in countless numbers by unjust governments. All too often, more people have been victimized by the law than by the lawless.

So, safeguards were set up by the founders and those who came before and after them. They wanted to assure that legal justice was first and foremost not violated by the government, the very agency that was supposed to dispense it. They set up boundaries and made it hard, or at least harder, to accuse and convict an innocent person.

But those safeguards can be manipulated and abused. They can be used to protect the guilty rather than the innocent. American law has done one of its jobs and mostly prevented the horror of arbitrary justice from living on American soil. But it's gone too far. It's protecting the weeds at the expense of the crops. That was never part of the Idea.

The saying, "It's better for ten guilty people to go free than for one innocent person to be convicted" sounds noble on first hearing. But it's a straw man. It's just as bad for the guilty to get away with it as it is for an innocent person to get stuck with it. Neither is acceptable. To protect the innocent who are falsely accused, it shouldn't be necessary to protect the guilty who are rightly accused.

Legal justice certainly includes all those who are accused, but this inclusion should never be at the expense of legal justice for those who are victims. What does this look like in practice?

- Someone confesses to a murder and takes police to the location of the body, a place that only the murderer could know. But he wasn't Mirandized before he told all, so the confession and everything related to it are thrown out.

- Incontrovertible evidence of a kidnapping is found during a search. But the warrant was faulty, so the evidence of the terrible crime is deliberately suppressed.

- Someone claims falsely that a verbal agreement exists that requires a business they worked in (and stole from) be sold to them at a certain low price. But although they can provide no evidence, and in fact evidence of their theft is clear, the judge is sympathetic to their demands as "the little guy" and swayed by the "deep pockets" of the owners.

Was the murder victim Mirandized? Was the kidnap victim served a warrant? Was the business owner given the benefit of the doubt? What we have is the triumph of technicality and misplaced empathy over truth. For those who are victims, the justice system has victimized them a second time.

If a police officer or some other government official violates an accused person's rights, we shouldn't have their "investigative crime" cancel out the actual evidence of the original crime. The truth is, two crimes have been committed. Justice demands that both of them be punished. The attempt to cancel out one crime with another crime has the effect of creating yet another crime.

And this is, like so many other assaults on the American Ideas, a fairly recent phenomenon. Truth wasn't excluded for any reason for most of our history. But "in 1961...the Fourth Amendment right against illegal search and seizure was nationalized, and the [supreme] court developed rules to exclude from trials evidence obtained illegally."[6] Anyone looking at excluded evidence knows it's true – but the jury can't know it at all.

The proper, primary focus of a legal justice system is securing justice for people on the receiving end of crime. This is what Americans have always wanted from their government but not always gotten. For Americans, a government is just if it secures our rights against anyone and everyone and a plague if it does not.

Americans have always been a direct people who want to know basic things like, "What are the facts?" and, "What's the deal here?" Because of this, legal justice requires us to revamp the legal system so that the goal is truth and not – as it is now – victory.

One of the enduring myths of the current American legal system is that it embodies a quest for truth. The concept is simple: let two sides battle it out in front of a judge or jury, and the truth will emerge from the process.

The Achilles' heel of this concept is that it puts the two sides in a position of presenting only their "truth," which may not be true at all. And worse – it encourages them to hide or shade some or all of the real truth that would harm their ability to "win." Sun-Tzu said that "the art of all war is deception,"[7] and this adversarial system – a war contained in a courtroom – invites this principle into the center of the action. Legal scholar Alan Dershowitz has said, "All sides in a trial want to hide at least some of the truth."[8]

In civil cases, the process achieves the pinnacle of search-for-victory rather than search-for-truth. The attorneys or law firms representing either side would, in most cases, not even take a case if they thought it had no merit – often meaning a strong chance to prevail more than anything else. Once they take a case, they know their mission is to defeat the other side – victory, after all, is what keeps the clients coming back and the fees rolling in.

Too often, this means that the truth they know about their own side that is harmful to their game plan is buried. Falsehoods or innuendos that can be imputed to the other side are crafted and launched. Since neither execution nor prison is on the line, attorneys can wage this war of deception in good conscience.

In criminal cases, the truth-defeating tendencies of the process get a bit uglier. Prosecutors can press their cases against people who are not clearly guilty and then let the process sort out guilt and innocence. Defense attorneys of any intelligence are going to know fairly quickly if their client or potential client is guilty. Even if they know they're guilty, they can still take the case and work hard to prove they aren't – as long as they believe they can win or at least make a fee or a name for themselves.

They do this under the pious-sounding "everyone deserves a defense" bromide. This is supported by the conscience-freeing belief that it is the system's responsibility to sort out the truth – even though they're part of the system and are working very hard to subvert the truth. Too often, it's only in the world of television where there are attorneys who will only defend the truly innocent.

This is compounded by the rules of evidence that have evolved through the years. Evidence should be let in on the primary criterion that it advances the truth. But it is usually let in based on whether it's the right "type" of evidence or was gathered "properly." Evidence of truth is regularly buried by competent, knowing, and fully-able-to-exploit-the-rules attorneys. Instead of punishing investigators and police who violate the rules of collection, and at the same time still allowing the truth that is now in the light of day to be seen, the system punishes the primary beneficiary of truth – the victim – by excluding the evidence. It merely reprimands the police (or less).

Witnesses are often at the center of this truth-masking charade. At the worst end of it, they can lie in their entire testimony, while they're guided into the lies by a skillful attorney. The deceits are only thwarted if the opposing attorney knows how to object and derail the runaway fabrication. Other witnesses shade the truth to tilt the balance to one side or the other. Witnesses are coached on what to say and what to leave out and what impressions they should leave with the jury or judge.

Even witnesses who intend to "tell the truth, the whole truth, and nothing but the truth" can be stymied and frustrated in their attempt to do the very thing they swore – were forced to swear – that they would do. Indeed, few things are more frustrating to an honest person than to have their truthful testimony chopped to pieces by the adversarial tools of objections and sustainings, and the continual demand to only answer "Yes," or "No." The fact is that few, if any, witnesses are ever allowed to tell "the whole truth."

This whole process turns judges into referees who have to make calls about what the truth really is. They aren't dispensers of truth or even arbiters of truth, but god-like creatures who decide what truth is and what they and the jury will be allowed to know of it.

But in the American Idea of Justice, the goal of the legal justice system should be truth. All evidence, no matter how it's gotten, should be used. We may have to punish those who get it illegally, but to act as though the evidence of a crime doesn't exist is to be willfully self-deceived. It makes the justice system a purveyor of injustice, and a second victimizer of the original victim. It completely misses the main point that every criminal should be punished.

Even if people attempt to administer justice perfectly, being imperfect, the best they can do is approximate justice. It's hard enough to approximate justice even when we have the truth. To deliberately choose to ignore the truth is to lose any real approximation of justice, if not reality. The greatest lies produce the greatest injustices and only in the exposition of all pertinent truth can a picture of justice emerge.

Truth and justice are inseparable. "Justice is truth in action," noted British Prime Minister Benjamin Disraeli.[9] This doesn't mean that justice has to be harsh; in fact,

Legal Justice Makes Room for Mercy, but Only If There Is a True Willingness to Change and to Make Restitution

Legal justice starts with the concept that something has been lost or taken. It declares that the lost should be found and the taken should be returned. Forgiveness depends on repentance and restitution. Rehabilitation depends on facing the truth and changing what you see.

Americans stand where few have ever stood – for moral justice, as well as legal justice. We don't allow murderers to rule us, whether they're killers or drug lords, terrorists or tyrants. We don't let them freely walk around, or come into our country, or perpetrate their nightmares on a desperate people. We always tell those murderers that they could make no greater mistake than to let us smell the stench of their foul deeds.

Americans also know the immeasurable value of mercy and tolerance. They know that it's often a good thing to strike one blow when two are deserved, that it's a mark of strength, not weakness, to follow the Golden Rule, that we must not become murderers to bring murderers to justice. We see – at least after the fact – that it's better to send ships to bring six million Jews to a land founded by escapees than to send ships to kill their tormentors after those Jews are dead.

Liberty, the second unalienable right, doesn't mean much if Life, the first unalienable right, is cheap and unprotected. No one can be truly free if they're threatened with looming crime against their person, their loved ones, or their property.

Potentially even worse is the current "solution" extended into the long-term future – the creation of a prison nation within the nation, where a criminal underclass advances a powerful culture diametrically opposed to the rule of law and civil society.

The problems are many. They all result from a faulty view of justice. But – very good news – they're all very, very solvable. Here they are:

> • *The loss of will to treat violent criminals as enemies of life, liberty, and humanity.* There's a recurring delusion that "all people are basically good." Some don't want to blame a supposed "good" person for the bad things that they do, so they look for the external causes of this otherwise inexplicable behavior. They often find a host of explanations that excuse nothing. Evil is as evil does. Societies that don't operate on this basis get more and more of the evil that they refuse to recognize. And compassion shown to unrepen-

tant criminals – like releasing them because they're terminally ill – shows, more than anything else, weakness of purpose and absence of wisdom. People in general aren't basically bad. But some people are.

• *The willingness to make excuses for bad actions.* The Idea at its best allows no excuses for evil behavior. Violent crime, for example, isn't explained away by poverty. Poverty was far worse in the first half of the 1900s, culminating in the Great Depression. There really was no middle class, and "poor" meant "not enough food or clothes or shelter," not, "I have to drive an old car and only have one television." And yet crime didn't explode as the economy imploded. With poverty greater by orders of magnitude compared to today, crime was a tiny fraction of what we now suffer. We've upgraded the definition of "poverty" even as we've downgraded its application. The endless list of excuses – abusive homes, bad neighborhoods, drugs, chemical imbalances, defective schools, ineffective churches – indeed represents problems that need to be addressed. But none of them justify harming another human being.

• *The belief that loss of freedom is sufficient to secure justice.* Our basic recourse is to strip people of their freedom. In some cases – violent crime – that is the just answer and, even then, it isn't enough. But loss of liberty is a terrible thing for a human being, no less for a criminal than for anyone else, and it's guaranteed to produce resentment, rebellion, degradation, and despair. It should be used sparingly and appropriately. Some crimes don't require loss of freedom. Right now, America has one tool, and it's a hammer. Unsurprisingly, all criminals look like a nail.

• *The inconsistency of punishing both too little and too much.* We don't seem to be sure how wrong some things really are. The result? We let appeals go on without end, have punishments that are minor compared with the crime, routinely shorten sentences, and parole because of limited budgets. Or we go the other way and make some things more wrong than they really are, so we vigorously prosecute victimless crimes, have punishments that are over the top compared with the crime, give people sentences that are way out of proportion to the crime (but directly related to their social and economic status or the quality of their attorney), and build ever more budget-crushing prisons. Consistency is crucial to any concept of justice.

• *A counterfeit belief that punishment magically contains the seeds of rehabilitation.* Punishment is part of the process. Criminals need to understand that touching a hot stove will cause pain. But it's only part of the process. Whether or not they're ever redeemed from their bad thought processes, a chance at rehabilitation for most will arise only from a rich combination of experiencing punishment, feeling remorse, declaring guilt, and making restitution. Restitution is the outstanding missing ingredient of our current justice system.

• *The false mind-set that criminals owe a debt to society rather than a debt to the ones they've harmed.* It's said so often and in so many ways that it seems to be a given – "They should pay their debt to society" or "I've paid my debt to society." It's true that all crime hurts society, but the debt is owed only to those who were harmed by it. A criminal attacking someone in some other city doesn't hurt me, but they certainly hurt their victim. That's where the obligation lies. This fuzzy "owing society" notion diminishes the idea of justice. How? Society is hurt, but it's big and doesn't hurt too much, so society can be magnanimous and punish lightly or not at all. Thinking the debt is some foggy thing owed to society is in part what's led to the prison mind-set – "You owe us time for your naughtiness." Even here, it's perverse because society, through the government, pays to house and care for the criminal rather than the criminal doing something useful for society or the society or criminal doing anything for the victim. There are in fact two other debts really owed in all of this, besides the debt owed to the victim by the criminal. First is the government's debt to the injured party, to require justice from the perpetrator and for the victim. If justice for the victim isn't forthcoming, the government has made them victims a second time. This debt is owed because we've vested the government with the trust, responsibility, authority, and resources to protect us. And second is society's debt to the injured party, to support them and encourage them and to insist that perpetrators and the government pay what they owe to the victims.

• *The absence of restitution.* The current approach also violates the rights of the victim a second time by denying her or him restitution. Working for the one you hurt makes everything real, personal, and meaningful. There's no substitute for the power of restitution from the perpetrator to the victim. But right now, there's virtually none of this in the justice system. The government needs to take concrete steps to ensure that the criminals make restitution, real restitution, to their victims. This could even be taken further by requiring the criminal to make restitution to the government for the costs of prosecuting him or her. People talk a lot about rehabilitation, but the best form of rehabilitation is restitution. In a criminal justice system, the low road is heavy-handed retribution and the dead-end road is soft-headed rehabilitation. The high road, the road to potentially better days for the victim, the perpetrator, and the society, is restitution.

There's hope for criminals and the society in which they live, but not with the current approach, which is so out of touch with the American Idea of Justice. It's a set of bad notions perfectly designed to get bad results.

It's folly to forgive criminals when they've spent time in prison but haven't really changed – or worse, when they've spent their time in prison honing and expanding their criminal skills. Shortening the sentence of a person who hasn't really changed isn't mercy, it's just processing. They've somehow complied – at least superficially – with a set of rules, and by doing this, they have given themselves a chance to commit more crimes. Their victim and society deserve much better than this.

But if they've really changed? If the combination of loss of freedom, having real and useful work, and making restitution has actually affected the way they think? Then we as a just society can, in many cases, offer mercy – something earned by a change of heart and not just by time served. A criminal who works hard to make restitution may very much deserve an early out and a second chance at life.

Ultimately, it isn't cruel to keep an unrepentant criminal locked up and locked down, costing taxpayers lots of money and producing nothing of value. Turning these people loose on fresh victims is the worst kind of injustice.

But even though it isn't cruel, in many cases, it's stupid. It's also wasteful, destructive, and destined to produce an ever-expanding, more creatively evil criminal class. We need to be smart, so we can be both just and merciful.

But legal justice isn't only the only great longing of people throughout history. So is the desire for social justice. What does that involve?

Social justice is a crucial part of the American Idea of Justice. It has always been so.

But social justice has never begun in America with groups. It has always started with the individual. The Idea reminds us that a society that treats one individual unjustly in an attempt to treat another justly has lost its way, if not its soul. The American Idea calls for social justice for every individual – no one put at unfair disadvantage, no one disadvantaged to somehow "advantage" another.

It's too easy to slice up social justice and then to fragment it and, ultimately, to annihilate it. Wrong begets wrong as we swing on a pendulum of social injustice – segregation and forced desegregation (like busing), exclusion and affirmative action (reverse discrimination), no voting rights and duped or bribed voting, forced prayer and no prayer. The one constant is that an individual gets harmed – stripped of social justice in the name of the "greater good." But in a just society, how can a "greater good" be good if it's founded on wronging an individual?

After the individual, social justice moves to the family. To say that the family is the building block of society is to go too far – the basic building block of a free society is the individual. But every individual is born into a family, for better or for worse, and this is where he or she starts learning or not learning about the responsibility, self-discipline, and care for others called for by the American Ideas.

But the family hasn't been getting much social justice lately. Declining religious conviction, drifting cultural values, expanding narcissism, and decaying personal responsibility have conspired with governmental tax and inflationary policies to place incredibly destructive pressures on the family – and this is true regardless of how conservatively or liberally we define "family." The American Idea has always been concerned with justice for the family to help them hold together and not crack under life's pressures.

But there's too little help for families today, too little to keep them from falling apart. And when those families crack, social justice for the adults or children – or both – can be decimated by legal processes and judges whose unchallenged power and unyielding certitude is often only exceeded by their ignorance of the issues at hand.

Few Americans realize how vulnerable they become when they marry and have children. But today, parental rights are only secure as long as there's no significant dispute between the parents – in other words, half the time or less. Family courts operate in complete contradiction to our legal heritage, as the one filed against in a separation or divorce or child custody action is often accused of being a psychological misfit or general pervert and is then presumed guilty until proven innocent. Bacon's dictum that "he who has a wife and children has given hostages to fortune"[10] could be updated to read "They who have spouses and children have given hostages to the judges, social workers, and psychologists."

Government social services have immense clout to manipulate and coerce supposedly free Americans with regard to their children. This is compounded by the regal judiciary in which judges who have no training in matters of relationships, marriage, family, child-rearing, psychology, or counseling sit in judgment over all of those things. Other lawyers – the judges are all lawyers – throw devastating and exaggerated charges against their clients' spouses.

To assist the courts, judges surround themselves with supposed experts who have only a passing connection to the people and facts of the case. These "experts" administer personality tests and spout platitudes that have no meaning in reality (like "the best interest of the child," even though the child is often not even heard or believed).

Social justice also includes groups. Groups have too often been the targets of irrational prejudice and violence. In the American Idea, the groups don't have rights – only individuals have rights – but when those individual rights are violated due to being part of a group, the Idea demands that justice be served for all members of that group.

When dealing with groups, though, attempts at justice can become a problem and can turn very quickly into social injustice. Whenever we try to solve injustice in a general way, it's almost inevitable that we'll end up with injustice of a different kind. For example, if we try – even good-heartedly – to give some people preference in hiring because of past injustice in the workplace, we can create injustice for those outside the favored group who've worked very hard themselves to come up from nowhere.

This has been magnified by the creation in recent decades of a cult of group rights. What? How can rights be a threat to justice (and even to freedom)? By the creation of "rights" that pit group against group, race against race, gender against gender, and individual against individual – rather than recognizing and defending rights that are essential to all human beings, regardless of types or categories.

The result? These multiplying "rights" limit the more general rights of freedom of speech and action. At the same time, they offer unlimited opportunities for people and lawyers to litigate, waste vast resources, and demolish liberty. If I've earned a chance to live the life I passionately want and I can't do this because of a conjured up set of "group rights" that I can't access, then my talent is lost and my freedom is destroyed.

So what does social justice for a group mean? That all barriers and obstacles which prevent the individuals in that group from fully experiencing the American Ideas are knocked down. The group may need to act to make its plight known or to bring the pressure to bear to correct that plight. The objective is – or should be – individual dignity. The group is just a vehicle for achieving that objective.

But this moves from justice to injustice when that group seeks to be treated not as one needing attention so its members can each have justice, but instead that it be given a separate and privileged position in the society.

This was once true for white Americans, and that was wrong. But it's now true for black Americans and brown Americans and Native Americans and a host of other groups, and that is no less wrong. There are no special rights for white or black or brown or other shades of Americans, but only unalienable rights for Americans. There is no "white majority" justice or "African-American" justice or "Latino" justice, but only justice.

The world has always been filled with social injustice and is so today. But few things are as ironic, or as pitiful, as a fight for social justice that uses injustice – labels and distinctions and divisions, blame and name-calling and insults, entitlements and regulations and heavy-handed courts – as its means.

The American Idea calls us to fight for social justice – but to do that justly. Even here, the fight begins with the individual. It's a recognition that

> *Social Justice Can't Be Coerced By Govement but Can Only Be Brought to Life by People of Courage and Character*

The truth is that government has many problems in its current quest to be the "social justice" dispenser. Not the least of these is that it never knows when to stop. Good intentions get mixed up with ambition, power, and keeping certain voters happy.

Government, for example, can make it illegal to keep members of certain groups out of neighborhoods or clubs or companies, and this is a good thing. But then it wants to do more, so it withholds government contracts from organizations without the "proper" percentage of minorities, even if there has been no apparent discrimination. It can go further and permit professional sports leagues to have an overwhelming majority of minority members – and, as it happens, even give those leagues exemptions from antitrust laws – because it seems "fair," since their great-great-great grandparents might have been slaves.

In other words, government, once it goes past eliminating the legal aspects of social injustice, is just as likely to create or support injustice as it is to eliminate it. Perhaps more likely. In fact, the greatest creator and sustainer of social injustice throughout world history has been government, with its penchant for monarchs and nobility and privileged classes and the vast majority of people expected to "know their place."

So, this leaves real social justice in the hands of people of courage and character. People who speak up or leave the conversation when low-life comments are made. People who help true victims of injustice but are sickened by "victimitis." People who hate discrimination and prejudice, whoever is dealing it out. People who stop passing around, or accepting, false guilt. People who know what Dr. King meant when he talked about people being judged "not by the color of their skin, but by the content of their character."[11]

These are good hands indeed.

This means that people of courage and character have to lead the way in eliminating some crippling illusions. What illusions? That we can:

- become a color-blind society by focusing our attention on color

- achieve racial, gender, and ethnic equality by constantly forcing one group up above another

- change people's hearts and minds by laws and penalties

- use the government as the primary means of achieving social justice

What does this mean for us? That we recognize this as the 21st century and stop fighting the old wars of half a century or a century ago.

If there can be no white-only entertainment awards or white-only entertainment channel, then there should be no black-only one or Asian-only one or Latino-only one. If a white radio personality can't insult a minority, the same should be true for the minority personality related to the majority. If a Mexican can't come to the USA illegally, neither can a German. If a man shouldn't get a job or promotion because he's a man, then a woman shouldn't get one because she isn't.

As the old saying goes, "What's good for the goose is good for the gander." Or to say it another way, we should do unto others as we would have them do unto us. This is still the best summary of social justice ever made.

Legal justice. Social justice. And there's yet a third leg to the stool of the American Idea of Justice, economic justice. We can and should say that

Economic Justice Includes Keeping What You've Earned and Getting What Is Due You and Should Be Related to Effort, Determination, and Ingenuity

Revolutionary leader Samuel Adams stated,

If ye love wealth better than liberty, the tranquility of servitude better than the animating contest of freedom, go home from us in peace.[12]

But it shouldn't have to be one or the other – wealth or liberty, earnings or freedom.

Let's say a person works hard and that this hard work is converted into currency. No one else did their job for them. No one else got up early, commuted, worked through problems, dealt with difficult people, persisted through tiredness and sickness, set the goals, created the ideas, or took the risks.

So why is it getting harder in America to say to that person, "You alone should get to keep what you alone have earned?"

The American Idea says this very thing. You get to keep – in fact, you have an unalienable right to keep – that which you've worked to have. It's yours and nobody else's.

The English thought leader John Locke, who so influenced America's founders, talked about the rights to life, liberty, and property. By "property," he didn't mean gaining by greed or getting tangible things at any cost. He meant the right of an individual to earn those tangible things and then to keep them and enjoy them undisturbed. He meant that those things couldn't and shouldn't be taken by hands that hadn't earned them, either by individual thieves or by the government.

Property was changed in American parlance to "the pursuit of happiness," but the concepts are connected because of the nature of government and rights. How so? Although happiness and its pursuit are wonderful things that include much more than property, those "other things" can't be defined in a way that government can protect them – or be prevented from stealing them.

Government can establish and enforce property rights, contract law, patents, trademarks, and copyrights, but it's an unlikely candidate to help us pursue other forms of happiness – to build satisfactory relationships, live a healthy lifestyle, or take just the right book to the beach.

Excepting ideologues and utopians, people have a fairly solid grasp of the basics of human nature. They operate with a lot of common sense. They know that most people

• Work hard if they get something in return and work little or not at all if they don't

• Are driven by recognition and reward and are degraded by handouts and bailouts

• Make an effort when it counts and stop trying when it doesn't

• Stick with something that has a potential payoff and give up when that payoff disappears or is stripped away

• Exhibit astonishing ingenuity if it can be turned into gold and exhibit astonishing lethargy if it can't

Most politicians know that they aren't going to change human nature, but some of them just don't care. They'll take the hit on the personal freedom and real success of their constituents if it will buy them some votes.

All too often, the government penalizes effort, determination, and ingenuity, and rewards spending, borrowing, and profligacy. If we've made ourselves into a more valuable employee, we pay an ever-larger percentage of our income in taxes. If we build our business and serve more customers and hire more employees, again we pay a bigger and bigger portion of what we earn in taxes. If we manage to save a few dollars after all of the taxes and invest them, we pay more taxes if we happen to make a good investment.

But if we borrow a lot of money to buy a house we can't really afford, the government reduces our taxes. If we borrow to buy a second house, it will reduce our taxes even more. If we are young and really not ready to buy a first house, it will reduce our taxes if we buy it anyway. If we take out a home-equity loan to fulfill short-term wants, again we get helped with tax reduction. Spending and borrowing are encouraged, while working and investing are devalued.

Government is now in a decade-long process of converting its role from protector of property to pilferer of property. It started this in the 1930s, picked up speed in the 1960s, and is now red-lining the economic engine. It's very close to converting America into a full-fledged dependency state, where political parties only differ on the amount of the dependency and the size of the state. Under the false banner of "government-led economic justice," they turn justice on its head and make dependents of us all.

Government has become very good at redistributing wealth to anyone who has a good enough claim on the proceeds – because they have a claim on the politicians who do the redistributing. Sometimes those undeserving claimants are the lazy poor (like people who could work but don't want to) and sometimes the lazy rich (like creators of unregulated financial schemes), but the result is the same – some people getting richer at other people's expense. Often it's the people of the lowest character gaining at the expense of the hardworking, thrifty, responsible American.

Government is also willing to fight to the last drop of our blood. "The power to tax is the power to destroy"[13] is a principle that has been understood for centuries. Taxes are necessary, but it's incredibly easy for them to become excessive and abusive.

Taxes can become excessive through politicians making promises with other people's money. This is often done in response to the insatiable demands of those who want to drink long and deep from the public trough. Taxes can grow geometrically when programs are allowed to expand beyond reason and without limit. When government says, "This will only cost..." wise people will hide their wallets.

Taxes become abusive when they're used to destroy life, limit freedom, direct personal choices, manipulate society, or steal from those who have earned to gratify those who have not. Politicians who love power can find endless ways to use our money to work against our values, control us, reengineer our culture, and redistribute our wealth. Who of us really gave our consent to this? Founding father John Jay observed that

> No power on earth has a right to take our property from us without our consent.[14]

When government talks about entitlement programs, wise people know that it always means "entitled by existence" or "entitled by demand" or "entitled by voting" and never mean "entitled by effort" or "entitled by merit."

It was not by chance that the Constitution prohibited taxes like the income tax. This destructive tool was finally handed to grasping politicians by constitutional amendment in 1913 on the promise that it would be a very small tax on a very few wealthy people. Opponents saw it instead as a powerful way for the government to be both excessive and abusive. And those opponents were right.

But it isn't just the harm to the individual that this distortion of the government's role causes. We want a society that produces the most for the most, and we've known since Adam Smith's Wealth of Nations in 1776 that this means a free-market, capitalistic system based on self-interest and merit.

And economic justice for the individual human being. The world has had far too much of the Soviet/Russian system, where it was said, "They pretend to pay us, and we pretend to work."[15]

The American Idea adds some crucial boundaries to this individual economic justice. It says, "You live in a society and there are some things that only a community can do," and "You live in a dangerous world and there are some things that only a government can do," and "Those communal and governmental things cost money." We have to pay taxes because we aren't hermits living in a cave.

But even the language of taxation has gotten turned upside down. Instead of, "The government has heard you and is reducing the burden it's placed on you, to leave you with more of your own money," it's, "The government is giving you a tax break," as though the money rightfully belongs to them. Legal tax avoidance gets all mixed up in politicians' speeches with illegal tax evasion. And the language is always the same, using that marvelously flexible and dangerous word "fair": "Everyone should pay their fair share."

The amounts of both taxation and regulation have gone far beyond reasonable or necessary. Tax cuts are redefined as "breaks for the rich" or "government giving up its revenues" or "adding to the deficit," rather than as "leaving people with their own property." Taxes are used as a tool to regulate behavior, rather than as a means to get revenue for providing essential government services. The tax system is used to get people to buy houses, renovate houses, buy cars, use less alcohol, and avoid tobacco.

This isn't a new game just invented by government. It's an old game, played by almost all governments all of the time. America didn't play it for over 300 years. It's time to stop playing it now.

Economic justice – getting what is due you – is severely injured by a government that adds borrowing and inflating to heavy and progressive taxation (with progressive meaning "you'll have more taken from you the more useful you are"). Borrowing and inflating are outstanding forms of economic injustice.

Government borrowing drives up interest rates, making it hard for productive citizens to build their businesses. And it contains the seeds of its own demise, as the interest it pays on the total amount borrowed grows geometrically and it needs to borrow more just to pay what it owes in interest. Eventually, it drives interest rates up, which greatly adds to the impossibility of paying the interest on the national debt.

The old saying is true: "Those who understand interest get it, and those who don't understand interest pay it." Our government obviously doesn't understand interest.

And then there's government inflation – the only kind there is. It ultimately destroys the value of everyone's income, savings, and investments. In *Wealth of Nations*, Adam Smith said that inflation

> *occasions a general and most pernicious subversion of the fortunes of private people; enriching in most cases the idle and profuse debtor at the expense of the industrious and frugal creditor, and transporting a great part of the national capital from the hands which were likely to increase and improve it to those which are likely to dissipate and destroy it.*[16]

The best thing the government can do for economic justice is to ensure a level playing field – and to remember that it is the referee and shouldn't play the game.

The founders knew how closely economic justice was tied to liberty. Founder Alexander Hamilton said,

In the main it will be found that a power over a man's support is a power over his will.[17]

The founders knew that

Economic Justice Shouldn't Be Subject to Anyone's Arbitrary Definition of "Fairness," or to the Selfish Demands of the Rich or Poor, the Powerful or Vulnerable

Economic justice is either a concept that means something important for responsible citizens over time or what it seems to be today – a high-sounding phrase that has everything wrong with it but still sounds too noble to be attacked.

A big part of the problem is that we've confused "economic justice" with the pliable, fit-any-occasion notion of "fairness." But there's a huge difference between justice and fairness. Justice is based on truth, fairness on opinion. Justice is solid and consistent over time, while fairness can change from person to person, situation to situation, place to place, and day to day.

With justice, we can agree that all who commit the same crime should receive the same punishment, with only the degree of punishment varying with the degree of the crime. We can agree that all who do the same work should be paid the same for it. Justice is common ground, a thing upon which all people of good will and intelligence can agree.

But with fairness, we move to a mushy place. Some can think it's fair to punish the less-responsible criminal more severely, while others think it's fair to consider those criminals less-advantaged and punish them less severely. Some wealthy people can think it's fair not to provide anything for the poor, while others can think it's fair to strip the wealthy for anything needed to provide for the poor. Fairness, it turns out, is in the eye of the beholder.

Government can set some parameters to give justice a boost, and it should. But it causes great harm when it starts operating on the nebulous notion of "fairness." It becomes a political balloon, blown this way and that depending on current stories in the news, polls, party agendas, and a host of other situational oddities.

Fairness itself could be a good concept, but in practice, it has become a very dangerous word. Which one it is depends on how the word is used. If we mean by fairness that "Everyone gets out based on what they put in," we're on solid, freedom-loving ground. If instead we mean, "Everyone gets out the same (or a lot) regardless of what they put in," we've ploughed freedom under the ground.

In fact, once we move beyond the grounded morality of merit, the connecting of effort with reward, fairness can mean anything we want it to mean. Personal preferences or perceived injustices can lead us to favor those who don't deserve and to penalize those who do. The only constant is that the group being favored can always make a case for the special treatment. "A government which robs Peter to pay Paul can always depend on the support of Paul," noted writer George Bernard Shaw.[7]

The rich (itself a fuzzy notion that can include everything from successful entrepreneurs to third-generation wastrels)? They can demand it because they're so necessary for the success of all of the "little people." We can be awed by the unbelievable wealth accumulated by an Andrew Carnegie or John D. Rockefeller until we realize how much of this was done by government-allowed bribery, kickbacks, collusion, few or no regulations on health and safety and working conditions, and government-created supports like tariffs, subsidies, and regulated monopolies. The rich can talk about free markets, which all too often mean "markets we're free to exploit."[18]

The poor (itself a fuzzy notion often arbitrarily defined, and based on an income level that excludes government assistance)? They can demand favor for a host of reasons – there are a lot of us and we vote, others should feel guilty for having more money than we do, the rich are keeping us down, our grandfathers faced discrimination. We can be taken in by this until we realize that a significant percentage of this poverty is caused by bad thinking, lousy values, miserable choices, laziness, and envy. They can talk about getting their share, when they really mean "getting your share."

Often, the ones in the middle suffer the most injustice in the face of these incessant demands from the rich and poor. These middle-class people don't have enough money to be treated like the rich or enough poverty to be treated like the poor. They're the silent majority, whether they want to be or not. They don't ask too much of their government, but their government asks too much of them.

In the American Idea, economic justice is a constant for all people at all times. Emotionally charged notions like fairness are left at the door. Demands for special treatment are all viewed as the cancers that they really are. And just because someone or some group feels unfairly treated, they have no just basis for treating others unjustly. President Franklin Roosevelt said,

In the long run economic morality pays.[19]

A true American wants economic justice for all. A false American wants "fairness," by which they mean "special favor for me and mine" or "handouts and bailouts paid for by someone other than me."

America is strong. It can survive, at least for a while, with a substitution of "fairness" for "justice."

It just won't be America.

President Benjamin Harrison said,

> God has placed upon our head a diadem and has laid at our feet power and wealth beyond definition or calculation. But we must not forget that we take these gifts upon the condition that justice and mercy shall hold the reins of power and that the upward avenues of hope shall be free to all the people.[20]

The American Idea of Justice bucks a long trend of mostly unjust world history. We can long enjoy the fruits of this powerful Idea if we will:

Take Action

Make justice a special word that is equally meaningful to everyone.

★

Avoid creating a "cult of group rights."

★

Refuse to leave justice to lawyers alone.

★

Create a restitution-based criminal justice system.

★

Simplify the law and then magnify what is left.

★

Focus the justice system on truth first and last, and insist that no truth ever be omitted or ignored.

★

Make perjurers receive the very punishment their lies would cause another person.

★

Convert the adversarial trial system to a truth-finding process.

★

Define crimes as "harming others" not "harming myself."

★

Make civil lawsuits civil by limiting punitive damages and having losers – including their attorneys – pay for all court and legal costs.

★

Refuse to let one individual be penalized so that any other individual or group can get ahead.

★

Protect families from the society and the government.

★

Consider groups as means, not ends.

★

Redefine "economic justice" to include merit and to eliminate arbitrary notions of "fairness."

★

Start with economic justice, not with what the government demands or thinks it needs.

★

Eliminate all taxes on productive effort and risk-taking.

To see detail on these Action Points and
to add your voice visit www.theamericanideas.com

These actions would be much more than the beginning of a return to justice. If we take them, it will feel…just like justice.

Justice and the American Idea

As the culture has strayed from the American Idea of Justice, it's brought about demands for more – better jobs, higher pay, "free" healthcare, "free" college education. There's nothing wrong with wanting more – that, too, is part of the American Ideas. But there's a huge difference between wanting and demanding, and there is a gulf between "deserve" and "expect."

But we haven't strayed too far. The way back is clear, carved out by 400 years of the American experiment. People came to America for freedom and opportunity, and they had hard experience telling them injustice was the great destroyer of both. They were able to see that those treasures were put at great risk everywhere when injustice was permitted to stand anywhere.

The American Idea of Justice represents a great break with the sordid, unjust past of most nations and empires of world history. Justice in America is a rich and powerful word with tremendous legal, social, and economic ramifications. It's too important to be lost or to allow it to be abused.

It's said that we have "blind justice." But in the American Idea, justice isn't really blind. More than almost anything else, it has permitted four centuries of Americans to see clearly how life should be lived.

CHAPTER 4

The American Idea of Equality

What was Thomas Jefferson thinking when he crafted the majestic declaration that "We hold these truths to be self-evident, that all men are created equal"?[1]

Nothing in the world around him would have made that truth self-evident. Women, Native Americans, and blacks had no real legal standing. The few rich owned almost everything compared with those of modest means, and only property owners could vote. Advanced education was available only to the select few, and even elementary education was out of the reach of many. Social class limited or eliminated the otherwise available opportunities.

So there was a lot that he didn't mean and couldn't mean. What he meant did go and *had* to go deeper than all of those physically observable realities.

He went to the deepest wells of what it means to be human. He sensed – he knew – that everyone was a created being, determined in personality, birth, talents, and abilities by God. No one had a choice about his or her origins, so no one had a legitimate basis for pride about those origins. God could look at humanity and ask of every one of them, "What do you have that you weren't given?"

The American Idea of Equality reminds us that differences between people that may appear huge from our limited perspective shrink in importance when viewed from historical, global, and eternal points of view. The only differences that ultimately count are the ones that we choose – the decisions we make to advance our skills or take advantage of our opportunities, the relationships that we build, the legacy that we leave behind.

The person who views all others as his or her equal will enjoy people more, benefit them more consistently, show them more deference, and be more understanding of others who share the same frail human nature. That, and more, is what Jefferson meant with his remarkable choice of words. This Idea of Equality is a total break from how people were viewed from the beginning of recorded history, right up until...America.

Equality

Equality isn't a right – equality is a given.

The equality of human beings before God is alone at the root of universal human rights and democracy.

Equality means no one is essentially better than anyone else, since all are both made in the image of God and capable of doing right and wrong.

Claiming superiority over others puts a person at great odds with the American character as well as the reality of life.

We know that equality doesn't mean that all should be judged the same but that all should be judged on their self-chosen character.

Everyone should have equality of citizenship, justice, opportunity, and responsibility but no guarantee of equality of income or outcome.

Let's see what this Idea means in detail. First, it is absolutely essential for us to know that

Equality Isn't a Right – Equality Is a Given

The founders of America didn't describe equality as an "unalienable right." They didn't say that we were endowed with unalienable rights to "equality, life, liberty, and the pursuit of happiness." In their formulation, equality comes even before rights.

That's because equality isn't a *right* at all – equality is a given. A right is something that you *have*, while "equal" is something that you *are*. "We hold these truths to be self-evident, that all men are created *equal*...."[2] Equality is a beginning point, a self-evident truth, the *first* self-evident truth.

In the language of the Declaration of Independence, equality is the point just before we get to rights. It's the first big truth, the one that precedes the second big truth about rights.

This is because the founders of America knew that equality was something more, something different from, a right. The unalienable rights they listed were "life, liberty, and the pursuit of happiness," but not "equality." They made equality a statement about who we are, and they made rights a statement about what we have *because* of who we are.

The core of the American Idea of Equality is that equality comes with being human. We've all been placed on common ground. We all share a common origin and a common destiny. People can set up endless pretensions and divisions so they can look down on others less equal than themselves, but the Idea says that this is all a pompous illusion.

At least until more recent decades, Americans might respect and admire – and in a few cases even revere – political leaders, barons of industry, and celebrities. But Americans always knew something very important. They knew that none of this respect, admiration, or reverence included a recognition – much less an acceptance – of superiority. Charles Lindbergh was a hero in part because he was one of us, not *because* he was better than us.

In fact, behind Americans' outward show of respect was a well-grounded (and given human nature, well-founded) skepticism, always ready for action. "You think you're better than us because you have more money? Education? Connections? Fame? Think again." There's always been an American disbelief in a better breed of human being. There's always been a distrust of people who claim to have superior value.

Not infrequently, this skepticism morphs into cynicism about those "high-level" people. Americans look at political leaders and don't automatically think, "Now there's our best and brightest." They're more likely to ask, "Is that the best we can do?" Part of the American spirit includes wanting leaders who excel in character and talent while remembering that they're made out of the same cheap clay as everyone else. And if they forget, we're very happy to remind them. If they get too big for their britches, we'll gladly cut them down to size.

Equality in the American Idea doesn't say, "I get to live at your expense," or "I get to do everything that you get to do," or "I get to have as much as you." In recent years, we've heard many of those kinds of statements. But they represent grasping human nature, not the American Idea of Equality.

That Idea says something much more profound. It says, "I'm as good as you." It might not look like it, but it's so. I'm as good as you.

Americans understand that this concept of equality is more than socially important, that somehow it's the foundation of their whole political system. They know that

The Equality of Human Beings Before God Is Alone at the Root of Universal Human Rights and Democracy

Equality is and always was a dreadful word to kings and queens, dictators and tyrants, aristocrats and snobs.

It means a degradation or loss of their special place and the unwelcome elevation of the "riff-raff" and "rabble." It forces those with power to maintain constant vigilance and a readiness to take action to preserve what they have and to get more if they can. To the criminals who have ruled most of human history, ruthlessness in defense of privilege has been no vice.

Everyone below the monarchy, nobility, generals, or clergy was equal, if by that we mean "equally worth nothing." Most of the human beings who have ever lived haven't been the practical equals of those in power. Not even close. The powerful's only nod to equality is generally to treat everyone below them equally badly.

So equality is an incredibly radical concept. No one with absolute or near-absolute power would ever come up with it, promote it, or even tolerate it. There's no advantage in it for them. From their vantage point, it's a sick joke: "Peasants, serfs, common laborers, uneducated – equal with me? I don't believe it."

And when we get down to it, equality is a belief. It's an intangible, like conviction about spiritual things or love between people. We can't see it, touch it, taste it, smell it, or hear it. Nothing "in the course of human events"[3] argues for its existence. In fact, everything we see, touch, taste, smell, and hear argues that it "just ain't so." We have to believe it as an article of faith – or not.

But a belief doesn't mean much unless we can tie it back to an unimpeachable source. That source isn't – can't be – charismatic leaders, government, society, or some miscellaneous notion of community. If history teaches anything, it teaches that these sources are excellent breeding grounds for creating differences and manufacturing inequalities. These other "sources" of human equality are ethical quicksand.

The founders knew what the impeccable source was, and most Americans knew it then and know it now too. That source is God.

God is the one who created us equal. And it's this created equality alone that paves the way for the concepts of equal, shared human rights and an equal, shared political voice.

What about those who claim that this is mush or religious mumbo-jumbo? They certainly have the freedom to do so. But there's no mush or mumbo-jumbo that can compare with what they have to offer as a foundation. Because it's either that God created us equal with identical human rights and equivalent political voices, or...

There is no "or."

There's no real alternative. If we're not equal before God, if all of us aren't equal before God, then there's no reasonable basis on which to give people who are less intelligent, capable, powerful, or rich the same rights as those who are brilliant, competent, mighty, or wealthy. Whenever God is left out of the equation – including those times when God is used as a slogan to win political support for bad plans or to start wars – human rights either get shredded, or they get redefined in terms that benefit the government.

Of course, the anti-God crowd would disagree. But they choose to ignore the evidence of even recent history, where anti-God states in Germany, Japan, Russia, and China – among many others – slaughtered tens of millions as though they had no rights at all.

And more. They imagine that people derived solely from mindless and meaningless processes can create mindfulness and meaning for themselves – and make them stick. They believe that people can create their own widely accepted egalitarianism and invent their own widely respected rights. They propose another basis for equality – a utopian world where all are equal because they magically share common beliefs, dreams, and goals.

But all of these utopian ideas and movements are fundamentally flawed and disastrously unreal. They have an unreal notion of human nature. They hold views of people that are unreal ("people are basically good," "people will see the wisdom of our movement") and offer solutions that are unreal ("people will perform unselfishly in collectives," "people with political power can be trusted to redistribute income equally and fairly"). They presume to speak for all people as though all of them are the same.

They call themselves "progressives" and "humanists." But when their illusions melt under the hot sun of actual life and circumstances, the only recourse for these utopians is governmental coercion and tyranny. What else can you do with people who refuse to cooperate? People who don't see the wisdom of being equal cogs in someone else's perfect machine?

The American Idea of Equality changed this forever. In this Idea, people aren't equal below power or before fantasies but are equal before God. God is the great leveler, the great destroyer of pomposity. In the old language of the Bible, God is "no respecter of persons."[4] So we shouldn't be, either.

This concept of equality flows right into thoughts about democracy. If we aren't equal before God, why should an illiterate, ignorant, homeless person have the same right to vote as the educated, well-read, influential person? In fact, pure logic would say that the latter person should have a hundred votes to one vote for the former (if we give that homeless person any votes at all).

One of the many problems of modern big-government, nation-building thinking is the erroneous belief that democracy is a stand-alone system – or worse, a political mechanism that can operate in a vacuum. "If we can just get them to have a relatively honest vote, then we'll have…"

Then we'll have *nothing*. If they don't start with God-created equality and God-endowed unalienable rights, they can vote until doomsday and they'll still have nothing. Or if they elect a Hitler or Chavez, worse than nothing.

Democracy is, first and foremost, a mindset. It's a set of beliefs rooted in human equality and the desire to see this equality well represented in the world of politics and government. It's a historical truth that democracy can't work without fundamentals like the rule of law and the peaceful transition between elections. But it isn't even *democracy* if it isn't rooted in God-created human equality.

Ultimately, the only ways in which we're all equal is before the Creator who made us so and in the rights that flow from that fundamental equality. In every other way, human beings are incredibly unequal.

Without the self-evident truth that all of us are created equal by God and endowed by that Creator with those wonderful unalienable rights, we're left with slogans and deceptions, with an Animal Farm where "all animals are equal, but some are more equal than others."[5]

But with this truth of God-created equality, we can clearly see that

> *Equality Means No One Is Essentially Better than Anyone Else, Since All Are Both Made in the Image of God and Capable of Doing Right and Wrong*

Part of the Idea, the part about being equal before God, is connected to another part, the part about being made in the image of God. It's a concept believed by Christians, Jews, Muslims, and in some way, by many other religions. It's a phenomenal thought, really, that frail human beings are somehow very much like the one who created them.

Eventually, this core belief was fully absorbed by Western civilization. People had value because they looked like God. This should affect how they're treated. They should no longer be thought of as a burden to be endured or a resource to be exploited.

This belief that human beings had immense value as individuals was expanded in the Reformation and Counter-Reformation. And it was taken to another level in the Enlightenment of the 1600s and 1700s and the Great Awakenings of the 1700s and 1800s, when the majesty of the individual human being – of all human beings – was forever recognized.

What does being made in the image of God really mean? It means that God put his stamp on each one of us. We all have a divine spark. All of us, in some way, look like God. We are all on common ground, and that ground is found in God. We have to say this because it's so. President Harry S. Truman said,

> We believe that all men are created equal because they are created in the image of God. From this faith we will not be moved.[6]

No one starts out more like God or less like God. And that means that no one is, in their origin, better or worse than anyone else.

Human actions just add to this formulation. Are people basically good or bad? Of course they are. All of us are equally capable of doing good or bad. No one is born a hero or philanthropist, and no one is born a murderer or thief. Some seem to have better nature and nurture than others, but much of this is illusion – saints can come from horrible backgrounds and surroundings, and sinners can come from well-bred parents living in luxury.

English writer Aldous Huxley reminded us that "experience is not what happens to a man; it is what a man does with what happens to him."[7] Our choices ultimately determine our value to ourselves and to others. We can add to the capability of doing good by doing good and to the capability of doing bad by doing bad. But at the start, we're no different.

We can say clearly that some lives are better lived than others. But we can never say that this is because one life was better favored by God at the beginning – or that those living those better lives have the right to cast a first stone.

Because of this essential equality, judgmentalism and self-righteousness have no place in the American Idea of Equality. In fact,

Claiming Superiority over Others Puts a Person at Great Odds with the American Character, As Well As the Reality of Life

President Dwight Eisenhower said that anyone

> Who seeks to deny equality among his brothers betrays the spirit of the free and invites the mockery of the tyrant.[8]

Because there are so many observable differences between human beings, it's remarkably easy to claim superiority over others. This can be in a specific area (like intelligence, education, physical ability, or beauty) or in general (as in, "I'm a much better person than most," or, "At least I'm better than them").

The American Idea of Equality acknowledges the differences. It admits that some of those differences are superior to others. But it refuses to allow that acknowledgment and admission to translate into arrogance, self-righteousness, false pride, and condescension.

Even many of the differences that we see that some people treat as so important are more illusion than reality. Mostly, we can't go by what we see. Historian Niall Ferguson noted that

> *Around 85 percent of the total amount of genetic variation in humans occurs among individuals in the average population; only 6 percent occurs among races. The genetic variants that affect skin colour, hair type and facial features involve an insignificant amount of the billions of nucleotides in an individual's DNA. To some biologists, this means that, strictly speaking, human races do not exist.*[9]

So the American character urges us to be indifferent about these differences. In part, this requires an act of faith. We have to go by what we believe to be true about human beings – about who we are at core, what we're worth, the impact we can have, the potential that each of us possesses – rather than the obvious but petty distinctions that simply don't matter.

That's what the American Idea demands. Imperfect as it may be in practice, it's part of the foundation of the American character.

But it's also part of the reality of life. What can a poor, sick, elderly person in a run-down neighborhood possibly have to say? A lot, if she's learned the way to build a lifetime relationship with another human being. How about an uneducated, illiterate, terminally ill patient in a hospice? Golden words, if he's learned how to live and how to die.

One person can have fifty billion dollars and the other a hundred dollars, but if the wealthy person dies first, at that moment the poor person still has a hundred dollars and the rich person has nothing. Their wealth ultimately counts for nothing – except for how they got it and how they used it along the way.

We all start out with nothing and end up the same way. At the beginning, we only get what is given to us. And the endgame is the same for us all.

The startgame is also the same for all, as everyone comes into life without even the simple ability to keep themselves alive. And more – where we start out, with whatever advantages or disadvantages, is totally not of our own choosing or doing. This is in part the basis of the radical notion that somehow there's a "self-evident truth"[10] that all people are created equal.

And even more. Who is really "more equal," the rich celebrity who struggles with life and dies young, or the anonymous, hardworking parent who improves lives and lives to be a hundred?

It's far better to understand that everyone has an equal claim on life and on the planet, to see the truth of Jefferson's expression that "the earth belongs to the living."[11] The poorest person alive today still has immeasurably more than all of the dead kings and queens. And the poorest person with happiness is much better off than the richest person without it.

So we're driven by this Idea to define Equality as having equal value and equal rights, not equal power or possessions. No one has built-in superiority on the things that really count, and no one has a basis for claiming superiority on the things that don't.

Using chess as an analogy for life, an old Italian proverb reminds us of a truth we should never forget: "When the game is over, the king and the pawn both go back into the box."[12] There may be bigger and smaller monuments in a graveyard, but everyone under them is equally dead.

This Idea of Equality can lead to excellent concepts like democracy and equal justice before the law. But it can lead to destructive notions like refusing to hold people accountable for their actions and scapegoating society for bad personal choices. In the American Idea,

We Know That Equality Doesn't Mean That All Should Be Judged the Same, but Rather That All Should Be Judged on Their Self-Chosen Character

It's very important to understand this American Idea of Equality – both what it means and what it doesn't mean. We've looked closely together at what it means, but great error can arise if we don't understand what it never said, what it never meant from the beginning of America.

Equality doesn't mean that:

• *All people are equally good.* People range from mostly good to all bad. Only bad things can come from pretending that evil people aren't evil or that they can be rehabilitated by talk. While good and bad can have degrees, they aren't relative – goodness may be hard to come by, but it is clearly better than the alternative.

• *All ways of living are equally good.* Saying that people are free to destroy their lives is different from saying this is a good plan. Living a wasted life is worthy of tears but has no defense. Most people want the good life, but whether they get a good life or not depends largely on their choices and actions.

• *All values are equally good.* Some people believe in protecting and elevating others, and some people believe in using and degrading them. Everyone operates from some sort of value system, from doctors and teachers to pimps and prostitutes. Value systems range in worth from platinum to garbage. Those that are garbage shouldn't be respected out of some wrongheaded notion of "equality."

• *All cultures are equally good.* Cultural relativism tries to teach us that no culture is better than another, just different. But some cultures have operated on notions that child sacrifice is beneficial, women are worthless, dictatorship is healthy, and "purifying" the land by slaughtering minorities is a holy thing to do. Cultures run the whole gamut from mostly elevating individuals to mostly wrecking their lives. The American Ideas are separated by an enormous distance from the values of a hundred dysfunctional cultural norms.

- *All political systems are equally good.* America's political system has flaws, some of them serious. But when we look at what it's done for its citizens and immigrants compared with other schemes – really, the ultimate measure of any political system – it is clearly a superior system.

- *All pathways to God are equally good.* There is a monumental difference between thinking on the one hand that the way to God is through faith and service and thinking on the other hand that the way to God is through ethnic cleansing and degradation of women. God can be found – but not every guide knows the way, and not every way will lead us home.

This Idea of equality doesn't require us to suspend judgment. Quite the contrary. It requires us to make good judgments based on first-class values and ideas. This aspect of the Idea lives in Dr. King's comment that "There is some good in the worst of us and some evil in the best of us. When we discover this, we are less prone to hate our enemies."[13]

There were of course exceptions, some of them huge, but Americans, from the beginning, learned to judge on the content of people's character. Often, their own lives depended on discerning good character – trusting people who had it, and avoiding those who didn't.

America was the place where it didn't matter where you came from or what you had right now. Where you started didn't establish where you'd end up, what you had to choose, or what you were allowed to do. Ralph Waldo Emerson called America a place where there was an aristocracy of merit, where people rose and fell by what they did, not by what titles they had or how much money they inherited.

The American spirit said, "I may not have much, but what I have I've earned myself. I earned it honestly. I didn't steal or cheat. I built this life myself. And that allows me to have genuine pride. It permits me to be content, and not to be ashamed of what I have – or what I don't have."

This is what kept people from accepting handouts or even the notion of handouts. Handouts meant that you no longer had control of your own life. Handouts spoke of dependency or not being your own person. They implied that you weren't up to the task, that in some way you weren't...equal.

What happened to the American spirit, where people went from not wanting handouts to demanding handouts, from earning their own bread to wanting to take the bread away from others? Whenever we see a politician offering us something for nothing – usually to the biggest groups with the most votes – we know one thing for sure: the American spirit isn't in the offer, and that spirit won't be in us if we take it.

In America, equality was a very different concept. Who you were inside would determine in large part where you ended up outside:

- If you were lazy, sloppy, careless, narcissistic, and profligate, you didn't get very far. No one was there to bail you out from your own disastrous lifestyle. Equality didn't mean you got multiple chances on someone else's effort or money. You have an equal opportunity to make good choices. If instead you choose not to study, listen, finish school, apply for jobs, show up, work hard, act respectfully, watch your language, save, spend wisely, avoid frivolous debt, lose bad relationships, skip drugs and gambling…well, Americans called the inevitable result "reaping what you sow."

• If you were industrious, ambitious, creative, caring, and frugal, you could go anywhere. Americans got past the nonsense that what counts is on the outside rather than on the inside. They knew that it's not what's in the genes that counts, but what's in the soul. Equality meant you got multiple chances, all on your own effort and money. If you made good choices, however limited in scope at first, you could build a life that mattered. Americans also called this "reaping what you sow."

America has been a relentless force against barriers to the success of good character. Were there exceptions? Terrible ones, to be sure. But, no matter how awful, they were exceptions. The American Idea worked on some of those exceptions for centuries, but work on them it did. And the Idea won. It has destroyed many of the inequalities of worth and justice.

But it's important for us as a society to stop there. We should never let a principled demand for priceless equality degenerate into a shrill demand for equal possessions and equal outcomes. The result of that degeneration is, ironically, always a less equal and less just society.

The power players at the top do well by catering to the growing masses who have less but want more, all paid for by the hardworking people in the middle who have too little political power and too small a voice to be heard. The handouts are always carved out of the productive middle – by people who do nothing for people who do nothing.

The American Idea never contained any illusions about equality. It focused on equality, not equivalence. There was never any pompous, high-sounding, inaccurate belief that equality meant that everyone is the same. The Idea stubbornly resisted any reduction of the individual or of individuality or of the immense value of individual differences.

The Enlightenment produced both legitimate and bastardized versions of equality, and they both were born in the last third of the 18th century – one in the American Revolution, the other in the French:

• The American Revolution, the child of John Locke, parented offspring – Jefferson, Franklin, Henry, Washington, Madison – who helped create unimaginable freedom and prosperity.

The American version of equality couples equality with individuality, freedom, opportunity, responsibility, dignity, and justice. Equality in this world means that every individual is valued as much as any other, that no one will be prevented from using their freedom to optimize their lives, and that every available opportunity can be taken by anyone who has the courage and energy to do it. Equality means that no one is more responsible for the society or government than any other, that everyone has a soul and is entitled to be treated with respect, and that justice for one is the prerequisite for justice for all.

The American cry could be stated as, "liberty, equality, society, diversity, opportunity." Liberty means freedom from artificial restraint and freedom to do all that you want and choose to do. Equality is of justice and legal standing and opportunity, not of forced outcomes. Society is open to anyone who wants to engage in it. Diversity is welcomed and seen as a societal and economic advantage, and opportunity is a doorway marked "welcome."

• The French Revolution, the child of Voltaire, parented offspring – Lenin, Stalin, Mao Zedong, Castro, Pol Pot – who helped create unimaginable suffering and the equality of death.

The French version of equality couples equality with "the people," regulation, limitation, entitlement, pretense, and "fairness." Equality in this world means that the community is more important than the individual, that everything should be regulated to ensure that inequalities of outcomes are minimized, and that limits have to be placed on freedom and ambition and innovation. Equality means that everyone is entitled to an equal share of government largesse and the communal pie, that we should pretend that differences in choices and actions shouldn't matter, and that "the people" should take by force whatever someone has that seems to make them too "unequal."

The French cry was "liberty, equality, fraternity." But these words don't mean the same thing as they do in the American Idea. Liberty means enjoying the good life as long as you don't enjoy it too much more than others or at the expense of brotherly (or sisterly) feelings. Fraternity means, "Our way is the only way." Diversity isn't even allowed in the way language is used and developed, much less in how immigrants are welcomed. Opportunity is allowed, but only within safe, well-defined boundaries. "From each according to their ability, to each according to their need"[14] – with an extra helping or two for the people at the top and crumbs off their table for the people who put them there.

The core problem addressed by both Revolutions was the same. Growing for centuries, there was an understandable and righteous disgust with the notions that some, by reason of birth, were better than others and that there were those who could exercise power ungranted by the people or God.

But the solutions to the problem were very, very different. One took solace in stripping away the layers of power and pretense and putting each person's life in his or her own hands. The other took solace in creating new authorities and agencies to assure that anyone taking their lives into their own hands would have to give them back.

The American Idea does recognize two kinds of differentiators – things that make people unequal in practice. The first is a product of circumstance: Some people are smarter or more beautiful or are born into families with better values or more wealth. The second is a product of pretense: Because of family name or position, racial or ethnic background, education or title, charter or decree, artificial levels and layers are built into government and society.

The American Idea of Equality accepts and even embraces the first kind of differentiator, seeing these as ways (if used wisely) to produce happiness for the individual and advancement for the society. But it rejects and loathes the second, seeing these as ways to produce happiness and advancement for the few at the expense of the many. And it sees how the first can easily lead to the second – how clever or wealthy people can conjure up many ways to embed themselves in phony privilege. The Idea demands ongoing watchfulness against this presumption and its ugly creations.

On its better days, a society expects equality of opportunity and *before* the law. On its poorer days, a society expects equality of incomes and outcomes. On its worst days, a society expects government to operate far outside its legitimate role to use its power to level incomes, legislate outcomes, and create – regardless of merit, at times opposite of merit – new favored classes.

The American Idea has always declared that favoritism is bad whether it's the favoritism of privileged class and great wealth, or the favoritism of voting blocks and great numbers. A tyranny is a tyranny, regardless of who pulls the strings.

In America, equality is far-reaching but has clear limits. Americans believe that

> *Everyone Should Have Equality of Citizenship, Justice, Opportunity, and Responsibility, but No Guarantee of Equality of Income or Outcome*

We discuss the American Ideas of Justice, Opportunity, and Responsibility in other chapters. Here we'll look at their connection to Equality. Much of this starts with a dual recognition – a strong equality of citizenship and a non-equality of income or outcome.

Equality of Citizenship

In the American Idea of Equality, every citizen has an equal claim on its government.

But no more than that.

No citizen is better than another or has a "higher" or "better" citizenship. Every citizen is different, but that difference is no basis for a stronger claim on the government that belongs to us all. President Martin Van Buren thought that American institutions would

> make our beloved land for a thousand generations that chosen spot where happiness springs from a perfect equality of political rights.[15]

This means that there's really no basis for white, black, Latino, Asian, Native American, male, or female superiority or special representation. If we shouldn't have a white congressional caucus, we shouldn't have a black or brown or yellow or red one. If we shouldn't have a male-only political meeting, we shouldn't have a female-only one. The excuse, "We're only trying to make up for past injustices and our minority status," is, in the American Idea, just another claim for special group treatment. President Harry Truman said,

> Government is established for the benefit of the individual, and is charged
> with the responsibility of protecting the rights of the individual and his free-
> dom in the exercise of his abilities.[16]

Why should

- Farmers get subsidies but not small manufacturers or retailers?

- Some get tax credits, but others don't?

- Some get help with mortgages, but not all?

- Some receive educational loans or grants or tax credits, but not every
citizen who applies?

- Some businesses get bailed out – "too big to fail," another way of saying,
"Too big to be run intelligently and honestly" – but not every business that
struggles gets bailed out?

- Government uses tariffs to protect some industries from competition, but
it lets others be gobbled up by foreigners?

- Some get tax abatement instead of all getting it equally?

- Some get 26 weeks of unemployment in one political climate, and others
get 99 weeks in a different climate?

In other words, what is the legitimate, principled basis for allowing one citizen or
one group of citizens to be favored by government action while others are not?

The American answer is, "None."

America will get back to its roots when it doesn't allow any citizen to be favored
over another based on anything. We all get the same things from the government
– the same tax credits, tax deductions, government loans, government subsidies,
government bailouts, government handouts – or we all get nothing from the government. Anything else is unequal, unfair, and un-American.

Nowhere is this inequality more obvious than in the most basic responsibility of citizenship in every nation – the duty to pay for your own government. The concept of
"equality of citizenship" is – even before "justice" or "simplification" – the principle
that should lead to a flat tax. Why? Because it's right, but also because it treats
every citizen as a true equal.

If there were a club, how well would it work if everyone wanted to be treated as
equal members with the same voting privileges and benefits, but some were required
to pay ten times the average dues and the majority of people weren't required to pay
anything? Well, it wouldn't work at all because it treats people unequally. And the
inequality and injustice would be even worse if the ones paying nothing received
more benefits than those keeping the club financially afloat.

In America, we now have something far more extreme than this club. The richest
citizens are required to pay almost all of the dues, while those paying nothing are
getting a huge and growing share of the benefits. But in a world where equality
means anything, the rich person's citizenship wouldn't be penalized to subsidize the

poor person's citizenship. The rich should have no greater advantage, to be sure – but neither should the poor.

If we really get down to equality in this crucial obligation of citizens, everyone, in principle, should pay the same tax – the same dues. Everyone should write out a check for the same amount – an equal amount – every April 15th. This isn't practical, especially given a government of gigantic proportions. And some may not think it's fair. But it would most certainly be equal.

As a fallback, we should each pay at least the exact same percentage – an *equal* percentage – of our income. This approach is good enough for God in the principle of the tithe: the contribution of 10% of your income whatever it is. And since government is not as important as God and is much less good, it should certainly expect no more.

Equality of Justice

In human affairs, justice has always been very hard to come by. Injustice has, sadly, really been the norm.

If justice is "getting what you deserve," most people in history haven't gotten justice. Fat cats have gotten everything, while the hardworking have gotten very little compensation (often well seasoned with oppression).

In the American Idea, justice really isn't blind. It is equal. We don't convict you because you're a certain race or ethnicity or gender or class, and we don't free you because of these, either. You don't get more because you're rich or less because you're poor – or in a "tyranny of the majority" case, less because you're rich or more because you're poor.

Justice is either the same for everyone, regardless of circumstances, or it isn't justice at all. It's only injustice with a fancy wrapper.

Equality of Opportunity

America offers...a shot.

You're born in the ghetto? In poverty? In a dysfunctional family? You don't need to stay there. You can leave. You can wake up in the morning, put on your shoes, if you have any, and start walking. You can go somewhere else – anywhere else – and find some kind of job. You can show up, work hard, be respectful, be grateful, and start building a life. If you have any kind of character, you can build a really good life in America.

And that's what this American Idea required – an equal shot at a really good life. The right kind of "fairness – not equal outcomes, but a fair chance for individual and group achievement – early on became an American watchword," noted writer Howard Fineman. "We just want a fair game."[17]

Did the American Ideas of Equality and Opportunity start with a philosophy or with the reality of a wide-open country with room for anyone and everyone or with immigrants eager to build something better than what they left behind? Yes and yes and yes. However they got started, those are the American Ideas, equality and opportunity and equality *of* opportunity – one of the great American differentiators.

But it can be lost. "You don't know what you've got until you lose it,"[18] echo the haunting words of the old rock-and-roll ballad. It can even be lost because of politically motivated good intentions like minimum wages that ends up preventing young, uneducated people from getting a foothold, and unemployment and welfare subsidies that end up preventing out-of-work people from moving on to different work, careers, or cities.

A lot of opportunity derives from pain and difficulty. But that opportunity is lost if the pain and difficulty are glossed over. There are far too many things designed to eliminate inequity that end up eliminating opportunity instead.

Equality of Responsibility

How can any society remain functional (or even survive) if many of its members take no responsibility for themselves, for their families, or for the society itself?

And what happens when the "many" turns into the "majority"? No great society has ever been built with a tolerance for shirkers and freeloaders.

Responsibility can seem hard, but it's one of the best things about being human. Few things are as encouraging as seeing people stand up, dust themselves off, and take responsibility for their lives.

In the American Idea of Equality, no one has more responsibility for himself or herself than for anyone else, and no one has less. No one has more responsibility for others than anyone else, and no one has less.

I may pay less in total taxes, but that doesn't lessen my responsibility for demanding effective, impartial government. I may have less public fame or influence, but that doesn't lessen my responsibility for demanding decent, civil society. In a free country where this equal responsibility isn't demanded, it is possible to end up at a terrible place. French observer Alexis de Tocqueville saw the end of this:

> When the bulk of the community are engrossed by private concerns, the smallest parties need not despair of getting the upper hand in public affairs.... They regulate everything by their own caprice; they change the laws and tyrannize at will over the manners of the country; and then men wonder to see into how small a number of weak and worthless hands a great people may fall.[19]

Early in the 21st century, it's easy to see the effect of so many people shedding their responsibility as equal citizens in a free, democratic republic. We no longer have representatives; rather, we have "lawmakers" who make up regulations on a whim and change them the same way – a few "weak and worthless hands" that have us in their oily political grip. We have an equal responsibility to ensure that these small parties of modern aristocrats are kept at bay.

We also have an equal responsibility to insist that it defend us from enemies, protect us from criminals, and ensure a sound financial system. And an equal responsibility to insist that it do little more than that.

Whatever this government is, it belongs to all of us, and it belongs to each of us. There's no one else to take responsibility for it and no one else to hold it responsible.

No Guarantee of Equality of Income or Outcome

In the American Idea, everyone should have equality of opportunity, but no one should have a guaranteed equality of income or outcome.

Why not? In part because forced equality of income or outcome is a sham. This is so for a number of reasons:

- First, the pursuit of happiness will automatically make us unequal in income and outcome because that pursuit will look very different to each human being. If someone believes that doing good work for a low salary is the path to happiness, have they really any business complaining about the high salaries of those in more prosperous fields or organizations? If an entertainer or athlete believes that seeking great celebrity is the path to happiness, have they any business complaining about not being able to do everyday things that non-celebrities take for granted? To be at all meaningful, the pursuit of happiness has to come with an understanding that different actions will always produce different incomes and outcomes.

- Second, this forced equality tends to drive everyone and everything to the lowest-common-denominator. Why should anyone live and work with focus and excellence when the fruits of that life will be stripped away and given to sluggards? Why care when caring gets you legally robbed? And why work hard when you don't have to? Why be responsible when irresponsibility gets rewarded?

- Third, this kind of forced equality produces rigid conformity, not dignity. We are all forced to have the same, even if that "same" pleases some and displeases others or lifts some up at the cost of taking others down. And it often has an ugly side. The "citizens" of the French Revolution discovered the sharp edge of this kind of conforming "equality" at the guillotine.

- Fourth, the people forcing this "equality" on others never consider themselves to be part of the equation. They may pretend to be a "comrade," but they still, like the Soviet commissars, live in their luxurious dachas and eat caviar. George Orwell was right with his summary of socialism in practice, that "all animals are equal, but some are more equal than others."[20] The percentage of politicians who resist the trappings of power is very small indeed. At least the aristocracy of earlier ages never pretended to produce equality.

- Fifth, equality of outcome can only be approached by treating everyone differently – favors for some, penalties for others, all unmerited. Another word for this is "injustice."

- Sixth, it can't be done. No matter how hard power tries to prevent it, people will differentiate themselves, for good and for bad. They may have to go outside the law, they may have to create and operate in an underground market, they may have to hide income or profits, but some will find a way around this coerced "equality." Unfortunately, as the coercion grows, many of those will be criminals who are willing to take big risks for big gains, while law-abiding citizens grow ever – but equally – poorer.

Getting the Idea of Equality right and getting the government on the right side of it is difficult but crucially important. As president Andrew Jackson observed,

Distinctions in society will always exist under every just government. Equality of talents, of education, or of wealth cannot be produced by hu-

man institutions. In the full enjoyment of the gifts of Heaven and the fruits of superior industry, economy, and virtue, every [one] is equally entitled to protection by law; but when the laws undertake to add to these natural and just advantages artificial distinctions, to grant titles, gratuities, and exclusive privileges...the humble members of society...have a right to complain of the injustice of their Government. There are no necessary evils in government. Its evils exist only in its abuses. If it would confine itself to equal protection, and, as Heaven does its rains, shower its favors alike on the high and low, the rich and the poor, it would be an unqualified blessing.[21]

Many "progressives" believe that everyone, regardless of how they've lived their lives, should have equal access to money, benefits, health care, and pensions. But they gloss over the fact that the only way to get this equality of income and outcome is to treat everyone unequally. As F. A. Hayek observed, "To produce the same result for different people, it is necessary to treat them differently."[22] Once a government or society does that, true equality goes out the window.

The American Idea of Equality never said, "You get these things just because you want them." But it has almost always given everyone at every level a very good shot at having those things. The working poor in America would still be considered prosperous by the standards of much of the world and most of history.

But the Idea's real glory is that it focuses its beautiful concept of equality on the big things, like justice and opportunity and responsibility – the deepest possessions a human being can ever claim.

The American Idea of Equality can once more become one of the great givens of an incredibly successful and satisfying culture if we will:

Take Action

Embrace God as the only legitimate source of equality.

★

Accept equality as a given rather than as a right.

★

Give up the unsustainable notion of human rights detached from God.

★

Abandon the growing favoritism of one group over another.

★

Stop offering reverence and awe to fellow human beings.

★

Be unafraid to call bad "bad" and evil "evil."

★

Define equality in a way that strengthens individualism, not governmentalism.

★

Expect equal access to, treatment by, and responsibility for the government.

★

Institute the Equal Tax, the Citizenship Tax

★

Recognize the wondrous and unique American dance of liberty and equality.

To see detail on these Action Points and
to add your voice visit www.theamericanideas.com

Few thoughts in the history of humanity have been as radical, as freeing, and as on-the-face-of-it preposterous as the American Idea of Equality.

But if we define it the American way, it's an Idea worth keeping, worth loving, and worth a good fight.

This Idea, this "self-evident truth that all men are created equal,"[23] is powerful indeed.

This power can be twisted and used for bad. Demagogues and dictators have used it repeatedly, like a favorite hammer from a toolbox, to do untold harm in the name of "equality" and "fraternity." More often than not, the equality that the people experience under these deceivers is the equality of poverty, abuse, and death.

But this power can also be used for good. The founders of America understood the ugly form of equality, where government forces the masses into equal misery and servitude or where it pits classes against each other and allows one to bring the other down to an equal state of hellishness.

Their Idea was very different. It was grounded in God, not government. It was based on individual dignity, not membership in a group.

We're created by God and are created to be equal. We should demand to be equal in our fundamental rights of life and liberty. We should expect to be equal in areas that elevate us as individuals, like citizenship, justice, opportunity, and responsibility.
And we shouldn't be surprised or upset to find, in the exercise of our God-given and unalienable right to pursue happiness, that we will end up with very different incomes and outcomes.

The American Idea of Equality isn't the only concept of equality that works – but it's the only one that treats human beings as majestic individuals rather than as expendable pawns, the only one that works to dignify and elevate every person in creation.

Totally free and utterly equal. It's the American way.

The American Idea of Dignity

In the cultural thinking that has dominated history and the lives of almost everyone who has ever lived, individual human beings are worth...nothing.

People are parts, components, census statistics, things to be accounted for, resources to be used, assets to be exploited. Their only value is in what they can contribute to the prevailing power – whatever nice words are used to describe that power. At times, people have been worth less than nothing – throwaways in wars, rabble to be starved, vermin to be exterminated. Only occasionally have they been respected.

But one of the hallmarks of Western civilization was its insistence very early on of the importance of the individual human being. She or he was no longer a cipher compared to the grandiose notion of "the people" or to the catch-alls of tribe or town, community or city, nation or state. At the start, individuals were still "small," but it was a very good start.

The American Idea of Dignity took this concept of the importance of the individual to the next level. It declared the individual to be not as valuable as the group, but much more valuable than the group. It went further, declaring the individual to be of enduring, even eternal, value. And it didn't stop there. It made the ultimate expression of dignity that the individual has *supreme* value.

Until America, no one had ever seen anything like this Idea – that individuals are worth everything, that each *individual* is worth everything. "Either everyone counts, or no one counts," says highly principled – and very American – fictional detective Harry Bosch.[1]

This Idea is anti-survival of the fittest to the core. It refuses to accept the notion that we're just another mammal, no different or better. It asserts that we have souls and possibilities and destinies. It rejects the belief that only the "select few" of us should be chosen and allowed to rule or prosper. It offers instead its "one person, one vote" democracy and its heady belief that ordinary people are the most extraordinary thing on the planet.

Dignity

Human life has immense value.

While nations and communities are important, the individual is the only thing of lasting value.

Each human life has enormous worth regardless of wealth, social status, position, age, gender, race, intelligence, talent, experience, education, or health.

We will never let anyone's strength, weakness, development, condition, beliefs, or choices influence the essential esteem that he or she deserves.

We will never accept the view that there is such a thing as a life not worthy of being lived.

We will always speak up for those who can't speak for themselves and defend them with unyielding conviction.

What does this Idea mean for us? It all starts with the foundational certainty that

Human Life Has Immense Value

President Dwight Eisenhower said

> We who are free must proclaim anew our faith. This faith is the abiding creed of our fathers. It is our faith in the deathless dignity of man, governed by eternal moral and natural laws. This faith defines our full view of life. It establishes, beyond debate, those gifts of the Creator that are man's inalienable rights, and that make all men equal in His sight.[2]

Throughout most of history, human life has had little value, especially to those with power. At times, it has had no value. It has been disposed of easily, like so much trash. We don't need to look very far today to see that this is still so in much of the world.

Western civilization changed that in theory and then, in many times and places, changed it in practice. The individual – or at least some individuals – began to be viewed as important entities in their own right. The process was slow, starting with nobility, then moving through the middle classes, and finally reaching, in some places, to most of the people in a society.

The signing of Magna Carta in 1215, when the English nobility extracted some rights from a king who confused himself with God, is a good place to call a beginning. The late 17th century brought the English Glorious Revolution that elevated the parliament to some sort of equivalence with the monarchy even while John Locke took the thinking about freedom and government – and individual rights that he called "natural" – far beyond that political change.

The American Idea of Dignity took this further. It connected each and every person's life and value directly to God, rather than to king or church, nation or tribe, family or class. Everyone was "endowed by their Creator with certain unalienable rights."[3] It took a long time for that wonderful Idea to sink in, but sink in it did.

It took even longer for that Idea to really incorporate everyone, and it is, of course, still a work in progress. But there it is. The Declaration of American Independence is, remarkably, a declaration of individual independence before it's a declaration of national independence. It proclaims in ringing tones that if you are a human being, you have value and that value was conferred on you directly by God. It eliminates government as a party to that sacred transaction.

If anyone is an American in citizenship or in spirit, he or she knows that this Idea of the dignity of the individual human being is both incomparably beautiful and immensely powerful. America, in the deepest sense, isn't a nation of 300 million human beings, but is 300 million enormously valuable human beings who have created a nation. They devised a government to serve them, to serve the people – but as individuals in their glory, not as a crowd with a label.

The individual human being isn't part of the story – she is the story. Her life is everything.

And so the first unalienable right in the American Declaration of Independence is life. Without security in this right, all other rights are meaningless. It is the foundation of liberty and the starting point of human dignity. This Idea has taken a beating. It has been attacked again and again by those who don't really believe that people are "endowed by their Creator"[4] (perhaps because they don't believe there is a creator).

But we can get it back in full because our dignity doesn't come from the government or community, parents or family, status or popularity. It comes to us, one person at a time, from the one-and-only Creator. This derives from the Western, Judeo-Christian, very American belief that

> *While Nations and Communities are Important, the Individual Is the Only Thing of Lasting Value*

Free people may be understandably interested in seeing the pyramids, Taj Mahals, Great Walls, and palaces like Versailles. But if they know the background of how these monuments were built, they'll utterly reject the cultural philosophy that built them. They were built by the many for the few, without the slightest regard on the part of those few for the many whose lives they were wasting.

Is a great civilization one that builds great works on the broken backs of a million immortal souls?

Free people know that great cultures don't focus on building up memorials for the power-mad at the top, for those who confuse themselves with God. Great cultures focus on building up people, one person at a time. You and I are their monuments.

If we aren't careful, we can greatly complicate our understanding about human dignity. We can make it some sort of communal or patriotic thing. But the fact is that the cornerstone for dignity was laid in a single sentence, the magisterial opening of the American Declaration of Independence:

> *We hold these truths to be self evident: that all men are created equal; that they are endowed by their Creator with certain unalienable rights; that among these are life, liberty, and the pursuit of happiness; that to secure these rights, governments are instituted among men; and when that government no longer secures those rights, we affirm the right of the people to alter or abolish it.[5]*

Let's unpack this astonishing statement, one with such resonance that almost all Americans have it in rough form somewhere in the back of their minds, one that other fledgling nations and peoples have copied, one that in so many ways says…it all.

We hold these truths to be self-evident

In our day, there are people who debate whether or not "truth" even exists. Not so in this statement. There is truth, and we can hold it clearly in our mind and firmly in our grasp. The revolutionaries were saying, in effect, "We're about to state some truths. We are confident you'll agree."

Not only are there truths, but we're told that they're self-evident truths. As soon as a moral, thinking person hears them, he or she knows that they're true. They're intuitively obvious. They need no further explanation.

In Jefferson's original draft of the Declaration, he called these truths "sacred and undeniable."[6] This shows us what Jefferson was thinking as the spokesperson of the American Idea of Dignity. "Sacred" reminds us that these truths originate from a hallowed somewhere else and have been conferred by a Noble Being on a noble being. "Undeniable" tells us that there is no plausible way to ignore or minimize these truths or to pretend they aren't so.

All men are created equal

As we saw in the last chapter on the American Idea of Equality, The Declaration starts off with a thunderous claim, a wondrous "Huh?"

At the time the founders wrote this delightfully peculiar phrase, most white Americans believed that Native Americans, African-Americans and other blacks, Latinos, and Asians were not only not created equal but were instead reasonable candidates for enslavement, servitude, degrading work, segregation, isolation on reservations, or abuse.

But the fact is, the Declaration says that everyone is equal. There's no getting around it. It's the first "self-evident" truth listed. But equal how? In what ways? Certainly not in origin, circumstances, talent, mental intelligence, emotional intelligence, physical ability, temperament, wisdom, knowledge, interests, motives, or ambitions. What then?

In value. All are created equal in value. They're equally valuable to the Creator, the one who gets the ultimate vote. People might not seem as though they're equally valuable, but they are. The founders knew that appearances can be deceiving and that appearances can be wrong.

How many vendors wish they could have known what Bill Gates was doing in his garage and joined him early on as a valued partner? Or given Warren Buffet $1,000 to invest when he was just starting out? On the other hand, who would have expected Lyndon Johnson, only a few years after winning one of the great presidential landslides in history, to live in vilified isolation and a descent into madness? Or to see Nixon, after another great landslide, driven from office in crushing disgrace?

No, appearances, in a sense, mean nothing. The value is intrinsic, regardless of great achievement or great failure. The original value is distributed by the Creator in equal amounts.

But there's more. All people are also equal in rights. Founder George Mason wrote,

> All men are created equally free and independent and have certain inherent rights, of which they cannot, by any compact, deprive or divest their posterity.[7]

We're all born free and independent. These rights are so built into who we are that any agreement to give them up, now or later, is automatically counterfeit.

Most of us may not have a silver spoon in our mouths, but we all have a Bill of Rights in our hands.

The founders told us that we're created to be equal in value and rights. If we lose either side – if we forget either that we're created to be equal or that this equality is one of value and rights rather than circumstance or ability – we're in trouble. So that we won't forget the first part, they emphasized it by saying,

They are endowed by their Creator

Where do liberties come from? Freedoms granted by powerful people or governments can be taken away by those same people or governments. We should be thankful that we're endowed by our Creator and not by the government or authorities or doctors or parents or family. Thank God there's a God.

And there really aren't many other options. Either we have freedom as a gift – an endowment – from our Creator, or we have natural selection and survival of the fittest.

However much we believe it to be the reality of existence, there's nothing even remotely comforting about a Darwinian world. If we really are driven and controlled only (or primarily) by natural selection and survival of the fittest, we'll find out soon enough that all people are not created equal and that rights are anything but unalienable. The strong will control and mistreat and destroy the weak – all those who aren't equal in power, all those whose rights can be stripped away like a tear-away jersey – because they can. And why not? It's the "natural order" of things.

And if people think they're living in a world without God, they have no right to call this dog-eat-dog existence a bad thing. You either get God and endowed unalienable rights, or you get no God and no rights except the right to struggle for existence. How can some people tell us that they believe in a survival-of-the-fittest world and in the same breath condemn the powerful who crush the weak? Isn't that what the powerful are built to do?

But forget the lack of comfort in such a world. What about logic? If it's a Darwinian world at its core, if there's no God watching and judging, then what on earth is the basis for equality? Why should we even care about the weak? Why should they have rights they can't defend? Nursing homes and hospices and intensive care units, Braille and handicapped parking spaces and programs to help the homeless and poor – these are all designed to perpetuate, even elevate, the disabled and weak. They are affronts to a Darwinian world.

In a world unendowed by a Creator, let the weak perish. And let the rest of us go about improving the gene pool – whatever "improve" means, and whatever value the "gene pool" has in a world without intrinsic meaning. If only the strong survive, then let's get on with it and let everyone be wary of everyone else.

Either human beings have special value, or they don't. But if they don't – if nothing's been conferred on them, if they're merely the product of an inexorable "climb from the slime" – then there's no logical premise for any rights other than the "right" to do battle with all others in a brutal fight for existence.

But the fact is that there is a God, a God who is watching and judging. This God is also generous, endowing people with unalienable rights – rights that no person can grant, rights that no person can take away except at their own mortal and immortal peril. Rights are not a made-up thing. Rights are an irrevocable gift.

This endowment is our birthright because God created us. And he created us to be something very special, just as Shakespeare exclaimed: "What a piece of worke is a man! How Noble in Reason! How infinite in faculty! In form and moving how express and admirable! In Action, how like an Angel! In apprehension, how like a God?"[8] And the God who made us endowed us

With certain unalienable rights

The rights we have as human beings are "certain" – very specific – and unalienable – can't and shouldn't be violated by anyone.

First, the founders affirm that these rights aren't ambiguous or changeable over time. They are certain – well-known, explicit, identifiable rights.

In the 18th century, these rights were thought to be "natural rights," or rights that flowed from nature. These rights had been written about and discussed for a very long time, with English political philosopher John Locke giving them their clearest form in the late 17th century. Locke spoke of life, liberty, and property, as did many of the founders.

In the Declaration, Jefferson replaced "property" with "the pursuit of happiness," a right that only a tiny percentage of humanity has ever gotten to experience. So if we combine Locke and Jefferson, we can say that we have four primary rights – life, liberty, property, and the pursuit of happiness. Long before Maslow's "hierarchy of needs," the founders saw them and called them a hierarchy of natural rights.

But of course these rights didn't flow from a mindless nature. They flowed from

God. When the revolutionaries talked about nature, they always had God in the back of it; they always knew that it was "nature and nature's God."[9] They didn't live long enough to see what intellectuals and antitheists would declare as "flowing from nature,"[10] and they would have been appalled by it. They meant by "natural rights" that we have rights that permeate nature, because God built them into the nature of things, into the natural order.

These rights are more than certain. They're also unalienable. They weren't given by people, so they can't be taken away by people. People can surely take away the manifestation of those rights – they can kill us or imprison us or steal our property or destroy our reputation – but they can't take away the rights themselves. Those come from a higher place, from living as a created human being in a Creator-endowed world.

And we should make no mistake about it: the rights that are about to be enumerated are indeed rights. People have them, have a claim on them, have the title to them, own them. Government didn't grant them, and it can't take them away.

Government, on its better days, might do a passable job of protecting our rights. In providing this protection or delivering justice, the government might have to impair the rights of rights-violators. But even here, the government has to play by the rules of the Fifth Amendment to the U.S. Constitution, which requires of the government that no one "be deprived of life, liberty, or property, without due process of law."[11]

Why? Because rights are supremely important and, even more than that, because they were given to people by God.

Only individuals have rights. A group of people might share the desire to get or secure a certain right, but the group is just a vehicle. Only its members, one soul at a time, have "certain unalienable rights."[12]

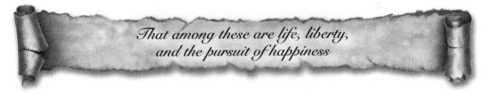

That among these are life, liberty, and the pursuit of happiness

Now the founders got down to ground level here: the endowed rights that make for a full life.

These are the building-block rights – life, then liberty, then the pursuit of happiness (encompassing the right to property). The right to the pursuit of happiness without the means (property) is a wish, not a possibility. The right to property without the freedom to use it as we see fit is a hoax. And liberty without a secured right to life is paper thin and mostly illusion.

The Declaration says "among these," so the rights listed aren't the only rights human beings have. Those listed are just the most important. The British have resisted listing rights in part out of fear that an omission or misstatement could be exploited by power gone mad. Americans have listed them and, unhappy in recent times with the results, have added to them and made some up.

But the rights that are listed are the big deals. These are the rights that are at the head of the list – the greatest grants from God, the most fundamental, the rights that are the prerequisites to all other rights, the ones that are sure to annoy tyrants. These basic rights are the ones most likely to need the protection of a good government and most likely to be violated by a bad one.

These three rights are the bedrock. Liberty is the great need of every human heart. We've presented the American Idea of Freedom as our first Idea. With liberty comes desires to be fulfilled, the pursuit of happiness (and the possession of your own property). We've presented this great right in the American Ideas of Opportunity, Religion, Society, Generosity, Diversity, and Justice.

But the first right listed is the right to life.

At the core of the rights that guard freedom is this fundamental right to life. People talk about "right-to-lifers" as though they're a minority or a small group of extremists, but anyone who understands rights has to be a right-to-lifer. This includes Jefferson and the signers of the Declaration.

The right to life is unalienable – in Jefferson's words, "sacred and undeniable."[13] If we respect that right – as we did for so much of our history – we put ourselves in a very small camp of nations indeed, perhaps a camp of one. If we disrespect that right – as we're doing now, and seem oriented toward doing more and more – then we're no different from all of the barbarous nations and peoples of history who care only about using and spending people, if indeed they think about them at all.

Either the right to life is sacred and undeniable for all, or in the long run, it isn't sacred and undeniable for anyone. If they can kill them today, they can kill us tomorrow. If we're ready to conclude that there's such a thing as a life not worthy of being lived, we can give up on all other rights; in fact, we can give up on rights altogether. Without this unalienable right to life, there are no other rights. When any human being is assaulted on this most basic right, all of their other rights are washed away in a river of blood.

Because this right has become so very alienable, every individual baby, every chronically ill and helpless and elderly person, and every terminally ill human being is at risk. They are now depending only on the good will of their mothers or relatives or caretakers. The degradation of this first unalienable right has put all of us, and even the future of society, at risk.

For example, although most Americans may not be aware of it, there's nothing except good will that prevents every baby conceived in the future from being aborted. In theory, in one generation, they could all be killed and the society would come to an end. Shockingly, there is nothing – nothing – in the law to prevent the ending of civilization.

And there's nothing to prevent others deemed no longer "useful" from being denied care – medicine, surgery, life support, even food and water. What can we say remains of Dignity in a society where sickness or disability or age can become a factor in determining whether an unalienable right to life still applies?

Either the right to life is unalienable, sacred, and undeniable, or it's a flimsy thing, determined by circumstances or the will of somebody else. If it's the former, we have a firm hold on Dignity. If it's the latter, we'll be welcomed into the large club of nations where life has never been worth much.

Freedom and choice do get into the equation – but only after the right to life is secure. We're free to do many things, but taking innocent life isn't one of them. That's going backward, using one fundamental right to annihilate an even more fundamental right.

Choice isn't the basic or most important thing. *Life* is the basic and most important thing.

The irony is that some who preach about "choice" are willing to drop the concept when it comes to the unalienable right to life. They're willing to let someone, like a preborn baby or person in a coma, be killed without having a voice or choice. And many of these "choicers" are at the same time unwilling to let someone, like a murderer or terrorist, be killed even though they have made their own life-ending choice, of forfeiting life for stealing life.

In the first instance, they support consequences without choice for the helpless. In the second, they suggest choice without consequences for the criminals. They aren't really defending the right to choose. They're defending the right to choose anything, including the right to kill others – but only as long as you are able.

People are rightly concerned about their right to choose – a key component of the right to liberty. The right to choose is a right worth defending, a right worth dying for. But it isn't a right worth killing for. It can't set all other rights aside. It isn't reasonable or moral to say that rights are unalienable but that some people's rights are more unalienable than others.

Women and men have an extensive right to choose when it comes to life. They can choose to be partners or not, to have sex or not, to use in-vitro fertilization or not, to use a surrogate mother or not, to use protection or not, to tempt fate or not, to keep the baby or not, to raise the child well or not, to have their family raise the child or not, to put the baby up for adoption or not. People have long had many of these choices, while some are new because of changing thinking and technology.

What about women's right to control their own bodies, their own lives? They indeed have such a right. They just don't have the right to control someone else's body, someone else's life. A baby is connected to her body but isn't her body. The baby needs her mother, but the baby isn't her mother.

The unalienable right to life, the first right, requires us to limit – to eliminate – only one choice, the choice to kill. The first thing, the primary thing that can't be set aside by this right to choose, is the right to life. There is no right to kill. In a civilized, right-defending society, there can't ever be a choice to kill.

This limitation is one imposed by any rational and principled culture. In a sane place, we can kill in self-defense or if someone forfeits their life by their evil actions. But no more than that.

Once a new human being comes into existence – a fully human being only needing to grow inside and outside the womb – an ancient and fully developed bill of rights is conferred on this child. This starts with the right to life – and then liberty, and then the pursuit of happiness. This baby may not be long on the ability to sustain herself without help, but she is chock full of the unalienable right to life.

Suggesting that one person's rights are bigger than or more than another's just because of greater size and ability to defend those rights is a brutal perspective that makes a mockery of all rights. If I can choose to kill you, you have no effective right to life. You only have a right to fight or flee. You have the most tenuous hold on life, only until someone stronger gets to you. No children, few elderly people, not many sick, and in the end, probably not many of us at all can hope to win this last-one-standing, might-makes-right contest.

If someone's "rights," like a "right to privacy," permit the destruction of the defenseless along with all of their rights, then that someone's "rights" are defective and not worth having or defending. It's finally time to separate the arguments for the freedom and equal treatment of women (which many men who pay for abortions don't really believe anyway) on the one hand from the right to life of another human being on the other hand.

In the final season of the television series *Law and Order,* in an episode titled "Dignity," the Assistant District Attorney, played by Alana De La Garza, says, "I grew up thinking Roe v. Wade was gospel and that a woman's privacy was inviolate [and now] I don't know where my privacy ends and her being's dignity begins." Her boss, played by Linus Roache, says,

> *In its day, Roe v. Wade conformed to what we knew then about human life and science....35 years later, birth defects can be corrected, disabled children are protected by a bill of rights, contraceptives of every kind are available....My God! Cats and dogs have more rights than the unborn. Roe v. Wade wasn't written in stone. It could stand another look.*

He concludes by telling the jury, "Despite our differences, we are joined in one belief, that every life is special and unique and imbued with unalienable rights."[14]

There's no need to try to legislate morality – make premarital sex and adultery illegal, insist that pregnant women get married. And we shouldn't treat having a baby outside of marriage as a punishment (just because we can't see your "mistake," whatever it is, doesn't mean it's any less serious). How life gets here has nothing to do with that life's value or rights.

The only differences between an unborn baby and the rest of us are that we've lived longer and can defend ourselves. Likewise, the disabled and deformed and sick and elderly are human beings, weaker than us in some ways perhaps, but no less human. If a society is judged by how it treats its weakest members – and in the end, it is – then we must always come down on the side of the weak.

"Give to every other human being every right that you claim for yourself,"[15] said founder Tom Paine. If we're ever going to be generous, let it be with a liberal definition of the unalienable right to life. Humanitarian Albert Schweitzer said that the person

> *Who has become a thinking being feels a compulsion to give to [others] the same reverence for life that he gives his own....He accepts as being good: To preserve life, to promote life, to raise to its highest value life which is capable of development; and as being evil: to destroy life, to injure life, to repress life which is capable of development. This is the absolute, fundamental principle of the moral.[16]*

The first unalienable right is life. Without security in this right, all other rights are meaningless. It is the foundation of liberty. Let's not let it be diminished in our great land. The term "right to life" wasn't created by interest groups in 1976 – it was created by Enlightenment thinkers and captured in the Declaration of Independence in 1776.

Some have proposed a human life amendment to the U.S. Constitution. Perhaps the best wording that could be used at the beginning of such an amendment would be the opening words of the American Declaration of Independence.

"There is no wealth but life,"[17] declared critic and social thinker John Ruskin.

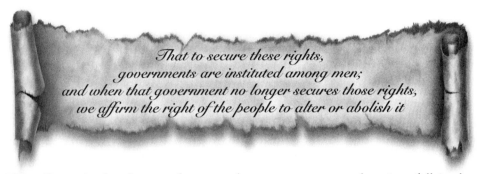

That to secure these rights, governments are instituted among men; and when that government no longer secures those rights, we affirm the right of the people to alter or abolish it

This tells us, in the clearest of terms, where governments and nations fall in the "relative worth" scale.

It declares that the whole *purpose* of government is to secure individual rights. Government isn't there to be our godfather or nanny, to tell us what to do or not to do, to provide jobs for civil servants or career paths for lawyers. It's there to secure our rights, our individual rights, to life and liberty and the pursuit of happiness.

But what happens when government stands idly by as rights are destroyed or even supports the destruction of rights? For example, Justice Byron White, in his tough dissent to the case in 1973 that made very bad law concerning unborn babies, called that decision an "exercise of raw judicial power."[18] He wrote that the court had created a "constitutionally protected right" to "exterminate human life."[19] This stands the purpose of government on its head.

When government doesn't secure our unalienable rights, the Declaration tells us that we have another right: a collective right to change that government or to get rid of it entirely.

This is an incredibly radical statement, a Declaration that government is nothing compared with individual human rights. This collective right to change or obliterate right-destroying governments is recognized nowhere in the world or in history except in one place: the American Idea of Dignity.

Throughout history, people have lived – or not – at the pleasure of government. But in the majestic, upside-down formulation of the Declaration of Independence, the government lives – or not – at the pleasure of the people.

This is because

Each Human Life Has Immense Worth Regardless of Wealth, Social Status, Position, Age, Gender, Race, Intelligence, Talent, Experience, Education, or Health

There's something in human nature that likes to focus on things that differentiate and then use those things to create barriers of distinction. With some people, it even seems to be a need.

What is a "barrier of distinction"? It isn't just noting the differences between people, of which there are many. Instead, it's making those differences say something about the worth of the people being compared.

But the American Idea of Dignity reminds us that these differences aren't differences in worth. It declares that you are worthy of the utmost respect because you have dignity – self-evident, equal, endowed-by-your-Creator, undeniable dignity. Not because you have money or fame or power, but regardless of any of those. Not because you have the individual birthright of the nobility, but because you have the noble birthright of the individual.

In powerful simplicity, we're told that no member of society is worth more than any other member and that barriers of distinction are a sham.

One of the really interesting things about these barriers of distinction is how they not only don't produce a person of good character but can contribute instead to bad character:

- Wealth can be gained dishonorably and spent in the same way

- Social status and celebrity can lead to narcissism and megalomania

- Positions of power can deeply corrupt even formerly decent souls

- Age, gender, and race disputes can lead to ugly categorizations and mistreatment

- Intelligence, talent, experience, and education can be highways to arrogance

- Good health and physical ability can move people toward judgmentalism and self-righteousness

It's not that these things aren't important. They can have a tremendous effect on our ability to have an impact or to achieve our goals. Good ideas can die because a person is short on one or more of these or has the wrong one. These things can do a lot. But what they don't do is differentiate worth.

Great leaders, great people, great societies minimize barriers of distinction. They know that these artificial constructs are good only for dividing people and pitting groups against each other. They give up the delusion that more of the "right" make-up makes someone a more valuable person. They insist that those who set up these barriers – pompous politicians, arrogant celebrities, wealthy snobs, racial manipulators, know-it-all academics – stop doing it.

There are many poor and uneducated people who have more wisdom than those who have formal authority in politics, business, education, and other spheres of life. "Freedom is the recognition that no single person, no single authority or government, has a monopoly on truth," observed President Ronald Reagan, "but that every individual life is infinitely precious, that every one of us put on this world has been put here for a reason and has something to offer."[20]

This Idea of Dignity doesn't guarantee – can't guarantee – that everyone will be treated respectfully. But it does guarantee that mistreatment is wrong. And it should guarantee that someone who violates another should themselves be disrespected, loathed, ostracized, and (if bad enough) prosecuted.

Often in American history, people were judged less on who they knew or what they had than on their character, common sense, and good work. That was a good place to be.

It would be good to get back to that good place. And we can. We as a people can determine that

> *We Will Never Let Anyone's Strength, Weakness, Development, Condition, Beliefs, or Choices Influence the Essential Esteem That He or She Deserves*

America has a long tradition of helping those with limitations. Americans hate watching people suffer from indignities.

Americans in World War II in the Pacific saw that "everywhere in Asia life is infused with a few terrible certainties – hunger, indignity, and violence. This was the world Americans perceived themselves advancing to save, not merely from the Japanese, but from imperialists of every hue – including their closest allies, the British."[21]

We make Braille available to the blind, sign language translations to the deaf, and accessible facilities to those with physical disabilities. We expect organizations to accommodate these special people in their work and careers. We provide specialized training and build camps for youth with disabilities. Volunteers teach English as a second language and tutor students with dyslexia.

But more and more frequently, those with deformations and disabilities and those who are incapacitated are treated with superficially dignifying words but intrinsically undignifying notions. We have the Americans with Disabilities Act and special grants, but the real goal is to make them go away. Pre-birth evaluations and tests can become "search and destroy" missions – searching for those whom we would honor with parking spots if they're born so that we can end their lives before we have to give them those spots.

The American Idea of Dignity causes us to look at this differently. Who's to say that life with a severe disability is less valuable or meaningful than an outwardly healthy life? People living lives that most of us would never want have, in fact, blessed and enriched the lives of others, while people living "healthy" lives have destroyed others' lives, started mindless wars, and caused untold destruction.

When opponents of the Idea of Dignity attack the existence of these people, they never say, "Let's get rid of the imperfect," or, "What we need is a good eugenics movement" (at least since pre-Nazi time). Instead, they use words loaded with sentiment to disguise the disrespect.

They talk about death with dignity, but too often what they really mean is death. There is no dignity in death ordered by others, only death. When death is handed out by other people, it's hard to find the dignity in the cruel transaction.

The Idea recoils at the theory that only the "best" of us should survive or be allowed to continue our existence. It declares its undying love for the underdog and its special concern for the "least of these."[22] Regardless of what might happen in the world of biology or the rough-and-tumble of animal nature, this Idea won't let some sort of "biological equivalence" strip away our majestic and unrivaled dignity.

Humanity left to its own devices always seems to revert to labeling and categories. You're weaker? Mentally disabled? Terminally ill? Believe what? Want to live how? Then you're not up to speed. You don't fit. You definitely don't belong with the "in" crowd.

The American Idea of Dignity changed all that. Not right away, of course, but over time. It was a wave of truth chipping away at the granite shore of privilege. Under this Idea, you may be more powerful, more intelligent, more fit, more mainstream, or more conventional, but there is one thing you are not and never will be.

And that's more worthy of respect. We believe this in the depths of our American soul. Because of it,

We Will Never Accept the View That There Is Such a Thing As a Life Not Worthy of Being Lived

Too many books, essays, and talking heads argue against the American Idea of Dignity. They say

- that "those people" are taking over our country and jobs

- that irremediable poverty is widespread in some minority culture communities

- that some racial and ethnic groups are less intelligent or able to be educated

- that desperate women are callous about human life

- that unborn babies aren't babies

- that children who have malformations or are chronically ill lack a necessary "quality of life"

- that people with disabilities need to make way for those better able to perform

- that incapacitated and elderly people have not only a right to die but a duty to die

What's the common ground in these un-American notions?

After the Second World War, American psychiatrist Leo Alexander studied what had gone wrong with German medicine under the Nazi regime. After completing a thorough investigation (reported in the New England Journal of Medicine in 1949), Dr. Alexander discovered that what went wrong with German medicine started before Nazi rule. He summed up the disaster this way:

> *Whatever proportions these crimes finally assumed, it became evident to all who investigated them that they had started from small beginnings. The beginnings at first were merely a subtle shift in emphasis in the basic attitude of physicians. It started with the acceptance of the attitude, basic in the euthanasia movement, that there is such a thing as life not worthy to be lived. This attitude in its early stages concerned itself merely with the severely and chronically sick. Gradually the sphere of those to be included in this category was enlarged.... But it is important to realize that the infinitely small wedged-in lever from which this entire trend of mind received its impetus was the attitude toward the nonrehabilitable sick.*[23]

The American Idea of Dignity stands in stark opposition to this terrible notion. The Idea says that there's no such thing as a life not worthy of being lived. Dr. Alexander elaborates:

> *Physicians have become dangerously close to being mere technicians of rehabilitation. This essentially Hegelian rational attitude has led them to make certain distinctions in the handling of acute and chronic diseases. The patient with the latter carries an obvious stigma as the one less likely to be fully rehabilitable for social usefulness. In an increasingly utilitarian society these patients are being looked down upon with increasing definiteness as unwanted ballast. A certain amount of rather open contempt for the people who cannot be rehabilitated with present knowledge has developed. This is probably due to a good deal of unconscious hostility, because these people for whom there seem to be no effective remedies have become a threat to newly acquired delusions of omnipotence.... From the attitude of easing patients with chronic diseases away from the doors of the best types of treatment facilities available to the actual dispatching of such patients to killing centers is a long but nevertheless logical step.... The killing center is the reduction ad absurdum of all health planning based only on rational principles and economy and not on humane compassion and divine law. To be sure, American physicians are still far from the point of thinking of killing centers, but they have arrived at a danger point in thinking, at which likelihood of full rehabilitation is considered a factor that should determine the amount of time, effort and cost to be devoted to a particular type of*

patient.... At this point Americans should remember that the enormity of a euthanasia movement is present in their own midst.[24]

And this was in 1949. To anyone paying the slightest attention, these signs have most certainly grown in size and force in America.

This appalling notion, that there is such a thing as a life not worthy of being lived, is a dreadful mindset that needs to be resisted at every turn. "There are a thousand hacking at the branches of evil to one who is striking at the root,"[25] noted Henry David Thoreau. This notion of "worthiness" is the root of all of the anti-right-to-life actions and movements. This is where the American Idea of Dignity meets its greatest enemy and where it must exercise its greatest influence.

Behind closed and sterile doors, many of our hospitals, hospices, nursing homes, and clinics have already begun to declare that some lives just...aren't worthy.

But this Idea shouts, "No!" and demands a return to a culture of unbroken dignity, a Dignity without exception. In the American Idea, where there's life, there's hope – and even more, the rock-solid protection of an individual's unalienable right to life. We can pretend this isn't going on, that life isn't being deemed "unworthy" all around us. But if we do, we can't really condemn the German civilians who didn't "know" where all those Jews were being taken during World War II.

In a certain sense, there's always arrogance at the root of a decree of "unworthiness." We compare a person or group to the norm (which usually translates as "us") and then measure the gap between them and the desired end (us). If the gap isn't too wide and can be closed, we might try to bring those confused heathens or barbarians along. But if the gap is too wide – as measured by our own criteria – then...they just have to go.

There are several components of this life-denying arrogance:

> • Part of it is the false assumption that who we are and what we believe is the ultimate measuring stick

> • Another part is forgetfulness about the simple fact that none of us decided where we would be born, to whom, in what condition, or in what time or place

> • A third part is the conclusion that we have the power to make decisions for others not as "fortunate" as us.

All of this is bad business, heartily rejected by the American Idea. It took a long time to get to handicapped parking spaces. Let's respect to the end of time those who will need them. As Americans, we can declare that

We Will Always Speak Up For Those Who Can't Speak For Themselves, and Defend Them with Unyielding Conviction

Something in this American Idea causes Americans to appreciate and root for the underdog.

Other people honor the kings and queens, the nobles and wealthy, the rulers and generals. We might do some of that. But not much. This comes from being the first nation to throw off the heavy chains of top-down authority, the millennia of the privileged and powerful few using – and crushing – the poor and padlocked many.

This was a very good event indeed: seeds of dignity sown in the early 1600s and coming to full bloom in the 1770s. Americans looked around and didn't see anyone more worthy of ruling themselves than themselves. They saw that there was only one person who ever lived who was good enough to rule over others – and he refused to do it.

What really stirs the American soul is the little against the big, the probable loser against the longest of odds, the desperate against the mighty, the Davids against the Goliaths. Instead of the underdog being marginalized or eliminated, the underdog is given a fighting chance, is surrounded by a rooting interest, is encouraged whenever possible.

Americans recognize that there can even be dignity in failure and disaster. They always respect and even admire a "good loser." They want to win. They recognize the truth in football legend Vince Lombardi's statement, "Winning isn't everything – it's the only thing."[26] But they also see the truth in another of his statements, "The real glory is being knocked to your knees and then coming back."[27]

But sometimes the underdog needs help. This magnificent Idea calls us to "speak up for those who cannot speak for themselves." The voiceless have never had a better friend than the American Idea of Dignity. It says, "Make no mistake – if you're discriminated against, poor, uneducated, unskilled, desperate, unborn, have a malformation, have a disability, or are incapacitated, you have friends in America. You have a champion in the American Idea of Dignity."

So if individual human beings are at the center, the right questions to ask would be along the lines of, "How do we protect and nurture her?" and, "How do we help her unleash her potential?" and, "What should we do with those who try to harm her?"

Instead, she finds herself under assault by a series of questions, questions that have a veneer of intellectual honesty that covers a deep-seated disregard for her most fundamental right, her right to life. The "wedge" into death today isn't the "nonrehabilitable sick," as it was in Dr. Alexander's review. The wedge is the most helpless class of all, pre-born human beings. The entry-level attack question is

What is a human being?

The Declaration of Independence doesn't even acknowledge this as a valid question. It uses the sweeping phrase "all men" – every person. But people of ignorance and ill will love this question. By asking it, they get to set up artificial ground rules and throw some people off the bus. In America, this included, in some way or other, women, blacks, Native Americans, Irish, Eastern Europeans, Chinese, Japanese-Americans, Jews, and others.

But the answer was always there, achingly clear in biology and in the minds of anyone not blinded by prejudice and propaganda. If you are Homo sapiens, you are – regardless of details – a human being. You aren't – cannot be – anything else.

But this question, "What is a human being?" has "legs" and refuses to die. It takes different forms, always trying to find a way to be asked that will allow some people to be dehumanized. One of its current variations is both devious and devastating and has now been asked for many years:

When does life begin?

In a surprising joint venture, religion led the push for the sanctity of life, but science sealed the deal. With religion only, life was still mysterious and its beginnings were shrouded in mist (like using "quickening," whatever that is, as a starting point for life).

But with science, all of the mystery and shadows are gone. We can see and hear and know there is a living being there. We are certain that all of that being's DNA is there at conception – no new ingredients are ever added. We know when the heart starts beating and the brain starts functioning.

The only way to support this question now is to abandon science and create your own mystery, as when we had an American president say that answering this "is above my pay grade."[28] This is a clever way to dodge a question that has somehow become controversial, but which really isn't difficult at all. In the 21st century, we don't even need to refer to religion or philosophy or ethics or intuition to answer it. It's well settled by basic biology.

Life begins when a human egg is fertilized. Whatever "it" is at that point, no thinking person can really believe that it isn't living. Every biologist knows that "it" is alive. Anyone who has heard a baby's heartbeat in the womb, just a few weeks into a pregnancy, knows first-hand that this being is alive.

So, perhaps recognizing the many deficiencies of this elementary question, some clever people upgraded it to

When does human life begin?

Now we're getting into the thick of it. Even if we agree that any being called Homo sapiens is fully human and that whatever is there is alive, how do we know when it becomes a human life?

But this question is no more than the last two questions or really even different.

Human life begins when a human egg is fertilized. That's it, and there's no mystery to it. Homo sapiens is there. The DNA of a human being is fully present in all of its complex splendor. That's the moment when Albert Einstein and Marie Curie, George Washington and Simon Bolivar, Mother Teresa and Martin Luther King, Chief John Ross and Lao-Tzu came into being.

All of the DNA, everything that would ever make them who they were, was created at that first moment. Before, there was no human life. After, there was a being who could change the world. No woman ever bore offspring that wasn't human.

In answer to the question, "When does life (or human life) begin?" the Idea of Dignity asks, "Doesn't life begin when it begins?" It asks us to consider how he can be a baby if we want him and a fetus if we don't. To say, "If I want this being, then he is a human baby with a right to life, and if I don't want this being, then it is a non-human fetus with no right to life" – to suggest, in other words, that this being's very identity is determined by the changeable wishes of someone else – takes us to a uniquely terrible place.

This massive cultural contradiction is seen first-hand in some medical facilities. If a person wants the child, she goes down one hallway, where she finds people who will try to save the life no matter how early in the pregnancy. If she doesn't want the child, she goes down another hallway, where she finds people who will try to end the life no matter how late in the pregnancy. This stark split in a medical facility is called a "full range of services." In an individual, it would be called insanity. As Ross Douthat observed in the New York Times,

> This is the paradox of America's unborn. No life is so sought after, so desired, so nurtured. And yet no life is so unprotected, and so destroyed.[29]

These two questions, "When does life begin?" and, "When does human life begin?" keep getting asked, but at this point of scientific understanding, they are in fact unintelligent questions. The answers have long been settled by science (and even longer by religion). The motive to keep asking them isn't scientific or even rational; rather, it is political and ideological. People who want the "right" to dispose of inconvenient life want these counterfeit questions to distract us from the American Idea of Dignity.

And so when they're pressed, they change the question again to

When does human life become viable?

The fascinating point here is that this question gives up the other questions. It agrees that we're talking about life, and not just any life but human life. But this new question wants to take the argument to another place, far from the Declaration's regal, well-designed simplicity, the elegant simplicity of "all."

So when does human life become viable?

Well, to answer this question, we first have to agree on what "viable" means. People who want to marginalize tiny human life say that viable means "able to live, on its own, outside the mother." But this is an artificial distinction that no thinking person is required to accept. Just because it's been said for decades doesn't make it so.

In fact, viable means "capable of living or developing normally under particular environmental conditions." And there it is. An unborn baby is capable of living and developing normally under its "particular environmental conditions,"[30] which for every person ever born has meant a mother's womb. When does human life become viable according to the dictionary definition? When she begins living and developing inside her mother.

But even if we accept that as a possible definition, what does it mean? Does viable mean "removed from the womb, physically disconnected from the mother, and able to breathe on his or her own"? As of this writing, this would mean little or no viability in the first trimester, some in the second, and very much in the third. The problem is that, using this definition, the "viability" time keeps getting pushed back. This version of viability is a self-limiting, shrinking notion heading relentlessly toward the first trimester and eventually to the first few weeks of life.

This argument about viability is full of opinions but very short on dignity and very long on dangerous extrapolations. If we accept this definition of viability as "able to live on its own outside the mother," then as of this writing, an unborn baby twelve weeks along is certainly not viable.

But what full-term baby, now born and one day old, can claim viability on those terms? Or at one month, or one year, or five years? They can breathe on their own but without constant care would be dead in hours or days. How many of the seriously sick people, people with disabilities, those with cognitive impairments or developmental delays, or people of advanced age would be able to retain their unalienable right to life?

If we make viability the measuring stick instead of dignity, it's a long list of people indeed who had better go into hiding.

"Viability" becomes a code word for unwanted life. It's a murky notion that opens doorways to death and shreds the American Idea of Dignity. This Idea asks us to be careful. It suggests that the unborn be given an unqualified chance at a dignified life.

This viability flight of the imagination is a distraction, not a real argument grounded in logic or morality. Many of the people who use it really want the right to end human life into the third trimester, and some want it up to the point of birth and, unbelievably, beyond. Instead of shrinking the time frame within which babies can be aborted in line with medical advances, they continue to fight for unrestricted abortion through all nine months.

If viability, even in their definition, were pushed back to 8 or 10 or 12 weeks, would they give up their Supreme Court-given "right" to end life whenever? Not likely. The people who argue for viability don't usually follow the logic anyway. This argument serves as nothing but a diversion. And it clouds the issue further, by asking,

What about the quality of this being's life?

Isn't the quality of life an important concern? For a life to have meaning, doesn't it have to have good quality?

This notion is thrown around a lot today. But if quality is the measure, who holds the yardstick? Who decides who has quality and who doesn't? Who gets to say how much quality is needed to allow you to keep living?

Quality is a powerful word, but it needs tight definition even in an industrial setting, where experts can take measurements down to miniscule ("Six Sigma") levels, identify even tiny deviations, and if not careful, can create a cost in less innovation and creativity. With human beings, quality can only be a personal, subjective idea. It is best left to each person to hold their own right to life in their own hands, and it is for no one else to help them end that life.

Don't we allow pets to be "put to sleep?" when the quality of their life has evaporated? "They shoot horses, don't they?"[31] asked an awful motion picture long ago, as it tried to make a plausible case for euthanasia. Carrying this over to human life is a huge error of logic and morality, seemingly made more palatable by the attempt to throw in a measure of compassion.

But human beings aren't animals. Only individual human beings are "endowed by their Creator with certain unalienable rights."[32] Animals are valuable, but people and animals aren't equivalent. We should love our pets and make necessary decisions at the end of their lives, but we should never confuse what we're doing with animals with what we must do with human beings who have sacred and undeniable rights.

The cutting edge of the anti-dignity movement is pressing its viability and quality arguments. Newborns with severe mental or physical defects have been allowed or even helped to die, because they aren't "viable," they can't live a "quality life," they're unpleasant to have around, they'll cause a lot of grief. Elderly people who are terminally ill (as all of us actually are) are allowed to die of secondary infections because they aren't "viable," they don't have enough "quality of life," they can no longer function on their own, they will create a lot of expense.

In fact, the twin arguments of viability and quality are the keys to unlocking the door of death, the dark passage into the eradication of people of all ages. We should recognize that this "unlocking" has a twisted logic all its own: If we will kill, sight unseen, potential Newtons and Nightingales and Beethovens, how can we justify not killing those we can see to be deficient or incapable, old or "useless"?

We're allowing the old adage, "Where there's life, there's hope," to be changed to, "Where there's life, it had better be viable," or, "Low quality, no life, no hope, no rights." Shouldn't we err on the side of life? Shouldn't we insist that people be found living until proven dead? In the long run, isn't it true that either everyone has an unalienable right to life or no one has? In the words of the Cleveland Clinic, "Every life deserves world class care."[33]

The many defenseless and America the defender

Any one of us could have been born in a time or place where we would be thought of as garbage and treated like trash. There are powerful people and always will be, but might still doesn't make right. There are majority groups, but numbers don't equate to truth or justice. There is no lesser race or gender or ethnicity. And there is no one in a greater category but only those who pretend to be so.

The poor can be given a helping hand and can break the cycle of poverty. Anyone willing to listen and learn can be educated and trained. Everyone should be given a chance because wherever they come from, those willing to come and work are American in their DNA.

Desperate women can be helped and encouraged. Babies, regardless of how they got here, can be treasured as our best investment in the future. The elderly and those with a tenuous grasp on life can be aided in holding on rather than pushed over the edge. Those with malformations, who are chronically ill, and who have disabilities can be treated as though they're just "us" with a different set of circumstances.

As Senator (later Vice President and presidential candidate) Hubert Humphrey said so well in 1977,

> *The moral test of a government is how that government treats those who are in the dawn of life – the children; the twilight of life – the elderly; and the shadows of life – the sick, the needy, and the handicapped.*[34]

Thomas Jefferson noted, "The care of human life and happiness, and not their destruction, is the first and only legitimate object of good government."[35] An America without the strongest defense of those who are defenseless is an America no longer special, no longer different, no longer ethical, no longer…America.

America At Its Best

The grand American Idea of Dignity is an affront to bad notions, like some people being worth more than others and some of those "others" not being people at all.

It has suffered some serious setbacks. But this immense American Idea can be revived, if we:

Take Action

Keep reminding each other of the origin of our rights.

★

End artificial definitions of who is or isn't a human being.

★

Allow all human beings full control of their own lives and health.

★

Avoid becoming a culture that willingly deals in death.

★

Take the debates about the unalienable right to life away from the courts and give them back to the people.

★

Eliminate the censoring – like not showing videos of abortions – that allows disrespect and destruction to grow in the dark.

★

Use fair language that describes a position without artificially elevating or degrading it.

★

Make the penalty for the destruction of human beings as severe as the crime.

★

Recognize that someone's right to life can only be surrendered by their own choice.

★

Refuse to make excuses for bad decisions and actions or allow a way out that costs others their dignity.

★

Instead of just condemning people for making bad choices, help them make good ones.

★

Always value the one more than the many.

★

Refuse to talk about or measure human worth in terms of externalities.

★

Remove barriers of distinction from our dialogue.

★

Respect everyone because the difference between us isn't that great.

★

Reject all discussion about whether lives are worthy of being lived.

★

Refuse to cross moral boundaries to save some at the expense of others.

★

Speak up for the voiceless.

To see detail on these Action Points and
to add your voice visit www.theamericanideas.com

Dignity isn't a small thing. The longer you live, the more valuable the Idea of personal dignity becomes.

For 6,000 years, the human race has been awash in death and degradation. It hasn't seemed to know where to start a change. Even with religion, the slaughter and violence has raged on. But the American Idea of Dignity was – is – a start.

With it, we have a very strong chance to finally get it right.

Dignity and the American Idea

Through the years, some people have claimed that people are basically good. History doesn't support that claim and, in fact, destroys it.

Then are people basically bad? No, not that either. The real truth is that the answer to the question, "Are people basically good or bad?" is "Yes."

Many people, truly great and magnanimous people, have spent their lives lifting others from the ash heaps. But even some of those efforts have been made with a condescending view toward their "inferiors." And many other people have treated their employees well and their families poorly or their families with great affection and their enemies with ruthless brutality.

So it should be no surprise that dignity has been a scarce commodity. It's too easy to steal it from others, too enticing to build up our own at the expense of others, too appealing to the dark side of human nature to strip it away from the helpless.

And so it has been, even in America, even as it tries to evaluate its actions and make its corrections. Native Americans, Female-Americans, and people of African, Chinese, Japanese, Irish, Mexican, and Jewish descent – these and more have been stripped of their dignity at times.

But this American Idea won't let these mistreatments and atrocities stand. These people were not finally given a seat at the table because they had influence or power, but in spite of the fact that they didn't. They've been treated with dignity – imperfectly, to be sure – because this Idea is unyielding, because it eventually gathers all into its exquisite embrace.

This American Idea of Dignity is unique in concept and scope. It insists on individual human dignity regardless of condition or situation. It includes every human being in its protective grip.

The Idea of Dignity clings hard to the stirring conviction that, although nations and leaders will come and go, you and I are forever.

CHAPTER 6

The American Idea of Opportunity

They came because they thought they had a chance. And they're still coming.

One of history's hardest lessons is that most people never have a chance. They're stuck where and how they start – unless things get even worse for them, which they often do.

There's nothing even resembling opportunity. Many end up fighting just to survive. The political, economic, and social systems that encase them are perfectly designed to benefit the few, more often than not at the expense of the many whose only "chance" is to be exploited.

And then along came America. For many generations now, America has been known as the Land of Opportunity. Not a land of mountains and valleys and rivers and fertile land, although it has all of those and more. A land of opportunity.

What a remarkable way to be known – as a place where what you want to be and do is possible, if you'll only imagine it and form it and work at it with all your heart and might. A place without artificial restraints. A place of open doors rather than closed minds. A place where you can start with nothing and end up with more of everything – more freedom, more security, more wealth, and – yes – even more opportunity.

There's nothing like it and never really has been in history or anywhere else in the world. It's the opposite of the song New York, New York, which says, "If I can make it here, I can make it anywhere."[1] This American Idea has a different, broader, and more inviting message: "If you can't make it anywhere else," it says to everyone, "you can make it here."

"We don't care what your name is, boy, we'll never turn you away," proclaimed a popular song in the 1960s.[2] Americans at their best don't care about your name or about the many unearned or overhyped trivialities so often used to limit human potential.

The only things Americans care about are the kind of person you are, what you want to accomplish, and how hard you're willing to work to win.

Opportunity

The possibilities are endless.

Every human being should have a real chance to be successful. All people deserve a life in which they can work and create and build.

We want a culture where the good limitations are generally few and the bad limitations can be shattered by determination and action.

We want an educational system that provides everyone a way out and up.

We expect government to ensure a level playing field but not a level victory stand.

We believe that merit will take you far and that you should be willing to compete against other people of merit to get there.

Success is never final but neither is failure.

You can try and fail and learn and then plan and work and try again and again. If you'll never give up, you can finally end up with more than your ancestors even dared to dream.

The first thing that Americans came to believe about the majestic concept of opportunity is that

The Possibilities Are Endless

Thomas Jefferson said,

> *You live in a country where talents, learning, and honesty are so much called for that every man who possesses these may be what he pleases.*[3]

"Possibility" is one of the grandest words in the dictionary. It tells us that whatever is, no matter how bad, it doesn't have to be. Whatever is, no matter how mediocre, it can be made better. Whatever is, no matter how good, it's just the starting point of something even much, much better. American poet T.S. Elliott defines this American sense of possibility: "Only those who risk going too far can possibly find out how far one can go."[4]

There's no end until we're gone. We can make tomorrow better than the past, different than today, and better than the future others might believe to be our destiny. Life has opportunities that we might not even imagine today but, if we're vigilant, might be right around the next bend in time.

Possibility has always been there for a small part of the human race, for the few who monopolized the money and power. Kings and queens expanded their holdings and empires and sometimes saw their dreams fulfilled. They almost always created nightmares for everyone else in the process.

Even today, for nearly a billion Chinese, nearly a billion Indians, and more than a billion Africans and Asians and Latin Americans, even imagining possibility is... impossible.

But even the very poor in America – in some places, even those with mental impairments or physical disabilities – have possibilities. They can:

- Read and think and grow into more than they are right now

- Go to school and learn useful skills

- Start a little business with no hassles

- Work hard and be respectful and make themselves valuable to an employer

- Move if necessary and, except where there are still pockets of oddness and bigotry, find a job at some level

- Do what Mark Twain did to get his first job when he arrived in San Francisco – offered to work for nothing until it became obvious that he was worth something

- Spend what money they do have to advance their lives rather than to wreck their minds and bodies

America is inarguably the land of possibilities. Remarkably, "With 5 percent of the world's population, the United States has generated between 20 and 30 percent of world output for 125 years.... The U. S. economy has been the world's largest since the middle of the 1880s, and it remains so today."[5] Some people wonder if there's such a thing as American exceptionalism. Just these few numbers on this one idea should put all of that wondering to rest.

The possibilities – self-actualization, creativity, productivity, persuasion, respect, and many more – are all there in the American Idea of Opportunity. It's our job to keep it so. And the possibilities are dynamic, always churning, always fresh. Ralph Waldo Emerson wrote that

> Trade.... was the principle of liberty...trade planted America and destroyed feudalism....It makes peace and keeps peace, and it will abolish slavery. We complain of its oppression of the poor, and of its building up a new aristocracy...but the aristocracy of trade has no permanence, is not entailed, was the result of toil and talent...and is continually falling, like the waves of the sea, before new claims of the same sort.[6]

The possibilities go far beyond work and subsistence in America. Here are just a few of the personal possibilities for which every American can strive.

Self-Actualization

In most cultures even today, people can't be whatever they want to be. In fact, "whatever they want to be" is often not even a legitimate concept. People have a destiny, a fate, a place, a position. Their duty is to accept it.

But not so in free societies, especially not so in America. Who the person is inside is considered to be more important than peripheral life facts like ancestry, tradition, role definition, race, gender, or current circumstances. People are thought to have enormous and unique potential to be and to do...something very special.

In truly free societies that honor the individual, we recognize the unique possibilities for advancement and development of each human life. We see that freeing these inherent energies produces a magnificent portrait of individuals who own themselves. It's liberty that allows people to be what they will be, limited only by their own talents, abilities, desires, interests, and perseverance. Compared to the beacon of one such life, the flicker of any ten governments taken together pales and vanishes.

America didn't become wealthy by stripping colonies of their natural wealth. That was the perverted "critical success factor" of the European colonial empire-builders and "wannabes." America has dabbled in it to be sure and is in danger of becoming a de facto imperial power, but that hasn't been representative of the better angels of its nature. America became prosperous not by freeing poor countries of their wealth but by freeing poor people of their limitations.

Although self-actualization can't be guaranteed, the fact that it's now possible is an amazing human achievement. As class distinctions and barriers are minimized or eliminated, opportunity moves from the classes to the masses.

Creativity

President Franklin Roosevelt said, "Happiness lies…in the joy of achievement, in the thrill of creative effort."[7] But here's a fundamental truth of nations, organizations, and families: Scared people do not innovate.

Because human beings are fundamentally designed to be creative, bits and pieces of innovation will occur even in repressive societies. But not in earth-shaking, world-dominating proportions. Americans aren't more creative than others because they're smarter. Intelligence, regardless of the breast-beating of various groups, roughly follows a normal distribution. They're more creative because they're freer than others. President James Polk observed that in America,

> Mind, no longer tasked in devising means to accomplish or resist schemes of ambition, usurpation, or conquest, is devoting itself to man's true interest in developing his faculties and powers and the capacity of nature to minister to his enjoyments. Genius is free to announce its inventions and discoveries, and the hand is free to accomplish whatever the head conceives not incompatible with the rights of a fellow-being.[8]

Leaders in other nations can look for other reasons and invent other reasons. They can claim that Americans benefit from dominance and hegemony and natural advantage. They can imagine that Americans have always been wealthy.

But the fact remains that a nation formed out of mostly poor immigrants has innovated itself into unprecedented prosperity and economic leadership. President Ronald Reagan observed, "Freedom and incentives unleash the drive and entrepreneurial genius that are the core of human progress."[9]

Productivity

What incentives do unfree people have to work harder, smarter, or more efficiently? To expect people to be productive when none of the advantages accrue to them is to be indisputably ignorant of human nature.

What Pharaohs got done with thousands of brutalized slaves, we've learned to do with a few who are well treated and paid – to design the machines and operate them, to design the buildings and engineer them, to make everything better. What kings and queens extracted from thousands of peasants, we've learned to receive from a few independent farmers – who are paid even better if they use innovative methods.

A slave who is whipped, no matter how motivational fear might be to stir short-term performance, cannot and will not think of ways to improve the whipper's lot. A serf who has to turn over the better part of the crop to someone who didn't work for it is an unlikely candidate for creative farming.

Unfree societies try to achieve productivity under one of the truly outstanding political illusions – that strong effort and, ultimately, prosperity can be achieved by control, domination, or slavery.

But these tools of tyrants are no match for free people, however poor or ignorant they start out.

Persuasion

Only free societies make persuasion an important skill.

Why use persuasion if you can simply order it done? Why should I deal with you if I can dispose of you? Absolute monarchs never even had the concept of persuasion float through their minds.

If power corrupts, one of its major points of corruption is at the more social and subtle ways of living: listening, thinking, convincing, negotiating, compromising. These disappear in the face of brute force. They're unnecessary, and they only seem to diminish the autocratic power.

Some in unfree societies might ridicule America's highly developed skills in marketing and advertising, and indeed, there are times when these are insulting, offensive, and over-the-top. But having these skills is a thousand times better than having a society where there's no need for them, where people can only have what they're told they can have.

Leaders in free societies have to rely on practical wisdom and persuasion rather than coercion and punishment. They might try to use manipulation or deception as a substitute, but we can trust that their sin – as well as the people – will find them out.

Respect

Freedom produces respect, in part because freedom unleashes merit. It's hard to respect people who have achieved nothing, even if their lack of accomplishment is largely due to living in an unfree society. We can and should choose to respect them for their humanity. But that's far from what we would feel for them if they were living valuable lives.

How much sooner could Europe have climbed out of its primitive tribal culture if it had moved more quickly away from the false respect for landed aristocracy? If it had doubted rulers who got their privilege first by taking and then by anointing and then by inheritance? If it had had the smarts to unleash the potential of its peasant masses and the grace to watch them succeed?

No one can reasonably believe that all of the smartest and ablest people lived in castles. In fact, looking at how they acted and fought and grabbed, it's hard to believe that any of the smartest and ablest people lived in castles.

Europe's leaders today might claim good intentions and care for the poor, but one of the reasons that so many of these nations became welfare states is because they'd never given the poor real opportunity. Most people expected to be ruled and provided for by the patriarchy. When they got enough political voice, they insisted on the only thing they knew – to be provided for. So political leaders had to buy them off. Like the Romans, they gave people bread and circuses, now called "entitlements." These are incredibly poor substitutes for opportunity and achievement... and respect.

We can encourage respect based on the humanness of others, and that's good. But it's mostly just theory until we see them accomplish what no one thought they could do. Now our respect can be rich and deep because it derives from observation and acknowledgment and not just from good will towards fellow human beings.

This is deeply ingrained in the American spirit. Americans believe that

Every Human Being Should Have a Real Chance to Be Successful

Because we have an unalienable right to the pursuit of happiness, we should also have the logical corollary to that right – a chance to be successful, however we define "successful." This is partly because success can be a strong pathway to happiness and partly because success can bring us happiness all by itself.

This is much different from saying we have a "right" to be happy or a "right" to be successful. The Declaration of Independence is clear: We have a right to the pursuit of happiness – not happiness itself. Happiness is too dependent on a host of choices and variables to be codified into law.

In the same way, that right includes a chance to be successful but not a guarantee of success. Success is too dependent on a host of decisions and actions to be guaranteed. President Bill Clinton said that the goal is

> To give all Americans an opportunity – not a guarantee, but a real opportunity – to build better lives.[10]

But we're free people, and freedom is, in great measure, about opportunity, about having a chance. Among other things, freedom is the opportunity to lead a self-determined, satisfying, self-controlled, responsible life.

- *Self-determined.* I'm free to choose the kind of life I will live – for big causes or small causes or no causes, for others or myself or both. I can make my life fall anywhere along Henry David Thoreau's continuum of making my life a mansion to making it a shack.[11] But whatever the choice, it's mine and mine alone to make. No one else may take my life or my freedom to choose how I'll live it.

- *Satisfying.* I'm free to pursue happiness. There's no guarantee that I'll find it, but I have a right to search for it. I'm free to seek it with all my heart. I'm free from interference by people and governments who want to keep me from it or to take it away once I find it. The Declaration of Independence calls this pursuit a "right." But even before it was a right, it was a fundamental human passion.

- *Self-Controlled.* I'm free to control myself. I recognize that freedom without boundaries isn't freedom at all, but rather a way to wreck my life. I will not be a freedom-without-boundaries advocate because there is no freedom without boundaries. I know that this kind of freedom can't survive itself. I'm certain that the best kind of control – the only kind compatible with freedom – is the kind I impose upon myself. People who practice freedom without self-control will lose much of their freedom and all of their chances to be successful. A culture that preaches freedom without teaching self-control won't have either for very long.

• *Responsible.* I'm free to take full responsibility for myself and appropriate responsibility for others. I know that all responsibility begins with individual responsibility. A free society is one in which all people are free to carve out their own territory, to win their own successes, and to grapple with their own failures. We need to be free not only from interference by do-gooders, but also from the burden of mandatory care of do-badders. I may need help, but I won't let it be because I avoided taking responsibility for myself. I may be needed, but I won't let it be because others are dodging responsibility and asking me to enable their dodging.

Millions of human beings would give almost anything to have this great chance, the real chance to be successful. We should be careful not to squander either our chance or our way of life that makes it possible. As President Bill Clinton said,

> *The American dream that we were all raised on is a simple but powerful one – if you work hard and play by the rules you should be given a chance to go as far as your God-given ability will take you.*[12]

Americans indeed are certain that

All People Deserve a Life in Which They Can Work and Create and Build

Building on the great sense of possibilities and the breathtaking chance to be successful, the American Idea of Opportunity advocates an active role for our culture and institutions: They should assist individuals in leading productive, creative, and expansive lives.

For a variety of reasons, including religious beliefs, American culture has long been favorable to leading this kind of life. The culture as a whole has supported the industrious, the innovative, the increasers. The results of this can be seen in many realities, like the enormous size of an American economy that has been built by such a tiny fraction of the world's population.

Although American institutions have contributed to this, they have, at times, had a less-supportive history:

• *Society.* American society has largely encouraged industriousness and the concept of leaving a legacy to future generations. But it has also featured bigotry, discrimination, favoritism, cronyism, corruption, and theft – not to mention segregation and slavery.

Every time society has favored the wrong people or one group over another or the few over the many or the many over the few, it has worked against helping everyone get the lives they deserve. Any time people are given an edge based on anything other than character and merit, those not given the edge are relegated to second-class opportunities.

• *Education.* "I never let schooling interfere with my education,"[13] Mark Twain declared. His humor contains an important truth – learning is the key, not the way we get that learning. Education has been the way up and out for millions of Americans.

But too often, schools haven't been an asset in that quest for knowledge and improvement. As schools and school systems have become both mammoth and government-controlled, learning has too often become secondary to ideological goals and big-administration, big-labor demands. All of this is destructive of the potential opportunities of those being educated – or too often, not being educated.

• *Religion.* The religiously inspired work ethic of early Americans was an extremely positive influence. It drove people to strive, build, and create.

But religion has often treated business as a tainted way of life and glibly called hard work "greed" or "runaway ambition." It has treated money, rather than the love of money, as evil. It has treated practical interests as commercialism, an enemy rather than a component of the spiritual life.

We can see the flawed thinking today in the high-sounding term "giving back," as in, "Now you've made your money or built your business, so you should give back some of what you've taken." Better to recognize that what they did to make the money or build the business was already a great gift to others. In a culture that favors opportunity, a better term would be "giving more if you choose," not "giving back because you owe it."

• *Government.* For centuries, American government aided people in their quest to build a worthy life, mostly by what it didn't do. It didn't

- Damage people and businesses with high taxes

- Overwhelm entrepreneurs and businesses with voluminous and incomprehensible regulations

- Borrow money that would never be repaid

- Eat away the value of the currency with inflation, continuously at a lower level and periodically (like in the 1970s) at a monstrous level

- Provide government workers more security, higher wages, and better benefits than those who employed them

- Expect business to check for illegal immigrants rather than itself stopping illegal immigration

- Think its job was to elevate some citizens at the expense of others

- Give tort lawyers the keys to the bank

- Enter European and other wars and their destruction of worthy lives for the better part of three hundred years.

Now, for decades, it's been doing all of the above. We may be at a point where the strongest economy the world has ever seen has been chipped away at for too long and in too many ways and is bucking under the controlling hand and dead weight of the government.

For opportunity to flourish, American citizens need political leaders who will be both strong and self-restrained. We desperately need real leaders who are secure and satisfied in who they are, needing neither the approval of the crowds (causing them to follow polls and shatter fragile liberties) or kudos from the nations (causing them to meddle in international disputes and conflicts).

It is weak leaders who cater to bad notions – who bellow and roar and lead nations into economic disaster and wars, who destroy opportunity in their quest to create it.

• *Business.* For centuries, the American economy was driven by many self-starting, self-employed people – farmers, craftsmen, merchants. Even today, a huge number of people are employed in smaller businesses, where most of the new jobs and new ideas are created. Entrepreneurs generate up to 70% of economic growth and two thirds of technological innovation. Although less than 10% of companies, entrepreneurial organizations create up to two thirds of all new jobs.[14]

Thomas Jefferson envisioned a future where all people would essentially be the leader of their own lives. If Britain was a "nation of shopkeepers," America was a "nation of CEOs."

But then big business happened. It started with the railroads, which based themselves (and still do) on the only large-scale models available – hierarchical, autocratic kingdoms, armies, and churches from the Middle Ages. This led to chains of command, with systematic management, control, and too often degradation of people.

Freedom of thought and action are often limited or eliminated. In the midst of the freest nation on earth exists some of the most authoritarian – even totalitarian – of organizations. It's a statement about the size and nature of our government that it bails out the very organizations that are contrary in so many ways to the American Idea of Opportunity – often those which are the greatest destroyers of wealth.

Sadly, entrepreneurs often don't improve on this. We can and should honor entrepreneurship as a concept and entrepreneurs as a class, but that doesn't mean we should honor every entrepreneur or support every one of their plans. Some entrepreneurs are arrogant, others are ignorant, yet more are incompetent, and none of them deserve to have their businesses survive just because they are entrepreneurs who are trying to make good. Entrepreneurs can be all about themselves and not at all about those they're using and abusing.

Any business people worth their salt care about people – and have the sense to know that this will add to performance (as long as it doesn't lead to entitlement thinking).

• *Labor.* Unions and other labor sympathizers once rightly stood for the many who were dealt unsafe, unsanitary, grueling, insecure, and undignified lives. But they've too often forgotten their grand mission – to help workers to achieve and to live a life of value.

All too frequently, unions have protected the few at the expense of the many. They've kept wages high for the dwindling number that the company can still afford to employ – steel, automobiles, airlines, so many others. They've put their companies at risk with their dual destructive demands of ever more money and ever less work.

They've made state and local government, their last real bastion of power, unsustainably expensive and far too entitled. They've made professional sports inaccessible to the average American and his or her family. And when big labor conspires with big business and big government? Watch the opportunity disappear.

Not all Americans may want to be wealthy, but all do want to have a good life. They want to give a good life to their children and bequeath a good life to their grandchildren. They want to make sure those descendents have an even better life than they do – and more, that they have the marvelous opportunity of finding and exploring and living their passions.

America is the place where there's actually opportunity to focus on passions, to make a living doing what you really love to do. At least it was. And surely, with fresh thinking and strong commitment, can be so again.

Because we believe so strongly in individual opportunity,

We Want a Culture Where the Good Limitations Are Generally Few and the Bad Limitations Can Be Shattered by Determination and Action

Limitations? What do they have to do with freedom and opportunity? Aren't they always bad?

Some limitations are not only reasonable, but are necessary to produce and take advantage of real opportunity. Here are the big personal ones:

• *Passions and Interests.* It's really hard to be successful at something which elicits no passion or commitment.

• *Talents and Skills.* It really isn't true that we can be anything we want to be. If we aren't good at math, we're not likely to be a successful engineer or physicist.

- *Knowledge.* We'd better know something if we're going to try something. Someone once said, "If you think education is expensive, try ignorance."[15]

- *Experience.* Starting a business or investing our money in a field where we have no background is a fairly solid formula for failure.

- *Prior Commitments.* If we've already committed our time or money to one effort, we can't – shouldn't – commit them to something else. Distractions are opportunity killers.

- *Money.* Short of stealing or deceiving, we can't do more than what we have (or can access) the financial resources to do.

- *Time.* We only have so long to apply for an open position, take a product idea to market, or get the knowledge we need to exploit an opportunity. As someone once said, "Someday is not a day of the week."[16]

One of government's important roles is to provide good limitations. Protections against fraud, collusion, market manipulation, and coercion are all crucial to maintaining and maximizing opportunity for all.

But the American Idea of Opportunity, at its core, is about shredding bad limitations. While things like minority status, ethnicity, gender, religious affiliation, educational deficiencies, poverty, work heritage, and physical disability are defining boundaries elsewhere, in America, they're only hurdles. They can be high hurdles indeed. But they've always been crossed, and when they're crossed, it becomes easier for everyone who comes behind to cross them too.

There are many bad structural limitations in life. For example, there's an opportunity if an organization is good enough to create a temporary monopoly. It can briefly limit the opportunity of others who would like to engage in that work.

But even here, the danger is eventually destroyed by this American Idea – if it is allowed to operate. If someone dominates a market by providing a product or service that is so excellent or inexpensive (or both) that no one can compete against it, this means they are serving their customers very well indeed. In the fairest of ways, they may prevent others from providing this product or service. But this just means that these others will have to find some other place to compete. And if this monopoly of excellence at last becomes arrogant and sloppy – which they almost always do – the Land of Opportunity always has its replacements waiting in the wings.

This leads us to one of the most powerful of bad limitations – government monopoly. This is the only "legal" monopoly we ultimately need to fear. When it's a monopoly of legislation and special favor rather than a monopoly of excellence, it becomes an entrenched, overbearing, and very inefficient thing.

When a license or franchise is granted by government – as has been done with utilities, transportation, communication, and other industries – we're always promised that the government will act as our watchdog and protect our interests, that we don't need a free market because we have...them. Government-regulated monopolies can work, but never very well and never to the advantage of the consumer. Comparing airline pricing from today with the government-controlled days of the 1970s (and before) is one simple way to remember the unbearable cost of government-created monopoly.

Government has created or protected other monopolies with a variety of tools:

- Tariffs to protect high-cost producers from facing competition and from giving their customers the best pricing

- Import quotas to limit the number of competitive products that the producers will have to face

- Unnecessary regulation, which burdens smaller and more nimble competitors who have no lobby or armies of lawyers

- Subsidies, where some are provided artificial support at the expense of everyone else

- And bailouts, where inefficient producers are protected from the consequences of bad management and greedy workers

Government manipulation can also create artificial opportunities. It can lower interest rates so much that it creates an unsustainable housing boom and an ever-shakier mortgage system to support it. It can create "easy money" policies that produce bubbles in stocks, commodities, and acquisitions. It can "stimulate" and throw money it often doesn't even have at projects guaranteed to attract corruption and waste.

Government monetary and fiscal policy has a role to play in optimizing opportunities. But its misapplication can lead to overdoing and then underdoing, all of it hurting the American Idea of Opportunity.

If it's a sin to kill a mockingbird, it's a much bigger sin to kill opportunity. We should insist that the government remove itself from limiting real opportunity or from creating false opportunity. Government-created limitations always favor the select few over the ignored many and have no place in America.

The free market doesn't mean – never has meant – "no rules." Free markets and free trade should mean "markets and trade free from bad limitations, bad actors, bad actions, and bad government." This American Idea says, "Of course there are limitations, but in America, your only important, deal-making, or deal-breaking limitation should be yourself. If you believe in yourself and have the passions, talents, knowledge, experience, freedom, money, and time to accomplish a goal, you can do it."

This Idea of Opportunity puts a premium on initiative. Wherever you are in life, you can do something different, something better, something that will improve your lot, your standing, your "place"...something that will make your life soar.

But soaring is impossible without learning. This is why

We Want an Educational System That Provides Everyone a Way Out and Up

British philosopher Samuel Johnson said,

> *The supreme end of education is expert discernment in all things – the power to tell the good from the bad, the genuine from the counterfeit, and to prefer the good and the genuine to the bad and the counterfeit.*[17]

Everyone, no matter how poor, no matter how impoverished their background, can find opportunity if they will choose to learn. Those opportunities are expanded dramatically when their choice to learn finds a good place to learn. For generations, schools have been a way out and up for countless Americans.

This is mainly because schools knew what their mission was. The training in particular areas – reading, writing, arithmetic – were important things, but not the main thing. Learning didn't stop with the acquisition of technical skills. As social critic John Ruskin reminded us,

> *Education does not mean teaching people what they do not know.... It is not teaching the youth the shape of letters and the tricks of numbers, and leaving them to turn their arithmetic to roguery and their literature to lust. It means, on the contrary, training them into the perfect exercise and kingly continence of their bodies and souls.*[18]

When schools get trapped by any other focus – such as indoctrinating young minds, using children as vehicles to achieve social goals, experimenting with teaching methods, building bigger schools and school systems – education, learning, and discernment die. Even the technical skills aren't learned very well, if at all. President Rutherford B. Hayes said,

> *At the basis of all prosperity...lies the improvement of the intellectual and moral condition of the people.*[19]

The problem, in part, is that we got confused along the way about the meaning of "public" education. Originally, it meant that the local community, led by parents and thoughtful neighbors, would start and run a school. There was tight accountability because everyone had a stake in the outcome – better students, better community, better opportunity for all. Everyone was invested and results were usually good – even in poor, marginalized, segregated schools.

Education can once more be the powerful force for good that it was in American life for so long. For that to be so, it must be returned to the children, the parents, and all those who have a stake in learning rather than in receiving the spoils of a rotten system.

Government's only role should be to ensure that the unalienable rights of all involved are protected. In education, as in all other areas of opportunity,

We Expect Government to Ensure a Level Playing Field but Not a Level Victory Stand

Government is needed to ensure that the rules of honesty and impartiality are followed. But when it bypasses all of that and turns the game upside down, calling winners losers and losers winners, true opportunity is severely harmed. Founder James Madison wrote,

> That alone is a just government, which impartially secures to every man, whatever is his own.... That is not a just government, nor is property secure under it, where arbitrary restrictions, exemptions, and monopolies deny to part of its citizens that free use of their faculties, and free choice of their occupations, which not only constitute their property in the general sense of the word; but are the means of acquiring property strictly so called.[20]

Equality of opportunity and equality of outcome are opposites, at times even enemies. Equality of opportunity is vital to the survival of the free-enterprise system and the expansion of individual opportunity. Equality of outcome is the perfect way to destroy both the system and the opportunity.

The government can and often needs to be a referee. But it has been a player in the details of economic life for too long and to poor effect. The government makes loans and loan guarantees and provides myriad other ways of supporting big, failing organizations. As of this writing, this includes banks, automobiles, airlines, steel – and state and local government. But how can this be economically reasonable, much less just?

By definition, the government will only step in to prop up failing businesses or industries. There's no need to save a successful one. Failing in America means "they can't figure out how to compete on their own." They have a flawed (if not stupid) business model, a product or service that isn't needed or can't command the prices they're charging, a cost structure (including wages) that's unsustainable given the market – something that makes them a millstone around the economy's neck.

But our government now seems to love millstones. There are powerful influences – money, notable people, lobbies, labor unions– at work to save the albatrosses. Government talks about saving companies that are "too big to fail," when obviously they weren't. Government loves to ride to the rescue, even – perhaps especially – when it's the cause of the catastrophe. "Americans are angry in part because they sense that the government was as much a cause of the [financial] crisis as its cure," noted a Federal Reserve Bank president.[21]

At the same time, government doesn't intervene to save the tens of thousands of small businesses that fail every year, each one causing personal pain and economic hardship and loss of jobs. Many of them may have even failed because of the disastrous actions of the big companies that destroyed their industry or crippled their markets. But only the big companies will get media attention and government largesse.

This is the same manner in which the national government now deals with other nations – cater to and support the big ones no matter how evil and let the small ones flounder and fail no matter how decent. Government can only think big in part because it is so big. It can only relate to its peers – big business, big banks, big lobbyists, big labor, big movements, big nations.

There's only justice, naked and alone, to prevent all of this. Justice would demand either that all businesses be allowed to rise and fall on their own merits or that all businesses be saved regardless of size or influence. If support is to be given in any form, it should be provided equally to all organizations – big and small, healthy and unhealthy, popular and hated.

But government at all levels gives the most advantages to those who may need them or deserve them least. The big business is lured with tax breaks and other bribes, while the small business (that may create more jobs in the long run) is ignored and saddled with a government-created competitive disadvantage. The big business that has driven to its own destruction on a path readily observable to outsiders is bailed out, while the small business caught up in its wake passes away without help or mourning.

How destructive is this constant manipulation and interference by government? In writing about the causes of the Great Depression, one expert noted that "the deepest problem was the intervention, the lack of faith in the marketplace."[22] When we give up on freedom, when we allow the government to be the biggest player rather than the referee, the result is often disaster of fantastic proportions. This is in part because the government is "competing with the private sector, and frightening it.... The story of the mid-1930s is the story of a heroic economy struggling to recuperate but failing to do so because of perverse federal policy."[23]

And this is all based on a fallacy, the notion of government impartiality on the one hand and marketplace wickedness on the other. Economist John Maynard Keynes, who was a believer in government intervention, still wrote, "It is a mistake to think businessmen are more immoral than politicians."[24]

Thomas Jefferson pointed the way to a special kind of politics with his promise of a "frugal government, which...shall not take from the mouth of labor the bread it has earned."[25] He knew, as all the founders did, that government can too easily take a direct role in destroying opportunity. Here are the seven main ways it does just that – we could call these government's financial "7 Deadly Sins":

1. Unequal, high, manipulative taxes

2. Endless borrowing with no plan for repayment

3. Cancerous inflation, the monstrous "invisible tax"

4. Ponzi schemes renamed "entitlement programs"

5. Safety nets that catch people in dependency

6. Insurance against accountability

7. Intervention to maintain prosperity (or its illusion)

Because of their gigantic negative effect on opportunity, let's take a look at each of these in more detail.

Opportunity Threat 1: The Tax-Man Cometh

What kind of freedom is it that doesn't include the freedom to keep and use what you alone have worked for and produced? President Calvin Coolidge said,

> *The collection of any taxes which are not absolutely required, which do not beyond reasonable doubt contribute to the public welfare, is only a species of legalized larceny. Under this republic the rewards of industry belong to*

those who earn them. The only constitutional tax is the tax which ministers to public necessity. The property of the country belongs to the people of the country. Their title is absolute.... We can not finance the country, we can not improve social conditions, through any system of injustice, even if we attempt to inflict it upon the rich.... The wise and correct course to follow in taxation and all other economic legislation is not to destroy those who have already secured success but to create conditions under which every one will have a better chance to be successful.[26]

As a country, we had that freedom for centuries. Historian Paul Johnson has noted that it is "one of the most important facts in the country's history that America remained a low-tax country until the second half of the twentieth century."[27] What opportunities could Americans have exploited if they'd gotten to keep another 20 or 30 or 40 percent of what they earned over the past 50 years?

The attitude of many people in powerful places can be seen by their reaction to tax cuts, deductions, and exemptions. They will call these things a bad use of government revenues instead of acknowledging the reality that it is simply allowing people to keep their own money. As their demand for more revenues to spend and give away goes up, they try to rename tax avoidance "tax evasion" and call paying taxes a "patriotic duty."

As of this writing, the top 10% of earners pay about 73% of all of the individual income taxes collected by the federal government, while the bottom 49% of earners pay no tax at all – "a number so high that it undermines notions of shared sacrifice and mutual investment in the core functions of government."[28] Incredibly, the bottom 40% of earners actually makes a profit from the federal income tax system, by getting "more money in tax credits than they would otherwise owe in taxes."[29] This partly turns the tax system into another welfare program and redistribution scheme, only partially hidden from public view. In just two short years, the percentage of households paying no federal income tax went from 38% to 49%.[30] How is all of this just? How is it sustainable? Founder James Madison wrote,

A just security to property is not afforded by that government, under which unequal taxes oppress one species of property and reward another species: where arbitrary taxes invade the domestic sanctuaries of the rich, and excessive taxes grind the face of the poor...[31]

Government produces nothing but can only take from the fruit of others' labor. And the more money they have available, the more they have to keep themselves in power and create new schemes to transfer funds (always with a cut for the government), to manipulate or mangle the economy, or to engage in foreign misadventures.

"Simplify, simplify, simplify," exhorted Henry David Thoreau.[32] Even God only asks for a flat 10%. A "citizenship tax" of 10% for all is equitable, reasonable, and the only security against financial injustice. And there's no real freedom without economic freedom.

There is a special need to eliminate corporate income taxes. If we want to have a vibrant, job-creating economy, we have to maximize the money we happily let businesses keep to do it. With zero taxes on income earned in America, businesses would have every incentive to keep facilities and jobs in America. The alternatives, like protective tariffs and currency manipulation, only get us into the business of playing games and destroying opportunities.

In the meantime, corporations should also pay an equal tax, without the distortions due to lobbying and special exemptions, deductions and credits. When average middle-class workers are paying taxes, while a giant General Electric can pay no tax on over $14 billion in profits, justice has left the building.[33]

Opportunity Threat 2: Borrowing

President Ronald Reagan said,

> *You and I, as individuals, can, by borrowing, live beyond our means, but only for a limited period of time. Why, then, should we think that collectively, as a nation, we are not bound by the same limitation?*[34]

Why does the government – any government – need to borrow? More specifically, why does a government with revenues measured in the trillions need to borrow?

None of the possible reasons are good:

- It can't live within its means. It's prepared to mortgage the future to score political points and achieve short-term political goals.

- It has already raised taxes to the skies. It knows that any further taxes will bring avoidance, evasion, and possibly revolution.

- It's afraid that if it prints any more phony money, inflation will get out of control. It has already accepted inflation and the demolition of the dollar as a given.

- It wants to use deficit spending – also known as borrowing – to manipulate the economy. It might call it "stimulus," but it's actually a few arrogant people in Washington who think they can manage the most complex economy in the world.

All of this borrowing soaks up resources that could be used to create vast opportunity. It drives up interest rates and borrowing costs over the long term for everyone, further crimping the creation of opportunity. Ultimately, the borrowing gets out of hand, pushing the government to its last-stand weapon, inflation and the destruction of what's left of the dollar.

Until fairly recently, America was a creditor nation, not the king of debtors. The federal government was able to operate without debt for most of its first century and a half, so we know it can be done. We just need to insist that it do it again.

Opportunity Threat 3: Money Games

Inflation is the scourge of people and nations. It joins high taxes and expanding debt as keys to economic destruction. President Grover Cleveland said,

> *Manifestly nothing is more vital to our supremacy as a nation and to the beneficent purposes of our Government than a sound and stable currency. Its exposure to degradation should at once arouse to activity the most enlightened statesmanship, and the danger of depreciation in the purchasing power of the wages paid to toil should furnish the strongest incentive to prompt and conservative precaution.... We will be wise if we temper our confidence and faith in our national strength and resources with the frank concession that even these will not permit us to defy with impunity the inexorable laws of finance and trade.*[35]

What causes inflation? The government would like us to believe that inflation is caused by rising prices and wages because that distracts citizens from understanding the truth: Inflation is caused by – in fact, inflation is – creating more dollars than are necessary for the current level of economic activity.

Currency not tied to gold or anything else is subject to the laws of supply and demand, which are the only laws that still apply. What this means is that more dollars supplied for the same level of demand makes each dollar worth less. Inflation is a continuous change in the meaning of the word "dollar."

And saying that inflation is caused by rising prices is like saying that snow is caused by slick streets. Inflation is caused by the Federal Reserve, which "informally has said its goal is inflation of around 2%."[36] Its *goal*? A terrible goal – but it also has the means to achieve it.

Inflation, the great "invisible tax," devalues savings. It gives people higher nominal wages while it drives them into the associated higher tax brackets. The higher related interest rates – banks have to charge more than inflation to make any money – add another burden to people buying homes or other property or trying to start or run a business. It's a wasting disease that turns into a tragic death. President Ronald Reagan said, "[Inflation] distorts our economic decisions, penalizes thrift, and crushes the struggling young and the fixed-income elderly alike. It threatens to shatter the lives of millions of our people."[37]

The institutionalizing of inflation, by indexing many government payouts to the inflation rate, guarantees that the few will prosper at the expense of the many who have no such protection. This isn't a formula for anyone's continued economic freedom. And it won't make for peace between the citizens who get to keep up with inflation because of the unwilling sacrifice of those who don't.

All of this is assuming that anyone can accurately calculate the inflation rate, which has been consistently and deliberately understated. At first, government changed the formula so that the basket of goods used in the formula was no longer fixed, and cheaper items would be substituted for those that had higher inflation. Now government officials talk about – and the media goes along with – the notion of "core inflation." This is a number that excludes "volatile" items like…food and energy. Americans see past the magician's tricks and know that the value of their dollars is disappearing over time.

People talk about moderate inflation, which is akin to talking about moderate cancer. Inflation, like cancer, is always bad and to be avoided at all costs. There is no reasonable level of either one. Inflation hurts the hardest-working and most-vulnerable people first, but in the end, the cancer devours even the government that triggered it (as Germany found out in the 1920s and 1930s).

Ultimately, only the government can create inflation. Until the end, the government profits handsomely by having it, along with everyone who has borrowed at a fixed rate and is now in a position to destroy their creditors.

Opportunity Threat 4: Government Ponzi Schemes

The essence of a Ponzi scheme? The first people brought in actually have no real accounts set up in their name or investments made on their behalf. Their money is used to set up the system and pay the administrators. The money of everyone else brought in as time goes on is used to pay the earlier entrants along with a generous cut to the administrators. If a lot of people are brought in during any period, their money can be put on reserve for future payouts. More likely, it will be used for current administrative rewards and for loans or gifts to collaborators. But it will never be invested.

Bernie Madoff did the above for a long time and on a large scale. The federal government, with Social Security, has done the above for a much longer time and on a mammoth scale.

In fact, we now have three entitlement programs that are built on the principles of the Ponzi scheme. The first in always make out nicely, and the last in always make out with nothing.

Nothing is ever really invested, and the Ponzi manager (or in this case, the government) takes a cut without ever incurring a personal financial risk. Bernie Madoff ran the largest private Ponzi scheme, but it was nothing compared with the public Ponzi schemes of the federal government, all created after the first successful 150 years of American independence:

> • Social Security. Many people today still believe that the money taken out of their paychecks is being put aside and invested on their behalf, like any good and legal 401(k) plan. But nothing could be further from the truth.

The money contributed by the early retirees was nothing compared to what they took out. Those now receiving benefits had their contributions spent long ago, on people long retired or dead. They are actually living off the contributions of those of us still working. Baby boomers retiring over the next twenty years will be supported some day by people who are now too young to work or who haven't even been born.

To add to the ugliness, surpluses accumulated in earlier years have been loaned to the federal government to be spent on pork and subsidies and bailouts and wars. Those loans will never be repaid because they can't be repaid.

The commitments that have been made to the future elderly that are unfunded – meaning, in reality, that there is no way or plan to pay for them – totaled $21.4 trillion as of 2011 (not counting an additional $5.6 trillion promised to military and federal employees).[38] Unless math is no longer relevant, any hopes that this will work out are the triumph of wishful thinking over demographically certain disaster.

If the politicians want to continue with a government-run program, they should at least convert it from a generational transfer scheme to a true pension plan. They should have to put the money contributed by employees and their employers into individual accounts, invest it broadly – not just in buying government securities – and report out regularly to the account holders. In the meantime, we should stop pretending that it is a savings/pension plan and call it what it is – a taxing/redistribution plan.

In any case, people should be given the choice of opting out of social security. Some might think of this as an alien concept. But this has already been done in Chile, to the benefit of both the people and the government, which had no way to make good on its promises. If Chile could do it, why not the land of the free?

• Medicare and Medicaid. In a general sense, of course everyone wants elderly (Medicare) and poor (Medicaid) people to be cared for. But what does that mean in a specific sense? Can the few really provide unlimited health care to the many?

When Medicare Part A was launched in 1965, the estimated cost by 1990 was expected to be $9 billion. As of this writing, just 45 years later, its cost is $500 billion. This projection was made by the same government that is now giving us estimates on health care. The total of unfunded commitments – promises made that can't be kept – is $24.8 trillion as of 2011. Medicaid is set to further bankrupt states, which, along with local governments, have rung up $5.2 trillion of phony promises of their own.[39]

Who would pay for this? All of us. Who can pay for this? No one. Rationing is inevitable. All of this money taken from paychecks needs actually to be used to buy a set of really large group insurance policies, with large deductibles, starting in...1965.

• Health Care. Like throwing a rock to someone who is drowning, we've now added a general health care entitlement to the already impossible burdens of Social Security and Medicare/Medicaid. Why? Because health insurance and health care have somehow become "rights."

But if they're rights, what does that mean? That everyone gets to go to the same top doctors? Be treated in the same top hospitals? If it's a right, why do some people get to go to the Mayo Clinic and not others? Are there any limitations to this right? Shouldn't it be that if everyone can't get an organ transplant that no one should be able to get one?

No one even knows what this will really cost. Based on every bit of history, we can assume that it will be a huge multiple of the highest of current estimates. If what has actually happened with Medicare is a guide, the cost will be...enough to finish off the American economy forever.

All of these schemes remove wealth and resources from the economy and opportunities from countless Americans. The fact that they are administered by giant unaccountable bureaucracies and are ridden with waste just adds to the tragedy.

Is the American Idea opposed to the care of the elderly and the sick? By no means. On the contrary, it wants to preserve the care of the elderly and sick of all time and not just this time – for future generations of the elderly and sick and not just those who need help today.

Opportunity Threat 5: Unsafety Nets

There have always been poor and needy people, and there always will be. Half a century and multiple trillions of dollars later, what has become of Lyndon Johnson's War on Poverty? Its goal to eliminate "poor and needy" as a category has been shown to be the illusion that it always was.

But the desire to help those who are down and out is very American indeed. As we'll see in the American Idea of Generosity, no people have ever been more charitable to those in need than Americans. But when government gets involved, "helping the needy" morphs into "creating the programs." Politics, waste, and corruption (in part because of the huge size of the unmanageable programs), and a growing chorus of people demanding their fair share (how much is that, and who decides it?) combine to obliterate resources that could be used to create real opportunities for the needy and many others.

As of this writing, one in six Americans receives assistance from the federal government.[40] This is presented to us as economic rights that give people freedom rather than what it really is: an allowance that produces dependency on the "lord of the manor." We should be honest enough to admit that this represents the creation of an economic underclass and of economic neutering rather than economic opportunity.

It's also time for a new definition of what it means to be underprivileged or disadvantaged. When these words were first applied to the poor and needy, they left the sense that if they were underprivileged, someone deprived them of their privileges. Someone took them away. In some cases, that may have even been true.

But people can be poor and needy for a host of reasons, only one of which is exploitation. Many people were simply born into poverty. Others have ended up there because of their own choices. When we call them all "underprivileged," the tendency is to make up for that by giving them a lot of privileges – by granting to them what no one else can get.

Government's efforts can turn the meanings upside down. There's no way to make someone "overprivileged"[41] without taking something away from someone else – without making someone else truly underprivileged by government fiat. Those who receive without work or merit are overprivileged. Those who are forced to give without getting anything in return are certainly underprivileged.

The problem here isn't just with welfare programs. Even something as apparently helpful and benign as unemployment insurance, extended forever by a poll-and-vote savvy government, can pay people to stay out of the workplace and turn down jobs that are "beneath" them or that don't pay them what they think they're worth. If this is now a right – if everyone out of work can claim this as something owed to them – then there are no limits. If it's a right, it should be extended to the unemployed not for a year or two but...forever.

Any decent society wants to care for the truly down-and-out. But the key word here is "society." The path to a better life runs through the enabling generosity of individual Americans, rather than the deadening handouts of government.

Opportunity Threat 6: Insuring Against Disaster and thus Guaranteeing It

Insurance is a marvelous invention.

Before insurance, everyone was just out there, unprotected and hoping hard against a tragedy that could wipe out a lifetime of work. Insurance allows all of us to pay a small amount on a regular basis instead of a large or impossible amount after a tragedy strikes. We hope that all of those small payments will be wasted – we're buying security and peace of mind, not a big payoff after the storm.

When provided by companies who have a stake in a successful financial outcome, insurance can work very well. But when provided by a government that is long on promise and short on good insurance practices, four huge problems occur:

1)   The government actually turns out to be us, the taxpayers. When something goes wrong, we're the ones who have to make good on all of the promises made by people who had no stake in the outcome.

2)   The government makes promises for political rather than economic reasons. Their reasons can end up being illogical and even corrupt. We the taxpayers end up providing insurance for people to build houses in flood zones because those people have a powerful representative who knows how to bring home the pork.

3)   Government insurance is, by definition, a bad bet. If it was a good bet, private companies would be all over it and clamoring for the business. Government is the insurer of last resort – another way of saying, "the insurer who should stay out of the business."

4)   Government insurance is almost guaranteed to create moral hazard. When huge scale is combined with bureaucratic ineptness and lack of oversight, the disaster is actually magnified by the availability of the insurance. Greedy people use the coverage to make flaky deals look secure. The most destructive examples include the government's backing of Savings & Loans in the 1980s and mortgage giants Fannie Mae, Freddie Mac, and Ginnie Mae in the 2000s (these are called GSEs, or Government Sponsored Entities – sort of private but fully backed by…us).

Government should generally stop insuring against and thus ensuring disaster. There's only one solution to this, and that's to minimize the government's role in providing insurance. Beyond providing backup to individual depositors so they'll feel safe depositing their money in banks, it's hard to create a case for government insurance. Even in the case of deposits, it would be far better to require banks to have real and substantial reserves so that the depositor is covered by assets instead of by a government promise.

Opportunity Threat 7: Manipulating Our Way to Prosperity

Can liberty survive desperate times? Freedom in America outlasted the Great Depression and some very major recessions, so the answer would appear to be "yes."

But merely the promise of prosperity – of better times – caused people in the 1930s to be willing to accept government programs and involvement at a level that would never have been permitted before.

And just as important, can liberty survive good times?

What will people be willing to do to hang on to their prosperity? Give up the liberty that produced it? It's relatively easy to fight for liberty when you have nothing to lose. How hard is it when wealth is at stake? Will a retreat in economic fortunes cause a bigger retreat in our respect for liberty? "A people that values its privileges above its principles soon loses both," said President Dwight Eisenhower.[42]

And what role does greed play in destroying liberty? Can we survive a large proportion of our citizenry operating on the destructive principle of jealousy? Too many already seek to gain by force – by government – what they could never gain by freedom and by their own initiative and competence. These are powerful forces that represent some of the worst of human nature. "Envy is more implacable than hatred," observed Francois De La Rochefoucauld.[43]

At some point, expecting a giant government to provide for us is the same as requesting it to control us. We forget the connection between our own prosperity and the survival of liberty. We fall for the notion that we can gain things on the back of freedom and still somehow preserve our gains even after freedom's demise.

Yielding liberty for prosperity is like giving up the hen to keep the eggs. Many in history have done just that, and America is in the process of doing the same. Prosperity is a great byproduct of a great people living the American Ideas. But it's a very poor goal and a terrible god.

What do these 7 threats mean to America? As they have been reaching critical mass in the last decade, they've been primary drivers of a monumental decline in opportunity. From 1940 to 1999, the American economy grew 3.9% a year and employment grew an average of 27% each decade. From 2000 to 2009, the economy grew 1.9% a year and employment only a meager 0.8%.[44] The government has grown fantastically in size and scope and reach, while opportunity has faded away.

There has been a dastardly attack on the American Idea of Opportunity, amazingly, most Americans still say,

We Believe That Merit Will Take You Far and That You Should Be Willing to Compete Against Other People of Merit to Get There

The American Idea of Opportunity is built around merit.

Opportunity is not using political or organizing or other coercive power to get what we want. It's using personal power to get what we want. We have to do something well to take advantage of available opportunities and to give us other opportunities. In the American Idea, opportunity is a chance to earn, not to take.

In fact, it goes far beyond just "not taking." Because this Idea includes a free and open-market system, personal opportunity is usually maximized by service to others. We can't get what we want unless we help other people get what they want. Adam Smith, in his groundbreaking Wealth of Nations, saw that the free-market system was the best and only way not only to minimize the effect of human selfishness, but also to actually turn it to good. He observed that

> The individual's self-interest is always to be found in the common interest... and that justice to others is charity for ourselves.[45]

A free and open market means that there will be competition. This may sound unkind to some, but it's the only way for better products and services –and the opportunity they represent – to be created. Athletes get better when they compete, as do workers and leaders and organizations.

Competition always produces winners and losers, of course. According to the Small Business Administration, 50% of new businesses disappear in the first 5 years.[46] But in America, even winning and losing aren't permanent. We have what Ralph Waldo Emerson would have called an aristocracy of merit.[47] The winners can become arrogant or lazy or stale and turn into losers. And the losers can become humble and energized and fresh and turn into winners.

The key to winning – the key to taking full advantage of the opportunity that America offers – is to work hard. As basketball hall-of-famer Ed Macauley said, "When you're not practicing, remember, someone somewhere is practicing, and when you meet him he will win."[48]

Free people accept untidiness in their political and social lives. They do this because it's impossible to have imposed order and still be free – but also because it's impossible to maximize freedom and not have a lot of creativity and some measure of chaos.

Even though it brings disruption, free people also have to accept untidiness in their economic lives. In a dynamic society – the only kind worth having – free people innovate (which produces change) and compete (which produces casualties).

People often refer to a free-market, capitalistic economy as an "unplanned economy." This makes it sound unruly, even primitive. But the free market isn't unplanned. It's planned in immensely detailed fashion – but by millions of individual planners, rather than by a few "geniuses" that too often have been given (or have taken) the impossible charge to plan an entire economy.

Individual planners – you and me – work on a human scale and thrive on personal merit. Government planners work on a global scale far beyond their ability to understand – much less plan intelligently – and thrive by selling their plans up the line. Individual planners make decisions quickly and revise their decisions as conditions change. Government planners can make huge decisions that take months to enact and years to rescind when mistaken.

All economies are planned, but the cost of mistakes goes up dramatically when a society moves from an individual-planned to a government-planned economy. And the availability of individual opportunity goes way down.

Capital in a free economy does nothing on its own. It follows an order – perceived need, then innovation and technology, then capital. Government planning reverses the order, throwing someone else's capital at an undefined need and without the appropriate means of satisfying that need. Government takes the pot of gold at the end of the rainbow and throws it at profligate industry (finance, housing), dying industry (automobiles, steel), and optional industry (ethanol, space exploration).

To waste capital is to spit on the future and on posterity. Capital that could be multiplied many times by the time that it reaches our descendants is squandered on current excesses and even on things that will destroy our descendants – like misused technology.

There is a moral dimension to the use of technology and capital. To abuse technology is to take an amoral human creation and turn it to immoral ends. If our values are solid, technology can improve their practical application. If not, technology can increase the rate of decline. Technology can be used to start wars or end them, kill the innocent or preserve their lives, feed the world or poison it. If the American Ideas are gone, technology can be used for unprecedented evil. But, in the end, technology doesn't kill people – bad ideas kill people.

If necessity is the mother of invention, freedom is the father. When people are free to sow their own effort and reap their own rewards, creativity and prosperity are unleashed. All societies have needs. But only free societies meet those needs – and they do this through the free market, not the free lunch.

Although gloss and fancy footwork might win something in the short run, only merit wins in the end. But even merit needs to keep proving itself, and in an opportunistic society, even mistakes can become the basis for future merit. This is so because in the American Idea,

Success Is Never Final, but Neither Is Failure

In America, the only thing that is permanent is the future – that there will always be another opportunity.

In a market free of collusion and government manipulation, no one can rest on his or her past successes. When those offering mutual funds say that "past performance is no guarantee of future gains," they're covering themselves legally but also speaking a powerful truth. You won yesterday? Great – now what about today?

A review of the Fortune 500 that looks back 20 years from any point in time produces surprising, even shocking, results. Many of those great companies have dropped far down the list. Many have dropped off the list. And many have gone off of every list – out of existence, taken over, bought out, or demolished.

In spite of the dislocations this economic churn can cause for individuals, this isn't a bad thing at the core. Organizations that lose their way and their market through arrogance, laziness, greed, or lack of creativity don't deserve to stay around. Individuals who lose their way for the same reasons don't deserve to have a job. And the money and resources that are freed up can be put to fresh and better uses.

But this Idea means more. It means that even the opportunity to fail is a good thing. It gives us the opportunity to learn and grow, and then, if we persist, another opportunity to win. It's too easy to forget that it's all right to fail – that failure in America doesn't mean we're finished, but it simply means that we're at a personal strategic inflection point. It means that we can start again and still succeed anew.

Only in America can failure be embraced and turned into opportunity. Only in America can failure be honored because it means that we had the courage to try and then were humble and smart and persistent enough to try again.

The free and open markets lead naturally to innovation. The only way to hold onto or expand an opportunity is to do whatever you have chosen to do smarter or faster or better or cheaper than others. America really is the place where the future is today, where what will be is born now. "The child is father of the man," says the old proverb.[49] In America, the Idea of Opportunity is father – and mother – to the future.

Innovation means change. And the change leads to more innovation, which produces more change – over and over, round and round. Compared with other cultures, the amount and speed of change in America are enormous. Others like familiarity and tradition too much, while Americans always seem willing to discard the past when it has been drained of its opportunity. Others like the status quo, while Americans are annoyed by it. They're stirred to challenge it, always. Many dream about the past. Americans always dream about the future.

This means that America always looks unfinished, rough around the edges, full of disorder, if not outright chaos. And it looks this way because it is this way.

And here's a critical place where this powerful American Idea is under attack. America creates opportunity on a grand scale, but it also creates dislocations, losses, and casualties. There is almost always an opportunity to overcome these byproducts of dynamic opportunity, but these byproducts will always be there as long as this is the Land of Opportunity. Why? Because the only way to be that wonderful place is to be wide open and innovative, always ready to embrace and exploit change, and forever willing to suffer setbacks.

But even well-intentioned people can work to artificially and forcefully negate these disorderly events – and with them this American Idea. Tariffs that protect badly run businesses, laws against inefficient plant closings, restrictions on trade with "unfair" competitors, closed shops – all of these and more can protect a few from reality for a time at the expense of the good of all for a much longer time. "Capitalism without failure is like Christianity without hell," noted famed investor Warren Buffet.[50]

Orderly, controlled systems have a certain appeal. They look like they can level out the bumps and eliminate the chaos. But they are a destructive illusion. They never produce opportunity except for the few who create and manage them. And even a cursory review of the planned economies of the past century shows that they aren't really that good at leveling out the bumps.

This American Idea reminds us that the only way to have widespread opportunity for everyone is to insist that our political and social leaders leave people alone – to succeed on their own and to get knocked to their knees and come back on their own. They need to let people help others when that is in their interest, relying on the grand fact that the only way that really works is to do things in the interests of others.

The government now locates Americans in classes – upper class, upper-middle class, middle class, and so on. But all Americans who have even a faint echo of this Idea of Opportunity in his or her mind believe that this location is only temporary. It's why, on their better days, Americans are never quite comfortable with soak-the-rich tax schemes – they have a belief that they too have a chance to be the rich, or at least richer than they are, because it's...possible.

And possibility is a heady brew. It tells people that

You Can Try and Fail and Learn and Plan and Work and Try Again – and Again

"The people I want to hear about are the people who take risks," declared American poet Robert Frost.[51]

The old saying, "There are no second acts in American lives,"[52] isn't true. In American politics, Lincoln lost his bid for the Senate just two years before he won the presidency. Grover Cleveland lost a bid for a second term and then won that term four years later. Reagan lost his bid for the Republican nomination, and then won both the nomination and the presidency the next time around.

But it's also untrue to say that there are no second acts in American opportunity. As long as the failure wasn't due to bad ethics or criminal activity, America is the only place where failure doesn't mark a person forever.

It's an American paradox. The country that loves winners also loves those who try. It loves underdogs and hopeless cases, dogged persistence and spectacular failures. Somehow, the soul-freeing concept that honoring good failure is a brilliant way to get a lot more successes was woven into America's DNA from the beginning.

The failure leads to learning. If the learning is taken seriously and used for a better plan the next time, learners are onto something. If they work that plan and refuse to let the ghosts of past failure haunt their determination, they can win where they didn't know enough to win before. And they can now win even bigger than they could have won before.

The Land of Opportunity is the land of the second chance – and the third and fourth and fifth chances, too. Maybe even the sixth and seventh if you're still standing and will not quit. In America, you should keep trying, because

If You'll Never Give Up, You Can Finally End Up with More Than Your Ancestors Even Dared to Dream

Many people, including Americans, tend to put too much emphasis on talent as the key to a successful life. Having talent certainly helps, but unless that talent is totally unique or just happens to find itself in the right place at the right time (or both), it will be insufficient by itself to assure success.

In America, the only ingredient really indispensible to a successful life is persistenc- Writers with lesser talent get published, while special talents are unknown, and the difference is usually one of tenacity.

So which came first, an open land of boundless opportunity or a driven people with a tenacious spirit? Both. The new land offered opportunities, and those who had the will to grasp those opportunities did so. And then those persistent, dynamic opportunists innovated and built, creating opportunities for themselves and many others – embedding real opportunity into the soul of America.

No one is excluded from having determination. No one can have his or her tenacity taken away. If any citizen or future citizen is willing to work harder and longer than others, there's simply no stopping that American.

Ever.

What does it take to be the Land of Opportunity? Well, this doesn't just happen. In fact, the default historical position is "no opportunity."

If we want to remain the place where opportunity rules, if we want to repair the damage inflicted on these great gifts by power mongering from above and greed from below, we need to take action. We should:

Take Action

Love a place like America where everyone can win, rather than hate it because everyone doesn't.

★

Make the concept of "possibility" our personal watch-word, and strip the use of it away from the politicians.

★

Keep the concept of opportunity alive by maximizing our own opportunities and the opportunities of others.

★

Hate the artificial distinctions and regulations that reduce people's opportunities.

★

Appreciate good limitations that prevent the lazy and undeserving from ruining other people's opportunity.

★

Expect education first and last to be about developing character-driven opportunities for students.

★

Prize and praise merit.

★

Encourage healthy competition.

★

Reward the underdog, not the underperformer.

★

Build opportunity around principles, and treat success and examples of success with skepticism.

★

Help the poor with a vibrant economy & ways to join it.

★

Celebrate good failure and condemn the bad.

★

Accept the ups and downs of a vibrant economy and refuse to let government manipulate it.

★

Keep the government out of the opportunity business.

★

Get the government out of the opportunity-destruction business.

★

Refuse to let the government diminish private-sector opportunity to benefit public-sector opportunity.

★

Institute a Citizenship Tax in place of the "progressive" income tax.

★

Eliminate all anti-growth taxes, such as corporate income taxes – especially on money earned or investments made in America.

★

Set property taxes at a fixed rate based on true spending needs, not a variable rate based on supposed market value.

★

Eliminate the "vulture tax" and the government hovering over the dead.

★

Expect the government to let us keep our own money while they keep the money sound.

★

Force each generation to pay for itself by ending government's ability to borrow.

★

Banish the Cancer Tax (inflation) and its endless destruction of value.

★

Require people to provide for their own retirement expenses and healthcare.

★

Keep the government out of the insurance business.

★

Prevent "big finance" from being the tail that wags the dog – to death.

★

Refuse to equate "opportunity" with "big business."

★

Treasure and nurture small business, the real engine of growth.

★

Refuse to equate "opportunity" with "entrepreneurship."

★

Encourage people to win rather than whine.

To see detail on these Action Points and
to add your voice visit www.theamericanideas.com

World history argues strongly against the concept of widespread opportunity. There's nothing written in stone that allows America to automatically continue being the Land of Opportunity. And once this concept evaporates, it can be difficult or impossible to bring back.

Ultimately, the business of America isn't business – the business of America is people. We want to see business and all of our other institutions pave the way for people to have more opportunity. We want to lower taxes and regulations so we can raise expectations and hopes – real opportunities and real jobs so every American can feel valuable, and have the sense of worth and self-respect that can only come from making a difference and paying your own way.

Opportunity is too valuable a concept to allow it to dissipate, or to be stolen away by the elite of government, business, or labor. It is critically important to the thriving of freedom and the pursuit of happiness. But it can be destroyed by well-meaning people who, in the name of opportunity for more, end up giving us opportunity for none.

Opportunity in the American Idea is about opening more doors for everyone. It involves pulling those on the lower rungs up, not pulling those on the higher rungs down. That view of opportunity is worse than a zero-sum game, as the higher levels are beaten down and the short-term gains of the lower levels evaporate. The American motto is, "A rising tide lifts all boats," not, "Let's go raid those boats."

Opportunity is part of the promise of liberty. There are few things in the American story more thrilling and more available to all.

I know this as an American writer, one from a family with no money and no connections and no writers – but one who nonetheless could sit down and write and then persist until the book you are holding in your hands was published. Could this only happen in America? Probably not.

Not only in America. But almost.

Opportunity and the American Idea

The American Idea of Opportunity is about climbing. It tells us that where we are now is just a starting point, a foothold on the future. The mountain is there, with beautiful things to see and experience as we climb, a mountain full of rich food and refreshing lakes and maybe gold, if we look hard enough.

And the mountain is ours if we want it enough. We'll have to think and work and sweat to get to the top, however we define that summit. But no one will tell us that we can't try. We can stop anywhere we want – but no one will stand in our way.

This Idea is about achievement and self-worth. Human beings aren't designed to feel as good about their work and lives if their opportunity came ready-made, packaged and handed to them as a gift – an inheritance, a business, a job. And few diseases are more crippling to the human spirit than entitlement, the notion that everything is about me and should be given to me when I want it.

We are designed to succeed, to live a life worth living, to make a difference in others' lives, to do something useful. If we can create a future out of nothing – take hard work and street smarts and education and dreams and turn them into something new and valuable – we have much to feel good about and much to enjoy. Opportunity delivers the chance for prosperity and options, but it offers even more – the chance for meaning and deep satisfaction.

The American Idea of Opportunity is that everyone has a chance – because innovation is honored, because no one is controlling the game, and because the limitations have been reduced to you.

CHAPTER 7

The American Idea of Responsibility

One of the most remarkable of all thoughts took root in the minds of the millions who came to America. It was the idea that drove so many of them to come – the insight that they could run their own lives by themselves.

They decided that they didn't need to depend on a king or queen, premier or prime minister, dictator or tyrant – or, amazingly, on government of any kind. Instead, they saw dependence on government as always crippling, often abusive, and sometimes fatal.

They practiced self-government in its most fundamental sense: They thought it was their job to govern themselves. Their motto was "Yes we should, and yes we will."

They conceived the American Idea of Responsibility. It involved taking charge of your own life. Taking care of yourself and your own. Not looking for handouts or free passes. Refusing to be a victim, full of excuses and expert at finger-pointing.

And paying for your freedom in the rock-solid currency of responsibility.

This Idea grew. It included resisting others' claims on you or their desire to control you, often done under the banner of "good intentions." It said "no thanks" to anyone else providing for you, making life easier for you, or helping you avoid the pain and consequences of your own decisions and actions. And it made you resent being treated like a helpless dependent, lost without its master.

This great Idea mocks the notion that anyone – least of all a government – knows better how to take care of our lives than we the people do. It's our life. We own it. And we'll take responsibility for all of it – the good and bad, happy and sad, victories and mistakes, successes and failures.

It's a wild idea. And as you look through history, you discover that it isn't a very common idea.

But it's the American Idea.

Responsibility

We won't expect anyone to do for us what we can do for ourselves.

We should provide for our families, friends, and communities and not require others to do it for us.

We aren't victims and won't be treated as such.

We can't claim to be free if we won't take responsibility for ourselves, and we can't claim a freedom for which someone else must take responsibility.

We can't separate freedom from responsibility, either within a person or between people.

Freedom is meaningless without responsibility but is enhanced by proper limitations.

Last but not least, we're responsible for our government, not the other way around.

The American Idea of Responsibility starts with a strong mindset that

We Won't Expect Anyone to Do for Us
What We Can Do for Ourselves

In an imperfect and often broken world, it can become very hard to keep going. Even the best of us can tire out and want to give up. Can't someone else do this work? Why am I the only one who seems to care? How did I end up with all of this pressure? Why is it that I work harder than other people do, yet they have so much more?

So we can be tempted to shift some of the load. Even if we're an Atlas, we might think about shrugging. We can feel it welling up, the reasonable but deadly opinion that starts the march away from responsibility: "Let someone else do it."

It is understandable. But it's also a bad plan that leads to bad attitudes, bad relationships, bad society, and bad government.

From the beginning, the American Idea was to do for yourself. If you can do it, you should do it. Not because someone is threatening you but because it's your life and there are no more threats.

So you should stand tall. Make your own decisions. Live with the consequences. Don't require others to bail you out. Take pride in standing on your own two feet without crutches. Expect things from yourself, and leave others out of your expectations. "Individually Americans have the responsibility to pursue the American Dream and achieve what they can through their talents, character, and hard work," noted American scholar Samuel Huntington.[1]

Now, the Idea was never, "do for yourself, even if you can't." There's always been room in this Idea – a lot of room – for being a good Samaritan, aiding the widow and orphan, loving your neighbor. American responsibility was a treasure to possess, not a cross to bear alone.

But there's never been room for slothfulness or entitlement. Until recent times, there was never a requirement that responsible people provide for others who are faking it – people who could do for themselves but just don't want to or who want more than they're willing to work for or who would simply rather drink and smoke and watch television and play videogames instead of doing anything useful.

For too many people today, responsibility has been reduced to "being responsible to vote for those who will take what others have earned and then give it to you." Sadly, the meaning of responsibility has been moved away from, "you be responsible for yourself," to, "you be responsible for me."

Most people want to be respected. That has to start with respecting ourselves. There's no better way to be respected than to take full responsibility for whatever is in front of us – no matter how tough, no matter how unpleasant, no matter how much of it we've brought on ourselves. As President Bill Clinton said,

> We must do what America does best, offer more opportunity to all and demand more responsibility from all. It is time to break the bad habit of expecting something for nothing: from our government, or from each other. Let us all take more responsibility, not only for ourselves and our families, but for our communities and our country.[2]

He rightly points out that taking responsibility for what's in front of us includes caring for those in our circle of responsibility. Americans have believed – and most Americans still believe – that

We Should Provide for Our Families, Friends, and Communities and Not Require Others to Do It for Us

The American Idea was always more than just taking responsibility for yourself. It was taking responsibility for those that either God or you had implanted deeply into your life.

It included your family of origin, with a person's character and generosity determining how broadly "family of origin" was defined. Your aging grandmother needs help around her house? Do it. Siblings, uncles, aunts, cousins, nephews, nieces – they aren't there by accident. And if they have an accident, if they fall on hard times and just can't take care of themselves, a responsible human being who is related to them just...helps.

If you get married or make a commitment to another human being, if you create your own new family in any way, if children are birthed or adopted or taken in as foster children, if you commit to a deep and enduring friendship, you do whatever it takes for as long as you must.

You don't trade them in. You don't run away. You don't quit. You don't define commitment as, "I'll be involved with you unless it costs me something or until it costs too much."

And then there are the children. One of the biggest areas of necessary responsibility, usually accepted in the past but now more and more neglected, is with children. So here's the question: If we bring children into the world, if we father them or bear them, who should be responsible for them?

For generations, for centuries, the American answer was straightforward. If you have them, you take care of them. They're yours. You get to ooh and aah and have fun with them, but you also get to teach and guide and set boundaries and discipline and pay for what they need.

With children, we really have to take responsibility. They can't take care of themselves and shouldn't have to. They can't provide for themselves. They can't teach themselves. They don't know what the boundaries should be or how to set them and enforce them if they knew. We've lost some of the Idea in these crucial areas of childrearing.

• *Providing.* What level of bad is neglecting or abusing a child? As a society, we've become far too lax in requiring parents to provide for their children. We don't even insist that parents do them no harm. Deadbeat parents get to father or birth more children instead of caring for the ones they already have. If they can't parent but they can work, we only sporadically make them pay for someone else to raise or take care of those children. This isn't a small failure. The Apostle Paul noted that "if anyone does not provide for his relatives....[he] is worse than an unbeliever."[3]

Providing includes more than just material things. It includes giving children a safe and healthy environment, spiritually and emotionally as well as physically. It means we don't always put our own comfort first. And we never, ever, use them or hurt them. There may or may not be things lower than neglecting or abusing a child, but there are none more heinous.

We can go the other way and over-provide for children. We can take it to the point of erasing their own sense of responsibility. We can buy for them until they have a strong sense of entitlement but no sense of gratitude. Instead of requiring them to invest in their own future, we can fully provide unending post-high-school education to "college kids" – actually, adults in their 20s who should be acting like mature adults because we've helped them to become mature adults.

Children don't get on well when they're treated like they're the center of the universe. A wealth manager for the super-rich once told me that the one common attribute of their children was lack of self-confidence. They'd never had to take responsibility for anything, and they didn't even know how.

• *Teaching.* Mark Twain said, "I never let schooling interfere with my education."[4] But we can let educational monopolies and bureaucracies interfere with our children's education daily. Government wants to move from being Uncle Sam to Father Sam, and education is a key to this transition. "Wherever is found what is called paternal government," observed British Prime Minister Benjamin Disraeli, "there is found state education."[5]

Isn't it government's job to teach our children? Absolutely not. That job belongs to their parents, from the moment children are born – individual parents and parents joined together in a common cause. Parents have the responsibility and the right to educate their children as they, not paternalistic government bodies, see fit.

For much of American history, education wasn't a responsibility assigned to government at all. Much education was indeed "public" (controlled by the community) but was not "government" (controlled by the state). The error originates with a monumental misunderstanding: We can too easily think – in fact, we've been taught to think – that "public schools" mean "government schools."

Having public schools can be a great positive for a community – as long as we define public as "paid for and administered by the community and its parents," not as "run by the government." People worry about a nanny state when, in the most crucial development area of all, we already have a nanny state. Spanish philosopher and educator Francisco Ferrer noted,

> Governments have ever been careful to hold a high hand over the education of the people. They know, better than anyone else, that their power is based almost entirely on the school. Hence, they monopolize it more and more.[6]

It's bad business to have government running education. It becomes political, with too many hierarchies, funding battles, bad decisions, union demands and political correctness and too little academic freedom, open inquiry, diversity of thought and excellence. It eliminates the teaching of morals and elevates the teaching of approved government positions. It causes the closing of local schools because of governmental strategic blunders and financial legerdemain. Worst of all, it leads to youthanasia, the senseless slaughter of young minds.

Parents are robbed of their responsibility and instead get to spend their time blaming the schools, which in reality means ever-larger unified school districts. Children can be taught anything, as long as the government approves. And we end up with the hypocritical spectacle of politicians praising the public schools while they send their children to the best private schools that money can buy.

It's time – way past time – for the separation of school and state. And for the reuniting of school and community. All schools not privately run need to be community schools – schools of the community, by the community, and for all the community's kids.

• *Setting Boundaries.* One of the biggest boundaries that used to get set for children? It was to be responsible. Go to school. Get good grades. Be punctual. Do your chores. Be respectful. Apologize when you make a mistake. Make restitution when you hurt someone.

A child could run wild and wreak havoc, but his or her parents and the community were going to come down hard. But those who were raising Baby Boomers started worrying about being too restrictive and hurting their children's "self-esteem" or "creativity." They thought that many of the ways of raising children were too rigid, and in some ways they were right. But that pendulum long ago swung too far the other way.

Now, when children run amok and wreak havoc, no one comes down hard – or easy. Parents are loath to quash it, forgetting that this is how monsters are formed. Relatives, friends, and kindly strangers are loath to intervene, lest they be viewed as meddlers and busybodies. In the boundary vacuum, bad behavior grows. When those children are old enough, their lives become their responsibility. But, from the beginning, it's their parents' responsibility.

If set properly, boundaries don't diminish or kill freedom. They unleash it. Children find and test the boundaries, and when they're sure of where those boundaries are, they're free to operate joyously and safely within them. A life without boundaries, on the other hand, lets children test everything, gives no guidance on choices, and lets freedom disintegrate into selfish and self-destructive behavior. A life blossoms with good boundaries, as composers discovered with the flourishing of musical creativity after the development of the boundary of octaves.

A wise culture once knew – and can choose to remember – that boundaries for children assure the passing on of a civilization worthy of the name.

Real Americans take responsibility for themselves and, where needed, for their own. And they insist that their own do the same.

Part of taking responsibility involves avoiding a dread disease of the soul. Standing on their own two feet, Americans have almost always declared,

We Aren't Victims and Won't Be Treated as Such

There are true victims. There are abused and neglected children, battered spouses, people on the wrong end of violent crime. We can be robbed, cheated, and left with nothing. We can be the subjects of despicable gossip and slander. We can be fired for telling the truth and cast aside for trying to do the right thing.

But this American Idea challenges any claim to victimhood when it goes beyond these obvious and true claims. Whether we admit it or not, we are responsible for our lives as we received them – poor or rich, minority or majority, bad neighborhood or good, terrific parents or bums. And we're responsible for our lives as we live them – decisions, choices, and actions; stupidities, mistakes, and failures; successes, victories, and generosities.

So is it nature or nurture or choice that determines the direction of our lives? Of course. All of the above.

But somehow, in a culture built on personal responsibility, we've ended up with an infectious disease. We could call it "victimitis." With victimitis, whatever is bad is still there – in fact, we enlarge it and work hard to keep it going. But we also get to make the attempt to lay it off on someone or something else. At some point, it goes from being an explanation to being an excuse. Finally, if left untreated, it becomes the sorrowful, self-demeaning way we look at ourselves and others like us.

The advantage of feeling like a victim is that we can explain our problems by blaming them on that someone or something else. It feels like we're lightening our loads. But it comes at a huge price. We voluntarily disempower ourselves and turn our future over to that someone or something else. "If only they…" is not a formula for a successful life or culture.

It's both too easy and too hard to live in a no-fault society. It's easy because we don't have to take responsibility for our own choices and mistakes and disasters. But it's hard because if it's not our fault but it seems to be wrong, then someone else must be to blame. No-fault divorce, no-fault parenting, no-fault careers, no-fault lives – driving us to blame the partner or finances, the schools or culture, the boss or company, nature or nurture.

All of us have had bad, perhaps even terrible, experiences. I nearly died when I was 7, spending Christmas in intensive care. I was nearly kidnapped at gunpoint when I was 14. These were immensely disturbing events. But those are only the end if we allow them to dominate our lives. "Experience is not what happens to you," noted writer Aldous Huxley. "It is what you do with what happens to you."[7]

If, as a consequence of a bad experience, you choose to be a victim, your progress and hope are ended. The only joy you have is the diminishing, twisted pleasure of getting to blame…someone else.

But if you choose to move forward, to pick yourself up, and to see life as a place for second chances, you've captured some of the power of this American Idea. You'll experience the powerful truth that you can't be a willing victim and be truly free.

Americans know that freedom is intimately connected to responsibility. They cut through the nonsense of carefree freedom, the freedom of the fictional "noble savage" of Rousseau, and talk instead about responsible freedom. They believe that

We Can't Claim to Be Free If We Won't Take Responsibility for Ourselves, and We Can't Claim a Freedom for Which Someone Else Must Take Responsibility

"Liberty means responsibility," said playwright George Bernard Shaw. "That is why most men dread it."[8]

Even like children, we're prone to love the rights and loathe the responsibility. We want to stay up late but not get up on time. We want to buy things but not do our chores. We want to be treated with respect but still boss around or even degrade other children.

The problem is that it's hard to outgrow this problem of "doing what I want to, not what I have to." Given human nature, it takes a powerful culture of responsibility, from the society at large to the individual family, to weed it out or box it in. Wanting comes quite naturally. Duty must be taught and reinforced. But we've gone soft on "duty." An article in Newsweek said,

> We have built a society of safety nets, a lawyer-constructed web where no one really has to take responsibility, where there's always someone else to blame, where all the children are above average, or at least deserve a trophy for participation…. But deep down, I think, people are perfectly aware that something needs to change.[9]

Of course, there's nothing wrong with wanting the good life. Americans – all people, really – want "life, liberty, and the pursuit of happiness."[10] What's not to like about these?

But we can too easily want someone else to pay for those rights. I get to smoke or do drugs or drink too much or eat badly or to excess, and you have to pay for my medical costs. I get to buy a house twice as big as yours and twice as big as I can afford, and you have to help me keep it. I get to do nothing, and you get to support me. I get to have as many children as I want, and you have to pay for their health care and education. I get to run a business as I see fit and make terrible decisions, and you have to bail it out (if you're a taxpayer) or lose your job (if you're an employee) or forfeit your money (if you're an investor or creditor).

When that happens – when someone else is actually conned or forced into paying for our rights, when we've created a culture of extreme injustice – we've created two downward forces. These forces are perfectly designed to create an irresponsible culture.

One downward force is on the person or group doing the paying. They'll begin to see "being responsible" as "being a sucker." They won't want to pay for anything, good or bad, because it all feels bad. They'll see "patriotic" calls to pay ever-higher taxes as political-speak for robbery. They'll finally see what people in all times and places have understood: that redistribution means "taking from the responsible to pamper the irresponsible." This is true whether the irresponsible ones are the rich, the poor, or the neighbor down the street.

The other downward force is on the person doing the taking. There's no way for them to avoid losing respect for themselves. But the downward slide still has its enticements. This loss of respect can take place even while they demand more and become blinded by the tantalizing power of "entitlement" – a terrible, destructive, anti-responsibility word.

Sooner or later – often too late – these people who love what they want to have and hate what they should do to get it can come to a terrible realization. They can see that what they had to give up in their quest to get someone else to take on their responsibility was their freedom. They've become slaves in their minds, if not in fact. They owe what they have only to their ability to exploit an inherently unjust system and to take advantage of those being exploited.

We simply can't separate freedom from responsibility – not and have either of them make sense. Ultimately, we can't separate any rights from responsibility. Nobel prize-winning economist F. A. Hayek noted that economic freedom, that critical component of both liberty and the pursuit of happiness,

> *Must be the freedom of our economic activity which, with the right of choice, inevitably also carries the risk and the responsibility of that right.... Responsibility, not to a superior, but to one's conscience, the awareness of a duty not exacted by compulsion, the necessity to decide which of the things one values are to be sacrificed to others, and to bear the consequences of one's own decision, are the very essence of any morals which deserve the name.[11]*

Rights, freedom, and responsibility are always connected in a healthy society, as they have been in America. When we try to separate them, bad things happen.

One of those bad things is the injustice that is created. It's especially repugnant to this American Idea when one person or group is granted the rights and another person or group is granted the responsibility for those rights. This responsibility can come in many forms – assuming the guilt and financing the rights being the most usual. It's both ironic and evil that people can convert their own false or exaggerated claims of victimhood into the heartless victimization of their responsible fellow citizens.

Someone has said that we should have a Statue of Responsibility on the West Coast to correspond with the Statue of Liberty on the East Coast. Would Americans contribute to its design and construction?

Maybe so. Why? Because that could be the responsible thing to do to prevent us from having half of a good Idea or all of a bad one. It would make a loud, visible statement that

> *We Can't Separate Freedom from Responsibility,*
> *Either within a Person or Between People*

President Bill Clinton said,

> *Our Founders taught us that the preservation of our liberty and our Union depends upon responsible citizenship. And we need a new sense of responsibility.... Each and every one of us, in our own way, must assume personal responsibility....*[12]

All of this leads us back to this idea of freedom, our first American Idea. There is good freedom, the kind we've been talking about, and then there is bad freedom

We've had a lot of good freedom. We can continue to have the freest and most prosperous nation ever, if we keep the American Idea of Freedom in mind – and if we don't trash it ourselves.

The problem is more fundamental than ignorance, apathy, or taking freedom for granted, although all of those can pose threats. There's a danger in a free society that a lowest-common-denominator, self-centered definition of freedom will evolve, something along the lines of, "Freedom means I get to do whatever I want." Often, because it sounds so...selfish, people might add, "as long as I don't hurt anyone else."

But it never seems to stop there. It's all too easy for this loose definition to further evolve into an ever-growing interpretation of the "whatever I want" part, and an ever-shrinking interpretation of the "hurt anyone else" qualifier.

Another name for the "whatever I want" view of freedom is decadence. This doesn't mean everyone attending orgies. American historian and philosopher Jacques Barzun defined decadence as "Falling off!" He said that a decadent time is

A very active time, full of deep concerns, but peculiarly restless, for it sees no clear lines of advance. The loss it faces is that of Possibility. The forms of art as of life seem exhausted, the stages of development have been run through. Institutions function painfully. Repetition and frustration are the intolerable result... [along with] boredom and fatigue....[13]

There's no anchor, no core. Decadence too easily degenerates into anarchy, where every person is a law unto himself or herself. Barzun warns us that freedom can devour itself. Freedom to do whatever we want is guaranteed to bring a clash of people, passions, and rights.

Even the great concept of the "pursuit of happiness" can be converted into a declaration of decadence. In fact, that conversion is rapidly taking place. The "pursuit" as defined by our founders isn't decadence – it's a fine thing, a good thing, a human thing. But when it shifts to rampant narcissism, when everyone is focused on themselves and little else, how can we retain civil society or self-government?

In fact, how can we prevent evil from tearing us apart? Free people have to work very hard to ensure that freedom doesn't become a cover-up for evil. We can too easily lose sight of the "as long as it doesn't hurt anyone else" part of the equation. For freedom to thrive, this has to be just as important to us as the "whatever I want" part.

In short, we have to know the difference between the toleration of difference and the toleration of evil.

  • *Toleration of difference.* Different isn't always – or even often – evil. As we saw in the great American Idea of Diversity, differences can be good and rich and constructive, as long as they're held together by a common core. Differences can vary in appeal, effectiveness, or value, but as long as they aren't evil, a great culture will make room for them all.

  • *Toleration of evil.* There are some differences that are evil. Things like murder, robbery, physical and emotional abuse, and sexual abuse of children are obvious, although even here, we've become way too tolerant. Polluting public discourse and media, destroying reputations, lying, cheating – a great culture never winks at these or helplessly asks, "What can we do?"

A people that can't tell the difference is destined to get more evil, which will ultimately bring about more restrictions on freedom. If a free people won't exercise self-control, they will end up buying – whether they want it or not – government control. Tolerance isn't a good thing or a bad thing in itself. The goodness or badness depends totally on what is being tolerated.

The relentless focus on "whatever I want" can drive personal responsibility underground and into the ground. I want something, so I should have it. I want this bigger house or car, even though I can't realistically afford it. I want to live an unhealthy life, even if someone else has to pay for its consequences. I want these entitlements, even if others need to be pillaged by the taxman. And that's where irresponsibility begins to "hurt anyone else."

Why? Because ultimately, someone has to be responsible for everything. If I won't do it, someone else will have to take over. It ends up in a very corrupt, anarchic, narcissistic, irresponsible formula: "I have the rights, and you have the responsibility."

At first, the "you" who has this bogus responsibility might be family, friends, neighbors, or fellow church members. But if the vast majority of people define freedom this badly, this far away from the American Idea, the "you" will eventually and inevitably be every responsible person, forced by the government to take on the load. In the end, the powers that be will take over our lives so they can "serve" others and will gladly charge us for the service.

There's no escaping it: Separating freedom from responsibility is hazardous to a culture's health. But freedom blossoms in the rich ground of responsibility. In the end, in fact,

Freedom Is Meaningless Without Responsibility but Is Enhanced by Proper Limitations

Freedom is always challenged by entropy, the law of deterioration. "The natural progress of things is for liberty to yield, and government to gain ground,"[14] noted Thomas Jefferson. Too easily, the great libertarian ideals of the Enlightenment can be reduced to a simplistic notion that "freedom means you should keep your hands off of my life," while communal responsibility disappears.

Ultimately, we lose freedom when we don't create a proper balance between the individual and the community, the needs of the one and the needs of the many. When the community overrides everything else, the individual becomes a cipher and freedom disappears. When the individual overrides everything else, the community fragments – producing either chaos or control as a response to the chaos – and freedom disappears.

If we insist that liberty means freedom from all restraint, we have demanded on a freedom that cannot survive. Why not? Because all true freedom begins with a proper view of limitations. As with all good things (like sex, ambition, power, productivity), freedom has to have limits in order to be good and in order to be enjoyed.

If we have no limits, we'll soon find that we have no freedom, since societies can't and won't function without boundaries. When order and peace are threatened at a certain level, the society will demand – and government will be happy to impose –severe restrictions. So how has America kept freedom from destroying itself? By protecting it with widespread personal responsibility and *self*-control.

We can't make widespread, externally imposed limits the main thing because they'll hurt and then crush freedom. Americans have always rightly been leery of too many limits, rules, and laws. They know that rules are great as tools and disasters as masters.

What does this all mean? We can lose freedom from either an absence or an excess of limitations. And there's more: The absence will relentlessly lead to the excess. Or to say it differently, a shortage of personal responsibility will always lead to a glut of government control.

Some politicians and their supporters have focused on one version of limitations – government shouldn't be allowed to interfere in the economy, to dominate the market, to use its power to control the economic life of the nation, or to take very much of our income in taxes or inflation (except where that interference would advance their social agenda).

Their opponents have focused on a different version of limitations – government shouldn't be allowed to interfere in the social life of the nation, to dominate society, to use its power to control individual decisions about life or work or relationships, or to enforce values (except where that interference would advance their social agenda).

In both cases, the opponents are often driven by interests and preferences, not by principle. The American Idea argues for both economic and social restraints – just enough to protect freedom and not enough to destroy it. There are greedy, ruthless people, and there are immoral, destructive people. No one in either group should be allowed to destroy American life. Short of that destruction, we should let freedom ring.

Thankfully, limitations in America have been about actions, not thoughts. The great American tradition of responsibility made complete room for freedom of conscience but at the same time put common-sense boundaries around freedom of action. In America, you could think anything you wanted. You just couldn't do everything you thought.

And last but not least is the issue of power-backed limitations and the related question of, "Who is responsible for governing?" Throughout history, government always claimed responsibility for those it ruled, which, in its definition, usually included control, coercion, and manipulation. It didn't just want to enforce limitations, it wanted to create and expand them.

Not so in the American Idea, which insisted that

We're Responsible for Our Government,
Not the Other Way Around

Government – and the politicians and bureaucrats who control it – all too often want to take responsibility. Got a problem? We'll take charge! But the only way the government can take responsibility for one person or group is to take resources or rights from another person or group.

Taking from one to give to another is a fundamental violation of this American Idea. This "taking" was happening prior to our nation's founding. It was objected to in the Declaration of Independence, which said of the British King,

> *He has erected a multitude of new offices and sent hither swarms of officers to harass our people, and eat out their substance.*[15]

The British were taking from one group – the colonists – in order to provide for other groups – local officials of the crown, as well as government and economic powers in Britain and other parts of the empire. It was one of the compelling justifications for revolution. That sentence from the Declaration rings uncomfortably true today.

The "taking" is usually in the form of taxes. If they're going to take over someone's responsibilities, they're also going to have to take over someone else's money. It has long been said that "the power to tax is the power to destroy."[16] This taxing/taking can cause immense destruction. Founder and President James Madison observed,

> *The apportionment of taxes on the various descriptions of property is an*
> *act which seems to require the most exact impartiality; yet there is, perhaps,*
> *no legislative act in which greater opportunity and temptation are given to*
> *a predominant party to trample on the rules of justice.*[17]

Unrestrained government always wants to take responsibility because it is the only way that power- and position-hungry people who have no ability to create value on their own can grow their jobs. They claim care and benevolence and use these as a cover to advance their personal interests and general control.

Often, they don't really even take responsibility then, except in name. They still blame others for failures – often the very people they are robbing. For example, after decades of the "war on poverty" and trillions of dollars spent, the government claims that the poverty level is still about the same (such a good excuse to keep spending and controlling). But who do they say are the culprits, the evildoers behind all of this entrenched poverty? Not failed government programs, of course, but the overtaxed wealthy who somehow find spare time to create and maintain systemic poverty.

There are people who are poor through no fault of their own. Perhaps they've made great effort to improve their situation but just can't catch a break. They are the truly needy who can rightly lay claim to our compassion. If government limited itself to helping these desperate souls, few would be concerned about government overreach. But its "help" too easily extends to those who've brought their problems on their own heads, to people who refuse to help themselves (except to other people's money). Let's look at one extreme but actual current example.

An America has a relative who has extended himself beyond his financial limits. He is, by all measures, in severe economic distress. He's gotten everything possible from his employer, including cost-of-living increases to cover inflation. He's borrowed from every bank and person that he can think of until no sane person would lend him any more. He's actually put up his collateral multiple times so that his creditors may have problems just as severe as his. His interest charges have swallowed him up. They dominate his current budgeting and drive him to continual acts of juggling accounts and borrowing from one source to pay another. He's become a financial sorcerer. He appears to have some possessions, but it's all illusion.

He's cut a few items in (but not from) his budget by a token amount, but he steadfastly refuses to cut back on his standard of living or his status. In fact, his total expenses have continued to grow at an alarming rate. He simply doesn't want to say, "No," to his dependents, friends, or himself, so he doesn't. He keeps giving out allowances and gifts because he wants others to like him. And he keeps making promises to his dependents and others in his family that he'll make ongoing payments for various expenses way into the future. He used to put money aside so he could be sure to deliver on his word but, for quite some time now, has saved nothing to cover his many current and future commitments.

Now, because of the unrelenting financial pressure, he's behaving in a peculiar manner. He has stopped including some of his bills in his budget. He didn't stop spending – incredibly, he just stopped counting. He seems to believe that what he doesn't count can't hurt him. He's getting advances against future income, even though he never intends to pay his employer back or fulfill his assigned job duties. He's trying to make others around him look bad so he can claim some of their work and compensation. He's keeping his creditors on the hook by using the threat of bankruptcy. He keeps hitting up the responsible people in the family for help. He's wicked enough to have no real friends but shrewd enough to have some allies.

But the game is nearly over. His many dependents now want more than he can deliver. His employer wants to recover what he'll never give back. His colleagues just want him to go away. And now it turns out that he's moved into illegal activities, like counterfeiting money, running Ponzi schemes, and blackmailing his coworkers.

What would you do if this is your relative? Well, you should give up on him. You should tell yourself that he deserves whatever punishment he gets. You've done your best to help him, but with great reluctance, you blow the whistle. You tried to save him because he was your family.

He was your Uncle Sam.

Reread the preceding paragraphs and see for yourself if this description fits. The out-of-control government that wants to help the poor is the poorest entity in America.

In their concern, some have called this government a Nanny State. But this is way off the mark because

  • A nanny takes care of a child and (unless they're completely self-centered or a monster) places the best interest of the child ahead of his or her own. But with paternalistic government, the best interest of the child – us – is only a vehicle to advance the political and other ambitions of the supposed caretaker.

  • A nanny doesn't take away one child's possessions to give them to another. The government specializes in this activity. The harder one child works to create and build, the more this caretaker takes away.

  • A nanny doesn't have final authority over a child. But this is far from the goal of power-hungry government. It wants to be the final authority. It wants to be the parent, not the parent's employee.

  • A nanny doesn't make the children pay his or her wages. This government, however, charges exorbitant rates for its services, all paid for by the hardest-working children.

  • A nanny has to be trusted in order to keep his or her job. A brief review of survey results shows that few entities are less trusted than the government and its branches.

  • A nanny can be dismissed. Try doing that with an outsized government.

Government may present itself as a relative, an uncle, or a nanny. But it's all about power and control. Always. It isn't the Benevolent State or the Nanny State. It's the Supremacy State.

The government isn't responsible for you or me, but it would like to be. Yet, all it can do is offer programs and manufactured opportunities and costly "solutions." Only we the people can actually take meaningful responsibility for our education, work, income, health, living conditions, and retirement.

The American Idea of Responsibility wholly rejects this notion that "government is responsible for me." The Idea does more: It turns this notion on its head. It declares that every citizen is actually responsible for the government.

I, the individual citizen, am the responsible party here. I'm the one with the good sense to know what to do. I'll take responsibility for myself, but I'll also take responsibility for my government. It needs nannying and watching and controlling, and I'm just the one for the job.

Once people exercise their rightful responsibility for their government, they have a number of specific responsibilities, including:

• *Limiting its responsibilities.* Government does have a few legitimate responsibilities in a free society, discussed in detail in The American Idea of Government. But intelligent people know that government and politicians won't willingly stick to those responsibilities. In fact, people see that government too easily forgets these first things, in part because it's spending its energies on worst things – like taking responsibilities away from the people.

• *Holding it accountable.* It's become commonplace to say, "They're politicians, so of course they aren't going to keep their promises." What kind of political system and government does that attitude foster? If they promise what they can't deliver, they're arrogant. If they promise what they won't deliver, they're dishonest. If they promise what they don't know how to deliver, they're stupid. In any of these cases, they should be directed toward employment elsewhere.

• *Preventing it from running wild.* Every violation of the American Ideas needs to be recognized and defeated in its infancy. There are no temporary encroachments by government. We have to be especially watchful during crises of any kind, when fear and confusion can be exploited by our government child run amok.

• *Paying for it.* When half the citizens pay no taxes, they have no investment in what government does – unless it's to "give" them more of what rightfully belongs to others. Every citizen should pay some tax, however small. At this minimum level, these are freedom dues, citizenship dues.

To ignore this responsibility we have for our government is to invite its disdain and its control. French observer Alexis de Tocqueville wrote,

If they are required to elect representatives, to support the government by personal service, to meet on public business, they have no time – they cannot waste their precious time in useless engagements…. These people think they are following the principle of self-interest, but the idea they entertain of that principle is a very crude one; and the better they look after what they call their business, they neglect their chief business, which is to remain their own masters.[18]

We've lost our edge in this crucial business of responsibility for government. In a recent poll, 68% thought that "most Americans do not live up to their responsibilities as citizens."[19]   But it wasn't always that way. We can change this. We can change our relationship with government so that it doesn't stay that way.

The American Idea here is simple: Either we take responsibility for our government, or it will take control of us.

America At Its Best

Through the centuries, America and Americans have, more than others, taken responsibility. And we can reclaim and rebuild that culture of responsibility. We can:

Take Action

Take care of ourselves and our own.

★

Be responsible for our own health and well-being.

★

Stop expecting others to bail us out as individuals, families, or groups.

★

Be generous with those who can't exercise responsibility for themselves.

★

Demand the separation of school and state.

★

Transform public schools into community schools run by parents and supported by the community.

★

Call out and reject "victimitis."

★

Replace political correctness with responsibly-delivered truth.

★

Measure freedom in terms of responsibility.

★

Welcome limitations that enhance freedom.

★

Take charge of government and politicians.

★

Refuse government offers of care that lead to government supremacy.

★

Remove government from the business of taking personal responsibility away from individuals.

★

Refuse to let the government "reverse delegate" its responsibilities back to us.

To see detail on these Action Points and
to add your voice visit www.theamericanideas.com

And so, happily, the American Idea says "take responsibility."

Taking responsibility can be hard, even unpleasant. But it's a walk in the park compared with the nasty results of adolescent irresponsibility.

Responsibility and the American Idea

"The future is purchased by the present," noted British philosopher Samuel Johnson.[20] Responsibility now is designed to purchase a free and prosperous future. Irresponsibility now is designed to purchase jealousy and envy, chaos and fear, and the poverty of pocketbook and soul.

When one person takes responsibility for himself or herself, it makes him or her a standout. When a society as a whole does it, it makes that society a remarkable place to live. America has been that place before.

And it can be so once again.

CHAPTER 8

The American Idea of Generosity

Americans certainly didn't invent generosity. But the American Idea of Generosity has always been innovative and exceptional, different in kind and degree from anything like it in human history.

Is it just coincidence that Americans are unswervingly generous, both with each other and with strangers? That, by the millions, they open up their pocketbooks and volunteer their time? That, at the same time, a society that has created a safe place for the opportunity to generate astounding wealth strongly condemns those who won't share that wealth?

And this generosity can't be explained by Americans having so much wealth. A basic reality of life is that the wealthiest have gone out of their way to keep it all to themselves, and more – they've all too often taken what little the poor still had left. But under the sway of this Idea, Americans have given out of their riches and their poverty. They've given away their wealth even when they had no wealth.

Generosity is built into the DNA of America, and it has been from the beginning. A brilliant foreign observer, the Frenchman Alexis de Tocqueville, was astonished by the level of generosity he saw in his travels throughout America in the middle of the nineteenth century. He noted, "When an American needs the assistance of his fellows, it is very rare for that to be refused, and I have often seen it given spontaneously and eagerly." He was fascinated by the unquenchable volunteer spirit, saying, "I have often admired the extreme skill they show in proposing a common object for the exertions of very many and in inducing them voluntarily to pursue it."[1]

When Europe was starving after World War I, it was America that fed it. When Europe and Japan were destroyed by World War II, it was America that rebuilt them. There's no precedent for a nation to rebuild enemy nations and give them their freedom, and there is certainly no obvious logic to it. The logic of realpolitik would argue the contrary and would argue for keeping the enemy beaten down and enslaved. But America is no ordinary place, and its generosity is greater than realpolitik.

People both inside and outside of America might condemn the society for its wild pursuit of happiness. They might even bite the hand that feeds them. But when they're starving, they know who'll be serving them their dinner.

Generosity

We remember that from those who have been given much,
much will be expected.

We won't give until it hurts – we'll give until it feels good.

We believe that expected but unforced generosity is a
high-water mark of a grand and self-reliant society.

We know that thriftiness is a good thing, partly so we can
be more generous, but miserliness is always a curse.

We'll lift others up and give away what was ours to keep.

But no one, including government, has the right to be
generous with other people's money.

True generosity can only grow out of hard work, earning,
saving, and investing.

And generosity isn't "giving back" because it's based on
living a bighearted life and not on making restitution for
taking away from others.

Let's take a closer look at this most felicitous of American Ideas.

It starts with a sense of being fortunate. Early Americans talked about being "blessed." They knew that they could have been born in a poorer time and place, yet here they were in a land of astounding abundance. This caused much serious reflection that helped lead to a collective societal gratitude. Americans said to each other,

We Remember That from Those Who Have Been Given Much, Much Will Be Expected

Part of this incredible Idea of Generosity is the belief that wealth is a trust. This belief is rooted in the concept that all wealth comes from God and is given not just for personal use. The intended use extends to family and friends. It goes beyond family and friends to fellow travelers and employees and people who supply our needs. And in the hardest-to-fathom version of the concept, it reaches total strangers.

Even those now criticized as being robber barons were captured by this outstanding American Idea. Andrew Carnegie gave away almost all of the wealth he accumulated in his dominating run to the top of the steel industry. He was the catalyst behind countless libraries and other facilities he built to benefit humankind.[2] He even took the time to set down his version of the philosophy of generosity in his book The Gospel of Wealth. He said, "Surplus wealth is a sacred trust which its possessor is bound to administer in his lifetime for the good of the community."[3]

From the Rockefellers and Fords to the Gates and Buffetts, the Idea makes its expectations known. American celebrities feel compelled to support humanitarian causes. Not-for-profits and foundations are established every day. Government is expected to provide tax deductions for charitable donations and to allow millions of generosity-driven organizations to pay no taxes at all.

Even the Federal Government itself can't escape the Idea, giving away more than $49 billion of our money through USAID, the State Department, and other agencies to people in foreign countries in 2008.[4] This is driven on the surface by realpolitik, but underneath by the power of this American Idea.

But this is only the tip of the American Idea of generosity. Americans are expected to give, not under the threat of a king or dictator, not because of legally mandated contribution to a state church, but under the inspiration of the Idea. And give we do. Here's what it looked like in 2009, in the middle of a terrible recession[5]:

- $307.7 billion in charitable giving. 75% of this was given by individuals.

- Donations of $10 billion or more to a host of causes – religion, education, grant-making foundations, human services, public-social benefits, health, international causes, and arts and culture.

• Of the $122.8 billion given in foreign aid by the United States in 2008, 79% ($95.5 billion) was from non-governmental sources such as churches, universities, and individuals. Americans gave – and give – more than all of the other 6 billion people on earth.

• 61.8 million people performing volunteer service. This added up to 8 billion hours of service, which is valued at an estimated $162 billion.

• Volunteering that included 29.4% of all women and 23.2% of all men. The more the education and professional responsibility (and presumably the wealth), the less the selfishness – 42% of people with a bachelor's degree volunteer.

Generally, this giving is done without expectation of return. It's the very picture of an open hand, receiving freely and giving just as freely. Americans give, and give a lot – even though they're constantly accused of being greedy, selfish, and profligate.

And Americans give with pleasure. We honor people who do it and put their names on lists and plaques. We measure people by commercial, business, and financial success, but we let few people reach the highest rungs of recognized achievement without generosity as a big part of their story. When a candidate for President is found to spend more on his exterminator than on charity, he has hung an American millstone around his own neck.

Some might try to rationalize, trivialize, or minimize this American Idea of generosity. They might:

• *Claim that this is done out of guilt because of the high level of American wealth.* But even a surface knowledge of history or human nature would remind them that the world's wealthy have almost never felt guilty about having a lot. And they've seldom felt guilty enough to share it. On the contrary, they've typically felt no compunctions about getting more however they could get it – a conscienceless, guilt-free accumulation.

• *Declare this a built-in, evolutionary response.* Isn't it "natural" to care for others? Not hardly. If they just briefly looked around the world, they'd know it isn't so. And how does their notion of care correlate with natural selection and survival of the fittest? According to that belief, aren't we already wired to let the weak die off, maybe helping them do so? American generosity is a historical exception to the self-centered, even brutal, norm. Although it doesn't by itself disprove the supposed overriding power of the "law of the jungle," it's a big enough exception that it certainly puts a huge hole in this supposition. And it points the way to a better place.

• *Assert that this is only an obligation Americans feel because they have so much.* But this does nothing to explain why Americans feel or have this "obligation." If they earned it, why should they automatically feel that they have to share it? If it's theirs, on what basis other than greed and theft should others be able to lay claim to it? And what other wealthy group or culture has ever felt this "obligation"?

• *Allege that this generosity is only possible because America has somehow gotten unfair advantage or pillaged the planet.* In reality, much if not most of this advantage has come from exploiting its other Ideas rather than exploiting other people or nations. And any truth in these claims – some

Americans have indeed abused the trust – still can't explain why Americans give so much away. Why would people who cheat and pillage recognize any such moral obligation?

• *Redefine generosity as a selfish act, as one that we do because it makes us feel good or important.* But is giving only virtuous if we feel bad about doing it? In fact, is badly motivated giving really authentic generosity? People with big hearts always feel good about helping others.

Some people may not like to think so, but this generosity impulse is spiritual in nature. It recognizes that all people are indeed created equal and endowed by God with unalienable rights. It sees that all people are made in God's image and so are worthy of a helping hand. It recognizes that God could have decided things differently and put me in the ghetto and them in the nice neighborhood.

This American Idea of Generosity is indeed odd. Generosity isn't thought to be a burden by Americans. Instead, it is viewed as an opportunity to have an enormous impact and as a way to personal greatness. This is why Americans can say

We Won't Give until It Hurts – We'll Give until It Feels Good

President Woodrow Wilson said,

> *Nowhere else in the world have noble men and women exhibited in more striking forms the beauty and the energy of sympathy and helpfulness and counsel in their efforts to rectify wrong, alleviate suffering, and set the weak in the way of strength and hope.*[6]

For many people, giving is a hard thing to do. It's unpleasant like a chore but without any corresponding personal benefit.

Somehow, some way, America changed that. Giving didn't just become easy to do – it became natural to do. It no doubt had a religious orientation, with people's strong belief in tithing and good works. But there was more to it than that. There was a cultural component. It was just what good people did.

In most societies, generosity the American way was and is unknown. If you gave it away, you wouldn't have it for your own needs when a time of scarcity came. And why would you give it away in any case? It is yours, isn't it?

Ironically, this withholding from others is often the most entrenched where the property rights are most ill-defined or least widely distributed. If your ownership is uncertain, it's only natural that you will cling to whatever you can get your hands on. Property rights and the pursuit of happiness are, in an American upside-down way, part of the foundation of generosity.

And although many rich Americans have given generously, "A number of...studies have shown that lower-income Americans give proportionally more of their incomes to charity than do upper-income Americans."[7]   At least in part, this must be driven by the permeating American Idea of Generosity.

The American Idea of Generosity is that we will give, freely and magnanimously, not because we must but because we can, because we want to…and because it feels good to love our neighbors.

This is so much a part of who we are that

> *We Believe That Expected but Unforced Generosity Is a High-Water Mark of a Grand and Self-Reliant Society*

Although there has been too little of it throughout human history, a tiny amount really compared with the cruelty and greed and selfishness, generosity has shown up from time to time.

Often, it has appeared in the unlikeliest of places, with the poorest and neediest being the most generous. Even in the Great Depression of the 1930s, extreme poverty led not to the currently fashionable idea of poverty-driven crime but to the reality of many people sharing their crumbs with others.

Although from the beginning there has been an American expectation of generosity, there was little coercion to it. Required tithing to an established church, a practice in some colonies, was phased out very early on. The Idea was, instead, "We expect you to give, but you don't have to give."

This giving was done in a big way. The fact that it wasn't forced allowed it to avoid the natural human resistance – always heightened in the American spirit – to being told what to do. People could decide for themselves. And they decided to give a lot of their money and their time.

The government has deeply intruded into that in recent decades. It made itself the giver of last resort in the 1930s and now has ordained itself too often as the giver of first resort. It wants to be the provider to the poor, the sick, the disabled, the elderly. Having no money of its own to give away, it takes from those who have it instead of letting them give it of their own accord.

This isn't generosity, and it isn't giving.

This is redistribution, with a bit of good intention mixed in with a lot of political posturing and vote-getting. But what else could it be? How can we expect politicians to avoid acting politically? The problem isn't with the individual politicians, although some of them do cold-bloodedly use our money to gain favor for themselves. The problem is with the system itself, where the American Idea of Generosity has been co-opted and perverted by government – which is, not surprisingly, never able to act non-politically.

This has led to debates on questions like whether government should fund faith-based charities. The real question is, "Why does the government have this money in the first place?" How much more could people give to these and other charities if their taxes were half or less of the current level? Who is likely to be better at determining a worthy charity, people who are close to the need or people who are close to Washington?

Foreign aid is another related issue. Some would say that only our government could meet some of the needs of poor and devastated people in other countries. But doesn't our government take from us all of the money that it is sending over there? Couldn't we just send it ourselves?

It's true that government can concentrate the giving. But too often that means concentrating it for political rather than humanitarian purposes. It also often means that the giving is done on a large scale to other governments and their agencies, a perfect formula for corruption, theft, and waste. Private charities aren't immune from these diseases, but they usually occur on a human scale, with people on the ground to ensure that the charity is dispensed with justice.

The attitude that all of this government intrusion is creating is the European stance: "Why doesn't the government take care of that?" Well, why not? In part because it can't. At its core, government isn't designed to be Mother Teresa. If we wait for government, clumsy and inefficient and twisted by political winds, to meet individual human needs in a just and satisfying way, we'll have a long wait indeed.

The American attitude used to be, "We can take care of that." We just did it, willingly and without coercion. We didn't wait for government. We thought using government for tender loving care was like trying to set a bone with a sledge hammer.

The American Idea has been assaulted, but it isn't dead. Not yet, not by a lot. Every time there's a disaster, there are Americans to address it. Every time there's a need, there are Americans to meet it. Where did this remarkable spirit come from? Why is relentless generosity an American Idea?

It starts, paradoxically, with the concept of self-reliance. Ralph Waldo Emerson, in his great essay *Self-Reliance*, said that the self-reliant person is

> *He who knows that power is inborn, that he is weak because he has looked for good out of him and elsewhere, and so perceiving, throws himself unhesitatingly on his thought, instantly rights himself, stands in erect position, commands his limbs, works miracles.... Nothing can bring you peace but yourself. Nothing can bring you peace but the triumph of principles.*[8]

Emerson adds,

> *It is easy to see that a greater self-reliance must work a revolution in all the offices and relations of men; in their religion; in their education; in their pursuits; their modes of living; their association; in their property; in their speculative views.*[9]

People came to America with an understanding that no one would be taking care of them. Even more than an understanding, it was a hope. There would be no grudgingly benevolent king or queen, no fifth-generation landowning noble, no top-down government taking the property from someone else to give it to them. They would have to take care of themselves because there was nowhere else to apply – but also because that's the way free people wanted it to be.

At the same time, they saw straight away that this business of living had a hard edge and that it was bloody hard to do it alone. There were times when something couldn't be done easily without help and other times when it couldn't be done at all.

So Americans shared. The first level of giving was based on mutual support. You help me clear my field, and next year I'll help you build your barn. You buy this from me, and next month I'll buy that from you. It wasn't a direct exchange or barter (although that occurred, too), but open-handed giving that would, as a rule, be repaid someday, somewhere, somehow. All of this made for better communities where, first and foremost, personal responsibility was admired and nurtured. Tocqueville said,

> The Americans make associations to give entertainment, to found seminaries, to build inns, to construct churches, to diffuse books, to send missionaries to the antipodes; in this manner, they found hospitals, prisons and schools.[10]

The next level was helping others who couldn't help you back – maybe not now, maybe not ever. Somehow, this American Idea grew to include more than just pragmatic give-and-take. There were widows who needed repairs to their homes, injured farmers who needed someone to bring in the harvest, orphans who needed a home. The attitude was, "I know you're not a slacker. I know you'd do this for yourself if you could because we're a self-reliant people. But you can't, so I will. And gladly." Was there a measure of watching out for others in case you needed help yourself? No doubt. But this isn't a bad thing. First of all, it's making an investment in other human beings, and that is just good in itself. But it's also admitting that life is too hard to go it alone. It's a form of insurance, relational insurance: "I'll freely put into the common pool. I hope I don't ever need to draw from it. I'll use it only if I must. And I know that to use it when I could really take care of myself would be shameful and degrading."

In the American Idea of Generosity, this self-reliant giving can be summarized like this: We won't ever give anything willingly if others demand it, but we'll often freely share what is ours to decide. We won't ever willingly help a freeloader, but we'll go out of our way to help a responsible person who happens to be broken by life.

People – not everyone, but a great many – were free in a whole new way to practice the great commandment to "Love Thy Neighbor." In 1939's Mr. Smith Goes to Washington, director Frank Capra captures this in Mr. Smith's (played by Jimmy Stewart) unforgettable closing speech to a corrupt senior senator, his former hero, on the floor of the Senate:

> I wouldn't give you two cents for all your fancy rules if, behind them, they didn't have a little bit of plain, ordinary, everyday kindness and a little lookin' out for the other fella, too. That's pretty important, all that. It's just the blood and bone and sinew of this democracy that some great men handed down to the human race, that's all![11]

This Idea is so embedded in America that even atheists practice it, with joy.

And it wasn't just giving away a few crumbs if we happened to have something left over. It involved living in such a way that there was guaranteed to be "give-away" money. As a people, we came to believe that

Thriftiness Is a Good Thing, Partly so We Can Be More Generous, but Miserliness Is Always a Curse

In recent years, America is often thought of as a commercialized and spendthrift place. Americans are viewed as profligates, borrowing wildly to support an unsupportable and out-of-control lifestyle. Sadly, this thinking has been painfully close to the truth of late.

But it wasn't always so.

Along with the religiously inspired concepts of hard work, saving, and giving came the religiously inspired concept of frugality. Thriftiness was viewed not only as street-smart, but also as moral.

Part of it was just common sense. You didn't spend and use up everything because you didn't know what tomorrow or next year might bring. You stored up in the fat years so you'd have something to eat in the lean years. In the American version if frugality, you practiced good old-fashioned horse-sense. The alternatives were poverty, begging, neediness and embarrassment.

But there was more to it. Thriftiness meant not buying more than what you needed. In America, you could define "need" in an expanding way as you prospered – you could build a bigger house or barn, buy more land, add some nicer clothes to the wardrobe, eat fresher food and better cuts of meat. But you didn't spend just to spend, to keep up with the Joneses or to outspend them, to have trinkets and extras, to own a house full of what four centuries of Americans would have called nonsense.

This frugality also meant not paying more than what you had to pay to get what you needed. Americans have always had a hard time "paying retail." They like a good deal and aren't afraid to ask for it. They wait for sales and put things on "lay-away" until they have the cash to pay for it.

So there were several forms of restraint embedded in this concept of thriftiness. Americans, so frequently thought to be naïve in a political or social sense, have always been thought of as shrewd in business, finance, and economics. People spoke with pride about "living within their means" and "getting a good deal" and "saving up to buy something."

And in the back of the American mind, rough-hewn but real, was the connection between frugality and generosity. In the first place, it just didn't seem right to live a gaudy lifestyle while there were people around us in need – and there were always people in need. But second, there was nothing to share in a life lived without frugality, in a life lived beyond one's means.

People cut away what they didn't need to spend so they could give away what they didn't need to keep.

The American Idea of Generosity is still very much alive, but it has been hampered by the loss of thriftiness. People buy what they don't need and won't use. They pay market rates because they can. They not only don't have any margin in their budgets, they have to borrow prodigious amounts to buy all of those "biggers and betters." They expect government to borrow to keep the good times going. All that debt is no friend to anyone – not to the borrowers or to the needy that will be helped less and less by individuals or to a debt-ridden, bankrupt government.

And there's the sad irony. People who have so much more than their ancestors had for four centuries now have so much less to give away. They feel so much financial pressure that they can't deal with the overwhelming needs of others. In too many cases, thoughtlessness and wastefulness have led to miserliness. Being a miser means grabbing and taking, hoarding and envying, wanting more and never being satisfied. Miserliness has never been the American way.

We've been a thrifty people and we can be so again. We can enjoy the good life, but sanely. We can live within our means and take the pressure off ourselves. We can relish the wholesome experience of helping others just because. We can break the trend that has Americans giving 3% or less of their incomes – in part if we cut back a government that takes ten or more times that amount, but also in part because we've recaptured the practice of American thriftiness.

So here in America is a giveaway spirit, a spirit that surely must confound any foreign observer focusing on American capitalism and innovation and growth, a spirit that says,

We Will Lift Others Up and Give Away What Was Ours to Keep

Strangely, America has often been viewed as a dog-eat-dog society. It's all about me, free-market madness, let the buyer beware, and sink-or-swim thoughtlessness about the needs of others.

But this has never been the case. America has always been a place where everyone has a chance to be and do more. There's fierce competition – a powerful tool to better the human condition and an engine of creativity and productivity. But at the same time, Americans have always understood that great things can often be built and accomplished only by collaboration.

And they've sensed that more can be gained by lifting people from their knees than by beating them into the ground.

So part of this American Idea is the magnanimous concept of the "helping hand." We see that life is a high-wire act, so we provide safety nets to keep people from hitting the ground. We think a lot about mentoring and coaching. We worry about being a good example and modeling good behavior. We're generous with our money, but we're just as generous with our time.

No place on earth has ever seen even a fraction of the voluntary effort or voluntary organizations that fill up America. A sign on Ellis Island, the great receiving point for millions of Americans in spirit, said,

> At a time when the government offered few social services, the burden of helping new arrivals make their first adjustments to life in America was carried by various ethnic and religious organizations, as well as by divisions of the Red Cross, the YWCA, the Daughters of the American Revolution, and others. On Ellis Island, representatives from over 40 of these private social welfare groups acted as interpreters for the immigrants, gave them clothing and money, unraveled bureaucratic tie-ups, located lost baggage, and contacted the immigrants' relatives and friends who were already living in the United States.[12]

Where else has anything like this ever been seen? What society has ever had such an open hand to aliens? The number of places where immigrants have been abused far exceeds the number where they've been welcomed. But there's only one place where they've been welcomed like this.

We don't have to give, but we do. We like helping others out. Even if they don't deserve it, we'll give people another chance – among other notable attributes, America is the land of the second chance. The only thing that thrills Americans as much as hearing a rags-to-riches story is hearing about someone who lost everything and then, in spite of long odds and huge challenges, made a comeback.

The American Idea of Generosity has always included the magnificent concept of "hospitality." There are many places around the world where foreigners feel their foreignness in every interaction. But even in the biggest cities of America, a foreigner can still stop a stranger on the street to ask for directions and expect to get a civil and helpful response.

One of the meanings of "hospitality" is "kindness to strangers."[13] This has always included the people who are Americans in spirit and who want to be Americans in fact – the immigrants, the latest contingent of a four-century throng. How can we hope to remain free if we treat others as though they aren't? We haven't always done a good job of welcoming immigrants, but on the whole, we've welcomed them as guests – with caution, to be sure, but also with great generosity.

We wouldn't invite just anyone into our homes, but once they've passed the test of "not harmful to society" – like criminals and idlers – we can warmly welcome them in all of their breathtaking diversity. We should have no problem making room for immigrants – as citizens or registered guests – since all of our ancestors (including even Native Americans) almost certainly came from another land.

Lifting others up, helping others out, welcoming others in – this is a glorious part of the American Idea of Generosity. But

No One, Including Government, Has the Right to Be Generous with Other People's Money

Americans have always had a clear-cut view of what is not generosity: People or groups anointing themselves as "benefactors" and then trying to win praise for confiscating and giving away other people's money.

It's strange, this fairly recent notion that helping someone by taking money forcefully from someone else is a good thing. It's a lot easier to see how this is robbery than how it is decent or just. This gunpoint generosity is an especially dangerous notion in a democracy, where the majority who has less can always vote themselves another share from the minority who has more.

Robin Hood is a great story, but it's based on taking money away from people who've gotten it through evil means, from people who are evil. It was like stealing from organized crime to help the Red Cross. That's not what we have today with the government taking money from people who have earned it legally and morally, often by providing a great service to other human beings. And many who are robbed by government would have used some of what was taken to help the needy.

The notion is, "If government doesn't do it, nobody else will." The reality is, "If government does it, no one else can." That's partly due to the fact that the government clogs up the philanthropic arteries, but it's also due to the fact that they're taking the money that we could be giving away.

The government – any government – isn't going to show us how to be generous. It doesn't even know what that means. Their giving is always about gaining power and influence, getting votes and satisfying constituents, listening to groups who vociferously demand their right to drink from the public trough, and taking property from one citizen to hand it over to another.

It isn't that some of the politicians who want government to be the biggest of all charitable organizations aren't generous. They're caring but misguided. They don't understand that generosity is an action of kind souls who are willing to give away what belongs to them. Generosity is not a government transaction. These politicians refuse to see the downside of their gunpoint generosity.

Far too many politicians are like the generals who are willing to fight to the last drop of your blood. Once they see no restraint in the law to transferring property by force from one citizen to another, once they believe that whatever we own isn't really owned, once they arrogate to themselves the mighty power to redistribute what isn't theirs, they've put a dagger into the heart of many American Ideas – of Generosity, Responsibility, Justice, Society, and Government.

It would be easier to believe these politicians were truly generous if they would start by giving away most of their own money.

Until recently, Americans have had a different and better Idea. They saw a need and, in the spirit of the American Idea of Generosity, they poured themselves into that need. The cumulative effect of this, while not as immediately obvious as a government intervention, is dramatic. As Alexis de Tocqueville said about Americans,

> *Suppose that an individual thinks of some enterprise, and that enterprise has a direct bearing on the welfare of society; it does not come into his head to appeal to public authority for help. He publishes his efforts, and personally struggles against all obstacles. No doubt he is less successful than the state would have been in his place, but in the long run the sum of all private undertakings far surpasses anything the government might have done.*[14]

For most of American history, Americans didn't expect the government to fill the generosity need, a need almost never filled in any way by governments. In fact, Americans didn't want the government to do this. They judged, rightly, that they could better decide who needed help, get the help there faster and better without a middleman, and receive the personal pleasure from providing the help themselves. They sensed, with that hard-boiled American realism, that they could provide it without the waste and corruption and bad prioritization that government is always perfectly designed to produce.

The Great Depression of the 1930s let the government's nose inside the tent. And its "generosity" didn't even help. The unemployment rate in 1938 was roughly the same as that of four years earlier when the New Deal was announced.[15] But no matter. The government began chipping away at this wonderful American Idea, changing its meaning and claiming it for its own. This was stepped up dramatically with the Great Society programs of the 1960s, and today we face another round of generosity destruction.

The government forgot Thomas Jefferson's rule that "no more good must be attempted than the public can bear."[16]

Americans always knew that government "generosity" was a freakish thing to be avoided. They knew that it came with demands, strings, politics, and pork barrels. And we still know it because the American Idea of Generosity is still alive.

We can take it back. It belongs to us, not to governments or critics or disparagers of the American ability to create wealth. We can reclaim the belief that the government cannot and should not interfere with our ability to be generous – by taxing us into poverty or by applauding itself for giving away our money or by taking upon itself what we have always done better.

We need our government to stand aside, to be awed by an Idea that no other government has ever even had to acknowledge, to support American generosity without presuming to exercise it. Government does have a role – to keep its hands off our property and to keep its taxing power off our charitable giving and work. Because

True Generosity Can Only Grow Out of Hard Work, Earning, Saving, and Investing

If we're not going to be generous with other people's money, we need to have our own. And in this world, that generally only happens as a result of working hard, smart, and creatively at something that other people value.

- Just working hard won't do it. Few people work as hard as those on hardscrabble farms, but they seldom have anything extra and often have too little even for themselves.

- Just being smart won't do it. The world is full of people who try to get by on their smarts alone but find that without hard work and creativity, they can't get very far.

• Just being creative won't do it. Countless great ideas have died for want of hard work and street smarts or have been exploited by other people who are smart and hardworking.

And just finding a need that people have and planning to meet it won't do it either. An observant person can see a need, and there are always many ways to improve products and services. But without the commitment, the focus, the willingness to learn, and the ability to meet that need creatively, little or nothing will be gained.

Simply put, it takes a lot of work to earn enough to have enough left over.

There are many options for the left-over part. It can be spent on personal needs and wants, wisely or foolishly. It can be saved for a bigger purchase down the road or for the lean years that almost always come. It can be invested in a new business or in money market funds or stocks or bonds or commodities. If it's saved and invested wisely, that growth can provide even more left overs to save and invest.

Or it can be given away. But we have to have before we can give it away. And the more we have, the more we can give away. The government creates terms like "excess profits" (for both political and taxing reasons), but it is generally only when we have excess – individually or corporately – that we have enough, and feel free enough, to give generously.

Some Americans even try to earn more so they'll have more to give. It's a worthwhile goal, and a peculiarly American one, to try to earn extra just for charitable purposes.

This American Idea was captured by that great lover of freedom and generosity John Wesley, who said, "Having, first, earned all you can, and, secondly, saved all you can, then give all you can."[17] He saw generosity not as the opposite of free-market, democratic capitalism, but as its exquisite outgrowth. He knew a simple but powerful truth – that you couldn't give away what you didn't have.

Americans may try to earn more than anyone else. At least for many, this is so they can give away more than anyone else.

And this giving isn't based on guilt or shame or embarrassment. It is a strange false guilt that critiques having more, when the whole world wants to have more.

Some people have stolen and need to make restitution, they *should* feel guilty – and that includes politicians and businessmen and financiers. They need to give back. But restitution and generosity are two very different actions. Most Americans know that

Generosity Isn't "Giving Back" Because It's Based on Living a Bighearted Life and Not on Making Restitution for Taking Away from Others

There's been much said in recent years about the notion of "giving back."

What is meant by this? At best, it's perhaps a rephrasing of the proverb that "from those who have been given much, much will be required."[18] We've been blessed by living in a free society and by having great opportunity, so we need to pay it forward and help others live with freedom and opportunity. We have a responsibility to enhance and advance the society and system that have allowed us to prosper. This may be all right, as long as it doesn't go too far.

But at worst, this is a statement about false guilt. We have to give back because we took what wasn't really ours to take or we took it by wrong means or we took too much – all as decided by others, who can be very "generous" about spreading sham guilt and generating bad press for successful people.

Giving in response to this kind of guilt really isn't generosity at all. It's making payment on a bad debt. It's paying off the blackmailers. It's hush money. In its own odd way, it's part of the cost of doing business, part of a good public relations program. Because if we're too successful...well, we should be ashamed and we should pay up.

If we really have taken wrongly from others, we do indeed have a debt. Now we have a matter of justice. But taking care of that is restitution, not generosity.

True generosity isn't really about giving back. It is a whole lot better than that:

- It's about giving away. It says, "I don't owe this to you, but I'm going to give it to you anyway because I want to be gracious and caring and selfless."

- It's about giving up. It says, "I have a rightful claim to this, but I freely give it up to help you – whom I may not even know."

- It's about giving more. It says, "I'm not going to work for thirty or forty years for money and then spend my retirement years giving back. I'm going to work for thirty or forty years to make a difference, and then I'm going to work for thirty or forty more years to make another difference."

It has been noted, "Americans give to charity for many reasons. The first and foremost of them is that they are a generous and civic-minded people – words that many other countries find hard to say. There are secondary reasons: the tax system encourages philanthropy, not because it is lax but because it is wise. There is a recognition that individuals give more shrewdly than the state."[19]

The American Idea of Generosity is unique for many reasons. Not the least of these is its separation from bogus guilt and imposed duty.

In America, people give because they want to, not because they have to. No wonder the place has been so blessed.

America At Its Best

TheAmericanIdeas.com

The American Idea of Generosity will continue to present a shining face to the world if we:

Take Action

Expect giving to start with me and not with the government or the rich.

★

Give for the right reasons.

★

Stop trying to explain American generosity apart from good-heartedness.

★

Remember to love our neighbors.

★

Live both a rich and frugal life.

★

Remember the connection between thriftiness & charity.

★

Value hard work.

★

Keep charitable organizations free from the burden of taxes and regulation.

★

Insist that the government be generosity-biased with individual and corporate givers as long as we have a "progressive" tax system.

★

Require people to provide real help for the truly needy directly, not allowing soul-crushing dependency through government, in a "fellow citizen" tax system.

★

Get the government out of the generosity business.

★

Refuse to buy into the lie that government welfare programs are needed because private generosity is insufficient.

★

Replace foreign aid by government with aid to foreigners by Americans.

To see detail on these Action Points and
to add your voice visit www.theamericanideas.com

In older English, "charity" was another word for "love."[20] Charity doesn't say everything there is to say about love, but it certainly says a lot.

Generosity and the American Idea

There have always been generous people. Even in the midst of the most horrifying poverty, people have shared the little they had. Battered by drought, they've still fed the hungry. Assaulted by disease, they've still provided care. Sometimes the poorest people have been the most generous, perhaps because they know so deeply what it feels like, perhaps because they know better than others how close we all are to having nothing.

But large-scale giving has never been commonplace. Governments required tithes to established churches, but often, that was just another tax for the powerful rather than true generosity. In that Old World, people watched as monarchs nestled in with state-supported churches and together gouged the people – including the poor, sometimes especially the poor. People gave because they had to, not because they wanted to.

That all changed with America. Although in recent years, too many Americans have come to expect the government to take money to help the poor as the politicians see fit, that is not the first choice of most Americans. They know this is just the Old World forced giving that their ancestors abhorred, money taken by a government-church rather than a religion-church.

Americans prefer to give as they see fit. They see the waste and abuse and vote-buying and fraud and corruption that go with government "charity," and they know this can't possibly be the best way.

They know there's a better way – and they still practice it, even in the face of mammoth government encroachment. No year passes without dozens, even hundreds, of new charitable organizations being formed. Americans support every conceivable cause as soon as they're aware of it, and even more after someone conceives an organization to channel that support. No matter how things are analyzed, the conclusion is clear: Americans – real people, not the government, never the government – are a generous lot.

Americans like to give. It makes them feel useful, significant, even spiritual. And they like the fact that it's done of their own free will. They like that they get to direct it to causes that are important to them. And they like to hold people accountable for how they spend those contributions.

We haven't lost this wonderful, surprisingly persistent spirit of generosity, and we don't have to lose it. To those who see life as nothing more than biochemical processes, the American Idea of Generosity – even though welcome – is inexplicable. This is because the Idea flies in the face of almost everything we see in nature and in history. It is an incredibly bold statement of decency.

May it always be so.

CHAPTER 9

The American Idea of Religion

The American Idea of Religion begins with this thought: Religion is the Great Paradox.

The paradox? Religion is the best of ideas and the worst of ideas. It can generate both love and hate. It's a force that is hard to live with and impossible to live without.

Although atheists and agnostics may try to deny it, America is now, and has always been, a spiritual and religious culture. From its beginnings, there was an unspoken agreement that God was heavily involved with this new place. People from many religious persuasions were drawn to America – not because it was finally free of religion, but because religion was finally free.

Here was a place where the worst of religious ideas from the Old World were purged. Religion could be respected as a guide rather than embedded as a tyrant. After millennia, people found a home where religion would be separated from its unholy and unhelpful alliance with government, a merger which always puffed up the ruling power even as it degraded the religion. Here at last was a human scarcity, freedom of religion.

But there's no point in having freedom of religion if there is no religion or if no one cares about the religions that exist. The Idea actually imagined religious vibrancy and dynamism on a large, new scale precisely because religion had finally been set free.

Part of the beauty – and success – of this Idea is that it includes deep clarity about the difference between spirituality and religion. Throughout most of history, and in much of the world today, this difference isn't even acknowledged. To be spiritual you must believe in this or that religion. In America, this has happily not been so. Here, spirituality can lead people to many different religious places.

Throughout the centuries, most Americans have accepted that there is without a doubt a God, a "paying attention" sort of God. They have deeply appreciated the widespread focus on individual faith, on relationship, on spirituality translating into good work and compassion. And they knew that religion rightly practiced was both very right and very American.

Religion

Religion is to be respected and valued because there is indeed a God behind it.

We know that if we only have a secular hope, we have no hope.

We believe in religious freedom, not low-level religious tolerance.

We want to be free from religious wars but not from religion.

We seek a proper understanding of the separation of church and state – that religion has freedom from government and not the other way around.

We want religion to flourish by keeping it and government at a proper distance and religion in the right place in American life.

Without establishing it in law or marginalizing those who believe otherwise, we know that American Ideas are established on a specific religious base and that severing or minimizing that foundation jeopardizes the whole dynamic structure of America.

Trying to explain America without understanding the central role of spirituality and religion is impossible, even preposterous. But trying to explain religion's impact merely as "tradition" or "community ritual" is no less absurd. In America

Religion Is To Be Respected and Valued Because There Is Indeed a God behind It

President George Washington launched the American government in his first inaugural address by declaring,

> It would be peculiarly improper to omit in this first official act my fervent supplications to that Almighty Being who rules over the universe, who presides in the councils of nations, and whose providential aids can supply every human defect, that His benediction may consecrate to the liberties and happiness of the people of the United States a Government instituted by themselves for these essential purposes, and may enable every instrument employed in its administration to execute with success the functions allotted to his charge. In tendering this homage to the Great Author of every public and private good, I assure myself that it expresses your sentiments not less than my own, nor those of my fellow-citizens at large less than either. No people can be bound to acknowledge and adore the Invisible Hand which conducts the affairs of men more than those of the United States. Every step by which they have advanced to the character of an independent nation seems to have been distinguished by some token of providential agency....[1]

President, founder, and lead drafter of the Constitution James Madison said without question,

> Before any man can be considered as a member of civil society, he must be considered as a subject of the Governor of the Universe.[2]

He knew that escapees from religious persecution in the Old World didn't disrespect or devalue religion. Quite the contrary. They respected and valued it so much that they refused to let an autocratic church, backed by an autocratic government, shove its version of religion down everyone's throats.

They wanted religious freedom, not freedom from religion. They wanted freedom for religion, not from it.

And why did they respect and value religion? Not for the soft-headed, soggy reason that "it makes for a better society" – although it does just that if constructed and practiced well.

No, they respected and valued religion because it was an earthly manifestation of something and someone outside of observable human existence. It made life better even as it explained it. Peter Drucker, the founder of modern management thinking, said,

There is an enormous need to build...the person. That's more than self-respect; it's also the awareness that there is something beyond you, and something beyond the moment, and something that is not only greater than you but different from you.[3]

Religion is defined as a "set of beliefs concerning the cause, nature, and purpose of the universe...usually involving devotional and ritual observances, and often containing a moral code governing the conduct of human affairs...a specific fundamental set of beliefs and practices generally agreed upon by a number of persons."[4] Religion attempts to answer the biggest questions and then to convert those answers into the practices and principles and community that make for a better life.

Those early Americans thought religion was important because they thought that God was important. If there is a God – and those who came to America and the founders and virtually every American for hundreds of years believed that there is – then God's religion was more important than society or government or anything else. As first President George Washington observed in his 1789 Thanksgiving proclamation,

It is the duty of all nations to acknowledge the providence of Almighty God, to obey his will, to be grateful for his benefits, and humbly to implore His protection and favor....[and] to promote the knowledge and practice of true religion and virtue.[5]

Contrary to a lot of discouraging talk, Americans have come to see this role of religion as more, not less, important as the years have gone by. They've become more involved. Research has shown that church attendance in America was actually higher in the 1800s than the 1700s, and higher in the 1900s than the 1800s.[6] Religions have become both greater in number and more varied, offering more avenues to the spiritual seeker.

Once freedom of religion – freedom of conscience – was embedded in thought and law, human spirituality was released to find its home. Spirituality – "of or pertaining to the spirit or soul, as distinguished from the physical nature; spiritual nature is shown in thought, life, etc."[7] – took everything deeper. Spirit came first, then religion. Americans viewed the spirit as "the seat of the moral or religious nature."[8] In America, like nowhere else, religion was organized spiritually.

In America, even the no-God religion of atheism and the maybe-God religion of agnosticism have free reign. They are still religions, talking about God constantly even though they deny or doubt God's existence. But they're free, and they're free to offer their doctrine to all comers – including those who are merely stopping there on their way to God.

Some of this religious impulse was converted into what Alexis de Tocqueville called America's "civil religion" – echoes and shadows of religion captured in beliefs, traditions, and laws. He said,

Religion, which never intervenes directly in the government of American society, should therefore be considered as the first of their political institutions.[9]

But even this civil religion was always tied back to a real God. This civil religion rightly practiced derived from Americans unshelling what they were taught in their churches and held in their hearts, and then practicing those unshelled values in their social, communal, political, and economic lives. Our institutions "presuppose a Supreme Being," said Supreme Court Justice William O. Douglas.[10]

Because of Americans' respect for true religion, they have attacked oppressive and violent and degrading perversions from the beginning. Americans have never had much patience with bad attitudes and behaviors dressed up in religious garb or religion designed to chain the soul or religion used as a club. They have made their disgust clearly known.

But for a very long time now, they refused to throw out the good with the bad. They knew it was foolish to ban religion from public life just because it was sometimes self-righteous or made mistakes, just as it was foolish to favor anarchy because government is sometimes arrogant or harbors a high level of corruption.

Today, however, religion is regularly and nastily mocked in the media and books and blogs. Religion is blamed for everything that the militant atheists believe is wrong with the world and America. God is described as a "fantasy" and God's followers as delusional.

Freedom is an American Idea, and it can and should be used to lambaste religious hypocrisy. Off-base religion should take its lumps. Unfortunately, freedom can be used for more – it can be used to denigrate religion as religion. But actually doing so is light years removed from the American Idea of Religion, which proclaims the religious basis of freedom itself.

In fact, Americans have usually sensed that good religion is primarily about freedom and possibilities, while bad religion is primarily about control and limitations. They know that the best religion finds ways to free people from their shackles, rather than finding new ways to chain them. They know that without good religion, freedom is vulnerable to misuse, abuse, and eradication.

Most Americans know that religion is the starting point, the great and irrevocable foundation of both individual and communal life and liberty. Most Americans have always said,

> ## We Know That If We Only Have a Secular Hope, We Have No Hope

The Continental Congress, on October 12, 1778, declared that

> *True religion and good morals are the only solid foundations of public liberty and happiness.*[11]

Without God, without the spiritual dimension, without spirituality's religious expression, there's no fallback position except natural selection and survival of the fittest.

That's it. What we see is what we've got and there isn't anything more. And what do the fundamentalist Atheists tell us that they see? Some of them are honest and tell us that this life leads to nothingness. But some don't want to face this obvious conclusion to life without God, so they create something beyond flimsy, one of the greatest delusions of them all – a faith in basic human goodness.

They would tell us – have told us – to be good for goodness' sake. But that is an empty platitude mocked by the obvious and massive evil done every day. What is "for goodness' sake," and why should anyone care? Why shouldn't we lie or cheat or steal if it gets us ahead in this war for survival? Virtue may be its own reward, but why shouldn't we discard it if vice makes a better offer? George Washington, always a realist, said,

> Reason and experience both forbid us to expect that national morality can prevail in exclusion of religious principles.[12]

Some non-religious Americans certainly make large contributions to the well-being of others, so faith isn't required to do good works. But they do this because it's built into human nature. Writer C.S. Lewis, referring to World War II, stated this about human beings:

> Taking the race as a whole, they thought that the human idea of decent behavior was obvious to everyone. And I believe they were right. If they were not, then all the things we said about the war were nonsense. What was the sense in saying the enemy were in the wrong unless Right is a real thing which the Nazis at bottom knew as well as we did and ought to have practiced? If they had no notion of what we mean by right, then, though we might still have had to fight them, we could no more have blamed them for that than for the colour of their hair.[13]

If this is so, why don't rich people in other countries make these contributions? Generosity and compassion may indeed be down there somewhere in the bowels of human nature – but it's the American Idea of Religion that brings them to the surface.

But why should anyone do these good things in a world without meaning? In fact, wouldn't they be working against the way things are? To be consistent with the atheists' Darwinian view of the universe and life, shouldn't they let all of these helpless, useless, non-contributing, unfit people die and get out of the way? How is helping them going to aid the human gene pool in its long-term grappling for survival?

All of this leads to a truth, a problem, and a danger:

- Here's the stark truth: Depending on anti-God, now-is-all-we-have beliefs to build a decent society that has respect for unalienable rights – including freedom of conscience – is a fool's errand. It would work, except for...people.

- Here's the big problem: Some of these anti-God believers – not all of them – are fanatical about their faith. They know that there's no God. They're certain that God is a humanly constructed flight of the imagination. They take offense at all religions. They can't really disprove God, so what they have is faith in No God. They're sure of what they can't hope for and certain that what they don't see can't exist.

- Here's the great danger: Although there have always been dogmatic religions – people who are convinced that they've found the one best way or even the only way – only one, in America, has managed in recent times to create the old and unholy alliance with power, the re-uniting of church and state: The secular religion of Dogmatic Atheism.

Dogmatic Atheism's insistence that its doctrine of "no God" be the only acceptable belief has deeply embedded itself into government, schools, and other facets of public life. This doctrinaire religious group has been influential all out of proportion to its numbers. It hides its religious agenda in a secular disguise – it doesn't look like a religion with churches and robes and hymnals, so it must not be one.

The American Idea forbids allowing any religion, including this religion of "no God," to oppress those who believe that there is in fact a special God. And more: Even though people are free to believe in "no God," the Idea warns us that this belief is a terrible foundation for a society that wants to be different, a nation that wants to be decent, and a government that wants to be just. Experience shows that zealotry designed to lead people away from a spiritual heaven can easily lead them to a secular hell.

This religious zealotry certainly doesn't include all atheists, many of whom are often spiritual in their own way without imposing their belief in "nothing higher or after" on others. Some have, in fact, spoken out against the Dogmatists. But a vocal minority of zealots, claiming that they're not a religion even though they are, has gained tremendous traction in making Dogmatic Atheism the American State Religion.

"My version of God at the helm of our country" is a frightening concept. It's just as frightening when that God is "no God" as when that God is the Christian, Islamic, or Jewish God. Samuel Huntington observed that atheists "do not have the right to impose their atheism on all those Americans whose beliefs now and historically have defined America as a religious nation."[14]

As one example of the Trojan Horse nature of this religion of fundamentalist, Dogmatic Atheism, look at the situation with the entrenched, narrow teaching about atheistic evolution. Evolution doesn't require the elimination of God from the equation, and many Americans believe in theistic evolution. But evolution has been transformed by Dogmatic Atheists from science into a religious doctrine, a key element in their creed.

Evolution itself is called a theory (and rightly so). It's a theory for many reasons, not the least of which is that it hasn't been proven. Even more, it may not ever be proven – not empirically, not scientifically. Does that prove that it's wrong? No. Does this mean that it shouldn't be taught? No. But does this mean that it's more than a theory? No. And whether proven or not, can it prove or disprove the existence of God? No.

And yet, what happens now when this is taught in a secular environment where God-based religion is suppressed? Evolution is asked to take on a role for which it is exceedingly unsuited. It's asked to be a technical substitute for God. It's still called a "theory," but that term is quickly discarded, along with any reference to God. Evolution is taught as fact, as indisputable science, and as a complete explanation of life that doesn't require God.

And perhaps worse, opposite to good science, any fact or idea that disagrees with the theory – the creed – is suppressed. Teachers in public schools are not only forbidden to teach about creation or intelligent design, they can't even talk about the holes in the theory of evolution, some of which are gaping still. Jerry A. Coyne, a professor of Ecology and Evolution at the University of Chicago, and a strong proponent of Atheistic Evolution, stated,

> No finding is deemed true...I can think of dozens of potential observations, for instance – one is a billion-year-old ape fossil – that would convince me that evolution didn't happen.[15]

But in this Evolution-without-God world, there is no open inquiry, no dialogue, no questioning, no disagreeing. In this hard-core version of evolution, God is not only absent, but also systematically eliminated.

This isn't science, it's religion. And it isn't even simple faith-based religion – it's dogmatic religion, religion that brooks no dissent. But if they can put "creation" under the topic of "religion," then others should be able to put "atheistic evolution" – some sort of "spontaneous creation" – right next to it under "religion."

It's no less wrong that a newer faith has replaced an older faith in having rigid claims about life and its origins. It's no less wrong that fundamentalism is ruling the class-room once more.

If creation is a religious concept because it offers an explanation that has to be accepted by faith, then atheistic evolution is also a religious concept. In other words, if we have something that isn't proven, that science has no way to prove and may not be able to prove, that has unaddressed gaps and issues, that addresses origins and God (at least by exclusion), but is nonetheless taught as unquestioned and unquestionable fact, then we have an established religion in the government-run schools.

This isn't an argument against evolution. "Should we teach evolution or not?" is too simple, too all or nothing at all. This is instead an argument against teaching religious dogma, against establishing an exclusive doctrine that closes minds, against pretending that a biological theory can substitute for faith and philosophy. This is an abuse of science, biology, and evolution as much as it is an abuse of faith and freedom. Americans generally respect science and revere God – and see no essential conflict between the two.

Why are these fundamentalist atheists so afraid of teaching and having discussions about alternative theories of origins? Because they have dogma that can't permit (or possibly survive) a minor crack in its pseudo-intellectual shield. The high priests of Dogmatic Atheism have to preserve the creed, and they need force and subterfuge to do it. Historian Jacques Barzun noted about evolution that "what is taught about its character and its mechanism is by no means consistent; yet the diversity of views is rarely confided to the student or educated reader."[16]

A vast majority of Americans don't believe this doctrine of evolution-without-God as truth.[17] They reject its dogmatic form and its relentless insistence that there is no God. Most Americans – even those who believe in some sort of evolution – believe in God as Creator. The founders did too, and famously claimed in the Declaration of Independence that this Creator was not only the source of life, but also the source of all rights. President Dwight Eisenhower said,

> Recognition of the Supreme Being is the first, the most basic expression of Americanism. Without God there could be no American form of government, nor an American way of life.[18]

The alternative to God as the source of rights is…what? The government, made up of people who are flawed like the rest of us, but who are also aiming for power over us? A consensus of people with different definitions of rights and different agendas for claiming them? The alternative to this bigger-than-life hope of being endowed by a Creator is hoping against historical and human reality. It is hoping that somehow we will be the one great exception to the irresistible forces of selection and survival, that we'll be able to do good even though there's no reason to do it.

This dogmatic push on atheistic evolution is part of, and is supported by, the "science is truth and religion isn't" mindset. Science can be a wonderful thing, clearing out the darkness and gaining knowledge that can vastly improve human life. But bad science is no better than bad religion, and at times (as with nuclear weapons) can even be more deadly. Science can be inaccurate, biased, untrue, even unscientific. As this essay in *The Atlantic* pointed out:

> We think of the scientific process as being objective, rigorous, and even ruthless in separating out what is true from what we merely wish to be true, but in fact it's easy to manipulate results, even unintentionally or unconsciously…. [A]ssuming modest levels of researcher bias, typically imperfect research techniques, and the well-known tendency to focus on exciting rather than highly plausible theories, researchers will come up with wrong findings most of the time….[T]hough scientists and science journalists are constantly talking up the value of the peer-review process, researchers admit among themselves that biased, erroneous, and even blatantly fraudulent studies easily slip through it.[19]

Saying, "It's only true if we can run it through a process," is arrogant and ignorant, no less than saying, "It's only true if we can find it in the Bible or Qur'an." It leads to a very narrow view of truth. It shuts down thought and discussion about everything that hasn't been or can't be "proven." And perhaps worst of all, making it the supposed fount of all truth turns an excellent human tool into a ridiculous god.

If we're going to keep God and monotheism out of public education and public discourse, then we should keep no-God and atheism out as well. Or we should do the reverse and include them all. How? By taking the crucial step of keeping the government – with its power-shaped values – out of deciding which belief systems are acceptable and out of setting up, through the back door, a state church of atheism.

Should Atheism be banished? By no means. But should it rule? By no means.

Americans learned that belief in God doesn't just offer spiritual salvation and eternal hope. It offers a better way to live in the here and now, a more certain way to secure human rights, and a realistic hope that a country founded on such a belief can lift all of us above the heartless doctrines of survival of the fittest and might-makes-right.

The Idea goes far beyond just putting up with the "unfit," odd people, and divergent beliefs. For centuries, Americans have said,

We Believe in Religious Freedom,
Not Low-Level Religious Tolerance

Freedom of religion has consistently prevailed in the American Idea of Religion. The stench of religious compulsion evaporated in the open space of human liberty. Theologian and founder of the Rhode Island Colony Roger Williams stated,

> *Enforced uniformity confounds civil and religious liberty and denies the principles of Christianity and civility. No man shall be required to worship or maintain a worship against his will.*[20]

In many ways, America was a place of personal spiritual refuge, a place to practice religion free of condemnation or persecution. This didn't always work out, at least right away, as Catholics, Jews, and certain Protestant sects discovered.

But the Idea of freedom of religion was always there, working its way through the American mindset. It pushed until those other religions were also accepted. Just as the powerful idea of everyone being created equal finally annihilated slavery and segregation, so the powerful idea of everyone owning their own soul is destroying religious haughtiness and bigotry.

"Freedom of conscience" was how the early Americans and the founders described it. It wasn't that they wanted someone to grant this freedom to them – they knew that they already had it, that everyone had it. They knew that no one grants this freedom, that it's arrogant to presume to do so, and that it is, in fact, foolish because no one can really control what another person believes.

From the earliest days, this freedom of conscience was something that people were free to live out in two ways:

- First, they had the freedom to practice it alone or in a community. As long as the practice didn't violate anyone's unalienable rights or the rule of law, neither the government nor the society had grounds to interfere.

- Second, they were free to impute their beliefs into the society and government. If they had better ideas about how to relate and govern, bring them on. Sanctity of life, dignity of the individual, equal justice before the law – these and many more began as religious concepts. The notion that beliefs and convictions should have no role in the public arena would have struck most Americans as nonsense. And what kind of religious system wouldn't want to make things better?

This freedom of religion and conscience is different from "tolerance" or "toleration." Tolerance has a wrong sound about it. It never really sat well with Americans. It implies that one religion or another is superior and dominant since someone in a higher place must be doing the "tolerating." And it implies that all other religions are inferior and subordinate because someone in a lower place must be being "tolerated."

Tolerance has a checkered history:

- Tolerance was the way station that Europe chose to try to get away from its endlessly destructive religious wars and persecutions and pogroms, right before it arrived at its destination of largely eliminating religion from its life.

- Tolerance is what certain rigid theocratic Islamic countries barely grant to Christians and other non-Muslims, in part because they need those "infidels" to make their countries "work."

• Tolerance is what many in the Old World offered Jews, right up to the moment that they pillaged or slaughtered them.

• Tolerance is what secularist dictatorships like today's China and the former Soviet empire sham-grant to religion, even while they find ways to make religious life difficult or impossible.

Tolerance is better than oppression and persecution. But it's a far cry from the American Idea of Religion.

While the vast majority of Americans have always shared a unifying belief that there is a God, they have also shared a diversifying belief that there are many ways to relate to that God. So the American Idea has not been about religious tolerance, but about religious freedom. As Alexis de Tocqueville observed in the mid-nineteenth century,

> The Americans combine the notions of Christianity and of liberty so intimately in their minds that it is impossible to make them conceive of the one without the other....[I]n France I had almost always seen the spirit of religion and the spirit of freedom pursuing courses diametrically opposed to each other; but in America I found that they were intimately united, and that they reigned in common over the same country.[21]

He was able to say that religion in America was held "to be indispensible to the maintenance of free institutions."[22]

This American concept of religious freedom was so important that Thomas Jefferson considered one of his three greatest achievements his writing of the Virginia Statutes for Religious Freedom. His other two were writing the Declaration of American Independence and founding the University of Virginia.

He didn't include being President, Vice President, or Secretary of State, and he didn't mention making the Louisiana Purchase. He understood that great concepts like religious freedom, independence from tyranny, and vigorous education were far more important than positions or purchases.

Freedom, not tolerance. That's the American way.

All too often in history, tolerance has slipped into intolerance. More often, unreformed, better-than-you tolerance has dominated cultures. Whatever forms it takes, intolerance is the breeding ground for conflict. Some have minimized or thrown out religion to reduce or avoid this conflict, but this is also not the American way. Americans say,

We Want to Be Free from Religious Wars,
Not from Religion

The most important question isn't "How much evil has religion caused?" (it certainly has caused much) but rather, "How much worse would the human condition be if there were no religion?" or, "How bad could things be if everyone believed that might makes right and that only the strong should survive?"

When a prominent, fundamentalist atheist like Bill Maher can claim that the really terrible wars have always been religious wars, it boggles the mind and should boggle his.[23] How can any intelligent person conveniently forget "tiny" non-religious conflicts like World War I, World War II, Mao Zedong's war on his own people that claimed tens of millions of Chinese lives, Pol Pot's genocide in Cambodia, the countless tribal slaughters in Africa?

Or perhaps, in an odd way, he was right about religion, but simply picked the wrong religion. Prominent Dogmatic Atheists like Maher, Richard Dawkins, and Christopher Hitchens might erroneously believe that monotheism started all of the great wars, but the worst ones in the last century were the atheistic religious wars (Hitler, Stalin, Mao). There is no doubt that these monsters were intolerant religious fanatics, zealous to replace God with...themselves.

Fundamentalist atheism doesn't only take murderous directions. In its no-God zeal, it can work hard to eliminate God and even the concept of God from the public sphere. In the book *Descartes' Bones*, the author finds "atheists such as Christopher Hitchens as intolerant as Islamic or Christian fundamentalists."[24]

But it isn't just Dogmatic Atheism that has threatened to destroy the fabric of the America Idea of Religion. Theistic Religion in America, at times, has had very unwelcome goals and results.

Perhaps the worst case of abuse of religion on American soil came in the support that most churches, by commission or omission, gave to slavery. Most churches in the South supported slavery and misapplied scriptures to justify it. Few churches in the North opposed it. Most churches in all parts of the country were silent on this breathtaking evil (as Henry David Thoreau so clearly pointed out).[25] The Civil War was in some ways a religious war, with both sides supporting their case and their slaughter with the Bible, sermons, and hymns.

Even after slavery was destroyed, the echoes of the old-time religion of divisiveness lived on, with people scouring religious texts to justify racial superiority, separation, or violence. They live on still, in Northern cities that once lambasted Southern cities for those very attitudes. They live on in the attitudes toward immigrants, legal and illegal. They live on because this Idea doesn't eliminate religious nonsense or demagoguery. It only reminds us not to let nonsense or demagoguery rule.

And then there's the war-creating potential of America's "civil" religion, the sometimes vaguely religious notions that get embedded in society and can lead to misguided notions of righteousness. Religious concepts built into civil society and government can be very good indeed, but a strong orientation toward higher things can become a problem when it loses its religious underpinnings and settles for being a civil religion.

This civil religion can combine with government to create a political messiah complex, a conviction of religious proportions that America is correct and sure and true. And more: That it has a right and obligation to help (or force) the unenlightened to see things "correctly." It can too easily cloak itself in exaggerated or erroneous patriotism. It can make flag-waving an unhealthy religious spectacle. Civil religion, no less than any other religion, is an ugly thing when combined with the power and folly of government.

In fact, the American Idea recognizes that religion in all of its manifestations has been one of the most destructive forces in history. Oppression, persecution, slaughter – the evil done in the name of religion stains the pages of history. The first to come from Europe to America had all of that long, terrible history in their minds, if not in their own lives, and wanted to escape it once and forever. The land of the free to millions meant, first and foremost, freedom of religion.

Those who came to America didn't always grant to others what they wanted for themselves. Just as children escaping from abusive homes can become abusive adults – because that is their only template – so religious sufferers have sometimes become the inflictors of religious suffering. But that didn't mean that they were wrong about the Idea. It just meant that they were wrong.

America found a way to have a complete society without having a "total" society – one in which everything is controlled by the same powers, directed from above, and integrated in all details. Having it all in America meant unity and diversity. In the area of religion, that meant a unifying belief in God and God's importance in individual and communal life, and a diversifying belief in how an individual and community could express and live their faith in God. Religion would be a force for good and change, rather than a tool to keep people in their place.

The American Idea is that there is a God who protects and reminds us. Washington said that we should "be devoted to the service of that great and glorious Being who is the beneficent author of all the good that was, that is, or that will be."[26] Lincoln knew that

> No human counsel hath devised nor hath any mortal hand worked out these great things. They are the gracious gifts of the Most High God, who, while dealing with us in anger for our sins, hath nevertheless remembered mercy. It has seemed to me fit and proper that they should be solemnly, reverently and gratefully acknowledged as with one heart and one voice by the whole American People…. I recommend to them that while offering up the ascriptions justly due to Him for such singular deliverances and blessings, they do also with humble penitence for our national perverseness and disobedience, commend to His tender care all those who have become widows, orphans, mourners or sufferers in the lamentable civil strife in which we are unavoidably engaged, and fervently implore the interposition of the Almighty Hand to heal the wounds of the nation and to restore it as soon as may be consistent with the Divine purposes to the full enjoyment of peace, harmony, tranquility, and Union.[27]

They didn't want religion leading to war, but they did want religion leading to greatness.

And religion, with its focus on values and ethics, is a critical component of our collective life. Founder Benjamin Franklin saw God as a driving force behind the American Constitution:

> I have so much Faith in the general Government of the world by Providence, that I can hardly conceive a Transaction of such momentous Importance to

the Welfare of Millions now existing, and to exist in the Posterity of a great Nation, should be suffered to pass without being in some degree influenc'd, guided, and governed by that omnipotent, omnipresent, and beneficent Ruler, in whom all inferior Spirits live, and move, and have their Being.[28]

De Tocqueville said that "in America it is religion which leads to enlightenment and the observance of divine laws which leads men to liberty."[29]   Enlightenment and liberty – not bad religious outcomes.   Founder and Secretary of the Treasury Alexander Hamilton wrote,

To all those dispositions which promote political happiness, Religion and Morality are essential props. In vain does that man claim the praise of patriotism who labours to subvert or undermine these pillars of human happiness these firmest foundations of the duties of men and citizens.... Let it simply be asked where is the security for property for reputation for life if the sense of moral and religious obligation deserts the oaths which are administered in Courts of Justice? Nor ought we to flatter ourselves that morality can be separated from religion....Tis essentially true that virtue or morality is a main & necessary spring of popular or republican Governments.[30]

Ralph Waldo Emerson said, "The end of all political struggle is to establish morality as the basis of all legislation."[31]   That struggle can't possibly be successful without the influence of religion and of religion's God.

Because of this, Americans wanted to create the best home for spiritual impulses and religious expression. Americans came to say,

We Seek a Proper Understanding of the Separation of Church and State – That Religion Has Freedom from Government and Not the Other Way Around

Religious wars? Of course no one wants any more of these. Enough is enough, and many who came to America did so to escape those wars.

But they also came because of the unholy alliance between religion and government, whether or not it led to wars. This alliance was often used to give the religion greater influence and power and the government greater authority and credibility. "A nation must have a religion," observed Napoleon, "and that religion must be under the control of the government."[32]

This connection often worked against religion. But it always worked against the people. Oppressive government was able to misuse religion as a stamp of approval for its lunacies – the egomaniacal "divine right of kings," wars of greed and conquest given a religious veneer, people worked to death as slaves and serfs while being admonished to serve their masters without complaint. Non-spiritual religion was able to misuse government to gain power and wealth and to practice servant leadership – the wrong kind, where the mass of people get to serve the religious leaders.

Hence the fruitful American concept of keeping these two powerful forces – religion and government – separate. The separation of church and state was a breakthrough insight, one that made freedom of religion and conscience viable.

The separation allows religion to work at its best, as an outsider – holding government accountable, being provocative, setting an example. And it has kept religion from being perverted, corrupted, or distracted by a close connection to secular power.

But government has gotten very confused about this whole "separation of church and state" business. They've also gotten very fuzzy about the constitutional guarantee of freedom of religion.

Thomas Jefferson's concern when he talked about the "wall of separation between church and state"[33] had everything to do with keeping government out of the religion business and nothing to do with keeping religious influence out of the government business. He was concerned about religious control of government, not religious influence on government.

Jefferson knew it was folly to eliminate God from public thinking and discourse. To say anything to the contrary about the person who drafted the Declaration of Independence, with its affirmation of a rights-endowing Creator, is gibberish. He said,

> I shall need, too, the favor of that Being in whose hands we are, who led our fathers, as Israel of old, from their native land and planted them in a country flowing with all the necessaries and comforts of life; who has covered our infancy with His providence and our riper years with His wisdom and power, and to whole goodness. I ask you to join in supplications with me that He will so enlighten the minds of your servants, guide their councils, and prosper their measures that whatsoever they do shall result in your good, and shall secure to you the peace, friendship, and approbation of all nations.[34]

The founders were more concerned about government's role in religion than religion's role in government. The constitutional guarantee of freedom of religion was designed in large part to keep the government out of creating a cabal with any religion. In the American Idea, government's response to religion should be to listen to it and absorb its wisdom. Its role in religion is to ensure that no religious group is allowed to take the reins of government and then use that position to make its religion the law of the land or to eliminate other religions.

Note the direction: It is always restricting government, not individuals or churches. The separation of church and state is maintained by controlling the state, not the church. The church – religions – should be free to affect the culture for good. Indeed, it would be a rare set of religious beliefs that wouldn't seek to improve people and their government, and many would question the value of such beliefs.

Because of this, Americans had a dual mission. They said,

There's a huge difference between making a religion the law of the land on the one hand and making religious beliefs a driving force behind government action on the other. Everything is driven by beliefs and values – some religious, some anti-religious, and some non-religious. Why should only religious beliefs and values be marginalized? And how can there be freedom of religion if religion isn't free to affect public policy?

There's a lot of peculiar thinking about this today. It goes something like this:

• Church and state should be separate

• "Church" means the teachings or actions of any religion as they relate to any issue

• These church concerns should be kept away from politics and government because we have this "separation" notion

• Therefore, this or that issue is a church issue that can't be discussed in the political arena ("Abortion a Matter for Theologians" is an actual editorial title that represents this chilling way of dealing with crucial, value-based issues)[35]

• Or it's an issue that the church is not free to discuss and debate (like questioning gunboat diplomacy or a foolish war)

With a flick of the wrist, religion – or any issue of great concern to religion – is eliminated from consideration.

But here's one of the biggest problems with this peculiar way of thinking: Excluding only certain religious beliefs and values is utterly discriminatory. And it perversely puts government in the role of establishing religion in violation of the American Idea and the Constitution.

And what religion has it been establishing for decades? The no-religion or anti-religion sect, the religion of fundamentalist, Dogmatic Atheism. If they say differently, that theirs is a non-religious belief system, they're lying. And they're attempting to use that lie to embed their belief system into the society and the government. And often, they're quite open about theirs being a belief system. The lawyer who has legally attacked having "In God We Trust" on our currency said that "devout atheists are forced to choose between what is often the only available legal tender and committing what they consider blasphemy."[36] Devout? Blasphemy? Totally religious terms.

"We're not an organized church," they counter, "so our belief system is different than a religion." But they're confused. They seem to think that the anti-establishment clause in the Constitution means that the government can't establish a church.

But it never talks about church. What that clause really says is that the government can't establish a *religion*.

That's exactly what it's doing now with its commitment to Dogmatic Atheism, that unshakable belief in nothing (apart from what we see). These fundamentalists may not have a church in the usual meaning of that word, but they most certainly have a religion with a capital "R." They've snuck in under the false claim, "We're not a church" – which isn't even relevant.

The result? Judicial rulings are consistently made against mono-theism and for atheism. They're both belief systems; one committed to a belief in one God, and the other to a belief in no God. Both religious systems require faith, have values, want to be heard, and yearn to have influence on the culture.

Governments and courts in earlier ages favored monotheistic religion and made it the only choice by fiat. Now they've changed the preference and made atheistic religion the government's favorite. Neither approach is aligned with the American Idea of Religion, which says that there should be no government preference whatsoever.

Religion in any form is in the wrong place when it is legislated or set up by government, but is in the right place when it influences what the government is trying to legislate or set up. In a free society, there's plenty of room for religion between the unappetizing choices of a harsh theocracy on the one hand and an established secular wasteland on the other. And there's plenty of room for all of that religion in the middle to strongly influence everything the government does.

The alternative is to try to run a government on beliefs and values deliberately stripped of any positive religious content. That's the real threat, not some "Joe McCarthy" scare tactic about a potential theocracy. We've already seen the end game, the result of a religion-erased approach in full swing – courtesy of Stalin, Zedong, Hitler, Idi Amin, Pol Pot, and other atheistic religious fanatics on a mission.

President James Polk said, "In assuming responsibilities so vast I fervently invoke the aid of that Almighty Ruler of the Universe in whose hands are the destinies of nations and of men to guard this Heaven-favored land against the mischiefs which without His guidance might arise from an unwise public policy."[37] Rulers-without-religion is a formula for "mischiefs."

America found a way to separate church and state without separating religion and state or spirituality and state. Americans didn't want the state to designate a church or religion as "the one" or to dictate what people could believe. But they also didn't want the state to be free from the influence of religion or religious people.

Americans never wanted an irreligious, unspiritual, amoral government. In fact, they wanted a vigorous religious community to help ensure that they wouldn't end up with one of those.

Americans were sure that the foundation of a successful society and government had to be religion. They said strongly that

Without Establishing It in Law or Marginalizing Those
Who Believe Otherwise, We Know That American Ideas
Are Established on a Specific Religious Base

What is the religious base of America?

Americans are "a Christian people," observed President Abraham Lincoln.[38]   We can say clearly and accurately that biblical Christianity – even with all of its flaws as practiced – was at the base of the experiment called America. President John Adams said,

> With humble reverence, I feel it to be my duty to add, if a veneration for the religion of a people who profess and call themselves Christians, and a fixed resolution to consider a decent respect for Christianity among the best recommendations for the public service, can enable me in any degree to comply with your wishes, it shall be my strenuous endeavor that this…shall not be without effect.[39]

We see it undeniably in the Mayflower Compact, a founding American document, signed on November 21, 1620. They wrote,

> Having undertaken, for the glory of God, and advancement of the Christian faith…a voyage to plant the first colony in the northern parts of Virginia, do by these presents, solemnly and mutually in the presence of God….[40]

President John Quincy Adams was unequivocal about the connection between America and Christianity:

> Is it not that the Declaration of Independence first organized the social compact on the foundation of the Redeemer's mission upon Earth? That it laid the cornerstone of human government upon the first precepts of Christianity?[41]

Those who came brought their beliefs with them, and those beliefs were overwhelmingly Christian. Even if they didn't read (or even have) a Bible, they generally accepted it as a book from a higher place, one to live by individually and collectively. And when they came to America, they found the Bible and Christianity literally at the door – the literacy test cards at Ellis Island were Bible verses, printed first in the immigrant's own language, and then in English.[42] President John Adams said that the Bible

> offers the only system that ever did or ever will preserve a republic in the world.[43]

There are those who say that America is "not a Christian nation."[44] A president said that, ironically, while standing in the city that was Christian and a Christian capital (of the Eastern Roman Empire, later the Byzantine Empire) for over a thousand years – until it was taken by force in 1453 by a nation that was most certainly "not a Christian nation." Europe was itself set to face the same fate as Constantinople until those same people were finally defeated by Eugene of Savoy at the gates of Vienna in 1683.[45]

217

Without that intervention by Christian armies, Europe wouldn't look today even as open as Turkey does. It would look like Turkey did before World War I when the Turkish Ottoman Empire was finally defeated by Christian Western Europe, and the Caliphate gave way to the somewhat secular and non-fundamentalist government of Ataturk. Europe instead would look like the Middle East without the oil.

Pandering to nations that are religious – but not Christian – by claiming that your own nation isn't Christian might, at best, gain some of the wrong kind of international popularity points. It's hard to see how that can amount to anything of value for America. And where do those who make these false claims about American origins think American Ideas came from, if not from Christian principles? What exactly does someone mean when they say that America isn't a Christian nation?

If someone means by "Christian nation" that everyone in that nation is, or has to be, a professing Christian, then of course America is not now and never has been a "Christian nation." But that's a straw man. We're talking about the foundation of American society as a whole, not the foundation of individual people.

So if we mean by "Christian nation" that the nation was founded on Christian principles – not Islamic, Buddhist, Hindu, Confucian, or Atheistic, but Christian – then of course America is a Christian nation. A few examples:

- It was said about the founder of Christianity that "it is for freedom that he has set us free,"[46] while other belief systems teach submission or acceptance of oppression and tyranny or that freedom itself is an illusion. Alexis de Tocqueville observed that

  > America is still the place where the Christian religion has kept the greatest real power over men's souls; and nothing better demonstrates how useful and natural it is to man, since the country where it now has the widest sway is both the most enlightened and the freest....For the Americans the ideas of Christianity and liberty are so completely mingled that it is almost impossible to get them to conceive of the one without the other.... [47]

- Christianity teaches that there are no distinctions between people and that no people are more valuable than others, while other religions teach that other people are outsiders, infidels to be used or killed, or dwellers in a lower caste.

- While the Christian principle is to "love your enemies,"[48] the ruling principle in many systems ranges from devaluing them to killing them. President Calvin Coolidge said about America, "The legions which she sends forth are armed, not with the sword, but with the cross. The higher state to which she seeks the allegiance of all mankind is not of human, but of divine origin. She cherishes no purpose save to merit the favor of Almighty God."[49]

It was Christianity that created the great regard for the individual human being rather than the community or the power structure. Look everywhere in America, and you see the Christian principles of individual value, dignity, justice, equality, and generosity. General Washington, in a general order to his troops announcing the Declaration of Independence, said that he

> Hopes and trusts, that every officer and man, will endeavor so to live, and

act, as becomes a Christian Soldier defending the dearest Rights and Liberties of his country.[50]

President and World War II General Dwight Eisenhower made the connection between America and the Bible clear:

The Bible is endorsed by the ages. Our civilization is built upon its words. In no other book is there such a collection of inspired wisdom, reality and hope....That's where our nation started. That's where my parents and forefathers started...a faithful reading of Scripture provides the courage and strength required for the living of our time.[51]

America was established on Christian principles, by Christians and people with Christian mindsets. To say anything else is to deny basic historical reality. In fact, America is much more than a Christian nation – America is a Christian society. And it's even more than that – America is a Christian civilization, the end product of 1700 years of Christianized Western culture. Abraham Lincoln, in his first inaugural address, said,

Intelligence, patriotism, Christianity, and a firm reliance on Him who has never yet forsaken this favored land are still competent to adjust in the best way all our present difficulty.[52]

Clearly he saw that Christianity and God were centerpieces of American life.

Americans who understand the American Idea of Religion don't want to establish the Bible as the law of the land, because they know from hard experience that this will mean a certain religion's or sect's version of the Bible, not the Bible itself. This is what happened in Europe, in Protestant and Catholic countries alike.

And it's what happened in some Muslim countries a thousand years ago, when the branch of Islam that wanted its rigid interpretation of the Qur'an to become the law of the land triumphed. This brought the rejection of openness and inquiry, invention and progress, and women as first-class citizens. Their theocratic imposition crippled a culture that was arguably one of the most advanced in the world.[53]

The American Idea also makes no room for marginalizing those with non-Christian beliefs. They have full rights as citizens, including a complete right to freedom of religion. They can and should be heard in the public square. If their beliefs and values serve to advance the society, it would be foolish not to welcome them and incorporate them. But if those beliefs and values set themselves against the American Ideas – like the dignity of all people, including women – they should be rejected, even as those who hold those beliefs and values are still fully respected.

What do people under the influence of this American Idea say? We don't want women to be treated as second-class or no-class citizens. We don't want "lower classes" to be degraded and allowed to die like dogs in the streets. We don't want a place where the "other" – the other religion or color or race or whatever – is disrespected or destroyed. We don't want a society where only the strong survive.

We've been there, done that, and don't want these things any more. We want better than what we see around the world. We want the American Idea, the one founded, as Lincoln noted, on the solid rock of Christian principles. Thomas Jefferson told us,

The Christian religion…is a religion of all others most friendly to liberty, science, and the freest expansion of the human mind.[54]

This foundation was both strong enough and broad enough to make room for all faiths and no faiths, unlike what we see even today in other countries with a dominant religious system. No one should ever be ashamed of, unaware of, or antagonistic toward the origin of so much that's great about America: the best of Christianity.

And we should remember that the first person in history to talk about the separation of church and state wasn't Thomas Jefferson. It was the first Christian, Jesus. He said, "Render unto Caesar that which is Caesar's, and unto God what is God's."[55]

Looking around the world and through the history books, we see a persistent (if, to some, annoying) truth: It is basically problematic for a society to be strongly influenced by any religion other than Christianity – and even it must be watched like a hawk.

Winston Churchill told us that democracy was the worst of all political systems, except for all of the others.[56] Some belief system is going to dominate every culture. Christianity, with its flaws, may be the worst – except for all the others.

You don't have to be a Christian to see its hand in the creation of America, to accept it as a force for dignity and freedom, to accept it as a framework for justice and equality, to want it as a driver of opportunity and responsibility – and perhaps most upside-down, to acknowledge it as the base of religious freedom. If you want to be free to believe and practice your religion, whatever it is, Christian America is the place for you.

The House Judiciary Committee reported in 1854,

> *At the time of the adoption of the Constitution and the amendments, the universal sentiment was that Christianity should be encouraged….In this age, there is no substitute for Christianity….That was the religion of the founders of the republic and they expected it to remain the religion of their descendants.*[57]

The Supreme Court agreed with this in 1931, when it reaffirmed Lincoln's declaration and said that,

> *We are a Christian people, according to one another the equal right of religious freedom, and acknowledging with reverence the duty of obedience to the will of God.*[58]

British historian Paul Johnson, in his magisterial *History of Christianity*, wrote about Christianity's value in giving freedom rather than taking it away. He said,

> *Its strength lies in its just estimate of man as a fallible creature with immortal longings. Its outstanding moral merit is to invest the individual with a conscience, and bid him follow it. This particular form of liberation is what St. Paul meant by the freedom men find in Christ. And, of course, it is the father of all other freedoms. For conscience is the enemy of tyranny and the compulsory society…. The notions of political and economic freedom both spring from the workings of the Christian conscience as a historical force; and it is thus no accident that all the implantations of freedom throughout the world have ultimately a Christian origin.*[59]

America wasn't founded as a Christian theocracy, and we can be thankful for that. But it was founded as a Christian nation, and we should be very thankful for that. Because of this reality,

We Know That Severing or Minimizing That Foundation Jeopardizes the Whole Dynamic Structure of America

Alexis de Tocqueville wrote, "It was religion that gave birth to the English colonies in America. One must never forget that."[60]

Without its Christian foundation, what does America look like?

We don't have to look hard for an answer. We can begin with those who also had a Christian influence. Europe, having largely abandoned its Christian roots, is eating its seed corn. It's living off the social and political capital of a religious heritage it no longer embraces or respects, one that it barely acknowledges. The account is nearly overdrawn, and no new deposits have been made for a very long time. It doesn't remember where its ideas came from, a sure formula for seeing those ideas fade away.

Europe's fortunes have declined in parallel with its decline in Christian belief – in France during its anti-clerical Revolution in the 18th century, in Germany with its destructive "higher criticism" of the Bible in the 19th century, and in Great Britain and the rest of Protestant Europe in its multi-war haze in the 20th century. Europe's new god is the welfare state – a state which has no divinity, no soul, and no ability to inspire a people to greatness and, ultimately, no way to deliver welfare.

And it's not just Europe where poor religious thinking negatively affects the direction of an entire culture. The former colonies of the ruthless Spanish and Portuguese imperialists in South and Central America have been crippled by a twisted religious teaching. "In the United States," noted Italian philosopher and novelist Umberto Eco, "there's a Puritan ethic....He who is successful is good. In Latin countries...a successful person is a sinner."[61]

Ideas have consequences. The consequences of religious ideas are almost always profound. The loss of good religious ideas can take with it a thousand magnificent benefits. As second President and founder John Adams warned,

> *We have no government armed with power capable of contending with human passions unbridled by morality and religion....Our Constitution was made only for a moral and religious people. It is wholly inadequate to the government of any other.*[62]

So we should work very hard not to lose the strong, positive Christian underpinnings of American culture. The application of this Idea in public (community) schools, for example, would sound something like this: "Whether we like it or not, this nation was founded on a belief in a real and powerful God, whether that God was called 'Almighty' or 'Father,' 'Jehovah' or 'Providence.' And that God was almost universally the Christian God."

Not just any religion could have driven the creation of the America we know. There is simply no way that America would be what it is without the Christian foundation. Not with Islam, Hinduism, Confucianism, Buddhism, Atheism, secularism, communism, or any other religious "ism." Simply looking around the world proves the point – the Middle East, India, Pakistan, China, really almost anywhere. There's no mystery about how America would look. Just look at them.

There may be many positive qualities in those other religions. But these attributes don't necessarily translate into things that are central to the life of the individual – a dynamic society, a vibrant economy, constant innovation, expanding opportunity… and above all else, freedom.

The problem isn't just other "formal" religions. Jefferson thought that atheism and freedom were fundamentally and ultimately incompatible. He wrote, "Can the liberties of a nation be thought secure when we have removed their only firm basis, a commitment in the minds of the people that these liberties are a gift of God?"[63] He said that America was

> [e]nlightened by a benign religion, professed, indeed, and practiced in various forms, yet all of them inculcating honesty, truth, temperance, gratitude, and the love of man; acknowledging and adoring an overruling Providence, which by all its dispensations proves that it delights in the happiness of man here and his greater happiness hereafter – with all these blessings, what more is necessary to make us a happy and prosperous people?[64]

Historian Paul Johnson observed that "the essential difference between the American Revolution and the French Revolution is that the American Revolution, in its origins, was a religious event, whereas the French Revolution was an anti-religious event."[65] The love of religion helped to create America. The hatred of religion helped to destroy France.

We want people to be able to practice any belief system that suits them. We just don't want to be ruled by them. Any of these belief systems may be one's individual religious preference, and that's perfectly fine. But that doesn't provide a free pass to deny the logic of where those systems will take a whole society.

The historical reality is this: All religions might provide some comfort to an individual, but only one has ever provided every individual with freedom, rights, and opportunity.

The vast majority of Americans has always believed in God and the Christian interpretation of who that God is, and they still do.[66] Americans have always wanted their laws to at least take account of that God. And Americans have always wanted their laws to protect their right to find their own spiritual way.

It is an outstanding place to be, unique in world history – a place where we know that we answer as a people to God, and yet answer as individuals to our own consciences.

"The ideas that define Western civilization, Nietzsche said, are based on Christianity," noted Dinesh D'Souza. "Because some of these ideas seem to have taken on a life of their own, we might have the illusion that we can abandon Christianity while retaining them. This illusion, Nietzsche warns us, is just that. Remove Christianity and the ideas fall too."[67]

Being ashamed of a foundation that has provided so much good is shameful. But it is where the Dogmatic Atheists are trying to take us. They want Americans to see Christianity as mushy at best and evil at worst. But they couldn't be more wrong.

Take away that foundation, and America may not instantly crumble. It just won't be America.

America At Its Best

The American Idea of Religion has incorporated a complete view of God. It is one that still includes demands for justice and righteousness and decency, but also one that includes demands for understanding and graciousness and respect. Keeping this Idea alive means that we should:

Take Action

Deeply appreciate the powerful and positive role that religion has had in American.

★

Welcome religious expression in the public square.

★

Encourage religious influence on government, while avoiding religious control of government.

★

Remember that the main reason to separate church and state is to protect the church.

★

Allow the people, not the unelected judges, to decide where the line should be between church and state.

★

Refuse to allow the government and its judges to curtail religious freedom.

★

Insist that God and religion be talked about freely in public schools and universities.

★

Refuse to allow science to be presented as opposed to religion, or to be offered as a substitute for religion.

★

Eliminate the "speak out and you lose your exemption" threat.

★

Boycott religion-mockers.

★

Avoid giving preferential treatment to religions, like Dogmatic Atheism, that pretend not to be religions.

★

Rejoice in the Christian roots that have elevated America, even if you aren't a Christian.

★

Remember well the alternatives to religion and Christianity.

To see detail on these Action Points and
to add your voice visit www.theamericanideas.com

The connection between religion and society has always been tight. It has only been considered highly problematic under the onslaught of highly religious but cleverly disguised religious Atheism and of unfounded religious relativism (all religions are equally valuable).

We can have that connection back. And we need it back. It has served us incredibly well for four hundred years.

Religion and the American Idea

I've lived, sir, a long time, and the longer I live, the more convincing proofs I see of this truth: That God governs in the affairs of men. If a sparrow cannot fall to the ground without His notice, is it probable that an empire can arise without his aid?[68]

The great wisdom of founder, statesman, and philosopher Benjamin Franklin represents what has always been at the root of this great American Idea: There is a God, this God is aware and powerful and involved, and a nation without God cannot ultimately be great.

Niccolo Machiavelli, who saw life without sentiment, wrote, "There is no surer sign of decay in a country than to see...religion held in contempt."[69]

America is still far from that sign of decay. But it has moved in that direction, and the forces in play are pushing hard to make that movement pick up speed. Decay is a very bad destination. We're heading there, but we can choose to change our direction.

The American Idea has been that religion is mainly a force for good. Even a relentless propagandist for the a-religious (or anti-religious) secular statists noted that some people "scoff [at religious faith], but the balm that comes with being part of a religious community – the Bible study, youth groups, choirs, and, yes, the moral absolutes that often accompany such communion – is real and comforting, unlike the promise of complicated and expensive government programs."[70]

America has somehow captured the way to be religious without giving up its secular street smarts. A senior official in the Vatican noted,

America is simultaneously a completely modern and a profoundly religious place. In the world, it is unique in this.[71]

America embodies a vital truth – that there's no necessary contradiction between religion and progress. There's no other place like it on the planet.

So what can we say about this American Idea of Religion? That spiritual things are too important to be ignored by individuals or high-jacked by religions. That religious things are too important to be ignored by society or hijacked by government.

And that all people should be free, right down to their souls, all the way down to where those souls touch forever.

CHAPTER 10

The American Idea of Society

What is this thing called "society"?

American revolutionary Tom Paine described it this way: "Society is produced by our wants, and government by our wickedness..."[1]

Wants. If we didn't want anything from other people, we wouldn't need society. We could become hermits or recluses. We could move to a mountain hideaway and grow our own food. We really could live out our lives as though we were an island, separated by a great distance from others of our kind.

But most people can't and won't live that way. They want to be in the midst of the swirl of human life, surrounded by family and friends and neighbors, co-workers and customers and vendors, artisans and entertainers and volunteers. They might not like many of their fellow citizens and travelers, but they don't like being alone even more.

Society makes its own demands in exchange for satisfying our wants. Society defines what's acceptable. Then it nurtures and defends the acceptable and diminishes or banishes everything else.

There are always those who chafe under society's demands and expectations. Sometimes this is good, when a society has become encrusted with artificial limits and oppressive boundaries and truthful revolutionaries come forward. And often this is bad, after society has found a happy place for people to tap into their best selves and lying revolutionaries steal their joy.

America constructed a unique society, one that enabled the good life in all that this means. Americans know the importance of that society, and they like its freedom and opportunity. They also see society being degraded and, somewhere deep inside, resent those who use freedom and opportunity to carry out their relentless attacks.

Long before Lyndon Johnson used the term, Americans constructed a great society. They want it back. Much more than their government, it defines who they are.

Society

Society is the communal environment in which relationships live and grow.

Society is valuable if it nurtures, edifies, and exalts each person who is a part of it.

Society has no rights, only obligations – to create a safe forum for ideas, communication, discussion, relationships, families, religion, commerce, and generosity.

Society can be multi-cultural but not omni-cultural.

While government is concerned with what is legal, society is concerned with what is appropriate.

We know that there is a vast gulf between an open society and an open sewer.

Societies that pollute and destroy should be condemned and changed, while societies that protect and defend should be commended and conserved.

Before it is anything else,

Society Is the Communal Environment in Which Relationships Live and Grow

Society is the way of life that human beings construct for themselves together. Sometimes it's deliberate, but more often grows out of countless interactions over decades and centuries. Norms develop and become entrenched – constructively if those norms are good, destructively if they aren't. Society, in many ways, is "the way things are."

Society is about identity and direction, values and behaviors. It answers extremely important questions that human beings have always asked:

- Who are we as a people?

- What makes us special?

- Where are we heading?

- Is that destination good or bad?

- How should we act?

- How should we treat each other?

- What makes for the good life?

Governments and rulers have tried to answer these questions. But these questions are too big and complex to be addressed by politicians, too difficult and meaningful to be addressed by government, and too easily misused and mis-answered to be addressed by those with power. Only we, the people, can answer them well.

Societies are as different as the people who make them up. Some emphasize the individual, while others focus on the community. Some honor life, while others degrade and end it. Some love freedom, while others loathe it. Some provide opportunities even for those who have little, while others concentrate opportunities with those who already have much.

Good societies nurture healthy communities and relationships. They provide healthy boundaries within which humanity's better side can flourish. They restrain without having to have the heavy, clumsy hand of government involved. They encourage freedom but prevent it from leading to decadence. They provide many opportunities to develop human potential, in part by boxing in the destructive forces inside every human being.

Toxic societies can go one of two ways. Neither appeals to Americans.

On the one hand, they can promise maximum freedom even as toxic societies deliver growing slavery. Freedom without boundaries becomes license, no limits becomes no commitments, and opportunity to try everything becomes entrapment by drugs, alcohol, gambling, sex, or a host of other pleasure-to-death transactions.

On the other hand, toxic societies can be so restrictive that they minimize or eliminate human freedom. Even healthy and innocent activities can be banished to a forbidden world. The pursuit of happiness becomes harder and eventually impossible.

Society is the source from which all relationships flow. One of the most important things any people can do is recognize the primal role of society in forming individual and communal life. Society is the great, unseen, character-forming sculptor.

Keeping that sculptor's hand steady can produce great people and culture over generations. Keeping that relational source as clean as possible is, along with maintaining a healthy regard for religion and respecting the dignity of the individual, indispensable to unleashing human potential. In fact,

*Society Is Valuable if It Nurtures, Edifies,
and Exalts Each Person Who Is a Part of It*

There have been many debates through the centuries about whether this or that custom or tradition is better than a similar custom or tradition in another society.

Is this a better way to eat and drink? Should meals be quick or leisurely? Is this a better way to dress? Is public transportation or driving preferred? Is it better to drive on the left or right side of the road? Should homes and apartments be large or small? There's plenty to debate in a wildly diverse world.

But this is the wrong measuring stick. The value of a society isn't in the fact that it has customs and traditions or that these are better in its eyes than some other society's customs and traditions. The value is in the society's ability to care for and improve the lives of the people who make it up.

There are many different and legitimate ways for people to live in community. If those ways build people and relationships up, they're good ways. They may be different from what others do, and they may not be the best ways, but in themselves they're good ways.

So what determines if this or that "good way" is better? The critical point is whether that society focuses on its members (the individual) or on itself (the community).

In the American Idea of Society, the greatest good comes from societal ways that focus on the individual. Given a choice between two good ways, the Idea comes down on the side of the one that most enhances individual life. Other societies may lean towards those ways that best advance the community. That's a choice some societies could make.

It just isn't the American choice.

If the community is elevated, the individual disappears into the faceless crowd. The community can become overbearing and oppressive as it is today in the Middle East, China, and other places. The community can pretend to speak for everyone when it only speaks for some, inaccurate at best and delusional at worst. Bad things can be done in the name of community – "nation," "country," the "people" – that are actually destructive to its members. This was a lesson learned in depth in the French Revolution. British philosopher John Stuart Mill wrote that if society

> *issues wrong mandates instead of right, or any mandates at all in things with which it ought not to meddle, it practises a social tyranny more formidable than many kinds of political oppression, since, though not usually upheld by such extreme penalties, it leaves fewer means of escape, penetrating much more deeply into the details of life, and enslaving the soul itself. Protection, therefore, against the tyranny of the magistrate is not enough...*[2]

Because of this, he says,

> *There needs protection also against the tyranny of the prevailing opinion and feeling; against the tendency of society to impose, by other means than civil penalties, its own ideas and practices as rules of conduct on those who dissent from them; to fetter the development, and, if possible, prevent the formation of any individuality not in harmony with its ways, and compel all characters to fashion themselves upon the model of its own.*[3]

If the individual is elevated, the community is still extremely important, in part because it is needed by the individual. But now community is a vehicle to meet individual needs rather than a vehicle to expand its own role and power. It's the difference between community as servant and community as master, community as influencer and community as coercer, community as persuader and community as manipulator.

We can have a vibrant individuality and a vibrant community at the same time. But one or the other has to take precedence. We can pretend to keep them in equal proportions, but unless the individual is deliberately made primary, the default position is always the community – or one of its powerhouse forms, the nation or the government.

Community first is the norm. Individual first is the American exception.

So the American Idea has been that society is there to meet people's wants as individuals. Part of those wants is a widespread desire to live in a healthy community, so that the "together" part isn't ignored. But the society is there primarily to nurture, edify, and exalt the individual – the only entity on the planet created by a higher power with rights. Society is there to:

• Nurture individuals. Is the society creating and maintaining a safe place for children? Do they feel respected regardless of their many differences? Is education really open, devoid of the dogmatic assertions of left or right? Are young people protected from unsought exposure to the slimy side of human life? Are they defended not only in their bodies, but also in their hearts and minds?

• Edify individuals. Does the society by and large provide people with positive experiences? Are citizens, neighbors, leaders, entrepreneurs, employers, employees, volunteers, partners, and customers made to feel valuable or like cogs in a faceless machine? Is rude behavior rejected and condemned? Are people told "no" graciously? Is gratitude freely given and highly prized?

• Exalt individuals. Does society honor those who make it better? Does it reward risk taking and sacrifice? Does it praise individuals for doing what's done in other societies by the government (or not at all)? Does it persuade its youth and citizens that they can be great people rather than dependents or self-designated victims? Are its members unembarrassed to talk about God?

The best that can be said about some societies, now and throughout history, is that they were no worse than any of the others. They all disregard the individual. Nurturing, edifying, and exalting haven't even been on their menu. But in America, these activities are the main course.

So is it better for a society to be conservative or progressive in order for it to carry out this nurturing, edifying, exalting mission well?

The answer is: of course.

Society is at its best where conservative and progressive are not only blended, but are also mutually reinforcing. This is the place where society conserves everything that is valuable and progresses beyond everything that isn't. It holds onto ideas like, "God is the Creator of equal human beings with unalienable rights," and loses ideas like, "Women and minorities are second-class or no-class citizens." It doesn't progress beyond God, and it doesn't conserve bigotry.

But great societies go well beyond this solid and necessary foundation.

They allow good "old" ideas not only to be conserved, but also to be improved. They want progressive thinking to update those valuable norms, to ensure their vitality and validity over time. They refine what it means to be equal and build solid protections around unalienable rights. They know that it's often folly to throw out the dilapidated old concept rather than to develop it. People in great societies want to be progressive conservatives.

And they allow good "new" ideas not only to be introduced, but also to be tethered to the social treasure that already exists. They want these new ideas to drive out bad ideas but not drive out good ideas in the bargain. They want to make sure that these progressive concepts don't invalidate those that have already improved society and made it a good place to inhabit. They conserve the real and immensely valuable differences between men and women and refuse to let minorities go beyond ensuring equality to tyrannizing the majority. People in great societies want to be conservative progressives.

So what is a society really worth? It depends on what it does. A society can be worth everything – or nothing.

Although a society can have worth, it doesn't have personhood. It wasn't created by God in God's image. The American Idea of Society includes the reminder that

Society isn't a human being with unalienable rights.

The only thing created by God with unalienable rights is the individual person. Groups can band together to secure these rights, but the groups themselves are right-less – whether those groups are voluntary associations of like-minded people, political parties, the government, or the society itself.

Society isn't a being without rights – it isn't a "being" at all. It's a description of our cultural life, of the way we are and the way we want to be. It is a cultural life that human beings have constructed to allow them to enjoy their unalienable rights to the full. It's there for a purpose. And as such, it has obligations to the members who grant it life.

What are those obligations? They're many, but at their core, they are related to the concept of creating a place – a safe place – for important human activity to take place. Society has obligations to create a safe forum for

- *Ideas.* Arabic Islamic culture became an unsafe place for most new ideas in the 11th and 12th centuries, the hangover of which is still felt today. European Christian culture followed suit in the 13th, 14th, and 15th centuries, only countermanded by a Renaissance, Reformation and Counter-Reformation, all sprinkled with countless political and religious wars. Secular culture has taken the baton in the 20th and 21st centuries, and the end will be just as unpleasant unless ideas are valued once more. Free, great societies make room for good ideas, new and old, and look askance at dogmatism and the closure of minds.

- *Communication.* Anti-individual, anti-freedom societies want to manage all communication. They want to eliminate anything that could stir up liberty, the eternal enemy of all tyranny. Their efforts range from spinning and staying "on message" to burying facts and controlling the internet. Someone has said that political correctness is the triumph of niceness over truth.[4] At its root, it's a prohibition of free speech and a demolition of the marketplace of ideas. Even programs that stake a claim to open dialogue can be infected by it, as evidenced by the ridicule heaped on people who defend disagreeable notions. Open, great societies say, "Yes," to all communication except that which directly encourages violence or societal destruction.

- *Discussion.* Crippling societies want to shut down discussion or set the rules about what can be discussed. They use declarations like "The debate is over," "All (scientists, educators, experts, authorities, etc.) agree," and, "Anyone who takes a contrary view is a flat-earther." We talk of the importance of diversity, and rightly so. But what about diversity of thought? Of opinion? A key element of a free society is the ability to permit people to believe and say obnoxious things as long as those things don't harm others or create an environment that clearly leads to the harming of others. Prejudices can't be legislated away – only putting those prejudices into harmful action can and should be. Vibrant, great societies encourage rich and continuous discussion and get nervous when no one disagrees.

- *Relationships.* Hierarchical, class-based societies set severe limits around relationships – what's possible, what's allowed, what's acceptable. They want relationships to form and exist only on the society's terms. Connected, great societies want every beneficial relationship that can be formed to have a chance to form – and blossom.

- *Families.* The worst societies have demolished families through slavery, feudalism, and oppression. Others burden families with onerous taxes and overwhelming expectations and an insistence that relational ugliness and abuse be tolerated. Stable, great societies know that every living and future human being comes from a family and needs family to give him or her context and support. They recognize that raising and maintaining a family is a difficult and expensive mission. They ask the question, "How can we make this easier?"

- *Religion.* Societies that fancy themselves brilliant and rational and above the "pie in the sky" of religion try to construct a fine a-religious or anti-religious culture and too easily end up with a Soviet Union full of tyranny and gulags or a China full of Cultural Revolution and dead bodies. Meaningful, great societies treasure a positive religious impulse. They welcome the grace, benevolence, and sacrifice that come from one of its hands and the truth, accountability, and admonition that come from the other.

- *Commerce.* Foolish societies denigrate business and finance, believing that commerce is the source (or at least the main source) of greed and corruption. They make it hard to start a business, hard to run a business, and hard to stay in business. They allow commerce as a necessary evil and debate what few things they might allow business to do. They also work hard to drain business (often to feed the greed and corruption of politicians, bureaucrats, and their supporters). Prosperous, great societies view commerce as a necessary good and debate what few things they might need to forbid business from doing.

- *Generosity.* Selfish societies view personal generosity as simple-minded and even wasteful. They think it's enough for each person to provide for themselves and to have the government take care of the problems. Gracious, great societies are notable for their volunteering, philanthropic spirit and take strong steps to encourage rather than diminish it.

In the American Idea, a society that fulfills these obligations in a consistently first-rate manner has achieved the most that can be expected out of human interaction.

This society may not be Utopia, but given prior attempts at Utopia – where one person's utopian dream becomes everyone else's utopian nightmare – that is a good thing. It may not be Utopia, but it's even better because it's real and produces real – not imagined – benefits to those who live there.

In the American Idea, this first-rate society doesn't have to be homogeneous, where everyone looks alike and sounds the same. In fact, it's understood that homogeneity can cripple the society and steal away its vibrancy. So the great society is the multi-cultural society. But here, there's a caution. The Idea recognizes that

Society Can Be Multi-Cultural but Not Omni-Cultural

Many societies have been uni-cultural. The society and the culture are one. There are no divergent ideas, voices, or faces. Japan is a current example of a uni-cultural society. It's easy to fit in if you're a member of the homogeneous culture, but it's difficult or impossible if you're not. It has the advantage of tight cohesiveness as well as the disadvantage of tight cohesiveness.

Others societies are unhappy omni-cultural societies – societies made up of many un-integrated, disconnected cultures. They often tend to drive toward uni-culturalism. This is pushed forward either by the majority culture, or the most powerful culture regardless of size, or an ad-hoc coalition of cultures united by their hatred of the "others." The methods they use involve marginalizing, driving out, or eliminating their minority sub-cultures.

European societies marginalized the Jews before driving them out and finally exterminating them. The Turks did the same with the Christian Armenians after World War I. Tribes in sub-Saharan Africa have done this for centuries, both before and after colonial rule. The Indians did this with the Muslims, and the Pakistanis did it with the Hindus. The Balkans have been a poster child for omni-cultural madness.

It's no different today. The majority culture doesn't know what to do with the minority culture – English with Indian, French with Muslim, German with Turk, Arab with Christian, Chinese with Tibetan.

These omni-cultural societies share the same geography but nothing else. Each grouping seeks to live out its life apart from the alien cultures around it, to live happily – or at least separately – in their clan. In this sense, another word for "omni-cultural" is "tribal."

We're living in a world where empires yielded to nationalism, and now nations are yielding to tribalism. In some cases, this has led to open warfare and destruction, as it did with the European tribalism that led to the World War of 1914-1945, and as it is doing now in the Middle East and much of Africa. But tribalism is also advancing within nations, as people identify with ever-smaller groups and then make these groups into their "whole."

The apparent short-term freedom to tribalize, to isolate and become hyphenated people, to have a variety of languages spoken, has only ever led to internal warfare, both political and actual. This is a curse on the liberty of all. To complicate matters, this is occurring in a world that is economically going the other way and globalizing. Building an ever more complex and integrated global economy on an ever more simplistic and fragmented cultural model is not a formula for success in either economy or society.

In a sense, tribalism is nationalism and self-identity carried too far. When my uniqueness separates me from others and excludes them from who I am rather than merely being one of the things that makes me who I am, it becomes one of the things that puts me and my "tribe" on the road to conflict and ruin.

It's difficult to achieve societal greatness if the source is either rigid sameness (the uni-cultural society) or spiraling diversity (the omni-cultural society). America is a living embodiment of the third way – the multi-cultural society.

What does a multi-cultural society look like?

First of all, it's a single society. It has very little of the cacophony and ruinous division of an omni-cultural society. It avoids the constant, pointless friction that is an everyday feature of the omni-cultural conglomeration of petty tribal societies.

Second, it's a diverse society. It has a smooth flow from the sub-cultures to the whole and back again. It avoids the inflexible and stifling homogeneity of a uni-cultural society. In fact, it uses its amazing diversity to enhance the whole society, as Fareed Zakaria reminds us:

> *American culture celebrates and reinforces problem solving, questioning authority, and thinking heretically. It allows people to fail and then gives them a second and third chance. It rewards self-starters and oddballs. These are all bottom-up forces that cannot be produced by government fiat.*[5]

America is a multi-cultural society that values all forms of diversity – racial, ethnic, color, gender, age, experience, and more. But it values just as much diversity of thought and wonders how valuable the other diversities are without it. Having cultural diversity with thought uniformity – like requiring political correctness – may be the worst of all possible combinations, since we would have the illusion of diversity without the reality, diversity of form without diversity of substance.

But it isn't the restless, limitless diversity alone that makes the American Idea of Society so powerful. It's the fact that all of this wild diversity is absorbed into the broader concept of a cohesive American society. As described in *The Economist*,

> *Nearly all Americans are descended from people who came from somewhere else.... And the variety of countries from which immigrants come – roughly all of them, and usually in significant numbers – is unmatched.... [T]heirs is an inclusive nationalism. Most believe that anyone can become American.... America has lost none of its capacity to absorb newcomers.*[6]

Real freedom thrives only where a society has learned to put unity and diversity into equilibrium, to create a true multi-cultural society, where the "uni" has been opened up and the "omni" has been shuttered.

In the American Idea, what does this all mean?

It means that I am first of all an individual and second, an American. Only after these meanings are secure am I a member of one or more of the countless ways to group human beings.

And I recognize that this society, while there to help me with my wants, is also there to limit wants. It has a responsibility – so that we can all live together successfully and peacefully – to fill the gap between anarchy on the one hand (there are no laws or rules) and government on the other (all that can be done is to make laws or rules).

Society fills a crucial role in setting boundaries without the political maneuvering and brute force of government. Thinking people know that

> ## *While Government Is Concerned with What Is Legal, Society Is Concerned with What Is Appropriate*

It's very, very easy to confuse a government with a society. Although they may inhabit the same geography, they are completely different in purpose, form, and function.

There's a real and important difference between America and American government. A president is hired to speak for the government but is only peripherally allowed – and then only if he or she is wise – to speak for American society.

Government's core purpose is to contain evil, overarching evil – foreign threats and wars, internal crime and violence, fraud and corruption. It requires a clear-cut and usually hierarchical form. It typically functions in a reactive way, through political and semi-political (like rallying and lobbying) processes. By its nature, it's at its best when it's dealing with rules and regulations.

Government is about what's legal. It can say, "This can't be done," or, "This must be done," and then – if it has the will and power – enforce its dictates. But it's on shaky ground when it tries to deal with what's appropriate – what's fitting or decent or fair. It is ham-fisted, gets confused by the posturing and politics, and ends up using its only familiar tools – laws and force – to try to get to "appropriate." It's like using a worker skilled in using a sledgehammer to align the tiles in a mosaic.

Society's core purpose is to promote good, in part by restraining most evil, everyday evil – laziness, irresponsibility, bigotry. Its form is fuzzy, complex, and amorphous, and it has no stable hierarchy. It functions in both proactive and reactive ways – pushing toward better ways while negating the seamy side of life. By its nature, it's at its best when it's dealing with relationships and restraints.

Society is about what's appropriate. It has little ability to command but a lot of ability to influence. It can say, "This shouldn't be done," or, "This should be done," and then – if it has the cohesiveness and moral authority – insist on its pronouncements. Peer pressure and the generally felt need to conform can operate for good. Society simply has to have the will to say, "This is inappropriate."

A society can expect the government to create laws to protect society at the extreme. For example, while society should set the tone on public manners and behavior, it can oblige government to establish laws regarding things like public decency and indecency (there are such things) and disrespect of others (hate speech, hate signs or t-shirts).

But society is on shaky ground when it tries to deal with what's legal – with laws and crime and punishment. It is too soft and fluid to deal with very real destructive behavior that has crossed the line. It's like using an artist to drive a pile. Only on over-the-line or life-and-death issues should society insist that government create laws to protect and punish. For the most part, government is a poorly chosen vehicle to deal with attitudes, opinions, and beliefs.

In a sense, government is society's last line of defense. When all of the positive influences and social restraints have been ignored, when someone has decided to violate all of society's norms and become a renegade, the government is there to stop them. President Woodrow Wilson observed,

The first duty of law is to keep sound the society it serves.[7]

Government is the outer ring. We shouldn't want the government operating in the inner rings or the society – in a vigilante way – becoming the outer ring. Government can't and shouldn't be the whole game, and it shouldn't be the primary decider of what is appropriate. Government should be the last resort, the point just beyond the Golden Rule.

Government and society can both become very entrenched, but government is the more fleeting of the two. People can throw out a government much more easily than they can throw out their society. It takes a lot longer to learn what's appropriate than it does to learn how to put a murderer in prison.

Many political leaders have claimed to speak in the name of The People, which is a grand term when talking about society – how people will live and love and work together. But it's a Trojan horse when talking about government, which, in The People's name, will enact more and heavier laws. It will overreach and often try to become synonymous with society.

And government, all about laws and rules, can make giant mistakes in permitting – even defending – what society has said is inappropriate. It can decide matters badly on narrow technical grounds when those matters go to the heart of the culture. Tremendously valuable societal norms can be destroyed in a moment by the heavy hand of a legislating government, especially one with an unchecked judiciary that generally gets the final (but not always the best) word.

Government may not even be able to comprehend what people in society know to be true. For example,

We Know That There Is a Vast Gulf between an Open Society and an Open Sewer

What is an open society?

There are two completely different ways of defining it. The first – solidly part of the

American Idea of Society – is "a culture focused on truth."[8] Government shouldn't operate in secret or tell the citizens lies or half-truths (whatever those are). Business and financial transactions should be transparent. Media should be able to report honestly and freely. People should be able to meet publicly, discuss any issue, express any concern, and protest any problem or direction.

Truth should be shared, even if it makes people uncomfortable, so that things can be improved. If a sub-culture is a breeding ground for drugs and crime, we talk about it. If another is set on destroying the concept of "family," we challenge it. If one degrades women and promotes absolutism, we let them know that doesn't work here. If another wants to work outside the law, we say, "No," because without the rule of law, everything falls apart. If television wants to push the envelope and maximize the amount of sensuality it shows, we protest no matter how loudly they claim it's "protected free speech."

The second way to define open society, in full opposition to the American Idea of Society, is "a culture where almost anything goes." Short of shouting "Fire!" falsely in a public place, people can say whatever comes into their heads no matter how corrupt or corrupting. Politicians can lie and spin and promise with no intention of delivering, and can create phony budgets, and people shrug and say, "What can you expect?" Businesses can exaggerate and create over-the-top billboards and advertisements and deaden whatever is fine and good in the culture. Financial organizations can manipulate numbers, publish lies, and draw people into destructive investments. Media can shout anything about anyone, no matter how personal or grotesque.

Oddly, in this second definition, the "almost" in "almost anything goes" takes the form of eliminating one thing – truth, the hallmark of a genuinely open society. This can appear as political correctness, where truth can't be shared because it might hurt a "protected group's" feelings (and wouldn't everyone like to know how to get in on that protection?). Whole areas of truth are banned from the public sphere, even as falsehood and filth are unleashed.

> *Falsehood.* Nations or courts that claim to worry about first-amendment rights and freedom of speech shouldn't gloss over this problem. When a nation debases truth – when it will not allow people to say things that are uncomfortable, even though they are true – then it is destined to reap the full fruit of violating the principle that "you will know the truth, and the truth will make you free."[9]

> *Filth.* At the same time, we now have access to anything and everything, no matter how evil or dehumanizing – as long as it isn't truth that might offend someone. We can get to the point where we're not open to uncomfortable and unvarnished truth, but we're open to unredeemable and unremitting grime. This is a terrible inversion of openness, a key factor in turning society upside down.

One writer notes, "[Pornography's] pervasiveness clearly exacerbates the growing moral nihilism of our culture." She observed that new feminists have "reached a new consensus: the ubiquity of pornography has brought the sex industry out of the margins and into the mainstream, and we're all the worse off for it."[10]

And the effects of this increasingly are on children. In a study of the film industry, "The sexualization of teen girls in the movies was the most troubling finding to the researchers.... Teen girls were as likely to appear partially naked as the older women (30%).... The sexualization of girls is rampant in films, television, music videos and the marketing of clothing to children." A researcher observed that "this is sending a powerful message that it's important for girls and young women to be sexual objects from a very early age."[11]

Some believe that free speech should trump everything else. If people don't like it, they should turn it off. If they have children, the parents should control what they watch. But what if the filth is everywhere? What if it can't all be shut out, no matter how diligent the person or parent? It's ironic that the only recommendation "anything goes" proponents of free speech have for parents is for them to become dictators.

In one sense, there is no free speech. The cost of having it is very, very high. It costs society a lot to earn it and a lot to keep it. Not many societies have managed to get it or sustain it. It seems a terrible shame to waste such a hard-earned right by spending it badly or foolishly on things like:

- Permitting lies and slander while prohibiting painful truth

- Protecting children from media that corrupts the body (like tobacco and sugar) but not that corrupts the soul (like pornography and sex-drenched PG-13 comedies)

- Making room for public rudeness and nastiness, while ridiculing and boxing in expressions of spiritual and religious beliefs

An open society has a focus on truth. An open sewer has a focus on slime. A great society sees the difference and refuses to let its openness be perverted and used to destroy the society. It is wise enough to protect freedom by refusing to let it be abused. It resists the pull of its members into individual or collective slavery. Historian Jacques Barzun observed that many people

> deplore violence and sexual promiscuity among the young, but pornography and violence in films and books, shops and clubs, on television and the internet, and in the lyrics of pop music cannot be suppressed, in the interests of "the free market of ideas".... Science fiction and film as well as novels keep teasing the mind with the unspeakable and possibly incite young and old to reenact the deeds in real life.[12]

And here we come to a problem. There are always rebels in any society – people who see what is, imagine what might be, and are willing to do whatever it takes to change what is to what might be. They're the ones who are willing to cross lines and shatter boundaries. Should they be praised or condemned?

The answer is, "Absolutely." They should be praised if they're helping a society lose bogus restraints, or prevent attacks on the rights to life, liberty, or the pursuit of happiness. And they should be condemned if they're helping a society eliminate good restraints that keep life safe, keep freedom free of destructive behavior, and prevent the pursuit of happiness from decaying into self-immolating narcissism.

Many thinkers, writers, artists, actors, and others think they should be praised for breaking down barriers or tearing down conventions or throwing out traditions. But the act alone isn't worthy of praise. If the person is annihilating the society – all too often as a corollary to annihilating themselves – then we should see it for what it is. We should denounce these champions of destruction.

Freedom can be used to build up or tear down. Fred Kaplan, in his book *1959: The Year Everything Changed*, noted,

> *the withering of the prudish Comstock laws uncorked gusts of freedom in bookstores, publishing houses, and movie theaters – but it also let in rank pornography....Sexual liberty infused millions of lives with relief and excitement – but also wrecked untold numbers of families....[T]oo many creative minds came to confuse freedom for license.*"[13]

Voltaire said, "Decadence was brought about by the easy way of producing works and laziness in doing it, by the surfeit of...art and the love of the bizarre."[14]

Free from religion, free from unwanted babies, free from decency in speech – is it really freedom at all? Sigmund Freud observed,

> *It is impossible to ignore the extent to which civilization is built up on renunciation of instinctual gratification, the degree to which the existence of civilization presupposes the non-gratification (suppression, repression, or something else?) of powerful instinctual energies.*[15]

Not every societal restraint or tradition is good or should be codified by the government and turned into yet more laws. In fact, we should keep our society strong in part so that we won't need more laws. In a Great Society, it means even more – that we should make our society stronger so we can eliminate many laws. Americans have always wanted more society and less government, more that is appropriate and less that is legal.

An open society is like a river moving from one point to another in a vibrant but channeled way. People work to keep the river clear of debris and kept within its boundaries. They strive to keep the communal river free from contamination and keep it concentrated to maximize its power.

But the river can be turned into an open sewer, where people gleefully throw debris into the river and compete to do so more and more. Some push the river beyond its banks and harm those nearby, while others make the river unnavigable with obstructions and unswimmable with garbage.

In some people's minds today, the line between open society and open sewer may not be that clear. This alone should make us realize how far we've drifted from this fabulous American Idea. Too many people have already forgotten that

Societies That Pollute and Destroy Should Be Condemned and Changed

Here's a historical truth: There have been no totally good societies.

America has been no exception. But the overall intention of those in positions of leadership in America was seldom to benefit the few and to use the many, the typical approach of leaders in other societies throughout history. The American intention was to have a society where circumstances of birth didn't determine people's destiny. It hasn't been perfect, but it has been generally decent.

But there have been some very bad societies and not a few totally bad ones. These societies create a degraded and degrading atmosphere and play to the worst of human nature. How do they do this? In many ways, such as by:

- Ridiculing and erasing religion

- Acting as though all restraints are anti-freedom and opposed to human rights

- Refusing to think clearly and speak truthfully

- Treating powerful forces, like sex, as a commodity or as just an ordinary bodily function like eating and sleeping

- Thrusting children into overwhelming situations for which they can't be prepared spiritually, intellectually, or emotionally

- Treating crime lightly and criminals well

- Claiming to have a "war on drugs" but instead doing just enough to create a drug sub-culture with both organized and violent crime to provide drugs, and disorganized and violent crime to buy them (Instead of treating major drug dealers for what they are – not criminals, but terrorists with chemical weapons that have already killed untold thousands)

- Permitting corruption at the highest levels of government and enterprise

- Living as though nothing is sacred or special, including human life

Here, the community itself becomes a threat to people's desire to live a decent life. Sadly, community can just as easily become a corrupting influence as an ennobling one. When this happens, it is time for a dramatic overhaul. This is what those who came from the corrupted societies of the Old World intended as they set up largely religious, high-minded societies in the New. And once established, it was those new, elevated societies that drew tens of millions more.

It was never just an economic opportunity. It was also the chance to breathe fresh cultural air.

The Old World is still tanking. After centuries of self-destructive wars, revolutions, and social unrest, they are still polluting and destroying human life. Sometimes it emanates from too little of the real God and too little respect for standards. Sometimes it comes from too much of a made-up god and too much respect for narcissism.

As before, these societies – regardless of how much wealth or the good life they seem to have right now – should be condemned as the empty shells that they are. They are vacuous and crying out for transformation. If they aren't changed, they'll find that the wealth and good life aren't guaranteed to the decadent and degenerate.

The worst thing the New World could do? Imitate the Old – then or now. That way leads to debauchery and devastation. Americans have condemned that path for four hundred years, and this isn't the time to stop that condemnation. That way has been tried many, many times. It failed on every try.

In a self-governing society, it is critical for us to pass along not only authority to new generations but also the character to exercise it well. President James Garfield said,

> The voters of the Union, who make and unmake constitutions, and upon whose will hang the destinies of our governments, can transmit their supreme authority to no successors save the coming generation of voters, who are the sole heirs of sovereign power. If that generation comes to its inheritance blinded by ignorance and corrupted by vice, the fall of the Republic will be certain and remediless.... It is the high privilege and sacred duty of those now living to educate their successors and fit them, by intelligence and virtue, for the inheritance which awaits them.[16]

On the other hand, Americans once knew, and should stir themselves to remember, that

Societies That Protect and Defend Should Be Commended and Conserved

A society that protects human life and souls and defends its members from harm is a pearl of great price. It is very rare and incredibly valuable. What it can do to enhance human life can't be measured by analysts or polls but can be felt by every person in that society.

Societies like this are Great Societies. They're worth bragging about and standing up for. They're worth fighting and dying for as well. But they're often vulnerable because they're free and open. And they have enemies, not the least of which is human nature when it's not having a good day (which is often). If those who understand its value don't constantly strive to conserve that Great Society, its enemies will take it apart. As Alexis de Tocqueville noted, with chilling questions that resonate today,

> What force can there be in the customs of a country which has changed, and is still perpetually changing, its aspect...in which there is nothing so old that its antiquity can save it from destruction, and nothing so unparalleled that its novelty can prevent it from being done? What resistance can be offered by manners of so pliant a make that they have already often yielded?[17]

When Lyndon Johnson talked about a Great Society, he meant one where the government becomes the great caretaker of the poor and needy, where government becomes the strongest force for good, where government becomes the major player in the life of the society. He looked at the General Welfare clause in the U. S. Constitution and saw an opportunity for government and society to be one.

But before him, many generations of Americans had a better Idea. They wanted a

Great Society that was full to the brim with freedom, dignity, opportunity, responsibility, and generosity. They knew that government was very different from society. They had in fact discovered a powerful truth – that society flourishes best when government flourishes least.

They wanted to create a Great Society and have it last. They knew that government and law had a role to play in protecting and defending a Great Society. But they also knew that government always had terrible fallback positions – molding the society to fit the needs of the rich and powerful, catering to the influential minority or misled majority, making society beholden to government. They saw that government could make it easier for families to fall apart and then arrive as the "savior" to clean up their catastrophe with social services – myriad programs and bureaucrats armed with good intentions and crippling notions.

For many generations, Americans believed that the only real beneficiary of intruding government was…intruding government.

If those earlier Americans could be brought back to life and shown the General Welfare clause in the U. S. Constitution, they would say that the best way the government could promote the general welfare of the people would be to conserve the best of the American Great Society, in large part by leaving it alone. They would say that promoting the general welfare is mostly good when talking about society and mostly bad when talking about government.

Society can be helped or hurt by government. Government is a big sword that can cut both ways. The truly Great Society uses the government in a limited role to help preserve the society and limits the government in all other ways.

Because Americans know this truth: no government can do for any society what only its free and committed members can do.

America At Its Best

TheAmericanIdeas.com

The American Idea of Society can thrive, if we:

Take Action

Realize that society is a living thing that can be nurtured or killed.

★

Make a personal commitment to elevate society.

★

Hate the corruption of society.

★

Make society the servant of the individual rather than her master.

★

Remember that society has obligations but not rights.

★

Resist letting freedom be used to degrade society.

★

Refuse to let "appropriate" be defined by those who use government to gut society.

★

Defend marriage and family with wisdom, care, and caution, not regulation.

★

Stop allowing people under 18 to get a free pass on reprehensible behavior.

★

Recognize that the long-standing War on Drugs is working just as well as Prohibition.

★

Put the slime in the sewer and keep it there.

To see detail on these Action Points and
to add your voice visit www.theamericanideas.com

Freedom is at its best when it has boundaries. And boundaries are at their best when they are established by society, not by government. To be sure, both society and government can create oppressive boundaries. But laws are more brutal instruments than customs. Will and Ariel Durant noted in *The Lessons of History*, "Morals are the rules by which a society exhorts (as laws are the rules by which it seeks to compel) its members…to behavior consistent with its order, security, and growth."[18]

In most countries, the absence of morals creates the necessity for more laws. But the American formulation was, "More morals, fewer laws."

Society, like so many critically important concepts, is an intangible. But its results can be dramatic and very tangible indeed. Look at societies around the world, and look at the kinds of outcomes they have spawned. Look at the governments they've created or allowed. Do we really want that?

Or do we want the American Idea?

American society was founded on Ideas born in the Renaissance, the Reformation, the Enlightenment, and the Great Awakening – and earlier, on Anglo-Saxon, Greco-Roman, and biblical foundations. It took a long time to form a society really and truly designed to benefit every member. But it won't take nearly as long to lose it.

Americans have never been hesitant to talk about decency and morality. They've never been ashamed of their Judeo-Christian roots or that their society was founded on better concepts. They have highly regarded humanity in general and individual human beings in particular. They've always been ferociously protective of innocents and especially partial to underdogs. They've never forgotten that values are valuable and that boundaries are essential.

And they've always wanted a society that was both free and good. They've wanted to be a people who "opt for good when good is not the only choice, giving their virtue a special luster."[19] They've believed with de Tocqueville, who said,

> *Liberty cannot be established without morality....[N]o free communities ever existed without morals.*[20]

Society can be one of the greatest of human blessings. That's what the founders of this new country had in mind when they sought to create a "shining city on a hill."[21] They weren't looking for a bigger and better government or a world-class economy.

They were looking for a bigger and better way of life and a world-class society.

CHAPTER 11

The American Idea of Government

Is government the solution, or is government the problem? In America, the answer has always been, "Absolutely."

The American Idea of Government is a paradox. It recognizes that government alone can provide solutions to a certain, narrow set of problems. It is the only creation of human beings that is designed to formally and forcefully thwart evil. Rather than diminishing the value of government, the American Idea insists that government is so important that everyone be involved in forming, shaping, and supporting it.

At the same time, The American Idea sees clearly that government can become a problem. If unchecked, it can become the problem. If there are any useful lessons from history, this would top the list. Government has power, and it always has at least some people who are ready to abuse it. The more the power, the more the seductive it is to bad people to use it for their own ends. We may disagree over who the Messiah is, but we can be certain that it isn't – and won't be – a political power-broker.

So to say that government is good or bad is to make something black-and-white that is actually a blend. It's like asking the question, "Are people basically good or bad?" The answer is, "Of course." Most people are a mix. And so is the government. If it stays in its defined areas, it at least has a chance of being mostly good. If it strays outside of those areas, history tells us that it has an even higher chance of being mostly bad.

Government is necessary. At times, it is even crucial. It can defend us, protect us, and ensure that the Rule of Law is followed. Contrary to the often well-meaning but always naïve claims of anarchists and extreme libertarians, people have found through hard experience that government is indispensable – a welcome adversary of badness.

People have also found out through hard experience that government is pompous – an unwelcome ringleader of trouble. They see that it is crucial – crucial to put it in cuffs. They understand that government can attack us and let others attack us, expose us to harm and allow others to harm us, and turn the Rule of Law into the rule of laws. In their moments of sober thinking, Americans often put the word "evil" at the end of "government is necessary" – in part because it puts massive power in the hands of flawed human beings.

Government

Government can be both the solution to problems and the problem itself.

We want good government but are skeptical that human beings can consistently provide it.

Government becomes more palatable when it is self-government, with issues democratically decided or resolved in a representative republic.

Whenever government is necessary, it is better to make as much of it as possible local and as little of it as possible national.

Since "that government is best which governs least,' limits are crucial.

Government can succeed if it has real and evolving checks and balances and stays within its assigned sphere.

It fails if it doesn't carry out its mission, strays from its assignment, or is hijacked by career politicians.

Something difficult for many people to acknowledge is that

Government Can Be the Solution to Problems

Governments have always been necessary. This is in spite of the fact that many people are decent and because of the fact that many people aren't. There is a set of human problems that can only be solved by people who have power, people who can force a society's will on those who don't care about – or who even hate – that society.

Government is the solution when it is focused on restraining our individual and collective "badness," as revolutionary thought leader Thomas Paine noted in the great manifesto of the American Revolution, *Common Sense:*

> *Society is produced by our wants, and government by our wickedness.... Society in every state is a blessing, but Government, even in its best state, is but a necessary evil....*[2]

Government is necessary because people can and will do bad things. So it is that government can solve some problems, problems that are particularly, if not uniquely, suited to government action. Where do these well-suited-to-government problems reside? Given the American Idea, in four areas:

- *External threats to our national well-being.* There is a human impulse, extremely strong in some people, to use power to intimidate, conquer, or destroy others. This is very old – Greek, Roman, Persian, Arab, Mongol, Turk – and very new – Hitler, Stalin, Tojo, Zedong, Idi Amin, Pol Pot, Saddam Hussein. Humanity has not gotten over and is not likely to cure this madness of power. Reason and diplomacy are insufficient to address it. We need a government to protect us from this violent insanity that – in the actual world in which we live – will never die.

- *Internal threats to our personal well-being.* The same human power-abusing impulse occurs at the level of individual encounters. Murder, armed robbery, kidnapping, sexual abuse, and rape (generally a problem of cruel power first and sensuality second) – all threaten to steal our personal peace and safety. We need government at the right level – national, state or province, local – to deal with this ongoing human tragedy.

- *Internal and external threats to our culture.* The American Idea of Society is one of both openness and decency as we saw in Chapter 10. Openness without decency is corruption, and decency without openness is dictatorship. This is in line with the advice one American has given to thousands of leaders, to encourage their people to "be clear and be kind" – tell me the hard-to-hear truth, but say it in a gracious way that makes it easy for me to hear it. We need government to protect us from cultural threats to both openness and decency – not using openness as an excuse for rampant vulgarity in the public sphere and not using decency as an excuse for rampant censorship in the public discourse. It's a tough balancing act, but there are no remotely competitive, palatable alternatives.

• *Internal and external threats to our commerce.* Like it or not, no economic system other than free-market capitalism has ever provided benefit to more than a privileged few. It's a strong, dynamic, flexible system. But since it (smartly) plays off self-interest, it can also be hijacked by the privileged few (or those who want to be). We need government to provide rules to keep the competition fair, like the rules committee or competition committee in any professional sport. But the government, like any good umpire, needs to stay out of the game. The goal should be an equal playing field for everyone, and no trophies for the government-referee.

If the government does these things well, it can be a very good "necessary evil" indeed, one for which its citizens can be thankful.

Why weren't threats to our political liberty added to this list? For one simple reason: The greatest threat to political liberty throughout history has always been...government. But something difficult for many people to acknowledge is that

Government Can Be the Problem Itself

"We are a nation that has a government – not the other way around," said President Ronald Reagan.[3]

Tom Paine, continuing the statement from *Common Sense* that opened the last section, elaborated on the necessary evil of government, declaring that government is

> *In its worst state an intolerable one; for when we suffer, or are exposed to the same miseries by a Government, which we might expect in a country without Government, our calamity is heightened by reflecting that we furnish the means by which we suffer.*[4]

Too often, government wants to horn in on other areas of life, to permeate society with its overbearing presence. It naturally hates restraints and fences, in large part because it's made up of people who have power, want more power, and intend to use power – sometimes to impose their ideology, sometimes to enhance their own lives, and sometimes both. President Woodrow Wilson said,

> *The great Government we love has too often been made use of for private and selfish purposes, and those who used it had forgotten the people.*[5]

Government is the problem in two ways. The first is when it goes beyond its mandate in its four legitimate areas of influence:

• *External threats to our national well-being.* When a government starts seeing foreign threats under every rock, it's ready to take us on a very bad journey. This can happen for a variety of reasons – when a foreign ideologue or demagogue takes charge and wants to be a world player, when someone wants to take our eyes off their domestic failures, or simply because they're evil or paranoid. Government can go off the rails when it doesn't perceive threats correctly or at their actual level of seriousness – as when the American government spent decades telling its citizens about a "missile gap" with the Soviet Union that did not exist. Government's uninformed or power-informed actions can create bigger threats and can even invent threats out of nothing. Government can also go the other way and not really protect us at all – for example, leaving us fully exposed to nuclear annihilation for over half a century.

• *Internal threats to our personal well-being.* In a safe and decent society, government is proactive. It creates an environment where evil has a hard time planting itself or taking root, even while protecting the rights of evildoers. But government can switch its priorities, allowing evil a safe haven and defending the evildoers at the expense of their victims or other law-abiding citizens. Government can blame society for causing the badness and can accept excuses that absolve the depraved of personal responsibility. It can lose sight of its role in dispensing justice (which it might do adequately) and try to go beyond that to perfecting society and individuals (which it has no chance of doing well). Government can go the other way and produce a high level of supposed "safety" by combining a low level of freedom with a high level of calling anyone different "evil."

• *Internal and external threats to our culture.* Government can easily misidentify threats. It can release psychopaths and murderers, and rapists repeat their crimes again under the false banners of "rehabilitation" and "humane treatment." It can permit a flood of degeneracy and pornography under the wrongly applied banner of "freedom." It can use psychobabble like "parental alienation" to keep children with bad parents and away from good ones under the all-purpose mantra of "the best interest of the child." It can diminish respect for the law by allowing, even encouraging, illegal immigration and all of the crime, corruption, and disrespect for the law that go with it. And government can get it wrong the other way, controlling what gets said on the public airwaves, crimping criticism with threats of loss of tax-exempt status, allowing minorities to do what is forbidden to majorities, and putting limits on which racial or ethnic groups are desirable as immigrants.

• *Internal and external threats to our commerce.* In the world of economics, government can and often does swing on a pendulum between too much control and too little. It's seldom done with enhancing commerce as its goal, but is often done with enhancing political careers as the objective. While money is like blood when it flows through a society's marketplace, it can be like poison when it flows through a party's candidates. All too often, someone with twice the war chest and half the brains can defeat a good candidate who would make life better for all. The direction of the wrong-headed efforts – too much or too little control internally, too much protectionism or too little insistence on true free trade externally, too few or too many regulations – too often depends on an ugly combination of the current economic and political climate with whatever groups are supporting a particular candidate or platform.

The harm government can do when it operates at the extremes in these four areas is immense.

The second problem with government occurs when it goes outside of those four areas. When it strays into areas that, in a free and open culture, should be reserved for the individual or the society, the harm can be incalculable and very hard to reverse.

What are those areas? Education, jobs or careers, healthcare, retirement, innovation, energy, company ownership, land ownership, and foreign aid, just to name a few. These areas always have problems, of course. Straying government finds a way to use these problems to enhance its power. It will force itself into the game and, ultimately, into controlling the game. It will use excessive taxation, borrowing against the future, and monetary manipulation to fund its misadventures. At its worst, it creates or worsens problems as a prelude to announcing itself as their solution.

But just because an area has problems doesn't mean that the government has solutions. Often it has none. Given an American view of the proper role of government, we should be pleased that it doesn't have any. Government, with its big guns and its mastery of force, simply isn't designed to do the work of society.

All too often, government's "solutions" are more of the same thing that created or exacerbated the problem and are often the opposite of what's needed. They give us more "progressive" taxes (meaning a bigger percentage, not more fair) to secure social justice, more debt to stimulate prosperity, more spending to create wealth, more inflation to make people feel like they're getting ahead, more regulation to give people a sense of security.

The fact that those problems are almost always better handled by the individual or society is secondary. There's simply nothing in the way that governments have to be structured that argues for any special expertise in these areas. But there are many things in the way they are structured – power gained on the cheap (by campaign rather than accomplishment), political considerations, competing interests, bureaucracy, hierarchy, the ability to spend other people's money – that makes both the problem and the government itself bigger.

Americans want to be proud of their government. But given who they are, they can only be proud if that government stays small, focused, and limited. A huge, wide-ranging, unbounded government run by honorable people (if such can be found) is not only insufficient to generate pride; in America, it is also perfectly designed to generate fierce opposition and even hatred.

After dealing with any government for any length of time, people can be left with a feeling of gloom. They can give up. Americans took a different course, a balanced course. They said,

We Want Good Government, but Are Skeptical That Human Beings Can Consistently Provide It

The American Idea of Government starts with not only a hope for good government, but also an understanding that this all depends on how we define "good."

If we define it as "decent people wonderfully and without fail looking out for others with no thought for themselves or their own agendas," then there's no such thing as "good government." Americans have always been a pragmatic, down-to-earth people, and they know that this kind of definition is nonsense.

If, on the other hand, we define good government as "limited government that is restricted to a few key activities and prohibited from everything else," then we have a shot at good government. We can have a government that does what only it can do. It can make life better for all of us.

Americans have usually had a healthy skepticism about the benevolence of people who have an abundance of power at their disposal. They resonate with Thomas Jefferson's question, "Sometimes it is said that man cannot be trusted with the government of himself. Can he, then, be trusted with the government of others?"[6]

They see power as a tool that has more often been used to dominate others rather than to liberate them. They see power as a tool that, in the hands of normal people, all too easily becomes a goal. They see it as a possession that usually works to the advantage of the few who have it at the expense of the many who don't.

The founders were immensely realistic. They knew that government had to be designed, in part, to address the laziness, greed, and badness of human beings. This applied not just to those being governed (which is why we need government in the first place), but also to those doing the governing (which is why the people being governed need to put checks on those who wield power). Utopias usually end up as dictatorships. The founders knew that and designed American government on a more modest – and sensible – basis.

They knew that something must govern the governors. Why? Because they're just like the rest of us, only more so. They have all of our flaws, but added to these, all too often, are a relentless drive for power and fame – and a willingness to do what it takes to get them. Benjamin Franklin observed,

> *There is no kind of dishonesty into which otherwise good people more easily and frequently fall than that of defrauding the government.*[7]

The founders knew that the primary goal of a tolerable government isn't to get good people – there are too few of them. They wanted good people in government, but they knew that getting them was a bonus. They knew that the primary goal of tolerable government – and, in their minds, tolerable government is good government – was to keep the bad people, as well as the bad inside of good people, in check.

Because of this built-in skepticism, the American Idea of Government never envisioned a professional political class. Giving people power as a part of their career was dangerous enough – giving people power as their whole career would be foolhardy, preposterous. The founders would have thought such people to be inherently corrupt. Benjamin Franklin said that

> *In free governments, the rulers are the servants and the people are their superiors. For the former to return among the latter does not degrade, but rather promotes them.*[8]

Alexander Hamilton stated that

> *The natural cure for an ill administration, in a popular or representative constitution, is a change of men.*[9]

They would have never imagined executive power becoming overbearing after George Washington set the right tone, or Franklin Roosevelt running for four terms (twice as many as anyone else with perhaps more to come). They would have been appalled at presidents using foreign crises, wars, and economic turmoil as paths to power. They wouldn't have conceived of members of congress ruling as elected representatives for half a century, using incumbency and voting district manipulation and truckloads of money to negate real democracy. They would never have believed that unelected Supreme Court judges would rule nearly as long – or, in fact, would rule at all.

But today, more and more power is accruing to the ruling elite – elected officials, unelected officials, appointees, and their royal courts of donors and lobbyists and interest groups. There's no clear way to get our power back from these people – except here or there, when one of them dies or goes over the top in abusing the public trust.

The only way to get the power away from these people is to get these people away from the power. Politics is too important to be left to the politicians. "The longer an incumbent stays in power," observed Democratic strategist Bob Beckel, "the greater the chance for corruption. Almost every scandal in congress, going back decades, involves senior members."[10] De Tocqueville said, "Duration is one of the basic elements of power. One loves or fears only that which exists for a long time."[11]

In the 21st century, the only way to really practice limited self-government is to force the professional politicians, seduced by power and staying on forever, to leave. Politicians today – including appointed judges, who almost always have an agenda – live much longer, know too many campaigning tricks, have too much money, represent too many special interests. The only way to have limited government is to have limited politicians.

Limited self-government can only exist if we limit the roles of the people who govern, if we once more have at least a semblance of the citizen-politician that differentiated the American Idea. Incumbents win over 90% of the time, not often because they are the best available person but nearly always because they are the incumbent – with visibility and power, patronage and earmarks, and a whole lot of money.[12] We need people who have politics as a career interruption, not as a career.

The greatest among us have "gotten it" and laid down power voluntarily. When King George III was told that George Washington – the "first president of a nation in the history of the world"[13] - would soon lay aside his power and return to his farm, the king replied with astonishment, "If he does that, he will be the greatest man in the world!"[14] Greatness in this American Idea is, in part, associated with people who lay down rather than cling to power. For a century and a half after the founding of the United States of America, presidents followed Washington and never sought a third term.

When this exceptional approach was violated, the reaction didn't take long. A constitutional amendment was passed, insisting that no president gets more than two terms. Without a formal limitation, it had become obvious that some people would now seek to be president for life (the president who broke the chain, Franklin Roosevelt, was indeed president till the day of his death).

But presidents are not alone. Few people can be trusted with power, and no one can be trusted with it indefinitely. We can't wait for every politician to be a George Washington. The natural American skepticism about people in power needs to find a legal expression with term limits across the board. Good or bad, smart or stupid, talented or inept – ultimately it doesn't matter. They all have to go.

But we, responsible and self-governing Americans, need to stay. Because while Americans have often thought that government was a tough pill to swallow, they also saw that

Government Becomes More Palatable When It Is Self-Government, with Issues Democratically Decided or Resolved in a Representative Republic

President Ronald Reagan said that

> From time to time, we have been tempted to believe that society has become too complex to be managed by self-rule, that government by an elite group is superior to government for, by, and of the people. But if no one among us is capable of governing himself, then who among us has the capacity to govern someone else?[15]

For anyone of independent spirit and mind, government can be a hard pill to swallow. The American Idea of Government made it much more tolerable when it introduced the radical concept of self-government. President James Garfield said,

> The colonists were struggling not only against the armies of a great nation, but against the settled opinions of mankind; for the world did not then believe that the supreme authority of government could be safely intrusted to the guardianship of the people themselves.[16]

At its core, self-government means that we get to decide for ourselves. Individually, we get to make most of the decisions about our own lives. Collectively, we get to decide directly on as many general issues as possible, including which issues we don't want to decide collectively. And on those few questions that remain, we get to collectively decide who decides them for us.

We can get confused and think that self-government only refers to the political realm. But the American concept of self-government included more than just a collaborative, democratic political system expressed in a representative, republican political structure – although it indeed included these. The Idea is much richer than that.

It meant that there are no kings. Or, in a sense, that each of us is somehow a king. We rule our own domain. We get to think about and decide what we want to do, where we want to live and travel, what kind of people we want in our lives, and what kind of people we want to become.

The origins of self-government and democracy produced the concept of *Vox Populi, Vox Dei* (The voice of the people is the voice of God). Rulers and intellectuals don't get to decide what's best for the "ignorant masses," to override what the people want, or to cram down their throats what the people don't want.

The voice of the people isn't the voice of God, of course, but it is and should be the final word. With self-government, the voice of the people is the Supreme Court (not nine unelected elites in robes). *Vox Populi, Vox Rex* (The voice of the people is the voice of the king) – if we really are a democracy, if we really want to have self-government.

In a representative self-government, that voice is generally heard through the people's chosen representatives in the Congress – the House of Representatives from the beginning and the Senate ever since the people got the ability to choose them directly in 1913 (the people may make mistakes, but at least those mistakes won't be made by power mongers in the smoke-filled back rooms of state capitols).

President James Monroe said,

> In this great nation there is but one order, that of the people, whose power, by a peculiarly happy improvement of the representative principle, is transferred from them, without impairing in the slightest degree their sovereignty, to bodies of their own creation, and to persons elected by themselves, in the full extent necessary for all the purposes of free, enlightened and efficient government.[17]

We also have the personal responsibility that goes along with this incredible, self-governing liberty. Self-government starts with individuals empowering, motivating, managing, controlling, and disciplining themselves. Americans don't expect others to do for us what we are capable of doing for ourselves. Ever.

Self-government is the ally of freedom. If well administered, it can even be the best friend of freedom. It eliminates the need for overarching structures and bulging bureaucracies because people are mostly governing themselves. Together, we know we're giving up some of our individual latitude in order to gain something collectively. But it seems all right because we're freely deciding how much to give up – and we're not giving up very much.

Self-government implies rule by the people, but also responsibility of the people. If everyone wants to be a full-fledged citizen – and of course they should want this – they should expect equal rights, equal respect, and equal say in what that government does. But they should also take their responsibility seriously. They should respect the American Ideas. They should obey the law. And they should pay something to support their government.

When a huge percentage of the citizenry pays nothing – or worse, gets "refunds" or "credits" on taxes they never paid – it becomes difficult to justify how those who only take should have an equal say with those who are always required to "give." No other form of human association would allow this – a situation where some members are discriminated against because they are successful and others are favored because they are not. De Tocqueville observed that "a democratic government is the only one in which those who vote for a tax can escape the obligation to pay it."[18]

Every citizen should have a minimum tax they should pay, even if it's only a few dollars. This isn't a poll tax. It's a citizenship tax. This is really requiring everyone to pay their fair share, as opposed to the usual and very peculiar definition, "the rich are already paying most of the taxes but should pay even more to get them up to their fair share." This view of "fairness" is in fact not only grossly unfair, but is also manifestly unjust.

To be really "fair" – to be just – every citizen would pay the exact same tax, the exact same number of dollars – the same citizenship dues. Why should one citizen be more responsible for the government than any other? Of course, this is extremely unlikely to happen in a democracy where the majority who aren't rich get to make demands on the minority who are. But at the least, moving away from the so-called "progressive tax" system – where the more you earn the higher percentage you pay – would make it considerably less unfair.

What is the middle ground between everyone paying the same amount in taxes and the wealthier paying almost all of the taxes? An equal-percentage system, where everyone pays the same percentage of his or her income. The more successful would still pay significantly more in taxes, since 10% of a million dollars is a lot more than 10% of $50,000 ($100,000 vs. only $5,000). But they wouldn't be treated like geese that can be forced to produce more and more golden eggs until they quit laying them or die of exhaustion or fly somewhere else.

The approach we have right now is a threat to the viability of self-government:

• Those who pay outsized percentages of their income in taxes are destined to become resentful, not only of the government but also of the non-payers who are always demanding more. Why start a business or make an investment?

• Those who pay nothing or get handouts are destined to become detached from expecting good government, as long as bad government keeps their checks coming. Why not ask for more? Why not spend other people's money?

• Government gets to grow fatter and more controlling by creating a huge dependency class, all of whom have the "right" to vote themselves more even as they lose respect for themselves in the process. Why not pander to the greed of the majority by – ironically – attacking the greed of the minority?

When the vote is used for the benefit of the majority at the expense of a minority, we've moved from self-government to the tyranny of the 51%. Founder James Madison said that

> The personal right to acquire property, which is a natural right, gives to property, when acquired, a right to protection, as a social right. The essence of Government is power; and power, lodged as it must be in human hands, will ever be liable to abuse.... In republics, the great danger is, that the majority may not sufficiently respect the rights of the minority.[19]

But self-government isn't just being assaulted by the gross inequities of the tax system. In many ways, we're not ruling ourselves any more, not in any real sense. Over the years, and especially since the Great Depression and World War II, government has moved away from self and toward rulers far away, in both place and attitude. Self-government is still there in name but, sadly, is deteriorating in practice because of the rise of a self-anointed nobility.

We've come to be ruled by an oligarchy, a new aristocracy that clings to incumbency and simply will not go away. It is made up largely of lawyers (although the profession of law is not the problem). Alexis de Tocqueville predicted the dominance of lawyers in American life in his mid-nineteenth century classic *Democracy in America*. He called them our true and only aristocracy:

> *Hidden at the bottom of a lawyer's soul one finds some of the tastes and habits of an aristocracy. They share its instinctive preference for order and its natural love of formalities; like it, they conceive a great distaste for the behavior of the multitude and secretly scorn the government of the people.... What lawyers love above all things is an ordered life, and authority is the greatest guarantee of order. Moreover, one must not forget that although they value liberty, they generally rate legality as far more precious... It is at the bar or on the bench that the American aristocracy is found.*[20]

As if to confirm his assessment, lawyers even use the aristocratic title "Esquire" after their names. But it isn't that hard to understand. In a nation devoid of monarchs and divine rights of kings and genetically transferred power, those who knew and understood the law and how to use it would rise to the top of the heap.

But is government-by-lawyers a good thing for the future of freedom in America?

A single professional group, lawyers, makes the laws, executes the laws, and decides cases based on the laws. While they're at it, they often make new law from the judicial bench. A congress dominated by lawyers, when combined with their total monopoly over the judiciary, gives lawyers effective control over two-thirds of the government. It becomes total control if the president is an attorney.

From one perspective, this makes sense. Isn't a government made up of, and administered on the basis of, laws? Shouldn't the ones who decide all of this have training in the "law" (whatever that is)? Because the word "law" is in "lawmakers" and "lawyers," we somehow believe that officials need nitty-gritty training in arcane legal details rather than the overarching values of The Law – freedom and justice.

But from many other perspectives, this single-background base poses serious problems:

- One of the most critical of all diversities, diversity of thought, is reduced dramatically. What difference does it make if we have a government that approximates diversity of such things as race, ethnic background, sex, and age, if there is little diversity of thought? We should begin adding to those other diversities a fair representation of professions and occupations – for example, entrepreneurs, businesspeople, technical and financial professionals, craftspeople, and people from public companies, private firms, and not-for-profit organizations. In short, lawyers need to be represented in our political process, but they don't need to be over-represented.

- We've given full power to people trained to believe in the preeminence of law, its application, and its interpretation – whether that law is right or not, whether it creates undue or unnecessary restrictions or not, whether it's a burden on free people or not. This is trusting our government to people who necessarily base their work on limitations and narrow legal readings, rather than to people trained to believe in the preeminence of freedom, justice, morality, and opportunity.

- We've lost the creative and effective solutions that can grow out of interactions between people with divergent, even opposing, points of view. One reason political parties don't seem that different is that they aren't that different. In the way they – and the lawyers who dominate them – view the law and government, they're on the same page. It's the rest of the book that isn't represented.

- We have come to assume that the questions of government are primarily legal, when, in fact, a huge percentage of them are social, cultural, and economic – and could best be addressed by people with training in other fields. When the question moves from "what is legal?" to "what is right?" or "what is effective?" lawyers have no more claim to a good answer than many other groups – and as a result of training and temperament, perhaps less.

- We've allowed not just credential-itis, but one-credential credential-itis to dictate who is fit and not fit for public office. A law degree has become the best entry ticket into political life and, in many ways, the only ticket.

We also need judges with a wide diversity of backgrounds, so they can address the wide diversity of cases that come before them. How can a judge without training in business, economics, or energy make intelligent decisions that affect business, the economy, or the energy industry? How can a judge without training in education and public administration make wise decisions about education or public administration? How can a judge without training in families and relationships make sensitive decisions about marriage, divorce, childcare, child custody, foster care, or adoption?

The answer is, they don't. They can't. People with a narrow slice of training and outlook are given control over a wide range of issues well outside of their competence. "Is it really the case," asks Jonah Goldberg, "that lawyers are better qualified to decide when human life begins or when it should end than are legislators or, for that matter, bus drivers?"[21]

One of the most astonishing contradictions in American culture – a world-class cognitive dissonance – is the fact that lawyers occupy some of the lowest places in our opinions and feelings and the highest places in our public life. In a recent Gallup poll, 37% of Americans felt that lawyers' honesty and ethics were lower than average.[22] Few think they're higher.

A profession held in almost universally low regard – rightly or wrongly – has claimed the tenured right to rule almost universally. And the problem isn't new. "If the Congress errs in too much talking," wrote Jefferson, "how can it be otherwise in a body to which the people send 150 lawyers, whose trade it is to question everything, yield nothing, & talk by the hour?"[23]

It isn't that the law is a bad profession or that most lawyers are bad people. It's that their role has been exaggerated far beyond their training, far beyond their viewpoint, and far beyond what is acceptable in a free, democratic country with a deliberately limited government. Lawyers are rightly concerned with legal matters – but the law itself is concerned with more, much more, with countless non-legal matters.

Lawyers, the natural "aristocracy," now have a firm stranglehold on the apparatus of government. They consider themselves to be the right and proper guardians of the people. Their squabbles are mostly intramural and, again, are one of the main reasons that so many people see no difference between Democrat and Republican, liberal and conservative. Instead of observing a vigorous debate among wide-ranging opinions and positions, we find that watching government in action is like attending a symposium at a trade association conference, where everyone has the same background.

Too much power for too long has corrupted too many. They have developed entangling alliances with the vested interests, have control over vast sums of money and other tools to keep themselves in power, and, in many ways, believe themselves beyond our reach. They wage their wars for reelection from a high and (in practice) virtually unassailable place.

We need a change in mindset. Self-government is too important to be left to others. And law is too important to be left to the lawyers.

But tenured politicians and narrow training are only part of the problem with government. Another is its location. Americans have always believed that

> *Whenever Government Is Necessary, It's Better to Make as Much of It as Possible Local and as Little of It as Possible National*

Self-government means that it's up to each person first to govern themselves, second to govern their families and other dependent relationships, third to govern their work, fourth to govern their communities and towns and cities, fifth to govern their states, and last to govern the nation.

From the beginning of America it was believed that all of this should be done from the fertile, solid ground up rather than from the sterile, ivory tower down.

Government is about governing, which is to "rule," "preside over," "oversee," "direct," "run," or "manage."[24] The core element needed to govern, to rule and preside over and oversee and direct and run and manage, is power. Governing is about amassing enough power in one place to accomplish some goal. The power can be gotten through elections or coups, trustworthiness or bloodthirstiness, honesty or treachery. Regardless of the method, however, power is the key.

But given human nature, power is inherently dangerous, even if it starts out in the hands of a decent person. And that danger is magnified as the power becomes bigger, more centralized, further away, and less accountable to those being governed. Power has a compounding sense to it, where two powerful people can get together and have the impact of many people operating alone.

So, the American Idea of Government turned the historical norm – top down, with power being trickled downward from a central ruling point – on its head. It instead created a bottom-up approach, with power being trickled to a central ruling point. And in the final turnabout, it didn't view this bottom-up approach as trickling up –

it put the people on top and made the government their servant. Power would be trickled down from the governed to the governors.

Throughout history, governments have been formed at the top and have ruled from the top down. The usual flow of power was downhill from the king (or dictator) to the royal court, to the aristocracy, to estates and towns, to peasants and craftspeople and merchants, and finally to serfs and slaves.

But de Tocqueville observed, "In America, on the contrary, it may be said that the township was organized before the county, the county before the State, the State before the Union."[25] President Ronald Reagan said, "All of us need to be reminded that the Federal Government did not create the States; the States created the Federal Government."[26]

The American Idea simply said, "No" to the "right" of a few to ride on the backs of the many. Power would now flow down from the people – to the community (city or town), then to the wider community (county), then to the state (a wonderful intermediary absent from most nations throughout history and today), and finally to the federal (but not national or central) government.

The Idea was to keep the power – all power – small, decentralized, close at hand, and relentlessly accountable to those who were agreeing to be governed. As Sun-Tzu wrote in *The Art of War*, "Keep your friends close and your enemies closer." The American Idea's version of this says, "Keep your society close and your government closer." Thomas Jefferson said,

> *When all government, domestic and foreign, in little as in great things, shall be drawn to Washington as the center of all power, it will render power-less the checks provided of one government on another, and will become as venal and oppressive as the government from which we separated.... I wish, therefore, to see maintained that wholesome distribution of powers established by the constitution for the limitation of both; and never to see all offices transferred to Washington, where, further withdrawn from the eyes of the people they may more secretly be bought and sold as at market.*[27]

Especially in the last half-century, the movement of power has all been in the wrong direction. Local communities, cities, and towns, along with their schools, are dominated by the counties or states. States are dominated by the federal government, which has undone its tie to the term federal (union) and become national (central) in practice. The national government makes more and more of the decisions that formerly were – and still should be – made at the state, local, or individual level. But founder Alexander Hamilton wrote that

> *the State Governments would clearly retain all the rights of sovereignty which they before had and which were not by the act exclusively delegated to the United States.*[28]

The question isn't one of "states' rights" or "community rights" or "local rights." Why not? Because these entities don't have any rights – only individuals have rights. These bodies do have obligations to their citizens, including resisting the theft of power by bigger bodies further away. But they have no rights.

What this is is a question of power, of who should have it and where it should be located. It's partly a matter of scope and scale. If we disagree with the mayor, we have a chance at getting an appointment. The governor? Beyond our reach. Representatives and senators? Only in staged group settings. The president? The last time a citizen could reasonably hope to see the president was in the nineteenth century. And the Supreme Court? Now we're talking about the ultimately inaccessible royalty, one that makes the president look like the neighbor next door.

Washington, the center, is absorbing all. This isn't because it is particularly wicked. It's because it is becoming the historical norm. Do we still have elected leaders at all levels of government? Mostly (except for the judiciary and the federal bureaucracy). But more and more, only the national ones count and they too easily forget the source of their power.

President Andrew Jackson said, "The will of the American people, expressed through their unsolicited suffrages, calls me before you to pass through the solemnities preparatory to taking upon myself the duties of President of the United States for another term."[29] He knew he was only an instrument of the citizens.

If there's to be any civilization at all, there must be a government. But that government must of necessity be small, or else it will – sooner or later – consign that civilization to an unmarked grave.

Americans learned from hard experience that

Since "That Government Is Best Which Governs Least," Limits Are Crucial

The American Idea of Government includes the remarkable concept that government has to be limited. American essayist and poet Henry David Thoreau wrote:

> I heartily accept the motto, - "That government is best which governs least"; and I should like to see it acted up to more rapidly and systematically.... Government is at best but an expedient; but most governments are usually, and all governments are sometimes, inexpedient.... [T]his government never of itself furthered any enterprise, but by the alacrity with which it got out of its way. It does not keep the country free. It does not settle the West. It does not educate. The character inherent in the American people has done all that has been accomplished; and it would have done somewhat more, if the government had not sometimes got in its way.[30]

Government needs fences, boundaries, even chains. The Idea reminds us that although we may need government, we don't need very much of it. Too much of anything can turn even good things – food, drink, sleep, leisure – into bad. Economist and philosopher F. A. Hayek noted that:

> Democratic government has worked successfully where, and so long as, the functions of government were, by a widely accepted creed, restricted to fields where agreement among a majority could be achieved by free discussion; and...it reduced the range of subjects on which agreement was neces-

sary to one on which it was likely to exist in a society of free [people].... [I]
t is not the source but the limitation of power which prevents it from being
arbitrary.... We shall never prevent the abuse of power if we are not pre-
pared to limit power in a way which occasionally may also prevent its use
for desirable purposes.[31]

Sometimes power-hungry people simply take power that isn't theirs to take, even at the point of the sword. But sometimes they use "desirable purposes" and real needs as their excuse for grasping more power. They hope that the short-term positive will mask the long-term disaster caused by this propagandized and likely irreversible shift of power.

With flawed human beings holding too much power and having too many ways to use it, a necessary evil like government can turn into an out-of-control evil – stealing and robbing, oppressing and manipulating, ruining the present and devouring the future, shortchanging peace and relishing war.

With regard to rights, the Idea reminds government that it has a limited role as a protector of rights, not as a giver of rights. It clings to the American belief that rights originate with God, not with executive orders and congressional votes and Supreme Court rulings. Rights are God-given, not government-given.

The Idea also reminds us that government is the likeliest usurper and destroyer of rights. A neighbor might infringe upon my rights, but a government can obliterate them. Americans have almost always been suspicious of politicians who trumpet their willingness to create and champion new "rights."

Instead, when they see expanding, voracious, all-consuming government, Americans worry about their real rights. They worry when they hear politicians talking about the "public interest" or the "good of society" or the "general welfare." When they hear this, they hide their actions, they hide their wallets, and – when government really runs amok and rushes into war – they hide their sons and daughters.

The American Idea of Government is that government needs to be restrained even more than any individual or group. And so the founders created a constitutional government – a government with a constitution, a government established by and with a constitution. It is a government limited and controlled by words, written by founders who had a lot of sense and who had had enough of unlimited government.

Americans once knew that the U. S. Constitution wasn't a law for them, but was instead a law for the government. The Constitution was the clear-cut, mutually agreed-upon document that put the fence around government, limited its movement, delegated to it specific and enumerated powers, and ordered it to stay out of everything else. Father of the Constitution James Madison

> *took notice of the peculiar manner in which the federal government is lim-*
> *ited. It is not a general grant, out of which particular powers are excepted*
> *– it is a grant of particular power only, leaving the general mass in other*
> *hands. So it had been understood by its friends and its foes, and so it was*
> *to be interpreted.... The Constitution of the U. States is a Constitution of*
> *limits and checks.*[32]

So when we hear about supposed constitutional rights to privacy or to an education or to health care or to a host of other in-and-of-themselves good things, the American Idea of Government asks simply, "Where did that come from?" It's a simple concept that we can too easily forget – that there are no constitutional rights unless the Constitution actually talks about them.

As individuals, we can, for example, claim a "right" to privacy. Now, privacy, without doubt, is a remarkably exquisite possession. But the government can't claim that "right," either for itself or for us. And we can't claim that "right" through the government, but only through our own actions. On privacy, the government has no voice because we have told it to be silent. It can only legally and rightly address the "right to privacy" if we re-write or amend the Constitution.

This is no small matter. With regard to the preservation of our unalienable rights, it's enormous. The conjured right to privacy, for example, has been used to void the unalienable right to life. A government without a respected constitutional restraint is a government without a real restraint of any kind.

We, of course, want to prevent government from doing anything truly bad or destructive. But we don't want the debate on limiting government to revolve around the notion that the things it wants to do are all or always bad. Sometimes they aren't bad. Sometimes the things it wants to do are good – and we shouldn't let it do them anyway. The key points are:

> • Most of those beneficial things can't be provided by government effectively, and perhaps not at all, because of the necessary nature of government. "The working of great institutions," noted philosopher George Santayana, "is mainly the result of a vast mass of routine, petty malice, self-interest, carelessness and sheer mistake. Only a residual fraction is thought."[33] Futurist Alvin Toffler noted, "It is not possible for the White House and the Congress and the federal bureaucracies to make intelligent decisions about one tenth of the many problems with which they now try to cope. Politicians are overwhelmed by the need to make instant decisions about thing they know very little about....[S]uch central manipulation produces uneven, irregular and contradictory effects."[34] The U.S. government has taken on so much that "the World Economic Forum puts America at 68th in the world for the effectiveness of its public-sector spending."[35]

> • Even if government could provide them effectively, the risk of power-madness is too great to allow it to try. Evil exists because people are capable of evil, but it is only completely destructive when it's institutionalized by a government on a large scale. And massive size works against the government having real and effective opposition. As de Tocqueville noted, for example, "[T]he number of newspapers must diminish or increase amongst a democratic people, in proportion as its administration is more or less centralized."[36] The dramatic decline of newspapers is, in part, a sign of how pyramidal and Washington-focused we have become. The government doesn't create freedom, but it can destroy freedom with an agenda of good deeds. Thomas Jefferson said, "If we can prevent the government from wasting the labors of the people, under the pretense of taking care of them, they must become happy."[37]

This American Idea of Government has taken a beating, especially since the Second World War. We're now expected to believe that it's normal for government to provide for us, educate us, train us, protect our employment, insure us, provide our health care, loan us money, care for us in our old age, care for the poor, and give us hope.

In a sense, they're right. It is normal for government to do these things. It just isn't normal, given the American Idea of Government, for American government to do them.

The result of this beating isn't good. We now have a powerhouse government full of itself, intruding into every area of life, flexing its muscles in every state and every part of the globe. While most of us were busy living and trying to do the right thing, government was busy growing and trying to do every thing.

We didn't create the all-consuming government – the top-down, unlimited, self-proclaimed giver of all that is good and taker of all that it wants. But it created itself on our watch. Power-mad politicians and their supporters, big money and small minds, have nearly destroyed the priceless concept of limited government. We need our American Idea of Government back, and soon, before our government is just like all the rest. Speaking of what America deserved, Thomas Jefferson called for,

> *A wise and frugal Government, which shall restrain men from injuring one another, shall leave them otherwise free to regulate their own pursuits of industry and improvement, and shall not take from the mouth of labor the bread it has earned. This is the sum of good government...* [38]

Or as Henry David Thoreau famously observed, "I heartily accept the motto, 'that government is best that governs least'; and i should like to see it acted up to more rapidly and systematically....Government is at best but an expedient; but most governments are usually, and all governments are sometimes, inexpedient."[39]

Jefferson knew that the best government is one that keeps itself on a diet, that keeps a light touch on the reins of power, that remembers the incredible American belief that whatever its accomplishments, it's still far less valuable than any one American.

The good news is that

Government Can Succeed If It Has Real and Evolving Checks and Balances and Stays Within Its Assigned Sphere

Plenty of checks and balances are needed to get a lean, effective, responsive self-government. The U. S. Constitution got many of them right, especially in keeping the executive and legislative branches under control. But there was at least one major constitutional defect with each of the branches of government.

Defect 1: The Warrior President

With the executive branch, not enough was included to prevent the "savage wars of peace."[40] The Constitution calls for the legislative branch, the one most directly responsible to the people – to the ones who will die or send their sons and daughters to die – to be the only one that can declare war. But the Constitution apparently didn't go far enough.

James Madison, the "father of the Constitution", observed,

> *If we consult for a moment, the nature and operation of the two powers to declare war and make treaties, it will be impossible not to see that they can never fall within a proper definition of executive powers....A declaration that there shall be war, is not an execution of laws: it does not suppose pre-existing laws to be executed: it is not in any respect, an act merely executive. It is, on the contrary, one of the most deliberative acts that can be performed...It remains to be enquired whether there be any thing in the constitution itself which shews that the powers of making war and peace are considered as of an executive nature, and as comprehended within a general grant of executive power. It will not be pretended that this appears from any direct position to be found in the [Constitution].*[41]

The president can start and engage in all sorts of things that look and smell and sound and feel like war, as long as he or she doesn't "declare" war. There have been no "declared" wars since World War II, but as of this writing, there have been five major wars (Korea, Vietnam, Persian Gulf, Iraq, and Afghanistan) and a host of minor wars.

All of this makes the "declaration" part of this war business more or less a joke. Presidents can commit troops and then insist that congress and the American people "support our troops," using our respect for the military against us. Congress joins in by passing resolutions of support and the necessary funding, but since it didn't "declare" war, it gets to blame the president if things don't go well.

The constitutional check on presidential adventures and misadventures has been rendered meaningless, with "declaring war" a nasty technicality to be avoided by all. This check needs to be resurrected as outlined in Chapter 13, the American Idea of Peace. Then we will have a check not only on a grasping presidency, but another check on an unaccountable, pass-the-buck congress.

Defect 2: The Profligate Congress

With the legislative branch, not enough check was put in place on compromise, greed and corruption. Bills are bloated and then loaded with pork and nonsense. Some are so large and convoluted that not even an exceptional person could know what he or she was voting on. Congresspeople trade pork for pork, influence for perks, and votes for financial support.

But at least two very important things aren't ideological, partisan, or able to be overridden by government fiat:

> • Math – No one can beat, or even negotiate with, math. Attempts to do so are futile and destined to fail. Making unsupportable pension promises. Spending more than you take in, forever. Making trillion-dollar interest payments on accumulated debt.[42] Lowering the value of the dollar to raise the standard of living. Supporting giant giveaways to government unions with giant takeaways from everyone else. Resisting cutbacks in hopes of a government savior. Math can be a friend or foe. But it can't be ignored.

> • Human Nature – It is intractable. It hasn't changed for six thousand years. If you tax people, they do less, no matter how useful. If you subsidize them, they do more, no matter how worthless. If they see government

and other people spending and borrowing wildly, they'll spend and borrow wildly. If you regulate and punish bad behavior, it slows down. If you deregulate and bail out bad behavior, you get corruption and meltdown. If you offer people a hand up, they'll take it, and they will just as eagerly take a handout. President Calvin Coolidge said,

> *We must realize that human nature is about the most constant thing in the universe and that the essentials of human relationship do not change.*[43]

The president has a veto on much of this, but it isn't much of a check. It's all or nothing. To get the meaningful part of the legislation – if there is any – the garbage has to be accepted along with it.

How did the founders miss it? In part because the government was still small enough and funds were limited enough that congressional bills couldn't get that big. Debt was viewed as a necessary evil, not as a fine tool or a doorway to prosperity. And more – the system hadn't yet been corrupted, and there were actually some statesmen in the lot. They didn't foresee what politicians and political parties could become.

The result is not only a congress run amok, but also a presidency that can duck responsibility and ask, "What could I do? We needed that bill, so I had to accept the bad with the good." With a line-item veto, we get not only a check on a grasping congress, but also another check on an unaccountable, pass-the-buck president. Every budget item becomes a joint responsibility – and a joint venture to incur public wrath.

We need a change to the constitution. President Ronald Reagan said that we should "make it unconstitutional for the Federal Government to spend more than the Federal Government takes in."[44] At a minimum, an amendment needs to do this.

And more. Real legal limits on taxing and spending – not just a "balanced budget" amendment without these limits, because it can be balanced at too high a level. Real legal limits on borrowing and debt – not "ceilings" and "resolutions" that prevent nothing. Real legal limits on the money supply – not arbitrary management by the Federal Reserve. Congress has too little concern about frugality, posterity, or economic reality. Like an out-of-control adolescent, it needs its checking account closed and its credit cards taken away.

Defect 3: The Unchecked Judiciary

Founder Alexander Hamilton, a proponent of strong national government, wrote about the judicial branch of government that

> *the general liberty of the people can never be endangered from that quarter; I mean, so long as the judiciary remains truly distinct from both the legislative and the executive. For I agree that 'there is no liberty, if the power of judging be not separated from the legislative and executive powers.'*[45]

And therein lies the problem. The judicial branch is no longer distinct from the legislative and executive. The "power of judging" has morphed into a power to legislate and execute its own "laws." We're in the process of getting Hamilton's predicted result, the terrible outcome of "no liberty."

The founders missed it almost completely with the judicial branch. They discovered their error almost immediately. Thomas Jefferson wrote these sobering words in his autobiography:

> But there was another amendment of which none of us thought at the time and in the omission of which lurks the germ that is to destroy this happy combination of National powers in the General government.... [W]e have gone even beyond the English caution, by requiring a vote of two thirds in one of the Houses for removing a judge, a vote so impossible...that our judges are effectively independent of the nation. But this ought not to be.... I deem it indispensable that they should be submitted to some practical & impartial control.[46]

Right in the middle of a free country founded on the concept of limited self-government, an anomaly was created by omission and allowed to grow. It is undemocratic, unlimited in scope and power, without checks and balances, and populated by old autocrats who simply will not go away. Abraham Lincoln said,

> The candid citizen must confess that if the policy of the government, upon vital questions, affecting the whole people, is to be irrevocably fixed by decisions of the Supreme Court, the instant they are made...the people will have ceased to be their own rulers, having to that extent practically resigned their government into the hands of that...tribunal.[47]

And we have often not received a good return for our acceptance of this regal court, complete with chambers and robes (De Tocqueville said, "I wish someone would take their robes away to see if, dressed as simple citizens, they might not be recalled to some of the dignity of the human race."[48]). They have decided, for example, that:

- Native Americans deserved no recourse for the several thousand treaties that were made and broken (all of them)

- Cherokees could not be citizens (Cherokee Nation v. Georgia)

- Black people were not people (Dred Scott v. Sanford, 7-2)

- "Separate but equal" was a valid way to compartmentalize and minimize minorities (Plessy v. Ferguson, 7-1)

- Americans of Japanese descent could be "relocated" to concentration camps during World War II (Korematsu v. United States, 6-3)

- Pre-born people were not people (Roe v. Wade, 7-2)

- George W. Bush should be president (Bush v. Gore, 5-4)

Where were the checks on any of these and scores of other actions? Who was allowed to balance these "supremes"? They don't even check or balance each other. Every Supreme Court justice operates in his or her own little fiefdom, voting for or against, concurring in opinions or not, expounding his or her own views in separate opinions that carry weight far beyond what is appropriate in a democratic government "of the people." It may be that "hard cases make bad law,"[49] but unchecked power makes even worse law.

It's not that every justice was or is a bad person. On the contrary, many have been extraordinary people. The problem is systemic. "Power tends to corrupt," noted British Lord Acton, "and absolute power corrupts absolutely."[50] What is absolute power? Power that's complete and unending, like the power of supreme court justices who always have the final word – and never have to face the people to explain that final word. Alexis de Tocqueville observed that:

> *The judge is a lawyer who, apart from the taste for order and for rules imparted by his legal studies, is given a liking for stability by the permanence of his own tenure of office....An American judge, armed with the right to declare laws unconstitutional, is constantly intervening in political affairs.... There is hardly a political question in the United States which does not sooner or later turn into a judicial one.*[51]

Judges as kings and lawmakers was never part of the American Idea. In fact, this notion is one of the surest ways to murder the Idea. President Andrew Jackson warned,

> *The authority of the Supreme Court must not, therefore, be permitted to control the Congress or the Executive when acting in their legislative capacities, but to have only such influence as the force of their reasoning may deserve.*[52]

Why did the writers of the Constitution miss it so badly? Because no one at the time saw any judiciary anywhere acting with any large-scale, global impact. Judges were ancillary to the real work of government. Because they were so unnoticed then, they've been allowed, in many ways, to become the real government now.

But the signers of the Declaration of Independence didn't miss the evil of judicial rule just a few years before. What they said about King George and the British government in that outstanding document could be said without change today about a Chief Justice and the Supreme Court:

> *He has combined with others to subject us to a jurisdiction foreign to our constitution, and unacknowledged by our laws; giving his Assent to their Acts of pretended legislation... For suspending our own Legislatures, and declaring themselves invested with power to legislate for us in all cases whatsoever.*[53]

The American Idea cries out for this great constitutional omission – one that allowed for the creation of a judicial monarchy – to be rectified. In a single stroke, a term limit of 12 years would help immensely by correcting the "people" side of the problem. Someone with unlimited power for 30 or 40 years is too much for anyone to bear. Thomas Jefferson saw this clearly:

> *At the establishment of our constitutions, the judiciary bodies were supposed to be the most helpless and harmless members of the government. Experience however soon showed in what way they were to become the most dangerous; that the insufficiency of the means provided for their removal gave them a free-hold and irresponsibility in office, that their decisions, seeming to concern individual suitors only, pass silent and unheeded by the public at large, that these decisions nevertheless become law by precedent, sapping by little and little the foundations of the Constitution, and working its change by construction, before any one has perceived that this invisible and helpless worm has been busily employed in consuming its substance. In truth, man is not made to be trusted for life, if secured against all liability to account.*[54]

But the systemic side has to be addressed as well. A group of nine people permitted 12 years of pontificating apiece is still too much opportunity for mischief. Simply put, in a real democracy, unelected judges can't be allowed to be lawmakers under the guise of interpretation. This is a problem that the Constitution didn't prevent, but rather inadvertently created. Before the Constitution, the unchecked power that was grasped so early on by Chief Justice John Marshall (and amplified over a 34-year tenure) would have been impossible.

In his later years, Thomas Jefferson wrote:

> *It is not enough that honest men are appointed judges. All know the influence of interest on the mind of man, and how unconsciously his judgment is warped by that influence.... [H]ow can we expect impartial decision between the General government, of which they are themselves so eminent a part, and an individual state from which they have nothing to hope or fear? We have seen too that, contrary to all correct example, they are in the habit of going out of the question before them, to throw an anchor ahead and grapple further hold for future advances of power.[55]*

Liberty can't be safe when the final word on law is left in the hands of unelected attorneys who both make and execute law. "Congress, being a political body," noted Justice Stephen Breyer, "expresses the people's will far more accurately than does an unelected Court."[56]

Scholar James MacGregor Burns summed up the argument against our current unchecked judiciary:

> *The Constitution never granted the judiciary a supremacy over the government, nor had the Framers ever conceived it....[T]he court today stands supreme and unaccountable, effectively immune to the checks and balances that otherwise fragment and disperse power throughout the constitutional system....[J]udicial rule [is] alien to the constitutional design....Against such a court armed with the dogma of its own supremacy, presidents often could win only by waiting for the next turn of the judicial roulette wheel....[57]*

He concludes that

> *deference to a court with extraconstitutional powers to summarily settle controversies over constitutional values has too often sapped our democracy of its vitality....[I]t is emphatically the province and duty of the American people, not of the nine justices of the United States Supreme Court, to say what the Constitution is.[58]*

After not very much time, we should have the wisdom to say to them Cromwell's words to the British King: "You have sat too long for any good you have been doing. Depart, I say, and let us have done with you. In the name of God, go."[59]

The Wandering Government

Aside from these three glaring defects, what about the government getting outside of its assigned sphere? This isn't necessarily evil or even abnormal – governments are always wandering or charging into forbidden areas. If there isn't a specific prohibition, government would rather ask forgiveness than permission (and it will almost never ask forgiveness).

According to the 10th Amendment to the Constitution, everything not specifically assigned to the federal government is reserved to "the States, or to the people."[60] But that has turned out to be too general. This "everything else" has been fair game for the federal – now national – government for decades.

We now know that we need to tell the government not only what it can do, but also what it can't do. If we don't do this, we basically have our own version of the unwritten British constitution – since it's not written down anywhere that government can't do it, government is clear to press ahead and take it over.

The other thing necessary to keeping government in its assigned sphere is to cut off its ways and means. It can't do something if it doesn't have the money. Government is always seeking new ways to raise revenues, using one of its longstanding approaches – taxing, borrowing, and printing money. Ways and means? All three of these ways can become means of destruction.

- "The power to tax is the power to destroy,"[61] noted Chief Justice John Marshall. This can be true due to the level of taxation, but also if taxes are used as an economic or social manipulation tool rather than simply supporting agreed-upon, legitimate government activity. Founder and president James Madison observed,

  The apportionment of taxes on the various descriptions of property is an act which seems to require the most exact impartiality; yet there is, perhaps, no legislative act in which greater opportunity and temptation are given to a predominant party to trample on the rules of justice.[62]

Founder Alexander Hamilton had a response to those who want to overtax specific groups like the "wealthy" or certain industries:

  There is no part of the administration of government that requires extensive information and a thorough knowledge of the principles of political economy so much as the business of taxation. The man who understands those principles best will be least likely to resort to oppressive expedients, or to sacrifice any particular class of citizens to the procurement of revenue.[63]

The key questions to ask are:

1) What should government really be doing?

2) What revenue level does government really need to do it?

3) Since we get more of what we exempt from taxes, what do we want more of (like investment, jobs, savings, industriousness, entrepreneurship)?

4) Since we get less of what we tax, what do we want less of (like borrowing and debt)?

The cost of government wandering is frightening, and the trend of its extravagances even more so. In just 9 years, from 2001 to 2010, the tax code grew from 1.4 to 3.8 million words.[64] It was reported in early 2010 that "public spending (federal, state, and local), which was 24% of GDP in 1950 and 35% before the current decision, could hit 44% this year."[65] There may be a limit, but government will never set that limit on itself. President Grover Cleveland said in 1885,

> *It is the duty of those serving the people in public place to closely limit public expenditures to the actual needs of the Government economically administered, because this bounds the right of the Government to exact tribute from the earnings of labor or the property of the citizen, and because public extravagance begets extravagance among the people.*[66]

• Government borrowing can become a tax on the future, in addition to crowding out the legitimate needs of the private sector.

National debt shouldn't be taken as a given. Ultimately, debt can be an enemy, a weapon of societal mass destruction. This is particularly true if debt only grows and never recedes, if it's used in good times as well as bad, if it's used to favor supporters or certain industries or powerful unions, or if it's deployed to manipulate and control the economy. President Andrew Jackson said,

> *Advantage must result from the observance of a strict and faithful economy. This I shall aim at the more anxiously both because it will facilitate the extinguishment of the national debt, the unnecessary duration of which is incompatible with real independence, and because it will counteract that tendency to public and private profligacy which a profuse expenditure of money by the Government is but too apt to engender.*[67]

This misuse of borrowing includes the penchant for professional politicians to make unfunded promises that can't be kept. Social Security, Medicare, Medicaid, "free" healthcare and education – whether or not these are good concepts, paying for them by sending backbreaking IOUs to the future is most assuredly not.

The government itself is now advising Americans that these IOUs are bogus. For example, "the Social Security system is facing serious financial problems…. [I]n 2016 we will begin paying more in benefits than we collect in taxes. Without changes, by 2037 the Social Security Trust Fund will be exhausted, and there will be enough money to pay only about 76 cents for each dollar of scheduled benefits."[68] What they don't tell us is that even this bad news is a lie, that there is, in reality, no Trust Fund "because the government uses the 'trust fund' to pay for other programs."[69]

It should disturb us immensely that a Chinese leader who oversees hundreds of billions of dollars of U. S. debt has been put in a position to lecture us. Concerning the new penchant of government to create massive financial stimulus to the economy, he said that we passed it "[f]inally, after months and months of struggling with [our] own ideology, with [our] own pride, [our] self-righteousness."[70]

He went on to say, "Now our people are joking that we look at the U.S. and see 'socialism with American characteristics.'"[71] Is this really what Americans want – socialism, and critiques from Chinese autocrats?

Great leaders from the past have weighed in on debt. President Johns Adams said,

> There are two ways to conquer and enslave a nation. One is by the sword. The other is by debt.[72]

President Rutherford B. Hayes said about debt,

> Let every man, every corporation, and especially let every village, town, and city, every county and State, get out of debt and keep out of debt. It is the debtor that is ruined by hard times.[73]

Secretary of the Treasury Alexander Hamilton said that we should

> avoid the accumulation of debt by avoiding occasions of expense and by vigorous exertions in time of peace to discharge the debts which unavoidable wars may have occasioned – not transferring to posterity the burthen which we ought to bear ourselves.[74]

For any real public servant, elimination of all debt should be a very large and ongoing concern.

• Inflating the money supply can become the cruelest tax of all, annihilating the value of assets painstakingly accumulated over a lifetime. Since the Federal Reserve was created in 1913, in part to preserve the soundness of the monetary system, the dollar has lost over 95% of its value.[75] A nickel then would require a dollar now. The government becomes a thief, as historian Niall Ferguson observed:

> By a continuing process of inflation, governments can confiscate, secretly and unobserved, an important part of the wealth of their citizens. By this method, they not only confiscate, but they confiscate arbitrarily...[76]

Adam Smith reminded us that inflation rewards and punishes the wrong people:

> It occasions a general and most pernicious subversion of the fortunes of private people; enriching in most cases the idle and profuse debtor at the expense of the industrious and frugal creditor, and transporting a great part of the national capital from the hands which were likely to increase and improve it to those which are likely to dissipate and destroy it.[77]

As one expert noted, "If the fiat dollar floats [in value], one has no idea what it will be worth when it comes time to spend it."[78]

Government can take and redistribute and diminish wealth, but it can't create it. It can only pretend to, as it uses its three-pronged assault on private property – taxes, debt, and inflation – to expand its scope and scale. As noted by Thomas Jefferson, government should "meet within the year all the expenses of the year without encroaching on the rights of future generations by burthening them with the debts of the past."[79]

People can try to play games with the government by things like minimizing their taxes, borrowing a lot at low fixed rates, and betting against the dollar, but – like a casino – ultimately, only the government wins the game.

The real questions aren't, "Should we cut taxes?" or, "Should we cut spending?" The key questions are, "What should government really do?" and, "How do we keep it from doing anything else?" Only when these questions are answered correctly can a tax plan be established that treats all of us as equal citizens and provides sufficient income so that government borrowing and inflating can be eliminated.

Anything else is arbitrary government that will, in the end, limit freedom and destroy immense value.

Failed government is a terrible thing. In the American Idea,

Government Fails If It Doesn't Carry Out Its Mission, Strays from Its Assignment, or is Hijacked by Career Politicians

Do we have too much government or too little?

Yes.

We can have too little government in places where its role is necessary but where it refuses to carry out its mission. As we saw earlier in this chapter, government can fail to carry out its four legitimate functions. It can leave us defenseless against foreign and domestic threats, excuse and coddle and release violent criminals, leave the elderly and unborn and sick and disabled vulnerable to discounting and death, allow insiders to rig and diminish the market, and permit vile and despicable people to pollute the public arena. All of these are attacks on a free people and on freedom itself.

We can have too much government in places where its role is unnecessary but where it insists on straying from its mission. All governments tend toward control. If permitted, they will quickly take on economic control, always for the "public good." This can be done with taxes and borrowing and inflation, but also with regulation, subsidies, tariffs, bailouts, legalized monopolies (like utilities), central planning, and nationalization of private companies.

For the more coercive, they will gladly take on social control, once again for the "general welfare." From favoring one group over another, to dictating what can be read or heard, to social engineering, they can go outside not only any constitution, but also outside reason and decency as well. Historian Jacques Barzun wrote,

> The modern individual has been emancipated from subjection to rank and has exchanged it for "inspection" over the whole range of life's activities. This control takes the form of permit, license, and stated limitations, as well as actual inspection.[80]

The first mission of the government of a free people is to preserve their freedom. If freedom is the proper end of all good government, government fails miserably if it doesn't protect and enhance liberty. Here's how our 7 Spirits of Freedom (see Chapter 1, The American Idea of Freedom) are being eroded by a government that is both failing to carry out its mission and straying outside of its mission:

1. Freedom from oppression. In recent decades, we've been morally and economically oppressed by unnecessary and badly managed wars in Korea, Vietnam, the Persian Gulf, Afghanistan, and Iraq. All the while, our government has grown in size, reach, and arrogance.

2. Freedom from control. We are now being controlled by so many laws that, as founder and president James Madison warned in the *Federalist*, there are too many for us to even know what they are:

> *It will be of little avail to the people that the laws are made by men of their own choice if the laws be so voluminous that they cannot be read, or so incoherent that they cannot be understood; if they... undergo such incessant changes that no man, who knows what the law is today, can guess what it will be tomorrow. Law is defined to be a rule of action; but how can that be a rule, which is little known, and less fixed?*[81]

"America needs fewer and clearer laws, so that citizens do not need a law degree to stay out of jail," noted one international magazine.[82] "There are over 4,000 federal crimes, and many times that number of regulations that carry criminal penalties. When analysts at the Congressional Research Service tried to count the number of separate offenses on the books, they were forced to give up, exhausted. Rules concerning corporate governance of the environment are often impossible to understand, yet breaking them can land you in prison."[83] I wonder what laws I am breaking by writing this book?

3. Freedom from fear. We are asked to give up our freedom bit by bit because of an ever-present fear that is kept before our eyes – of terrorists and rogue nations and biological weapons, or of pandemics and recessions and financial disasters. Although living itself can be scary, living without freedom is intolerable.

4. Freedom to count. Our freedom to count has been dwarfed by politico-celebrities who listen closely only to lobbyists and pollsters and money. They are far removed from listening to us and administering a government "of the people, by the people, for the people."[84] It is disturbing and disgraceful that in a country of liberty, unalienable rights, and self-government, we elevate presidents and other government officials so high. Do we just have an unnatural craving for kings and nobles? We can hope not. But even our representatives don't count when their legislation can be wiped out in a moment by one judge.

5. Freedom to achieve. Achievement is under assault by those in government who want to replace equality of opportunity with equality of results. Achievement is a hollow notion when achievers are stripped of many or most of their just rewards – which are then given too frequently to non-achievers. Presidents have taken to bringing up individual stories to make points about problems and needs and fairness. But in addition to the fact that they don't really know these people or their circumstances, they forget a great truth: Examples can illustrate but can never prove a point.

6.   Freedom to share. Government works ever harder to become the "Great Philanthropist" – with our money. A vice presidential candidate can lecture us on our "patriotic duty" to pay taxes so he will have a lot to give away, even though he personally contributes almost nothing to charity. Government makes promises – in Social Security, Medicare, Medicaid, pensions for military and other government employees – that it does not report honestly and that it cannot keep. It wants to do more – to control more – in areas like healthcare. And it does all of it badly and expensively. One of the collateral costs of this has been a growing willingness on the part of Americans to let the government take care of it.

7.   Freedom to come back. The ability to come back has been eased for the few through lax bankruptcy laws and made harder for the many through tax rates that would shock our ancestors – not just the Founding Fathers, but older people who are alive today. People speak with awe of the great industrialists of the 19th and early 20th centuries, but that's like praising athletes who are on performance-enhancing drugs. How would those industrial giants have done if they had income taxes, sales taxes, payroll taxes, capital gains taxes, ever-increasing regulation, and an aggressive legal system that allowed anyone to sue and try to rob what belonged to them?

Freedom is always a casualty whenever government misdirects its energies. Right along with freedom, both life and the pursuit of happiness can take some very large hits as well. "I own that I am not a friend to a very energetic government," observed Thomas Jefferson. "It is always oppressive."[85]

One of government's favorite tactics is creating a problem (like giving railroads or bankers too much latitude, protection, and subsidy), letting those receiving its favor take the heat when things inevitably go south, and then changing uniforms and riding in to save us from the bad railroads or banks. In these cases, they want to rescue us from the boogeyman when they are the boogeyman.

Another of government's tactics, honed over the past half century, is to mislead us and justify what it wants to do by...lying:

• It often does this with bogus terms and statistics – unemployment data that doesn't include all of the unemployed and "core" inflation that doesn't include "volatile" food and energy prices (which make up a large part of an American family's budget), "primary balance" of the federal budget, which excludes interest on debt.[86]

• It provides half the story to make a point – America with 5% of the world's population uses 25% of the world's resources (leaving out the fact that it produces about the same amount of the world's goods).[87] The whole truth makes America look amazing rather than gluttonous.

• It makes irrational comparisons – women only earn 77% of what men earn (without noting the vast differences in the career and life choices that lead to this discrepancy or recognizing that women often actually out-earn men when looking at roughly similar experience and positions).[88] Women don't earn anything. A woman does.

Why does government do this? Because whoever is currently in office has an agenda. They want to do something, so they "cook the books" to be able to do it. When presidents badly misstate facts and distort truth, they're either fools (they really don't know and aren't open or diligent enough to find out) or cynics (they know but want to advance their agenda and just don't care).

It's all right for them to draw different conclusions than we might, but it isn't all right for them to hide or distort the facts that disagree with their conclusions. They need to say to us, "Here is what appears to us to be happening. Here are all of the facts that pertain to this situation – pro, con, and neutral. Some advisors think the total picture is X, some Y, some Z. We're acting on Y for these reasons." Americans can understand difficult choices. But they've never been very supportive of treachery.

And then there is this relatively modern American creature, the career politician. At some point along the way, politics went from being a public service to a career path. But the power of government is too great to allow it to be hijacked by people who come into office and never go away. This problem is related to, but different from, the problem of missing term limits.

This new "principle" of "politics as profession" is disastrous, more or less so depending on the politician. "They saw all the consequences in the principle," noted founder and President James Madison, "and they avoided the consequences by denying the principle."[89] The consequences of this "principle" are arrogance, disconnection from real people and concerns, and frequently unbridled corruption.

The needed change – the indispensable change – is to put limits on all government positions other than civil service and military. Frequent elections aren't enough because the power of incumbency and inertia are too great and the same people linger on forever. The re-election rates to congress in the 2008 presidential election year were 94% in the House and 83% in the Senate (the equivalent numbers for the 2010 mid-terms were 87% and 84%). This is only slightly lower than the Soviet Union's Supreme Soviet in its heyday.[90]

Ten years is the longest a president could serve consecutively if he or she moved from vice president to president just after the halfway point of a term and then was elected twice. This is the most powerful position in government, so allowing others a little more time could be reasonable. Twelve years should be sufficient across the board. It's enough time to have to put up with anyone in a single public office, even if he or she is doing a decent job. In most cases, it's more than enough.

So we would have 2 terms of 6 years for a senator and 6 terms of 2 years for a representative. This is plenty of time to allow them a learning curve and for us to profit from both the freshness of their ideas and the depth of their experience. And it's a wonderful way to clear the decks and bring in some other dedicated Americans with their fresh ideas and rich experience.

Twelve years for a judicial position should be no different. In truth, the fact that they are unelected – and that there's no further accountability to the people – probably argues for less than twelve years. In practice, lifetime appointments, designed to protect justices from political exploitation, have served to protect the wrong things – to protect judges from accountability and to protect us from having judges in touch with the rule of law and constitutional limits. Lifetime tenure was thought to protect judges from political manipulation and public pressure. Instead, it has come to protect them from judicial restraint and popular will.

These mandatory limits make room for the possibility of some citizen politicians. It wouldn't bar professional politicians, but it would make it harder for them as they move from one position to another. And it might provide some needed humility even there, as a person with, say, two terms as a congressperson and two as a senator would have to go back to the lesser role if he or she wanted to stay in the federal government.

Professional politicians threaten our freedoms. Entrenched congresspeople, archaic senators, power-mad presidents, god-like judges – and all of their courtiers – have often been more concerned about extending their freedoms than protecting ours. It would be folly to believe that somehow "public servants" come from better stock than the rest of us do. "It is a mistake to think that businessmen are more immoral than politicians," observed economist John Maynard Keynes.[91] President Theodore Roosevelt said,

> The Presidency is a great office, and the power of the President can be effectively used to secure a renomination, especially if the President has the support of certain great political and financial interests. It is for this reason, and this reason alone, that the wholesome principle of continuing in office, so long as he is willing to serve, an incumbent who has proved capable, is not applicable to the Presidency.[92]

As corollary limits, we need to put real controls on how long political campaigns can be run and how much money can be spent. The temptation to campaign forever with money gotten from people who want influence and have interests is just too great. Six months with a reasonable level of public funding would be more than enough.

There is no way to control influence and interests, which are always present in human interaction. But we can limit the amount of time in which an individual can be influenced and give in to his or her interests. After that, the lobbyists and other influencers will have to start over with someone else, perhaps someone who just doesn't care about their influence.

Someone (perhaps Benjamin Franklin) said that "Democracy is two wolves and a lamb voting on what to have for dinner."[93] The wolves are out there, many of them in Washington, D.C. We, the lambs, need to contest their right to eat us.

The founders had a lot of savvy, but they didn't make enough allowance for out-of-control, never-ending crassness, ambition, and greed. They couldn't or didn't envision the "professional politician." As a people, we've already acknowledged their error with regard to an unlimited-duration presidency and corrected it.

If we did that, we can do the rest that needs to be done.

As is true with other recommendations in this book, there is a clear need to amend the work of the founders and all who have come along since. We should never fear making changes and creating a "more perfect union." Founder Elbridge Gerry wrote,

> However respectable the members may be who signed the Constitution, it must be admitted, that a free people are the proper guardians of their rights and liberties – that the greatest men may err, and that their errours are sometimes of the greatest magnitude.[94]

Before the Constitution was ratified, Gerry noted "that some of the powers of the Legislature are ambiguous, and others indefinite and dangerous – that the Executive is blended with and will have an undue influence over the Legislature – that the judicial department will be oppressive."[95] His concerns were justified and have proven to be correct. He also insisted that a Bill of Rights, missing from the original work, be added immediately. The Constitution started out being amended ten times. Thomas Jefferson wrote,

> Happy for us, that when we find our constitutions defective & insufficient to secure the happiness of our people, we can assemble with all the coolness of philosophers & set it to rights, while every other nation on earth must have recourse to arms to amend or to restore their constitutions.[96]

If it's true that people get the government they deserve, we haven't been doing enough to deserve better government. But we can raise our expectations, both of ourselves and of our government. The Declaration of Independence says that we have the right to alter our government, and it is certainly time to alter both the government and our thinking about government. We can:

Take Action

Respect good government and disrespect the bad.

★

Remember that self-government begins with each of us governing ourselves.

★

Give everyone the responsibility and honor to pay for his or her citizenship on an equal basis.

★

Put strict time limits on all government power.

★

Reverse the flow of power and money by enlarging individual and local government and shrinking state and national government.

★

Resist the notion that government can or should expand to meet needs or solve problems.

★

Pass a constitutional amendment stating clearly what the federal government can't do.

★

Fix constitutional defect 1, The Warrior President, with strict limits.

★

Move toward a non-royal, non-grasping executive branch.

★

Fix constitutional defect 2, The Profligate Congress, with strict limits.

★

Move toward the non-permanent, citizen congress.

★

Redefine the role of the legislative branch as being "representatives" rather than "lawmakers."

★

Put tight boundaries around politicians' ability to make promises for after they are gone.

★

Have public, limited financing of political campaigns.

★

Have limits on the amount of time a campaign can run in the public arena.

★

Fix constitutional defect 3, The Unchecked Judiciary, with strict limits and needed additions.

★

Move toward a non-tenured, non-regal judiciary.

★

Expect government to give us honest, consistent, understandable information.

To see detail on these Action Points and to add your voice visit www.theamericanideas.com

There's a tremendous amount for us to do to re-birth the American Idea of Government. But we can do it. We have to honor the work done by the founders while clearly facing its deficiencies. They themselves expected us to do it:

> *The basis of our political system is the right of the people to make and to alter their constitutions of government. (George Washington)*[97]

Each generation...has a right to choose for itself the form of government it believes most promotive of its own happiness. (Thomas Jefferson)[98]

Whenever [the people] shall grow weary of the existing Government, they can exercise their constitutional right of amending it, or their revolutionary right to dismember or overthrow it. (Abraham Lincoln)[99]

When the founders were creating the American government, they were on the political frontier, working their way through unknown territory – because people, as Tom Paine noted,

Have had so few opportunities of making the necessary trials on modes and principles of Government...that Government is but now beginning to be known, and experience is yet wanting to determine many particulars....[T]he best constitution that could now be devised, consistent with the condition of the present moment, may be far short of that excellence which a few years may afford.[100]

The alternatives to making a reasoned set of significant changes aren't pleasant. All we have to do to see them is to look around us – or look back through the pages of world history.

We have an excellent start with the inheritance received from the founders. And now we can do even better – using their Ideas as a guide.

This American Idea is totally at odds with the norms of human history. Those norms assume that people are stupid, helpless, and needy and require a government to manage and control them.

America was the first place of consequence where people rejected these notions, where they believed it to be both rational and doable that they govern themselves. This is an astonishing Idea, beautiful to behold and beneficial to practice – and uniformly opposed by people who feel in their bones that they were born to rule over others.

We need to treasure freedom, even though some people will abuse it and use it to do evil. Societies that focus on freeing the 95% who will lead responsible lives have a much greater chance of enduring and prospering than those that focus on controlling the 5% who won't. Outstanding societies follow the rule of the 95 and the 5: Don't design government to provide absolute control of the few who pervert freedom. This approach will actually oppress the compliant many – and the abusive few will get around the system anyway.

As we said before, the problem is this: In the age-old question, "Are people basically good or basically bad?" the answer is, "Yes." People have good, decent, social tendencies that cause the formation of societies. And people have evil, coarse, antisocial tendencies that precipitate the need for government. C.S. Lewis said,

> *These, then are the two points I wanted to make. First, that human beings, all over the earth, have this curious idea that they ought to behave in a certain way, and cannot really get rid of it. Secondly, that they do not in fact behave that way. They know the Law of Nature; they break it. These two facts are the foundation of all clear thinking about ourselves and the universe we live in.[101]*

Which people will we focus on? If the latter, we will build a gigantic government that, in addition to not stopping the 5%, will become a problem in its own right. Who has hurt others more – the people who pursue their own interests, or the government that pursues yours? Our troubles have only begun when we ask the government to be the chief tinkerer.

We aren't going to keep or earn the fruits of freedom if government is our primary means. In America, noted Fareed Zakaria, "society has asserted its dominance over the state."[102] America's society has always been more powerful than its government in the things that count. He goes on to say, "if America's economic system is its core strength, its political system is its core weakness."[103] Right now, America is hampered, not enhanced, by its government.

Zakaria concludes with an astonishing but true, observation: "America is also much more than its government."[104] America is its people, culture, opportunity and so much more. America isn't its government, and its government isn't America. America is the American people and the American Ideas – only one of which is government.

Of course, we need a government that deals with people as they actually are, not as we wish them to be or as they would be after a miracle or lobotomy. And this includes dealing with the people who, at any given time, make up the government. Jefferson observed,

> Sometimes it is said that man can not be trusted with the government of himself. Can he, then, be trusted with the government of others?[105]

Journalist Andrew Sullivan added his own take on this: "Democracy is rooted in the impertinent belief that our rulers are no better than we are."[106]

If we worry about what people will do without government, we should be at least as worried about what people will do with government. When government forgets that it is only a restrainer, it ceases being part of the solution and becomes part of the problem. The umpire can no longer do the job effectively or justly when he or she becomes a participant in the game.

The American Idea of Government wasn't rooted in the U.S. Constitution. It was rooted in early English history, initially expressed in the Magna Carta in 1215 and watered by John Locke in the 18th century.

It was brought to full flower by Thomas Jefferson in the Declaration of Independence in 1776. In his Gettysburg Address, Abraham Lincoln dated the beginning of the nation at the Declaration, not the Constitution. Why? Because the American Idea begins with the majesty of the individual, not with a structure of governance.

In the end, government isn't the goal, but only a tool. We want and need the rule of law rather than the rule of government. We need an empire of laws, not of people. We need a basic commitment to the principle that the law, not the people who administer it, is the foundation. As George Washington observed:

> The preservation of the sacred fire of liberty and the destiny of the Republican model of Government are justly considered as deeply, perhaps, as finally, staked on the experiment entrusted to the hands of the American people.[107]

He reminded us that the American people weren't put into the hands of government, but quite the reverse – the government, along with the whole American Idea, was "entrusted to the hands of the American people."[108] *And Americans* want people – the individual person – to be more important than the government.

Washington and the other founders knew that the American Idea of Government is about self-government. This starts – and ends – with you and me.

CHAPTER 12

The American Idea of Independence

Independence is...such a beautiful word.

We have a Declaration of Independence. We had a War of Independence. We celebrate Independence Day. The important question is: Do we really still have the kind of independence worth bragging about?

The Declaration of Independence deals in a majestic way with individual rights. But it was issued primarily as a declaration of national independence. For the individual, it was about freedom. For the people as a whole, it was about independence.

It said that we as a people would no longer be under the heels of anyone else. We would stand free and self-determined. And we'd be careful not to be drawn back into any crippling relationships. George Washington focused on this critical American Idea of national independence. He declared,

> *It is our true policy to steer clear of permanent alliances with any portion of the foreign world.*[1]

As a keen observer of human nature and power, he knew that involving the nation in alliances, policing the world, and engaging in power politics would end liberty in the long run – first for the nation, and finally for the individual.

Implied in the Declaration of American Independence was the conviction that no nation had a right, or even a business, to dominate other nations. We could be an example, a "shining city on a hill,"[2] but we wouldn't try to force our beliefs or needs on other nations. We would offer diamonds to all, but not force them on anyone.

And so the American Idea of Independence was born. It was independence at both ends – we would neither be dominated nor dominate others. We wouldn't play the game that nations play and had been playing from forever. There was always "great power politics," but America would be a great power...without the politics.

We've gotten far away from this grand Idea. Washington's voice – and many other voices – calls us to return to it once again.

Independence

Independence is freedom from foreign domination, affairs, entanglements, pettiness, greed, stupidity, and wars.

Independence doesn't mean isolation; rather, it means the right mix of involvement and separation.

We reject power politics and global chessboards.

We know that diplomacy usually isn't crucial when relating to civilized people and nations and usually isn't fruitful when relating to fanatics and monsters.

An independent spirit leads us to constructive engagement and the free exchange of goods and ideas, while a dependent spirit leads us to look to others for direction, approval, and resources.

Only an independent people can show the world a better way to live.

At its fundamental level, we know that

Independence Is Freedom from Foreign Domination, Affairs, Entanglements, Pettiness, Greed, Stupidity, and Wars

Given the degree of American entanglement with other nations and their problems, it's hard to imagine a time when it wasn't so. Or when it could be like that again. But it can be so.

Politicians talk about our "national interests," and we indeed have some. We want to be safe and prosperous. But what national interest can there possibly be in 95% of what our government now throws itself into outside of America?

Sometimes, our national interest comes down to merely protecting the embassy staff that is there to promote our interests. It's like a toll-booth system that collects just enough money to pay for the toll-booth system.

We have presidents holding forth on even minor events in places like Eastern Europe, Southeast Asia, and sub-Saharan Africa. Why? What does this mean to the daily lives and goals and dreams of Americans?

Nothing. It's just "great power politics," 21st century style.

The American Idea of Independence shattered all of that. It said that we will be free from

> • *Foreign domination.* We won't be dominated, and we won't dominate. We won't involve ourselves in anything that could lead either to being dominated or to dominating others.
>
> Right now, we have an unsightly mix. We're finding ourselves in situations where we're using power and pressure to get nations (or at least their leaders) to do what we want them to do. And oddly, we're finding ourselves dominated by world opinion and global sentiment.
>
> We had missteps in our first 150 years as a nation, but nothing compares to what we've been drawn into since World War II. Going back to the better Idea is not only possible – given our internal strength, it's simply a matter of choice. And Independence plays to our strength. De Tocqueville said that "foreign policy does not require the use of any of the good qualities peculiar to democracy but does demand that cultivation of almost all those which it lacks."[3]
>
> • *Foreign affairs.* There are always many things going on in the world, a great many of them bad. There are countless ways to get involved in all of them.
>
> This gives presidents a way to look important and gives the executive

branch something that seems important to do. It can make America seem important. But there's just no advantage in it for the independence of the American people.

Powerbrokers always know that empire extended abroad is power expanded at home. And the longer we engage in these affairs, the more likely that we will turn into a power-broking people, wondering as the British once did if the sun will ever set on our interests.

• *Foreign entanglements.* Before World War II, America generally steered clear of alliances and treaties that would require it to act against its real interests – the lives and well-being of its individual people.

Even America's entry into World War I wasn't required by any formal relationship, but only by an ambitious president and the "special interests." His master organization for interconnected foreign entanglements, the League of Nations, was soundly rejected by a Senate and American people that had never been quite sure about why they were involved in this Old World war and its aftermath.

The only reason for a nation to have alliances and treaties is to protect itself. As the most powerful nation in the world by a lot, we don't need the protection. So why do we have all of these alliances and treaties? They're only used to draw America into more power politics and never-ending involvement – with most of it, like in the Middle East, to no useful end. These relationships are double-edged swords – with other nations holding the handle and America grasping the blade.

• *Pettiness.* In the Marx Brothers' comedy classic *Duck Soup*, a war is started over a foreign leader calling Groucho Marx an "upstart."[4] It's ridiculous and hilarious. And it's based on human and historical truth – the smallest things can cause the biggest disasters.

The Vietnam War was taken to the next ugly level by American ships being assaulted in the Gulf of Tonkin – an assault which never took place. World War I was launched by an Austrian archduke (like other terms of nobility, a title without meaning in America) being assassinated by a Serbian nationalist, and then overreaching empires (British, French, German, Russian, Ottoman) taking their places on the bloody stage. The Spanish-American War was kicked off by the sinking of the USS Maine – which probably went down by internal explosion.

There's no limit to the petty and false things out there that can draw a nation into the abyss. The only safe course is to avoid them all.

• *Greed.* Greed, jealousy, and envy are the constant fellow-pilgrims of humanity. Empires were built on the notion of extracting much and returning less (or little or nothing, depending on the empire). Wars have been started to help the moneyed and industrial interests. Peoples have been sold out and slaughtered because they happened to be sitting on resources that somebody else wanted.

The American Idea was, "We'd rather be independent and poor than entangled and have your _____ [fill in the blank]." There's an old proverb, "When in doubt, look for the financial interest." There's truth in this that should make us constantly wary. It should make us look past the noble language and patriotic clarion calls to see if money is at the bottom of it all.

• *Stupidity.* We're in a world where the lunatics and deranged can get a big forum or a lot of power. They can claim that genocide never happened, that Slavic people are inferior, that people will be happy to lose their farms and live in a socialist cooperative, that women should be lower-class citizens, that terrorism will bend the will of great powers. In a recent survey, 1 in 7 Germans want to restore the Berlin wall![5]

The nation of Iran is a current embodiment of stupidity and willful ignorance. It's a country that has treated Jews as second-class (or no-class) citizens for over a thousand years. Not surprisingly, it hates Jews. It denies that the Holocaust happened. It believes that it can call for the annihilation of Israel and still have intelligent people consider it a civilized nation. But it is too stupid to be worthy of diplomacy and discussion. Reasoning and debating with people like this? A waste of time.

As someone has said, some ignorance is invincible. Human stupidity is widespread and continually renewing, and we can't make it go away. The only thing we can do is avoid it and let these people fall on their own swords.

• *Wars.* Leading the nation through a terrible war – this, we're told, is where great presidents are made. But how much greater is a president who keeps us out of war? Unless survival is at stake, fighting over things like "national honor" or "our rightful place in the world," for respect or resources, is a sign of weakness rather than strength.

The non-American world is expert on wars – starting them, dragging them out, letting the end of this one be the start of the next. They know violence and have the historical record to prove it.

With or without America, the world has always been an unstable and dangerous place. Matches have been struck by the thousands in modern times alone, but most burn out without lighting the fuse of a major bomb. It can be the very act of intervening that can provide the fuse necessary to set off a major explosion – the imposition of power that expands a local molehill into an international mountain.

The American Idea of Independence says, "No!" – No to all of these drivers of national misdirection and destruction, no to the lure of the Old World's ways. Revolutionary leader Tom Paine, in writing of America, said,

> *This new World hath been the asylum for the persecuted lovers of civil and religious liberty…. Hither have they fled…from the cruelty of the monster…. The Reformation was preceded by the discovery of America: as if the Almighty generously meant to open a sanctuary to the persecuted in future years…. Every spot of the old world is overrun with oppression. Freedom hath been hunted round the globe….[R]eceive the fugitive, and prepare in time an asylum for mankind.[6]*

It isn't a question of being either an isolationist or an internationalist. It's a question of being wise. It's a recognition that independence is much, much better than entanglement.

In Jefferson's grand words, Americans want "[p]eace, commerce, and honest friendship with all nations, entangling alliances with none."[7] They know that

Independence Doesn't Mean Isolation; Rather, It Means the Right Mix of Involvement and Separation

People have argued for many years over the question, "Should America be isolationist or not?"

As is true so often with either/or questions, the right answer is, "Certainly."

No nation, including America, has ever been totally isolated. Complete isolation – culturally, socially, economically – isn't even possible. In its early years of supposed isolation, America developed and maintained tremendous exchanges of goods and ideas. So we've never had – and we're not going to be able to ever get – true isolation.

But this doesn't mean that measured isolation – knowing when to be involved and when to be separate – is a poor or unobtainable goal. On the contrary, America went from being a tiny collection of colonies to being the largest economy in the world in less than a century because it knew when isolation was harmful and when it was the way to greatness.

There's been some notion that Americans, from the beginning, wanted to be involved in every way but moved toward isolation because the nation wasn't yet big or strong enough to be a player. But that misrepresents both early Americans and the American Idea of Independence.

There wasn't just acceptance of a temporary isolation until America could enter the game of great-power politics. There was gladness that there could be isolation from the worst of human nature and satisfaction that engagement could be on a new and very different set of rules.

This ability to know when to be involved and when to be separate represents incomparable wisdom. The founders of America had that wisdom. We have access to it and can live it once again.

When to Be Involved

Americans are citizens of the world. America was founded by bold explorers who came to find new worlds and by bold refugees who came to find new freedoms. It's continually re-founded by the same kinds of people.

Americans are sometimes belittled or even ridiculed for their ignorance of the ways of the rest of the world. It's true that most Americans don't travel abroad and can't speak a foreign language fluently. But in spite of these "deficiencies" – minor, and often raised by snobbish, jealous non-Americans – Americans make an incredible impact on every aspect of global life.

We make our mark with generosity of spirit and purse, with culture and economics and technology, with wild ideas of freedom and democracy and human and civil rights. America is an inescapable reality in every corner of the planet.

In part, Americans don't go abroad because abroad comes to America – to listen, to learn and to live, but also to engage, to enrich and to enlarge it. And they don't learn foreign languages in part because English has become the world's language in a special way, as it carries American culture throughout the earth.

The time to be involved is when that involvement benefits both sides and harms neither. Cross-cultural sharing, trade, and philanthropy are just a few of those ways. As Tom Paine said,

> *What have we to do with setting the world at defiance? Our plan is commerce, and that, well attended to, will secure us...peace and friendship.*[8]

The American Idea calls for deep involvement on everything that makes human life worthwhile – and on nothing that diminishes or destroys it.

When to Be Separate

When Americans are thinking clearly, we realize some very important concepts. We remember that:

- we're not the world's police or umpire or referee;

- we can't claim neutrality while we take sides;

- we shouldn't hold out a trading hand or a helping hand to oppressors who are tormenting helpless multitudes;

- involvement in civil wars and religious wars and balance-of-power wars, however noble in intent, is just as likely to make them worse than better;

- involvement in those conflicts is always worse for America, in the loss of blood and treasure and in the acquisition of a cynical spirit.

The time to be separate is when involvement will benefit only one side or harm either side.

There are many ways to fail this test. The spending of American lives to try to save other lives fails. An alliance that could cause one side to sacrifice itself for what its people don't value fails. A treaty that could cause the other side to act with destructive arrogance because it has a strong ally fails.

American hero Charles Lindbergh said non-intervention

> *is based upon the belief that the security of a nation lies in the strength and character of its own people....It demands faith in an independent American destiny....It is a policy not of isolation, but of independence; not of defeat, but of courage.*[9]

The American Idea calls for involvement when it benefits all parties and separation when it doesn't. At their best, Americans are deeply involved separatists. They are interested in everything. And meddle in nothing.

For generations, Americans said,

Founder and first president George Washington saw the world clearly and understood the priceless treasure America had found with its ocean-moat. He asked,

> *Why forgo the advantages of so peculiar a situation? Why quit our own to*
> *stand upon foreign ground? Why, by interweaving our destiny with that of*
> *any part of Europe, entangle our peace and prosperity in the toils of Euro-*
> *pean ambition, rivalship, interest, humor, or caprice?*[10]

Why indeed. For a very long time, America resisted the fatal seduction of the international power game. This was partly because it was small, but mostly because it was smart. It didn't take much observation of history to conclude that all of this power-broking did more to contribute to tension and conflict than it did to prevent or resolve it. Fifty years after Washington's death, President Zachary Taylor reminded Americans,

> *As American freemen we can not but sympathize with all efforts to extend*
> *the blessings of civil and political liberty, but at the same time we are warned*
> *by the admonitions of history and the voice of our own beloved Washington*
> *to abstain from entangling alliances with foreign nations.*[11]

America got off track after World War II. This was understandable, since it was the primary superpower left standing and the only nation that was essentially intact. There was a vacuum, and America stepped into it. It didn't have to fill the void. It didn't have to replace the British and French and German and Japanese empires, which, through "great power" politics, destroyed themselves and much of the world.

At that point, America could have followed the example of George Washington, who twice voluntarily laid down power that was in many ways absolute – first as the victorious general of the Revolution and second as the unanimously elected president in a time before term limits. Few generals or presidents in the Americas or anywhere else have ever done this, but this was America and its Idea of Independence – no absolute power, not even for a beloved and trusted hero. Like its first president, America could have walked away from power.

But it didn't. It started filling gaps – in Europe, Japan, Korea, Indochina, the Middle East. It didn't become an empire there, but it took over many of the responsibilities and expectations of empire – patrolling the seas, securing trade routes, exploiting resources, intervening in conflicts, forming and leading alliances, creating vassal states, overthrowing "unacceptable" governments.

Have there been advantages to America? Of course. But the disadvantages are greater. All of the disadvantages of empire – spending more than it gets in return, having to be in constant vigilance about everything all over the globe, being feared by all and hated by most, acting as the world's policeman and savior while potential enemies like China grow stronger in the absence of any such responsibility.

But thankfully, Americans are returning to their roots. In a respected survey, for the first time in over 40 years of polling, "a plurality of the general public (49%) say the United States should 'mind its own business internationally and let other countries get along the best they can on their own.'"[12]

So it turns out that James Monroe, our 5th president – the only president other than Washington elected unanimously (by the electors) – was right. In the game-changing words of The Monroe Doctrine, he declared the

> principle in which the rights and interests of the United States are involved,
> that the American continents, by the free and independent condition which
> they have assumed and maintain, are henceforth not to be considered as
> subjects for future colonization by any European powers.[13]

He goes on to say that America won't take part in Europe's wars – very powerful wisdom unfortunately bypassed in the 20th century. He then returns to his no-colonization theme. Contrary to some who have said that this was a policy to control of all the Americas, he delivered his doctrine in 1823, after peoples south of America had declared their own independence. Monroe says that we will stand with them and stand up for them if their freedom is attacked. He says,

> With the Governments who have declared their independence and main-
> tained it, and whose independence we have, on great consideration and on
> just principles, acknowledged, we could not view any interposition for the
> purpose of oppressing them, or controlling in any other manner their des-
> tiny, by any European power in any other light than as the manifestation
> of an unfriendly disposition toward the United States....[N]or can anyone
> believe that our southern brethren, if left to themselves, would adopt [colo-
> nization] of their own accord.[14]

Properly understood and applied, the Monroe Doctrine represented the willingness of an older sibling in freedom to defend any younger siblings who might be bullied by a strong outsider. At its best, it would surely include no bullying by the older sibling. Thirty years later, President Franklin Pierce advised Americans,

> With neighboring nations upon our continent we should cultivate kindly
> and fraternal relations. We can desire nothing in regard to them so much
> as to see them consolidate their strength and pursue the paths of prosperity
> and happiness. If in course of their growth we should open new channels
> of trade and create additional facilities for friendly intercourse, the benefits
> realized will be equal and mutual.[15]

The Old World then is still the Old World now. Then, they had their tribal wars and religious wars and domination wars. Now, they have their tribal wars (think the Balkans and central Africa), their religious wars (think the Middle East and Northern Ireland) and their domination wars (think China-Taiwan and Russia-Afghanistan). "There's nothing new under the sun"[16] is a horrible, living reality in the Old World.

This is why many of the people who came here for decades did so. They couldn't stand it. They had the guts to walk away. They brought some bad habits and some miserable learned behavior with them, but they left the old behind and went in search of something better. And then our more recent ancestors, through a combination of good intentions and naiveté, walked back into the Old World that still hasn't really changed. What were they thinking?

Our pilgrim ancestors were right to leave that nonsense behind. Washington was right when he warned of "entangling foreign alliances" and told us to treasure the oceans that separated us.[17] And Monroe was right when he told them to stay out. Period. As President John Kennedy said,

> *Let all our neighbors know that we shall join with them to oppose aggression or subversion anywhere in the Americas. And let every other power know that this Hemisphere intends to remain the master of its own house.*[18]

We need to draw lines. But not battle lines. We need to draw two vertical lines, right down the middle of the oceans, one just west of Hawaii and the other just west of Bermuda. Then, in a fresh restatement of the Monroe Doctrine, we need to tell the Old World to keep its insanity on the other side of the lines. And that restatement needs to say that America will honor those lines as well.

We should say to the Old World, we won't come over there and meddle. We won't try to improve you or save you or get you to see the light. Our ancestors knew, and we've now relearned, that these things can't be done. If you over there can't figure out that it's better to have peace and prosperity than war and poverty, good food and good movies instead of no food and bad jihad, then it's your funeral.

And we should say, on the other hand, don't you come over here. We don't need your destitute ways of thinking and living. We're tired of whatever you're doing, and we're even more weary of being drawn into it. Keep your hell to yourself, and let us take a stab at heaven.

In America, we've somehow ended up with a messianic government. But finally getting out of the muck of foreign entanglements will let us focus on scraping the Old-World mess off our shoes, sweeping the dirt off our own front porch, and living an independent American life once more.

The Old World is a great place to visit. I just wouldn't want to live there.

What about diplomacy? Isn't that important? This American Idea leads us to say,

We Know That Diplomacy Usually Isn't Crucial When Relating to Civilized People and Nations, and It Usually Isn't Fruitful when Relating to Fanatics and Monsters

Perhaps American political observer and humorist Will Rogers said it best: "Diplomacy is the art of saying 'Nice doggie' until you can find a rock."[19]

Diplomacy has been mother's milk for powers-that-be and powers-that-want-to-be for millennia. It has provided countless power-seekers with a way to make a name and a way for even more bureaucrats to make a living. Few occupations offer more avenues to self-importance, with the titles and diplomatic privilege, the ceremonies and pageantry.

Diplomacy has created endless opportunities for intrigues, back-room deals, and sell-outs. When poorly handled – as it often is – it can set the stage for misunderstanding and conflict. When operating in concentrated form, as in the lengthy diplomatic dealings at Versailles after the Great War (World War I), it can create inequity and bitterness that ruin nations and sow the seeds of even greater wars (like World War II).

But diplomacy isn't much of a useful skill for a nation that decides to be independent of foreign entanglements. What is it good for if we refuse to be involved with their politics, disputes, tensions, and wars? How much of a State Department do we really need then?

When relating to civilized people and nations – who respect human rights, operate under the rule of law, have open societies, practice free trade, believe war to be heinous – diplomacy isn't needed. If individuals or organizations in the different countries have a dispute, let them sort it out. Let's just get on with the business of sharing the good life with good people.

When relating to fanatics and monsters, diplomacy isn't fruitful. We can try every diplomatic move and trick in the book, and in the long run, they will still do whatever they want. Worse, they'll use all of the diplomatic maneuvering to their evil advantage – negotiating for time while they steal Czechoslovakia and Austria (Hitler), bring down an Iron Curtain on Eastern Europe (Stalin), and build nuclear weapons (North Korea and Iran).

George Washington advised us "that no nation is to be trusted farther than it is bound by its interest."[20] President Grover Cleveland reminded us in 1885 that

> *the resources of our vast territory dictate the scrupulous avoidance of departure from that foreign policy commended by the history, the traditions, and the prosperity of our Republic. It is the policy of independence, favored by our position and defended by our known love of justice and by our power. It is the policy of peace suitable to our interests. It is the policy of neutrality, rejecting any share in foreign broils and ambitions upon other continents and repelling their intrusion here. It is the policy of Monroe and Washington and Jefferson....*[21]

There's nothing wrong with "making nice." Americans are generally nice people. Treating others nicely is always a good approach to dealing with others.

As Will Rogers noted, there is a place for diplomacy. If a big, tough, nasty nation is ever moving toward war with us, we should of course use diplomacy…while we look for a rock.

But in the meantime,

An Independent Spirit Leads Us to Constructive Engagement and the Free Exchange of Goods and Ideas

This far into massive entanglement, it's harder than it should be to see the value of independence.

But an independent spirit opens up many splendid doors, even while it closes the dreadful doors to bloodshed and financial ruin.

If we can't look for some sort of political or diplomatic or military advantage, what then? Well, we'll have to rely on the creativity and ambition and energy of millions of Americans – traits that are fortunately still in great supply. Our advantage will be in our ability to bring a better way of living – morally, not just materially – to anyone willing to lay down their swords and abandon their deadly games.

Constructive engagement would then be the only kind of engagement available to Americans. In the absence of government-negotiated or government-forced trading and deal-making, we'll have to find ways to collaborate and trade with people and organizations from other nations. If we can't find those ways, then those others will have to suffer without the aid of American genius.

Even here, government works hard to cloud the picture and own the commerce. Protective tariffs, subsidies to favored industries, embargos to force political change, granting of "most favored nation" status to the governments of other nations (and their corporate sidekicks) – these and more raise questions:

  • What is government's involvement adding to everyone's wellbeing?

  • What are special interests – in America and in other nations – doing to get these government-generated advantages?

  • How is it fair that only a small minority benefits, often at the expense of the many (as when a high tariff gives higher wages to the few and higher costs to everyone else)?

  • Why is government even involved in international commerce?

Some say that without the government's involvement, American industries may go under and foreign nations may take advantage of us. But America is an extremely innovative and competitive place. American business is capable of taking on companies propped up by the dead and bloated hand of foreign government. Any organization that needs government props to stay alive is already dead, while any organization worth its salt can find a way to win.

There is one huge area where government could help by getting itself completely out of the way. We need an American Project for energy independence, far different from the government-led Manhattan Project to build bombs. All monies invested by organizations and individuals needs to be treated as tax deductions or credits, and all income from a successful innovation needs to be tax-free for years or forever.

America has always been at its best when bringing to the world useful products and services and when leading the world with uplifting and enhancing ideas. Contrary to the notion that Americans are insulated from others, Americans have always learned from others – and then immediately gone about improving and sharing what they've learned.

Americans used to know that the concept of unalienable rights was much more influential than a gunboat protecting oil sheiks and that exporting the American Ideas was even better than shipping wheat and computers. That knowledge is still there, just below the surface, and can be recaptured once more.

The other direction? Waiting for guidance, asking for permission, apologizing for strength, pleading for support. It means

A Dependent Spirit Leads Us to Look to Others for Direction, Approval, and Resources

Other nations may not like the way we live. In fact, they can be very critical about America.

They don't like America's violence or its capital punishment of serial killers. They don't like America's resistance to government-run healthcare or its struggles with race. They don't like America's untamed culture or the fact that this culture is so dominant. They don't like an America that uses much to produce even more. They don't like America because it's so big and strong and successful and its people are just so...confident.

But how well have these nations done?

> • How has Europe fared in the business of avoiding mind-numbing, murderous wars and the slaughter of innocents?

> • How have China and India done with their billions of people who are poor beyond imagining and with their religious and ethnic minorities? From 1958 – 1962, China systematically starved up to 45 million people to death and "clung rigidly to the view that the starvation of the people mattered less than the demands of the state."[22] Mao Zedong said, "When there is not enough to eat, people starve to death. It is better to let half of the people die so that the other half can eat their fill."[23]

> • How has too much of the Middle East done with education and innovation, with respect for women, and with treatment of Christians, Jews – and even other Muslims? Harvard economic historian David Landes observed, "No one can understand the economic performance of the Muslim nations without attending to the experience of Islam as faith and culture....Islam has long exercised a retardative influence on Arab intellectual and scientific activity."[24]

> • How well have Central and South America – freed from the Old World's grasp so soon after America – gotten along with their petty and oppressive governments, constant military coups, and debt and inflationary disasters?

> • How much has Africa achieved – before, during, or after colonialism?

We've been led to believe that somehow America needs other nations – needs their guidance and support, needs their agreement and authorization, needs their markets and materials. Don't we live in a small world where everyone needs everyone else? Shouldn't we lose this obsolete notion of independence?

But as you evaluate the world, you start to see that they need America more than America needs them. Do we really need their

- *Direction.* Isn't there wisdom out there? Shouldn't we let others guide us? Yes and no.

There is wisdom, and we should avail ourselves of it as individuals and as a people. But we should ignore their input when it's destructive of the American Ideas. Too much of it is – and startlingly, hasn't changed in centuries.

And we shouldn't let them guide us. First, we don't want them to lead us into the same ditches they've been falling into for millennia. Second, we should remember that their guidance will be driven – as it always is with nations – by their own interests, not ours. And third, their guidance will be based on their own history and experience – which could be imperialistic, socialistic, utopian, tribal, intolerant, fanatical – that often has little to do with the American Ideas.

- *Approval.* There's a growing notion that what others (primarily in the Old World) think of America is important. The behavior of presidents supposedly raises or lowers the opinion people have of us, and America's governmental leaders can be evaluated on whether other nations respect them (and because of this, respect us).

But even if all of this is true, is it important? What difference does it make to normal Americans that someone in China likes – or doesn't like – them? Why should we care if our presidents and diplomats are adept at saying things that people in Saudi Arabia like to hear?

Americans have always learned from others when there was wisdom to be found. But they've generally rejected seeking their approval. And Americans are returning to those roots. In a recent survey, 44% (the highest number since the question was first asked in 1964) said that America "should go our own way in international matters, not worrying about whether other countries agree with us or not."[25]

- *Resources.* The world runs on resources. Resources are crucial to the world economy and the well-being of its habitants.

Being resource-rich can be a tremendous competitive advantage (North America, by the English, French, and Germans) – or a path to domination by others (South America, by the Spanish and Portuguese). Being resource-poor can be a tremendous competitive disadvantage (North Korea and Mongolia) – or a path to creativity and innovation (South Korea and Japan).

But whatever the other pluses and minuses, the demand for resources is a particularly obnoxious route to foreign entanglement. This demand has caused us to lay aside basic American principles like freedom of conscience and religion to have access to commodities like oil.

Saudi Arabia, for example, is practically the embodiment of anti-American Ideas. It doesn't "respect religious freedom even in theory.... [P]ublic prayer by non-Muslims is out of the question. The Kingdom is one of eight nations listed by the State Department as 'countries of particular concern,' a category that normally incurs some punitive action. American governments have let the Saudis off, exercising a waiver on national-security grounds."[26] Is national security another way of saying "oil"? Benjamin Franklin, in a letter to Lord Howe just after the Declaration of Independence, challenged the notion of fighting over economics, what he called "trade":

> *To me it seems that neither the obtaining or retaining of any Trade, how valuable soever, is an Object for which Men may justly Spill each other's Blood; that the true and sure means of extending and securing Commerce is the goodness and cheapness of Commodities; and that the profits of no Trade can ever be equal to the Expence of compelling it, and of holding it, by Fleets and Armies. I consider this War against us therefore, as both unjust, and unwise; and I am persuaded cool dispassionate Posterity will condemn to Infamy those who advise it...*[27]

America should never compromise itself one iota to get its hands on...anything. If we don't have it and we can't find it peacefully and privately, then we'll find a way to change our economy – and the world – without it.

A nation can be dependent because it is weak and under the control or domination of a stronger nation – the usual case. Sometimes nations that were once largely independent have been coerced and battered until they accepted dependence on a "great power."

Or a nation can be dependent because it chooses to be. No nation is strong enough to control or dominate America. But all too often, America has chosen to be dependent, to care too much about what others think and say. This is, to say the least, unbecoming. And quite opposed to the American Idea of Independence. Founder and Secretary of the Treasury Alexander Hamilton wrote:

> *Toward the execution of such a plan nothing is more essential than that antipathies against particular nations and passionate attachments for others should be avoided - and that instead of them we should cultivate just and amicable feelings towards all. That nation, which indulges towards another a habitual hatred or a habitual fondness is in some degree a slave. It is a slave to its animosity or to its affection - either of which is sufficient to lead it astray from its duty and interest...As avenues to foreign influence in innummerable ways such attachments are peculiarly alarming to the enlightened independent Patriot.*[28]

This is also opposed to America's ability to make a difference because

Only an Independent People Can Show the World a Better Way to Live

President Dwight Eisenhower thought about the power that comes from not being part of the system. He wrote (specifically about the Vietnam War, but more generally about America's unique role),

> *The standing of the United States as the most powerful of the anti-colonial powers is an asset of incalculable value to the Free World.... Thus the moral position of the United States was more to be guarded than the Tonkin Delta, indeed than all of Indochina.*[29]

He calls us not a non-colonial power, but an anti-colonial power. America was the place that rejected being a part of the British Empire in the 18th century and rejected the notion of the continuance of that empire in the 20th.

Eisenhower said that this unique position was both an asset and a moral position. It was an asset because it allowed America to stand at the pinnacle of the Free World and to be a beacon to those whom Frantz Fannon called "the wretched of the earth."[30] And it was a moral position, higher ground rarely if ever taken by any nation. He admonished us to guard this moral high ground – a warning that has been repeatedly ignored in practice but is never proven wrong in principle.

What could be more appealing to other peoples than a nation of incomparable might and economic power that uses its position to oppose the ham-fisted use of might and power – starting with its own? It's easy for a tiny or weak nation to talk about the need for restraint because this is in their interest. But what about a large and powerful nation that talks about and practices restraint even when it isn't in its interest?

No one strains to listen to anyone more than a powerful person speaking in a whisper. Everyone will listen closely if America once again learns to speak in a clear and confident whisper. America can be the model for, but not the maker of, other societies.

Independence and restraint are in America's interest, its best interest. They will allow America to minimize its waste and wars and to maximize its influence and trade. James Fallows calls this "independence in its broadest sense: would the world respect a threadbare America? Will repressive values rise with an ascendant China – and liberal values sink with a foundering United States?"[31]

Independence and restraint will tell others in a new way what the American Ideas can bring to them. They will provide a way in which those Ideas can be heard once more.

America At It's Best

TheAmericanIdeas.com

Once again, we need the spirit that led to the writing of the Declaration of Independence. The American Idea of Independence can be revived, if we will only:

Take Action

Value national independence like our founders and ancestors did.

★

Let Independence be our foreign policy.

★

Thank God for the oceans and the unbeatable defense they provide America.

★

Re-declare, enforce, and live the Monroe Doctrine.

★

Radically change our way of thinking about America's role in the world from umpire and empire to freedom's great light.

★

Eliminate all military and political alliances.

★

Redefine what our international interests really are and shed everything else.

★

Redefine what we mean by "patriotism" and "the home of the brave."

★

Declare victory and leave – everywhere.

★

Tell them to keep their resources.

★

Create an American Project for Energy Innovation.

★

Refuse to trade with lunatics.

★

Refuse to supply any other nation with the means of war.

★

Realize that our own government is contributing to the problem of deteriorating American independence.

★

Eliminate foreign aid, including support for the IMF and World Bank, and encourage private philanthropy.

To see detail on these Action Points and
to add your voice visit www.theamericanideas.com

There's nothing quite like independence. Few nations have ever had it, and the rest would crave it if they even knew it was a possibility. Many have wanted to be free of oppression and control, the first stage of independence. Some with imaginations have wanted to be free of expectation and entanglement as well. America long ago found its way to all of this national freedom.

President Eisenhower was once asked how he would define America's purpose. He said that

> *America wants to live first in freedom, and the kind of liberty that is guaranteed to us through our founding documents; and secondly, they want to live at peace with all their neighbors, so that we may jointly find a better life for humanity as we go forward.*[32]

It would be hard to find a better statement of purpose – freedom for the individual, independence for the nation, and a better life for all.

Perhaps the biggest barrier that could keep America from a glorious and peaceful future is a loss of independence. Renewing that love is a path to unimaginable riches, in every sense of that word.

Before the American Revolution, the idea of a people – any people – declaring their independence was more than a stretch. It was unthinkable. And America's break-away was the most incredible of all – declaring independence against the strongest nation in the world while that nation was getting stronger (while all later successful revolutions were against weak nations that were getting weaker).

But that's what Americans did. It wasn't just a declaration of independence, it was a declaration of difference. It was a bold statement, in Lincoln's words, "This new nation, conceived in liberty...."[33] America didn't talk about the traditional balance of power – its freedom and independence was its balance of power. As John Quincy Adams observed,

> *Wherever the standard of freedom...there will be America's heart, her bene-dictions, and her prayers. But she goes not abroad in search of monsters to destroy. She is the well-wisher to the freedom and independence of all. She is the champion and vindicator only of her own.*[34]

America has not yet achieved the full meaning and received the incomparable value of its Declaration of Independence. But the good news – the great news – is that there is nothing in the world outside of America that can prevent it.

If we want to be independent – if we want to celebrate Independence Day in a way only hinted at even in our first 150 years – it's there, right in front of us, and ours for the taking.

CHAPTER 13

The American Idea of Peace

Americans have always had a love of peace and a hatred of war. "Peace is our passion," declared Thomas Jefferson.[1] This was built into the American spirit from the beginning. Immigrants came to America for many reasons, but one ingrained into the minds of so many was the desire to escape the endless wars of the Old World. They wanted a land flowing with milk and honey, not with rivers of blood.

George Washington warned the young nation about avoiding those wars and the foreign entanglements that led to them. For almost a century and a half, his advice was followed. But in the last 100 years, America has allowed itself to be drawn into the bloody cesspool of the Old World – in Europe (World War I), Europe again, but now with Asia and Africa thrown in (World War II), Korea, Vietnam, Kuwait, Bosnia, Afghanistan, Iraq, and countless other smaller but still "savage wars of peace."[2]

All too often, we've been a peace-loving people with a war-loving government. Our sense of justice and decency has been used against us. We've allowed ourselves to be fooled into wars, manipulated into wars, terrorized into wars, persuaded into wars, and even cheered into wars.

But war has never been an American idea. The American Idea is Peace. This means we hate war, stay out of war, won't be drawn into war, avoid steps that lead to war, and most certainly never start wars. We'll be strong enough that people will leave us alone, but we'll leave them alone in return. If we have to fight, we'll win – but we'll first make sure that it is necessary to fight.

At the core of their being, Americans know there are no good wars. Sometimes necessary wars, yes. But never good ones. They know that there are winners in war, but also know that even those victories are filled with huge losses – ugliness and cruelty, hatred and revenge, and above all, too many slaughtered in the springtime of their lives.

This American Idea is remarkable. Even while it represents the deepest desire of almost every human being who has ever lived, it embodies a clean break with the shameful and bloody norm of all of human history.

Peace

We love peace and hate war.

So no more wars.

That's what the founders of America wanted and what millions have sought here for themselves.

We know that war brings ruin in countless ways.

War isn't the "last stage of diplomacy," but rather the absence of peacekeeping.

Paradoxically, in a broken world, we're sure that we can have peace only through strength.

We are well-armed, always-prepared, military-appreciating pacifists.

We'll spend our ingenuity and resources to be so strong militarily that no one, even lunatics, would dare to attack us.

We will never attack others first, but if attacked, we will fight to win and we will win.

We're proud of what we stand for, an America that, at its best, loves, seeks, and delivers peace to its people.

The first thing others need to re-learn about Americans is that

We Love Peace and Hate War

Founder and Secretary of the Treasury Alexander Hamilton said

> *It is also known that the people of the UStates are firmly attached to peace.*[3]

Let's start with the unchanging truth about peace: Everyone who lives wins.

What's not to love about peace? Peace, unlike war, is a win-win proposition. We get to be born, live, and die in peace. To learn, work, achieve, love, marry, and enjoy, with no threat of a sudden and violent end. To raise our children with rich confidence that we won't be burying them. To be creative, not destructive. To spend our money on the care of the sick and needy, rather than on the care of the wounded and dead.

And here's the unchanging truth about war: Everyone who fights dies.

There are the obvious dead, those who die on the battlefield – over half a million Americans in the Civil War, a quarter of a million in World War II, tens of thousands in World War I, Korea, and Vietnam, thousands more in other godforsaken places. We rightly honor these soldiers in our memories, but we have to understand that for them, there is no glory – only death.

William T. Sherman, one of the toughest and most successful of American generals, declared unequivocally,

> *I am sick and tired of fighting – its glory is all moonshine; even success the most brilliant is over dead and mangled bodies....I've seen thousands of men lying on the ground, their dead faces looking up at the skies. I tell you, war is hell!*[4]

The truth is that dead soldiers – or civilians – have lost their lives. They are no longer aware of their lives, of our lives, of life itself. They've lost everything they have and everything they might ever have. They aren't thinking of glory because they've had their thoughts and their glory stripped away by death.

This doesn't mean that we shouldn't remember them and love them for their sacrifice. We owe them more than we can ever pay. We can hate war and still honor the dead – it's the least we can do. But the most we can do? Hate war so much that we have no more dead to honor.

But the immediate dead of war aren't the only casualties. There are those who die from their injuries, sometimes long after the combat ends – like the men exposed to nuclear materials in World War II who died half a century later from the ravages of

ALS. War has a long reach and a hard grip.

So many of those who don't die are terribly maimed. Part of them has died. They were healthy and in the prime of life one second, physically demolished the next.

But a piece of every combat veteran dies. There's the World War II army medic in New Guinea and the Philippines who wins two bronze stars – and dies in his fifties, at first glance from alcoholism but in reality from the long reach of war. "They brought us home," he said in a rare moment of openness, "and took us to a movie theater, where they told us, 'now you're back in civilization, and you have to forget everything you saw and did.'" He stared at the ground, shaking his head. "The only thing they didn't tell us was how to do it."

We talk about "disabled veterans" as though there is any other kind. It's illusion to believe that men and women can go into combat and not be disabled in some way. War is dehumanizing and barbaric. You can't be in it without it infecting you. William Manchester, a marine survivor of Okinawa, says of those who fought the Pacific war, "We were all psychotic, inmates of the greatest madhouse in history."[5] Historian Jacques Barzun observed that trying to determine the exact number of dead in World War I misses the point,

> *Because loss is a far wider category than death alone. The maimed, the tubercular, the incurables, the shell-shocked, the sorrowing, the driven mad, the suicides, the broken spirits, the destroyed careers, the budding geniuses plowed under, the missing births were losses, and they are incommensurable....The Armistice, moreover, did not halt the toll. It was escorted by an outbreak of typhus in Central Europe and a worldwide epidemic called Spanish flu, virulent and in most cases fatal....[T]he post-war state of large sections of the Continent was one of starvation, homelessness, and disease. One cannot pour all human and material resources into a fiery cauldron year after year and expect to resume normal life at the end of the prodigal enterprise.*[6]

Those left behind – families and loved ones and friends – die too. They die inside from the losses. Sometimes they literally die from the grief, or from the things they use to hide the heartache. Or from the war itself, if it spreads to cities and civilians.

Those who came to America from other lands knew these truths, knew them down to their bones. They saw a new land free of war and protected by oceans, and they wanted it. They were tired of watching the young die and seeing everyone else suffer. What they felt was captured by the people's writer, revolutionary Tom Paine:

> *We cannot help cursing the wretch, who, to the unavoidable misfortunes of nature, shall willfully add the calamities of war....If there is a sin superior to any other, it is that of willful and offensive war....[H]e who is the author of war, lets loose the whole contagion of hell, and opens a vein that bleeds a nation to death.*[7]

Within a war there is often a massive waste of life for little or no good reason. In his history of World War II in the Pacific, Max Hastings notes that "in every campaign in every war, sacrifices are routinely made that are out of all proportion to the significance of objectives."[8] It's only a short step from spending lives to wasting lives.

One of the incomprehensibly bad aspects of war is that many – perhaps most – had their lives thrown away. "In modern war...you will die like a dog for no good reason," said writer Ernest Hemingway.[9]

"War! What is it good for? Absolutely nothing!"[10] The words from the Vietnam-era song ask the most important question about war for Americans and offer the American answer.

Love of peace and hatred of war in all its masquerades are at the core of this American Idea.

So No More Wars

This hatred of war is why the American Idea of Peace offers a simple but uniquely powerful determination: No more wars.

If this idea resonates with you, you should know that it has resonated with Americans for four hundred years. People came to America for many reasons – political, economic, and religious drivers abounded – but nothing was as clear as the need to escape the endless wars.

Even though leaders of all stripes have dragged and enticed us into wars, something in our core has always sickened us and made us want to return to a place of peace. Many have understood that even if Americans are fully engaged in a war, they want it over as fast as possible. They question the reasons and are angered by the losses, even in a "good" war like World War II.

Although the American resistance to war has been beaten down by a century of madness, there's still an unbroken desire to have

> • No more wars – so we can build a decent and durable future and check the war-related growth of government and spend our ingenuity and wealth on building not destroying and be blessed by others rather than cursed.

> • No more wars – so we will not become what our ancestors loathed or destroy our young or become agents of death or drain away our resources or give others a thousand good reasons to hate our existence.

The amazing thing about this concept of "no more wars" is that America can actually pull it off. Could have pulled it off, in fact, for the past 100 years.

How do we have no more wars? It starts with getting back to the sentiments that brought people here – loving peace, hating the very concept of war, refusing to accept it as "diplomacy by other means," rejecting any and all arguments that present war as decent or honorable.

We have to hate what Tom Paine called "the whole contagion of hell."[11] We have to loathe the disease that introduces into a culture what President Woodrow Wilson saw accurately as "the spirit of ruthless brutality."[12] We have to remember what Mark Twain said about killing a man in the Civil War:

The thought of him got to preying upon me every night; I could not get rid of it. I could not drive it away, the taking of that unoffending life seemed such a wanton thing. And it seemed the epitome of war; that all war must be just that – the killing of strangers against whom you feel no personal animosity; strangers whom, in other circumstances, you would help if you found them in trouble, and who would help you if you needed it.[13]

No more wars means we have to set up bulwarks against war – the terrible idea that always kills but never dies. Here are seven of them:

1)   We can avoid wars in progress. We may have only the vaguest notion of the reasons for it, how deep its roots go, or who is in the right – if anyone. They started it, so let them finish it.

2)   We can be on the alert for enticements to war, from friend or foe. These can range from claims to common ancestry, common ground, or common cause on the one hand, to trying to take out evil on the other. President Harry Truman said, "The supreme need of our time is for men to learn to live together in peace and harmony."[14]

3)   We have to stop calling people "friends" who try to lead us to that ugly place. True friends don't do things that put their friends in harm's way. Along with that, we have to avoid power-driven alliances, where we can end up with ugly allies because of the horrible notion that "the enemy of my enemy is my friend."

4)   We have to resist saying, "If you blacken my eye, I'll burn down your house with your family inside." We can't let the relatively minor actions of others become the basis for major acts of revenge. We can't let the sinking of a Lusitania – with a few Americans inexplicably taking a British ship across the Atlantic while Germany is sinking British ships – lead us into a First World War. We have to be on the alert for the phantom gunboat battles in the Gulf of Tonkin that will be used to escalate a Vietnam beyond all reason.

5)   We should lose the imbalanced notion that it's alright to attack smaller armed countries but not larger armed countries, primarily because smaller ones are safer to attack. The U. S. attacked Iraq even though another pint-sized nation (North Korea) was actually more of a threat – perhaps in part because Iraq was an easier potential conquest. But more, what about Russia and China? Both have nuclear weapons, missiles pointed at us, huge armies, and values that certainly are misaligned with the American Ideas. Why not attack them? In part because they're so big. Policies that lead to attacks on the little nations but not the big ones make practical sense – but are very contrary to America's spirit, its street-smarts, and its sense of a fair fight.

6)   We should see phony calls to patriotism and "duty" for what they are: very real calls to kill and be killed. Reporter and Pulitzer Prize winner Walter Lippmann wrote,

A great power will make measured and limited use of its power. It will eschew the theory of universal duty, which not only commits it to unending wars of intervention, but intoxicates its thinking with the illusion that it is a crusader for righteousness.... I am in favor of

learning to behave like a great power, of getting rid of the globalism, which would not only entangle us everywhere, but is based on the totally vain notion that if we do not set the world in order, no matter what the price, we cannot live in the world safely.[15]

7)   And we need to find a way back to our long tradition of never starting a war. That was a powerful American concept, where even children knew that the good guy never shoots first. President Ronald Reagan declared that

> *Our defense policy is based on a very simple premise. The United States will not start fights. We will not be the first to use aggression. We will not seek to occupy other lands or control other people. Our strategy is defensive, our aim is to protect the peace by ensuring that no adversaries ever conclude they could best us in war of their own choosing.*[16]

We have to hate war in such a way that we condemn those who start them, while resisting every temptation to join the destructive madness. James Madison wrote

> *War should not only be declared by the authority of the people, whose toils and treasures are to support its burdens, instead of the government which is to reap its fruit; but that each generation should be made to bear the burden of its own wars, instead of carrying them on, at the expense of other generations.*[17]

We can focus once again on true national defense. We can change the question from, "How do we destroy them?" to, "How do we keep them from destroying us?" We can reverse the terrible word game of the last century by trading a current "Defense" Department that is concerned with war for the original "War" Department that was concerned with defense. Politicians changed the name while reversing the meaning. What we really need is a Defense Department that is really and truly concerned with defense.

We could not ever, and cannot now, defend the whole world from itself. If history teaches us anything, it's that the world has always been full of war. Americans – already here or wanting to be here – have always dreamed of a refuge from the storms of war, a place that was free from the terrible tragedy of destruction, a home where they could safely pursue their private interests without the daily fear of being transferred to the next life. In fact,

That's What the Founders of America Wanted and What Millions Have Sought Here for Themselves

American statesman, writer, and inventor Benjamin Franklin wrote in 1783,

> *At length we are in Peace, God be praised, and long, very long, may it continue. All Wars are Follies, very expensive, and very mischievous ones....*

I join with you most cordially in rejoicing at the return of Peace. I hope it will be lasting, and that Mankind will at length, as they call themselves reasonable Creatures, have Reason and Sense enough to settle their Differences without cutting throats....[18]

From its founding until 1917 – almost a century and a half – America didn't seriously venture across the sea to re-engage with the wars of the Old World. We didn't have to go. And we don't ever have to go again.

Of the utmost importance, no one wanted to go. Foreign wars struck Americans as unbounded insanity. They were thrilled to be so far away from it all. They knew with President Dwight Eisenhower, "Peace is the climate of freedom."[19]

It took another quarter of a century after 1917 and an even bigger foreign war before America finally gave up the incredible value of its moat, the unbreachable fortress of the two great oceans. Five-sixths of the world is covered by water, and no army yet has been able to march across it. They can't attack us, not with any hope of victory.

If we take care of the air and the terrorists, our moat is – and always has been – our best defense. Strong missile defense and strong homeland security added to a strong navy are all that America needs to have a safe and peaceful existence. Sadly, it's all we've needed since the middle of the 20th century.

People escaped the Old World, but somehow, brought that warfare spirit with them when they came. It's, in some way, part of the human heart. Given enough provocation or encouragement even peaceful people can be stirred to retribution.

But those who came largely repressed this warfare spirit. It lay dormant for a very long time. It's been awakened by too many wars, too much conflict, too much tension, and too much awareness of the violence that abounds. But this spirit can be repressed once again. The warrior can be driven into hibernation once more.

Some say that we inherited the "policing" role of the British Empire. If so, we have to remember that it didn't turn out so well for them, or for the other empires that preceded them (French, Spanish, Portuguese, Dutch, Ottoman) or the one that outlasted it (Soviet Russia). At long last, the role bankrupted the British – economically, politically, and, finally, morally.

If we inherited the role of world referee and enforcer, we should renounce our inheritance. The cost is too high and the payoff is too low.

And let's stop helping others start and fight wars. America should never be the arsenal for anyone else. It's the wrong business to be in. "Normally and generally men are judged by their ability to produce," observed historians Will and Ariel Durant, "except in war, when they are ranked according to their ability to destroy."[20] Who wants to be part of that ranking?

Let's give our thanks to and for those who have fought so valiantly for us. No nation should ever forget those who stood at the front lines to take the blows of violent enemies. All nations should be grateful for those willing to make the ultimate, irrecoverable sacrifice.

But at the same time, we can vow that as far as it is in our power, no more will have to fight or die. We can commit to a better way so that the lives of these good men and women can be spent better...living. No more wars. A fine American concept.

Americans are too honest and decent to believe that war is good in any way. In fact,

We Know That War Brings Ruin in Countless Ways

It has been said that "love is a many-splendored thing."[21] Its furthest opposite, war, has as many ways to destroy human beings as love has to enhance them. War is the ultimate human disaster, a many-ruined thing. President and General Dwight Eisenhower said, "Every war is going to astonish you."[22]

War always offers a promise of some kind. Domination, treasure, revenge, justice, security, freedom, even "peace in our time." The promises are usually false. War offers unimaginable cost but seldom delivers what it sets out to achieve.

But war always delivers ruin. Even those who take Americans into war, like President Woodrow Wilson, know this in their soul. On the night before he asked for a declaration of war to insert America into the mindless wasteland of World War I, he said:

> Once lead this people into war, and they'll forget there ever was such a thing as tolerance. To fight you must be brutal and ruthless, and the spirit of ruthless brutality will enter into the very fibre of our national life.[23]

The corruption of the character of a people is the first and often longest-lasting ruin. It changes us. It makes us think in violent terms. It causes us to take up war earlier than necessary or even when unnecessary. It's been said that when the only tool you have is a hammer, every problem looks like a nail. So it is that when the only tool you have is a dominant military, every problem looks like a war.

This corruption can also distort the concept of "tolerance." It can change it from "Your problems are your problems and we hope you can solve them" to "We'll leave you alone if you do things our way and remind us of us." Few have as good an understanding of this destruction of tolerance as the Americans of Japanese descent who were locked away in concentration camps during World War II. As one historian of World War II said,

> There was the saddest lesson, to be learned again and again…that war is corrupting, that it corrodes the soul and tarnishes the spirit, that even the excellent and the superior can be defiled, and that no heart would remain unstained.[24]

The truth even about victory is that the spirit of peace and peacefulness is lost, even if the war is won.

But the physical losses of war are phenomenal, overwhelming. Even in a war driven by the best and most-advanced technology, thousands of Americans die and many more are brutalized. Putting a good face on war doesn't diminish the ruin or bring back any of the lives. General William Sherman said, "War is cruelty and you cannot refine it."[25] Mahatma Gandhi asked,

> What difference does it make to the dead, the orphans and the homeless whether the mad destruction is wrought under the name of totalitarianism or the holy name of liberty or democracy?[26]

Not much difference to the dead. No difference.

The tentacles of war reach into everything. Aside from the loss of spirit and lives, one of the worst effects of war is that it expands the size and scope of government. Little if any of this is ever given back when the war ends. The quest for more power can even inspire the push toward conflict. French observer of America Alexis de Tocqueville reminded us that war

> must invariably and immeasurably increase the powers of civil government....All those who seek to destroy the freedom of the democratic nations must know that war is the surest and shortest means to accomplish this. This is the very first axiom of the science.[27]

Some of the destruction of liberty comes from regulation, like price and wage controls. Some comes from attacks on personal liberties, like Lincoln's suspension of habeas corpus and parts of the 21st century's Patriot Act. Some comes from massive financial dislocation, like the new taxes and government debt and inflation that stifle future opportunity. Some comes from critical attitudes, like telling people who question the war to "love America or leave it." And this destruction can occur in a short time under the threat – real or imagined – of war.

As we saw in the American Idea of Government, government has immense value – but only when it is "limited" in every sense of that word. Limits on government are hard to put in place and even harder to maintain. War is the most powerful way to push and finally destroy those hard-won limits.

When a government is managed badly, war can be used to cover up the incompetence. The war doesn't fix the mismanagement – it expands it. The great American writer Ernest Hemingway highlighted one of the great truths of history when he said,

> The first panacea for a mismanaged nation is inflation of the currency; the second is war. Both bring a temporary prosperity; both bring a permanent ruin. But both are the refuge of political and economic opportunists.[28]

Leaders with their own pitiable agendas have bad ways of looking good. They can debauch the currency. Since the creation of the Federal Reserve in 1913, the dollar has lost over 95% of its value.[29] A long line of "leaders" of all political persuasions have contributed to this short-term apparent prosperity and long-term actual ruin.

This is why smart, realistic leaders like Thomas Jefferson and Andrew Jackson vehemently opposed the national government being in control of banking and finance. And why many are rightly dubious about a currency backed only by the "full faith and credit of the federal government."[30] If politicians can inflate away their bad decisions and legislation, it turns out they will always do so in the end.

But even worse, they can try to cover up their sins and incompetencies with war. War can bring a temporary prosperity (as long as the homeland isn't on the receiving end). It was World War II, not the New Deal, that finally ended towering unemployment, economic experimentation, and the Great Depression. But the ruin of that war is still with us. As Jefferson noted, "The most successful war seldom pays for its losses."[31]

The two, war and fiscal mismanagement, can even work together, as war brings temporary financial relief but long-term financial wreckage. Economist Adam Smith said,

> *When war comes, [governments] are both unwilling and unable to increase their revenue in proportion to the increase of their expense. They are unwilling, for the fear of offending the people, who by so great and so sudden an increase of taxes, would soon be disgusted with the war....The facility of borrowing delivers them from the embarrassment which this fear...would otherwise occasion. [In addition,] the return of peace, indeed, seldom relieves them from the greater part of the taxes imposed during the war. These are mortgaged for the interest of the debt contracted in order to carry it on.*[32]

World War II changed America from a peace-first to a police-first mindset. Rather than remaining one of a kind, a people of peace, we became one more power in a long line that traced back through history from the British Empire to the Roman Empire. That war set the stage for the Korean War, which

> *was the occasion for transforming the United States into a very different country than it had ever been before: one with hundreds of permanent military bases abroad, a large standing army and a permanent national security state at home....into a country that the founding fathers would barely recognize....[I]t turned the United States into a country entirely remote from what the founding fathers had in mind, where every foreign threat, however small or unlikely, became magnified....*[33]

Korea made Vietnam, Kuwait, Bosnia, Afghanistan and Iraq thinkable, with all their death and destruction.

War makes us forget the many dangers of a large, standing military with all of its costs and economic distortions. Our founders worried a lot about standing armies and were always suspicious of making those armies bigger. Today, politicians and generals worry about avoiding two-front and three-front wars. Our ancestors worried about avoiding war.

Do we need a military? Absolutely. Do we need something so large that it cries to be used anywhere and everywhere? Absolutely not. America at its best isn't a military power – it is a peace-loving place, with military power to secure its own peace.

War and the prospect of war make us over-vigilant in all the wrong ways. They cause us to be over-focused on "hot spots" and "flashpoints." They make us less willing to let demented foreign leaders rattle their swords. They put an interventionist, threatening, violent twist to the otherwise good concept of globalization.

The overlarge military and its over-vigilant civilian master can lead to never-ending involvement that weakens not only the country, but also the military itself. We're doing so many things, we aren't able to do any of them well or finish what we start. This can lead a fine American general to say about the quagmire of Afghanistan, "I don't think you can win this war. I think you keep fighting....[T]his is the kind of fight we're in for the rest of our lives and probably our kids' lives."[34] Really? This is what America wants to be doing in 50 years?

Not least in war's destruction is the physical ruin. America has felt this primarily in the loss of life and treasure and less – so far – in destruction of the country. But that too can lay in wait if our nation forgets the unrelenting violence of war, doesn't quite count the cost of all of the intervention, dismisses the insanity of insane foreign leaders, and refuses to take steps to defend the country from nuclear holocaust (which it has refused to do for over half a century). Even short of that, Benjamin Franklin asks us to think about

> *What additions to the Conveniences and Comforts of Living might Mankind have acquired, if the Money spent in Wars had been employed in Works of public utility! What an extension of Agriculture, even to the Tops of our Mountains: what Rivers rendered navigable, or joined by canals: what Bridges, Aqueducts, new Roads, and other public Works, Edifices, and Improvements, rendering England a complete Paradise, might have been obtained by spending those Millions in doing good, which in the last War have been spent doing Mischief; in bringing Misery into thousands of families, and destroying the Lives of so many….* [35]

America spent a long time living by the plowshare rather than the sword. Now we're trying to live by the plowshare and the sword, rather than beating the unnecessary swords into plowshares. President and General Dwight Eisenhower said that an over focus on defense can lead to a terrible misallocation of resources:

> *Every gun that is made, every warship launched, every rocket fired signifies, in the final sense, a theft from those who hunger and are not fed, those who are cold and are not clothed….[O]ur nation] is spending the sweat of its laborers, the genius of its scientists, the hopes of its children….The cost of one modern heavy bomber is this: a modern brick school in more than 30 cities….We pay for a single fighter with a half million bushels of wheat. We pay for a single destroyer with new homes that could have housed more than 8,000 people.* [36]

We should remember that living by a sword – one that is so large and fierce, one that America has become too ready to wield – has always been a good way to die by that sword.

The greatest generation is not the one that fights and wins a war, however great the sacrifice, however valuable the victory. The greatest generation will be the one that fights to build a strong and lasting peace.

That generation will know that

War Isn't the "Last Stage of Diplomacy," but Rather the Absence of Peacekeeping

War has been called "diplomacy by other means." But this renders "diplomacy" a meaningless, even cynical, term.

Diplomacy is defined as "the management of international relations...adroitness in personal relations."[37] The key word is "relations." There are no "relations" in wars – only death and destruction, the relationship of one soldier's bullet to another soldier's heart.

Real diplomacy seeks to avoid war. In the American Idea, real diplomacy calls for the management of international relations by withdrawing from the field and discussions whenever war gets on the agenda. Real diplomacy – knowing when to talk and when to leave – is difficult, but it's not as difficult as war.

Of course, only a fool's diplomacy seeks to avoid war at any cost. Because the world houses evil and often sees monsters come into power, war is sometimes required. No amount of talking will make the evil and monsters go away. Some costs are too much to pay – destruction of life, loss of liberty, demolition of rights, slavery.

When the Ottoman Turks reached the gates of Vienna in the late 17th century, as they had the gates of Constantinople in the mid-15th century, no amount of diplomacy was going to turn them away from their long and relentless war of conquest against Asia Minor and Eastern Europe. Everyone knew what had happened to the great Christian capital of Constantinople – the murder, rape, pillage, and slavery. Only armies could stop the advance. Only war could prevent the slaughter of innocent lives, the loss of liberty and rights, the brutal slavery, the forced conversions to Islam.

But often those kinds of costs aren't even on the table. The British Empire tried to destroy itself in World War I by "guaranteeing" – in its self-appointed police role – the security of Belgium and the continent, an impossible commitment. The empire actually succeeded in destroying itself in World War II by learning nothing and extending its guarantees to Poland, a meaningless guarantee to a nation on the far side of a ferocious Germany. The hard truth is that Britain could have easily avoided the first war and – given that Hitler really didn't want to fight the British and had no way to cross the English channel – probably could have avoided the second. Shrewd diplomacy, combined with a hatred of war and a willingness to avoid it, could have rewritten British history.

America didn't even need the "diplomacy of withdrawal" to avoid World War I. All it needed to do was mind its own business and stay home. The diplomacy it actually did use in leading the settlement discussions after that war was really just bullying and helped pave the way for World War II. Real diplomacy after World War I may have prevented World War II. Without the retribution that bad diplomacy forced on Germany, America and Britain – the Germans themselves – could have marginalized Hitler as a loudmouthed clown.

A "diplomacy of restraint" could have dramatically changed America's history in World War II – and made it less of a world war. Would telling the Japanese that we were hands-off their activities in Asia have kept them away from Pearl Harbor and let them meet their demise in their long land war in China? Were we an object of conquest for Japan or an obstacle to be removed? Would China have been any worse than it was under Mao Zedong – the ultimate profiteer from America's involvement in the Pacific – who killed far more of his own people than the Japanese ever did?

And would saying to ourselves, "We can't tell the difference between Hitler and Stalin, so why don't we let these monsters beat each other to death?" have kept us out of that brutal war in Europe? And since then, from the never-ending wars in

Eurasia? Were we really fighting against tyranny and totalitarianism when we were fighting alongside the tyrannical and totalitarian Soviet Union?

September 1, 1939 is usually thought of as the start of World War II, when Hitler invaded Poland from the west. Less known – because the Soviet Union was later our "ally" – is that on the same day, Stalin invaded Poland from the east. Sadly, America helped take Eastern Europe from one monster and deliver it to another. A diplomacy of restraint could have said to both of them, "Send us your unwanted – Jews, Poles, whoever." We could have brought every persecuted person in Europe to America for a fraction of the cost of that merciless war and at no cost in American lives.

We can't rewrite history, and we will never know for sure. But one thing seems certain in retrospect: all of this could have been a very good thing to find out - simply to try - before we sent our boys to die at Normandy and Guadalcanal.

"I think I was unprepared for war," noted President George W. Bush on the faulty intelligence that was used to lead to war in Iraq.[38] Iraq was a sort-of nation that was already "free": weapons-of-mass-destruction-free, terrorist-free, and – for millennia and probably forever – free of unalienable rights.

But Bush was not alone. Truman in Korea, Kennedy and Johnson in Vietnam, George H. W. Bush in Kuwait, Clinton in Bosnia – all too often in recent decades, government leaders have looked harder for reasons to fight a war than they have for reasons to preserve the peace.

This concept that America could find a way to stay in perpetual peace is not a new one. This part of the American Idea of Peace is well summarized in a judgment by Civil War General and U. S. President Ulysses S. Grant:

> *There never was a time when, in my opinion, some way could not be found to prevent the drawing of the sword.* [39]

Americans, a peace-loving people, can only agree with him. There never was a time.

But

Paradoxically, in a Broken World, We're Sure That We Can Have Peace Only through Strength

President John Quincy Adams observed "that the firmest security of peace is the preparation during peace of the defenses of war.... [We] cherish peace while preparing for defensive war."[40]

One of the great paradoxes of human life is that weakness and (sadly) a pacifist spirit often lead to war, while strength and a willingness to fight if pushed are the surest way to avoid it. As Winston Churchill, one of the giants of 20th century politics, noted,

Peace is our aim, and strength is the only way of getting it....Indeed, it is only by having it both ways at once that we shall have a chance of getting anything at all.[41]

Peace presents us with a paradox. In the real world, we're not given the choice of war and strength on the one hand, or peace and weakness on the other. The only viable option for a sane people is strength and peace, peace through strength. President and General Dwight Eisenhower said,

We hold it to be the first task of statesmanship to develop the strength that will deter the forces of aggression and promote the conditions of peace.[42]

Strength is a non-negotiable aspect of real peace. Loving peace, hating war, minding our own business, and the diplomacy of restraint are all crucial aspects of securing the peace. But having both the power to resist power and the strength to raise doubts in the minds of predators are no less crucial. At times, strength can be the determining factor between backing down or beating down an adversary. President James Monroe said that American actions had been

Dictated by a love of peace, of economy, and an earnest desire to save the lives of our fellow-citizens from that destruction and our country from that devastation which are inseparable from war when it finds us unprepared for it. It is believed, and experience has shown, that such a preparation is the best expedient that can be resorted to prevent war.[43]

Building strength can often be a good investment. Secretary of the Treasury Alexander Hamilton wrote

Avoid occasions of expense by cultivating peace – remembering always that the preparation against danger by timely and provident disbursements is often a mean of avoiding greater disbursements to repel it.[44]

Strength presents us with a potential problem, of course – it's hard not to exercise power when you have it. Having strength and using it well requires wisdom, patience, and restraint. It's obvious that strong nations throughout history have not fared well on the wise use of power. America has the character to be the first. We need to eliminate artificial ways to prop up long, bad wars – like a military draft – and expand solid ways to support peace – like a relentless focus on free trade.

A perversion of this American Idea of Peace starts out in an accurate and welcoming way: War is bad. Who would disagree with that? But some would incorrectly extrapolate that concept to say that if war is bad, defense and weapons are bad too – that we can have peace if everyone just agrees to be peaceful and lays down all of their weapons, that peace is the elimination of war (even the very concept of war) rather than the absence of war because of superior strength.

People aren't basically bad. But they're bad enough. And some are very bad indeed. A few of these who find a way to great power are basically bad. They won't understand the American Ideas or care about diplomacy of restraint. They only want to conquer and control, enjoying some killing along the way. The only thing they will understand and respect is superior strength. President Harry Truman said,

If we can make it sufficiently clear, in advance, that any armed attack affecting our national security would be met with overwhelming force, the armed attack might never occur.[45]

America has been the strongest power on earth for a long time. If it has enough love of peace and hatred of war – and wisdom – it will work hard to remain so forever. Disarmament may be the way to Utopia, but it isn't the way to peace. Laying down our sword just makes it easier for them to run us through with theirs. "Whatever enables us to go to war, secures our peace," noted Thomas Jefferson.[46]

President Ronald Reagan said,

> *We will maintain sufficient strength to prevail if need be, knowing that if we do so we have the best chance of never having to use that strength…[and] no arsenal, or no weapon in arsenals of the world, is so formidable as the will and moral courage of free men and women. It is a weapon our adversaries in today's world do not have.*[47]

American power is based first on the American Ideas and only second on a particular military strategy or weapons system. Fareed Zakaria wrote that "American military power is not the cause of its strength but the consequence."[48] America is strong in so many fundamental ways, and its military strength is a product of those core strengths as encapsulated in the American Ideas. As President Jimmy Carter said,

> *We are a strong nation, and we will maintain strength so sufficient that it need not be proven in combat – a quiet strength based not merely on the size of an arsenal, but on the nobility of ideas.*[49]

Some of those fundamental strengths, so important to maintaining military superiority, are:

- Values and Ideas, the most important things that give America the passion and will to win;

- Effective institutions, which philosopher and management expert Peter Drucker said were so important to remaining independent and secure;[50]

- A vigorous economy, which provides the resources to keep the military strong without making Americans' lives weak;

- An innovative culture, which drives research and development and the creation of outstanding, cutting-edge technology and weaponry.

But in spite of this, America has allowed itself to remain weak – has deliberately chosen to be weak – in the face of the only military action that can utterly destroy it. America is the strongest military power in the history of the world, yet is completely unable to protect itself from annihilation.

If a single madman in Russia – and soon in China, and then in other nations – gives the order and the nuclear button is pushed, all Americans will die within the hour. Whatever else this is, it isn't peace through strength. So, it's time to say,

We'll Spend Our Ingenuity and Resources to be so Strong Militarily That No One, Even Lunatics, Would Dare to Attack Us

President John Kennedy said,

> *We dare not tempt them with weakness. For only when our arms are sufficient beyond doubt can we be certain beyond doubt that they will never be employed.*[51]

Remarkably, America has chosen not to defend itself.

America is relying on the notion that no one would be crazy enough to start a nuclear war. But there are insane people, some of them even now running countries that have – or will soon have – nuclear weapons. And it is clear that insane people with power often start wars that make no sense. Why would we trust our peace, our safety, and our lives to the hoped-for good sense of lunatics? Founder James Madison asked

> *How could a readiness for war in time of peace be safely prohibited unless we could prohibit in like manner the preparations and establishments of every hostile nation?*[52]

The astonishing truth is that there are no other gaps in American strength. Other than this glaring deficiency, America is invincible from any reasonable perspective. Our air force rules the skies, and our navy rules the seas. If needed, our army and marines can take on any invading force with ease. We need to keep these grand forces far ahead of any potential enemy.

But here, in the most critical area of all – possible nuclear annihilation – we're weak. Very weak. We frantically rush around the world trying to limit new entrants into the nuclear "club," in part because we know we have no way to stop any of them.

Peace through strength has to begin with real defense against nuclear weapons. We have to take the club out of their hands. Talk and treaties are insufficient. Hoping that the nations will deactivate these weapons and forget how to make them is naïve, even foolish. The threat of "mutual assured destruction" – since they know we can kill all of them, it would be stupid for them to attack us – is not only insufficient but also insane (and appropriately called MAD).

We have a Department of "Defense" that has, after more than half a century, no answer to the nuclear threat. If Russia – often in the hands of madmen in the past century – decides to launch or merely makes a mistake, Americans die. If China – which is developing a missile-defense system and is now the only other nation besides America to use a missile to destroy another missile in space[53] – builds a defense against our nuclear weapons, what prevents them from using their nuclear weapons to destroy America?

Peace-through-weakness people have tried to diminish the concept of missile defense, calling it "Star Wars." But using their own analogy, isn't the lesson of Star Wars that the good side had better be strong or the dark side will destroy it? A nuclear launch would be a very real star war, with fire and brimstone raining down on helpless Americans. One expert asked,

> *Can any government claim to occupy the moral high ground when it willingly, knowingly, and purposely keeps its people nakedly vulnerable to nuclear missiles?*[54]

If we could invent nuclear weapons and missile systems, we can invent the antidote.

We created the atomic bomb, and we can create the means to stop it. President Ronald Reagan said that we need "to find, if we can, a security shield that would destroy nuclear missiles before they reach their target. It wouldn't kill people, it would destroy weapons. It wouldn't militarize space, it would help demilitarize the arsenals of Earth. It would render nuclear weapons obsolete."[55]

Will it be expensive? Yes. But not as expensive as nuclear holocaust. Not as expensive as living under a global death threat. There's a lot of money already being spent on "defense" that could be switched over to really defending us. Why are we spending billions on military bases in the middle of the country while the sky is a boulevard of death?

This concept of missile defense is so basic, so logical, so crucial, that in 1994, polls showed "that most Americans mistakenly believe the U. S. already has a missile shield."[56] But decades later, it's still just a dream. We don't have a missile gap – we have a *sanity* gap.

So we have to close this remarkably absurd gap, even while keeping ourselves strong and superior in every other part of our military capacity. There are second chances in life and, often, opportunities to overcome lack of preparation, but very few of these are available when an overwhelming and instantaneous attack comes from a relentless foe.

We need to be strong beyond the slightest doubt. President and general Andrew Jackson said,

> There is a rank due to the United States among nations which will be withheld, if not absolutely lost, by the reputation of weakness.... If we desire to secure peace, one of the most powerful instruments of our rising prosperity, it must be known that we are at all times, ready for war.[57]

We want peace. And we want to be immeasurably stronger than any other nation so we can secure that peace forever. The goal? It isn't to have a strong, unbeatable military so we can fight. The goal is to have a strong, unbeatable military so we don't have to.

We also need to recommit to a long American practice – no first blows, but all of the last ones. We should say again,

We Will Never Attack Others First, but If Attacked, We Will Fight to Win and We Will Win

Thomas Jefferson said,

> But I hope our wisdom will grow with our power, and teach us, that the less we use our power, the greater it will be.[58]

In spite of recent events, attacking first is just not the American way.

History tells us that most nations have no problem with starting wars. But we just don't think it's right to attack others first. We are like – or at least want to be like – the heroic western sheriff who never draws his gun before the outlaw does.

For too much of history, too many people have been eager to start or join wars. Their motto is, when you're in doubt, fight; when you want something, fight; when you fear something, fight; when your passions run hot, fight. Almost none have chosen a "no first attack" policy, but America was one of them. We haven't followed this perfectly, but it has always been the American ideal.

Too often, people are willing to go along with the war-starters. Few sights in history are more bizarre, more macabre, than watching people cheer their soldiers into battle and watching soldiers talking excitedly about their part in the violence to come. People went with buggies and parasols to watch the first major battle of the Civil War. People sent the doughboys to Europe in World War I with parades and songs.

We've lost our way on this grand concept of not starting wars, and not just with Iraq. We now have "rapid deployment forces," which can involve us in a war anywhere in the world on short notice. We have too much military presence in too many places to stay out of the violence when it inevitably comes.

Government leaders now have "a vision for remaking the military to be far more engaged in heading off threats prior to hostilities and serve a larger purpose of enhancing U. S. influence around the world."[59] "Heading off threats prior to hostilities" means we strike first. And since there's always tension or conflict somewhere – threats and hostilities – we can be assured that we will never have to miss out on any more wars.

But perhaps the most frightening of all is this notion of American influence equating to military influence. Do we really want to use our military to "serve a larger purpose of enhancing U. S. influence around the world?" Do we want that in their mission statement? Wouldn't this be better done by American culture, innovation, and trade?

America has somehow become the "hired gun" of the world. We're like mercenaries who fight for issues that we don't even understand – but unlike mercenaries in that we don't get paid for our efforts. We're the most desirable of hired guns because we pay our own wages. Our "allies" can build better businesses because we're building their bombs.

Examples of this new attack-first attitude abound. "If we have to use force," noted Secretary of State Madeleine Albright not so long ago, "it is because we are America; we are the indispensable nation. We stand tall. We see further than other countries into the future."[60] But we used to see further in a different way. We used to see the bloodshed, see where war leads, see that no one is indispensable in the midst of violence, and see the brutal lessons of history without having to repeat them. As President John F. Kennedy stated,

> We must face the fact that the United States is neither omnipotent nor omniscient – that we are only 6% of the world's population – that we cannot impose our will upon the other 94% of mankind – that we cannot right every wrong or reverse each adversity – and that therefore there cannot be an American solution to every world problem.[61]

There have always been, and will always be, countless reasons to become involved in other people's wars. There's no limit to the list of international things that need fixing. There will always be another Korea, Vietnam, or Iraq. But America from its founding and even before never accepted these reasons or lists.

But if war can't be avoided, we should fight to *win*. In war, General Douglas MacArthur was right when he said that "there is no substitute for victory."[62] But what is "winning"? What is "victory"?

Winning? In war, winning throughout human history has meant completely destroying the enemy's ability to wage war. Completely. No pockets of resistance. No "areas not under our control." No "trying to pacify the countryside." There are war games, but war is not a game. If America is in a war, it should fight to win – or it should go home.

Victory? Victory has meant being able to dictate to the enemy the terms of peace – reparations, their form of economy and government, what can continue in their culture and traditions and what must go away. This dictating can be magnanimous, as it was by America with Germany and Japan after World War II. Or it can be harsh, as it was by the allies with Germany after World War I. But either way, "to the victor belong the spoils"[63] – Americanized as, "to the victor belong the terms."

But America can't dictate anything if it doesn't annihilate the enemy's military and reduce the enemy to a position of full submission. America has fought every war since World War II with one arm tied behind its back and its heart on the other sleeve. Too often we

- Expose our soldiers to harm in an attempt to not hurt or anger any civilians;

- Hold back and don't hit them with everything we've got;

- Apologize for causing destruction, inescapable in war;

- Let things drag out so they don't seem so bad;

- Demand that our military be goodwill ambassadors;

- Expect warriors to reconstruct societies;

- Fight without a declaration of war and all-in support of the nation;

- Engage without clear goals (Bob Woodward noted in 2010 about the Afghanistan War that "eight years into the war, [the president's advisors] were struggling to refine what the core objectives were."[64]);

- Stop short of victory.

Completely rebuilding another nation from scratch, as America did with Germany and Japan, only works if they have been reduced to "scratch." What if we had left Nazis in complete charge of half of the German cities and used the Gestapo as a "reformed" police force?

But this is now the burden our leaders lay on our soldiers. We ask them to rebuild before the old has been knocked down, to contain rather than eliminate the enemy, to partner with people who are still collaborating with an energetic enemy, to become part of societies that are repugnant to the American Ideas.[65]

We ask warriors to be a combination of the Peace Corps, the Red Cross, and the Girl Scouts.

Let our warriors be warriors. Don't put them in harm's way unless we're serious and intend to win. Don't commit them unless we commit *to* them that we'll let them do what it takes to achieve total victory. Let them go in fast and hard and leave no bad guys standing. Then we can send in the Peace Corps, the Red Cross, and the Girl Scouts.

But the main thing is to avoid conflict. We haven't always stayed out of stupid wars. But we can stay out forever, starting now.

Because

We're Proud of What We Stand For — an America that, at Its Best, Loves, Seeks, and Delivers Peace to Its People

America used to be clear in its desires and intentions. We were friendly with all nations and peoples, but entangled with none. We wanted the best for all people of good will, but no relationship with them that could drag us into conflict. And we wanted no part of warmongers, saber-rattlers, or people who were quick to throw a punch.

The goal of these desires and intentions was to have a place of peace on earth. Americans don't just want peace – they love it. They love not having to worry about having bombs dropped on them and then having to drop bombs in return. They love not having their future drained away by endless conflict. Mostly, they love not having their children, spouses, parents, and grandchildren slaughtered for the next "good cause."

They love what peace does to and for a people. They know that it fosters a positive and generous spirit toward other human beings. It takes the edge off of judgmentalism. It reduces tension and the human tendency toward violence. It creates room for people to live and breathe and grow. It leads to deep and enduring prosperity.

For all these reasons and more, Americans have sought peace. Even when America has gone to war in the last century, the core goal has been to bring about peace, not to conquer and rule. American soldiers haven't fought wars so they could fight more wars. On the contrary, they've fought wars to end war and to bring about a lasting peace.

America has been a society of peace-seekers. Few attributes could be as fine as that. Most people in the world live in fear that war will break out, and they have good reason to fear. Americans have always hoped instead that peace will break out.

And America has, by and large, delivered peace to its people. We've used our natural defenses well, and have added to them powerful man-made defenses. Aside from the

Civil War, Americans have generally been safe on American soil. Americans have had to go elsewhere to die. If we could find a way to keep them home, we have the prospect of peace being delivered into the hands of every American...forever.

Has America been perfect in any of this? Of course not. But the easiest thing in the world to do is to point out where great people or great nations aren't perfect – or even great, or even right. There are no flawless people or nations.

America hasn't been perfect in its love of peace. But it has wanted to be so in the past and can want to be so again. Trying to be peacekeepers while having failed from time to time is infinitely better than not trying to be peacekeepers and failing all of the time.

We have the power and the means to make war. If we really unleashed our military in an all-out, no-holds-barred, conventional war, no nation could stand against us. It is always extremely tempting to use a power that is at your fingertips. In fact, history reminds us that no great nation has ever had an immense military capacity and not used it. Thomas Jefferson said,

> Wars & contentions indeed fill the pages of history with more matter. But more blest is that nation whose silent course of happiness furnishes nothing for history to say. This is what I ambition for my own country.[66]

So it takes a high-quality, self-assured, and self-controlled people to have mighty power and not use it, to have the quiet wisdom to resist the enticements to involvement, to persistently love and seek and deliver peace.

But that's the American way.

At its best, America loves peace. We'd rather spend our time thinking about careers and families and the pursuit of happiness.

We seek peace. We're a very pragmatic and reasonable people, who instinctively see the folly of war and the ways to avoid it.

And we deliver peace. Since the Civil War, we've had a bountiful internal peace, without sacrificing the freedom and rights that so many in other countries are required to pay for their security.

And we can, far into the future, love peace and seek peace and deliver peace to generations yet unborn. We can take specific actions to secure the peace and regain the old mindset of no more wars. We can:

Take Action

Love peace and its promise with a passion.

★

Hate war and its lies with a passion.

★

Honor the military but stop talking about the glory of war.

★

Always remember the devastation of all wars.

★

Make it much harder to start or join a war.

★

Whenever possible, involve all Americans in a decision to make war.

★

Establish strong fences around a declared war to keep it from expanding.

★

Pay for any declared war as we go.

★

Understand that America didn't lose the war in Vietnam.

★

Get out of stupid and ruinous wars...now.

★

Resist any call for a draft or mandatory service.

★

Remember the many limitations, misdirections, and potential dangers of diplomacy.

★

Observe strict neutrality with all warring nations.

★

Lose the terrible notion of "the enemy of my enemy is my friend."

★

Bring all the troops home from everywhere.

★

Stop selling weaponry to other governments.

★

Refuse to allow anyone to get rich through an American war.

★

Remember that the best offense is a good defense.

★

Focus at last on the true defense of American lives against nuclear holocaust.

★

Simplify the concept of "national security," and dismantle much of the national security "industry."

★

If war is absolutely necessary, fight to win and have no more half-way wars.

★

Take stupendously good care of the combat veterans from the moment combat ends.

★

Keep the trade routes open and use them to minimize the chance of warfare.

To see detail on these Action Points and
to add your voice visit www.theamericanideas.com

Few things are as important in the life of a people as having clarity about war. A certain lack of clarity threads its way through American history, through the Civil War, Spanish-American War, First World War, Second World War, Korean War, Vietnam War, three wars in the Middle East, and a host of smaller conflicts. Why are we really doing this? Often, the answers are muddied, sometimes deliberately so.

But lying underneath that history of war – and the government that keeps taking the nation into war – is a people who love peace, who have a hatred of war in their souls, and who want no more of it. Americans are ready at long last to be the quiet superpower.

And it will be quite remarkable because America will be the first one in history.

"War is the unfolding of miscalculations," noted the brilliant American historian Barbara Tuchman.[67] For Americans, war both unfolds miscalculations and is a miscalculation. America has stumbled into – or been manipulated, cajoled, pressured, or pushed into – a great many wars. But none of them have been to our liking or to our benefit. And we can finally and really learn from these calculations. As Secretary of Defense Robert Gates said at West Point in 2011,

> *In my opinion, any future defense secretary who advises the president to again send a big American land army into Asia or into the Middle East or Africa should "have his head examined," as General MacArthur so delicately put it.*[68]

War wasn't the American way. But it is becoming the American way – in spite of the reality that Americans hate war. And love peace.

To be sure, once engaged, this peace-loving people can wreak holy hell on its enemies. But that isn't what Americans want. They want peace. They really like the sound of "life, liberty, and the pursuit of happiness," which is hard to have in the midst of war. Peace is in the cultural DNA of America.

Benjamin Franklin summed it up for America when he observed,

> *There never was a good war, or a bad peace.*[69]

He spoke – he still speaks – for the America he loved.

When it comes to war in America, it should never be "my country right or wrong." It should be "I love my country too much to let it be wrong." We don't like war, and we want a good fight about whether or not we should have a fight. We're a nation of rabble-rousers and dissenters. We want a mighty good reason for a mighty bad war.

Americans are not a nation of sheep. We don't want to be led into any more wars. Instead, we want to be a nation of peace-mongers, led by peacekeepers.

Americans love peace. It's our Idea. From our founding as a country until now, all we've been saying, all we are saying, is give peace a chance.

THE FUTURE

An American Renaissance

The excellent documentarian Ken Burns named a recent film project *The National Parks: America's Best Idea*. Certainly we can agree that America's national parks are an incredible treasure that belongs to us all.

But America's best idea? Better than the American Ideas of Freedom, Diversity, Equality, and Dignity? More valuable than the American Ideas of Opportunity, Responsibility, Generosity, and Religion? More crucial to the life of the nation than the American Ideas of Society, Government, Independence, and Peace?

I don't think so. And I don't think you do, either. His project has a catchy title about a magnificent subject. But if our best idea is a park, we have very little hope for the future.

The Opportunity

American philosopher and essayist Ralph Waldo Emerson reminds us,

We are very near to greatness

One step and we are safe

Can we not take the leap?[1]

No matter how tattered we might feel as a people, we're only one reach, one step, one leap away from renewed greatness.

The truth is, we've gotten somewhat off track. But happily, we can still see the track. It's right there in front of us. We don't have to reinvent the track because the track is already ours.

The 13 American Ideas are that track. They are rich and deep and full of potential. They are no less vibrant than they were 100 or 200 years ago. In fact, with so much more experience – both good and bad – we should be capable of applying these marvelous Ideas even more effectively in the years ahead of us.

To say it differently, for four centuries, Americans have believed and articulated principles that have stood the test of time. We don't need to discard or, for the most part, even change them. But the application of those principles needs some work, for several reasons:

- We're a lot more informed about what works and doesn't work in a democratic republic. The founders were working from a nearly blank board, with little in history to show them the way on implementation. They even knew this, allowing for constitutional amendments and a checked-and-balanced government to prevent any of their concepts from running amok.

- As of this writing, we've had nearly 80 years of government expansion far beyond what the founders imagined in their worst nightmares and far beyond what the plain language of the constitution would allow. The government's tentacles reach into every corner of life. It's time for a serious pruning of something wildly overgrown.

- If we don't change the application fairly soon, the principles themselves will be lost, covered over by years of neglect and abuse. Worse, the principles will be perverted, said to mean what they never meant, used to appeal to some distant memory in the service of some very nearby ugliness.

Wise, pragmatic Americans – what we are, for the most part – can understand this need for change. We can solidify the principles by modifying the application and cutting away the excess. We can honor and admire the work of the founders without worshipping it and treating it like a sacred text that can't be modified.

But we have to understand the Ideas before we can apply them. If you've made it this far, you should have that understanding – some of what you've read reminding you of what you already knew and believed, some of it adding color to what you already knew and believed, some of it reminding you of part of your heritage that might have been mislaid along the way.

Armed with a common understanding, we can have an expansive dialogue about the best way to apply these Ideas. We can have dialogue that is related deeply to the core of who we are as Americans – instead of to what some other culture is or what people in other countries are doing or what nifty experiment some politician has conjured up to make his or her name at our expense.

In light of this, I encourage you to go to our closely integrated website, www.theamericanideas.com, and read about the many ways to apply these Ideas, ways that were only listed as bullet points in each chapter under the heading of "America at Its Best."

And then add your voice to the dialogue. On that site, you'll see how you can send your insights to us. We'll select the best of them – most thoughtful, truest to that American Idea, most likely to support an American renaissance – and post them, with a credit to you, alongside what this American has written there.

Why did we do it this way instead of including all of that detail in this book?

• First, we wanted this book to be a handbook that could truly arm a new generation of American revolutionaries. We didn't want that to be overwhelmed with the many details of application.

• Second, we wanted the applications to keep up with the ever-changing political, economic, cultural, and technological landscape. Bad notions can take on a life of their own, and we want good concepts to demolish them.

• And third, we wanted you to be a partner with us in fleshing out the ways to renewal – building something better, the American way.

Those who see the beauty of these American Ideas may at first be a minority. But that's all right. Henry David Thoreau declared,

> *I hear many condemn these men because they were so few. When were the good and the brave ever in a majority?*[2]

We know from Malcolm Gladwell's fine work in *The Tipping Point* that a majority is hardly ever necessary to effect even monumental change.[3] "It doesn't take a majority to make a rebellion," noted American social critic H. L. Mencken; "it takes only a few determined leaders and a good cause."[4]

We have the good cause. You and I can be those determined leaders.

The Challenge

In the 19th century, French observer of America Alexis de Tocqueville envisioned the challenge we're facing now when he wrote,

> *There is, indeed, a most dangerous passage in the history of a democratic people. When the taste for physical gratifications among them has grown more rapidly than their education and their experience of free institutions, the time will come when men are carried away and lose all self-restraint at the sight of the new possessions they are about to obtain. In their intense and exclusive anxiety to make a fortune they lose sight of the close connection that exists between the private fortune of each and the prosperity of all.*[5]

America is a very prosperous society. We have more than most people have even been able to imagine. But he reminds us that this can put us at a cultural inflection point, where we're more attuned to the prosperity than the Ideas that produced it. He goes on to say,

> *Men who are possessed by the passion for physical gratification generally find out that the turmoil of freedom disturbs their welfare before they discover how freedom itself serves to promote it.*[6]

The biggest challenge we have in achieving an American renaissance is not how much labor it would take to accomplish it. Given an understanding of the Ideas, that is not an overwhelming amount of effort – certainly not much compared with founding cities in a New World, building a new nation against the wishes of the then most powerful nation on earth, or ending slavery and surviving a brutal civil war.

The biggest challenge is our willingness to make the effort that's required. As de Tocqueville pointed out, we've arrived at a dangerous passage, a moment when we have so much that it would be easy to forget how we got it, a time when having and enjoying things is more important than preserving and extending our freedom and our other grand American Ideas.

And he tells us to make no mistake: The Ideas that we could cast aside are the true foundation of our prosperity and well-being. Letting them deteriorate will eventually bring losses across the whole range of life, including that prosperity and well-being. If we don't care for the ground, future harvests will be ever smaller. "Civilizations die from suicide, not by murder," warned famed historian Arnold Toynbee.[7]

We have options. We can use these Ideas as the benchmark for all collective action, the course that will take us to an even better place. Or we can move toward other philosophies, useless or suboptimal or even terrible notions that have been foisted off on people for millennia. Or perhaps worse, we can just try to make it up in a pragmatic way as we go along, ignoring the Ideas as well as the lessons of history.

Winston Churchill, British statesman and son of an American woman, reminded the British of their great treasure – one to which the American Ideas owe much:

> We must recognize that we have a great inheritance in our possession, which represents the prolonged achievement of the centuries; that there is not one of our simple, uncounted rights today for which better men than we have not died on the scaffold or the battlefield. We have not only a great treasure, we have a great cause. Are we taking every measure within our power to defend that cause?[8]

If we want these fruits of freedom, we're going to have to earn them. Just desiring them won't be enough. His own great nation has largely abandoned the cause, wavering between trying already discredited notions on the one hand and making up new approaches to try to fix the results of those discredited notions on the other.

What about our Ideas? What about our fruits of freedom? We're going to have to earn them through personal wisdom and conviction that are effectively translated into a renaissance of the individual, a renewal of the society, and a reformation of government.

The Problem

One noted historian expressed a concern, saying, "A wealthy and complacent populace would allow the construction of 'palaces in which British or American despots…will guide mighty empires to ruin, amidst the acclamation of flatterers.'"[9]

We've gotten far enough away from enough American Ideas that we have the first part of this – ambitious, power-seeking, wealth-collecting political leaders, who are taking advantage of the product of centuries of American growth. And they're driving us all too rapidly to the second part – political, financial, and cultural ruin – while their courtiers hail each of these mini-messiahs as nobility. Alexis de Tocqueville went into more detail:

> *When the bulk of the community are engrossed in private concerns, the smallest parties need not despair of getting the upper hand in public affairs…. They regulate everything by their own whim; they change the laws and tyrannize at will over the manners of the country; and then men wonder to see into how small a number of weak and worthless hands a great people may fall.*[10]

America has long been represented by the eagle. But the eagle's wings have been clipped, and we can't fly like we used to. Few Americans would deny that small parties of extremists lurk around the corridors of power, that regulations and laws are outlandish in almost every respect, or – perhaps most clearly of all – that they've fallen into the hands of a host of weak and worthless people.

We can still walk to our destination, eat what we find, and live where we will. We appear to be free. But our choices have been severely limited, both in scope and in number. Since we're still free to travel, change jobs, buy what we want, and live where we want, we can believe that we're still a free people.

But liberty isn't what we still can do. It's what we could do before but can't do anymore. Sadly, the trend in societies has always been downward. First, the eagle can't fly anymore. Then it's in a cage. Then it's in chains. And then…the gun.

American revolutionary and statesman Patrick Henry warned us,

> *You are not to inquire how your trade may be increased, nor how you are to become a great and powerful people, but how your liberties can be secured; for liberty ought to be the direct end of your government.*[11]

Liberty ought to be our main concern. But government hasn't been concerned with our liberty for a long time or with most of the American Ideas at all. Our political leaders have been concerned with how they can become great and powerful and, too often, with how their "trade may be increased."

There has always been an unrelenting contest between the individual and the state, no less so in recent America. "The natural progress of things," noted Jefferson, "is for liberty to yield and government to gain ground."[12] American critic H. L. Mencken said it even tougher: "All government, of course, is against liberty."[13]

While most of those who love liberty accept the need for a power to limit the destructive potential of imperfect human nature, they never forget a simple truth: another individual can restrict or destroy our liberty in one or more ways, but the government can restrict or destroy our liberty in all ways.

We should be concerned about individuals but terrified of the state. It will take our own possessions from us and use them to further its own ends – always, of course, while calling these ends the "greater good" (as it determines what is "good"). Even high-minded intentions degenerate too soon into high-handed actions.

Liberty is secured rather than ruined by government only when power is allocated to it sparingly – when government is viewed as a possible aid but a miserable savior. Power has to be divided among local, state, and national governments in ever-decreasing amounts as that government gets further away, bigger, less under our potential to control, and harder to revolt against successfully should the need arise.

Far-away, delegated power should be minimal, clearly defined, and unflinchingly restricted. We write constitutions to control governments, not individuals. In the matter of limiting government power, it doesn't matter whether people are basically good or evil – the large government state often isn't needed in the first case and can't be trusted in the second.

Government must be limited, or there is no liberty. Government must be big enough to provide the individual with viable protection, but no bigger. It must be small enough to allow the individual maximum opportunity and latitude, but no smaller than needed to protect others from him or her.

And government must be decentralized – reduced to the smallest level possible and made closest to the individual. As government becomes larger and more removed, two things happen. First, the individual loses more and more control over its activities, thus becoming apathetic and cynical – this, and not difficulties in voter registration, is the reason for declining voter turnout. Second, government becomes less and less knowledgeable and interested in its real and needed role in the individual's life.

Personal involvement and responsibility are what allows the American Ideas to become a real and pleasant reality.

People are immortal, but their governments are finite. It doesn't appear that way, with the United States still here and all its founders dead. But the government, without spirit or mind or heart or soul, is less than any individual. Individuals are armed with immortality, while government is often only armed with a gun.

Government will try to trick us out of our liberty. "The people never give up their liberties but under some delusion," noted British statesman Edmund Burke.[14] And governments can be very good at it. How could it be otherwise? If governments are formed because individuals and groups will try to interfere with and control other people's lives, how can a government made up of the same individuals keep from perpetrating the same offenses?

Think of the number of ways that 535 congresspeople and their army of helpers can conjure to deceive us. We call them "lawmakers," as though this is automatically a good thing. But all too often, a piece of the American Ideas dies with each new law.

Government and politicians will try to lead us on their path by confusing freedom to with freedom from. "Look at all you're free to do," we're told. But at its root, liberty includes freedom from – from bondage, from captivity, from external control, from interference, from robbery, from destruction.

The Bill of Rights gets very specific: We're free from such things as unreasonable search and seizure, made-up indictments, double jeopardy, self-incrimination, drawn-out or secret trials, uncertainty about accusations, secret witnesses, and excessive bail or fines or punishment. The "freedom from" guaranteed by our constitution allows everyone who isn't a criminal to exercise their "freedom to" in the way that best advances their own interests.

But the "freedom from" concept, by necessity, has to include freedom from artificial support as well. Each person in a free society needs to understand that there are no cripplers and there are no crutches. You're free from all bondage, whether it's oppressive or supportive, despotic or paternalistic.

This can be frightening, this concept of not being controlled or directed or placed in an "order" by an all-wise authority. But a right-thinking society can't allow this fear to drive its government into what ours, unfortunately, is becoming. Franklin Roosevelt said, "There is nothing to fear but fear itself,"[15] but he missed it by some distance: Worse than fearing fear is having to fear the consoling government that promises to alleviate our fears.

It's a paradox that people who seek order through rigid control by government never find it (at least in lasting form), while an individual who freely seeks the best way to spend a unique life in the chaos of liberty can find order – and peace – for himself or herself.

We should also be free from the pollution of our public square. We don't have to talk about controlling what people do in private, as long as the rights of other people aren't being violated.

But the public square is common ground. People with perversions say they only want to be left alone. But then they go on crusades to get everyone else to accept their perversities. And then the government uses its power to support, defend, and protect their right to pollute. The same government that won't allow the actual rivers to be polluted allows the rivers of social discourse to be polluted beyond recognition.

What is this? A government gone wild. What is permitted and supported isn't true freedom – it's the wild binge of immature and unruly children (us), supported by a deranged adult with a gun (government).

Because we want to be free from interference or control by others, we can be willing to give up a small portion of our liberty to a governing body so that the balance of our liberty might be preserved. But if we're thinking clearly, we also recognize the dangerous drivers that can turn governors who preserve individual liberty into rulers who demolish it. This should lead us to mold a government with a minimum number of laws, strictly construed and justly administered, with the impact of individuals in government reduced to the minimum regardless of their supposed goodness and virtue.

The true sports fan doesn't want the umpire or referee to decide the game. The true lover of the American Ideas doesn't want the government to decide the game.

And it isn't possible to pursue happiness or maintain control of material possessions if our liberty becomes restricted by oppressive forces. In fact, a frequent assault on liberty is often made in the form of an attack against economic freedoms. We allow our property to be taxed away, taken away, devalued, and controlled, and we forget the unbreakable bond that exists between economic and political freedom. Once the "block" of economic freedom has been chipped away, the "block" of liberty lays exposed, vulnerable to assault.

It's so much the worse because people can voluntarily give up their rights to liberty and the pursuit of happiness to gain their dream of continual, secure, trouble-free prosperity – which in their selfish and ignorant definition becomes their pursuit of happiness.

The American Ideas are better – much better – than this.

Answers That Aren't Answers

A well-respected writer recently noted,

> We are the Arguing Country, born in, and born to, debate. The habit of doing so...makes us unique and gives us our freedom, creativity, and strength.... The United States stands out in sharp relief for one reason. We are an endless argument. [16]

While correctly observing an American trait – the willingness to vigorously disagree with anyone on any issue – he misses several fundamental points. First, arguing and debate are just as likely to lead to slavery, rigidity, and weakness. Second, it's only safe to argue and debate if we agree on core Ideas – otherwise every argument can become a basis for disintegration and a sense of betrayal.

But he misses an even more fundamental point: America stands out not because of the omnipresence of its disagreements but because of the quality of its Ideas.

He admits as much when he later writes, "If our disputes don't produce results, one reason is because we have lost a shared sense of – and pride in – ourselves as Americans."[17] That sense and pride can only come from the majesty of our Ideas. Arguments about application are welcome, but they are only productive if those who engage in the argument share the same common Ideas.

True leaders understand this. They don't ask, "Should we have this mammoth version of big government, or should we have this smaller version of big government?" Instead, they ask, "Given the American Idea of Government, how much of this government is allowable? Or tolerable?"

Renowned historian James MacGregor Burns observed, "Leadership emerges from the conflict over core principles."[18] There's much truth in this. But the quality of that leadership, and whether or not people and posterity bless it or curse it, emerges from which core principles are chosen as table stakes.

As a people, we've somehow ended up in "tinker" mode. We've got this big mess, and we have hundreds of politicians and special interests offering their tinkering. They start with the current situation as a given and then push or pull, add or subtract, twist or straighten – tinkering with something so huge that almost anyone who deals with it should admit the obvious truth, that they don't even understand it in the first place.

This is situational ethics: "Here we are; now what do we do?" The essential problem is that it's easier to see the situation than it is to see the ethics. If the principle is absent before the situation is encountered, it's foolish to believe that it will magically materialize along with the situation. If we don't take a stand against lying before we encounter a situation where lying will benefit us, the push to lie may be irresistible.

German Chancellor Otto Von Bismarck once said, "God has a special providence for fools, drunks, and the United States of America."[19] We can appreciate the sentiment and sense the truth of it. But we don't want to keep going the wrong way and hope that God will bail us out.

The alternative? To take a step or two back from our present situation so that we can rediscover the American Ideas. We need to reestablish them for the American centuries to come. We don't need to limit our future choices and directions by current events and problems. In fact, we shouldn't do this.

It's much better to visualize the kinds of Ideas we'd like to have, the kind of individual dignity we would like to see, the kind of society in which we would like to live, and the kind of government with which we can stand to live. And we can do it. As President Bill Clinton said,

> There is nothing wrong with America that cannot be cured by what is right with America.[20]

An American Renaissance

President Ronald Reagan said,

> It is the American sound. It is hopeful, big-hearted, idealistic, daring, decent, and fair. That's our heritage; that is our song.[21]

We have, and can continue to have, the freest and most prosperous nation ever – if we cling to the Ideas that made us so. We are at an inflection point, a point in time and space where we can solidify the American Ideas – or look the other way and let them fade away to nothingness.

We have to take action. Politicians won't do it. Government can't do it and is often the problem rather than the solution. If we think that there's any value in the American Ideas, we can't let them die while we simply agree on the reasons for their passing. Founder James Madison wrote about our representatitve republic that

> To secure all the advantages of such a system, every good citizen will be at once a sentinel over the rights of the people [and] over the authorities of the confederal government.[22]

We need to be a people – in all our omni-cultural glory – who are different in kind. We're not going to allow ourselves to take the gift of these majestic American Ideas and squander it. We're going to earn it again for ourselves. We need to be new Americans, willing to commit ourselves to this splendid cause for the ages. We were born originals and should live that way. "The people I want to hear about," noted

American poet Robert Frost, "are the people who take risks."[23] It's time to take some American risks.

Our rich, sumptuous, multi-course, four-centuries-long dinner of freedom has made us heavy-lidded and complacent. "Slavery is ever preceded by sleep," warned French political and legal theorist Baron de Montesquieu.[24] It's time to wake up. Imposed restrictions are already inside the door. Cultural pollution is flowing in torrents. And slavery is knocking.

The American Ideas are precious commodities, but they are highly vulnerable to both direct assault and to slow, sinister annihilation. There are things we can do to assure their continued existence, to revitalize them, and to give them the impact that they deserve and that we so dearly need. We can start by

1) Thinking for ourselves. We can think incisively and without illusions. Do we want a culture designed by power politics, greed, and ambition? Or do we want a culture designed by Ideas that have differentiated America from the beginning, Ideas that have made America great? Indifference fosters cultural death, silence fosters increasing degradation, and following the powers-that-be fosters…nothing.

2) Rejecting arguments made from self-interest. Of course there will be people in office who argue against term limits and campaign finance reform, judges who argue for lifetime terms and having the final word, presidents (commanders-in-chief) who argue for the right to start wars. The only way to avoid this would be to find something other than people to vote for and appoint. But we don't have to accept their arguments. If they want to earn glory for themselves, let them do it with their own money and time and blood, not with our lives and liberty and property.

3) Rejecting solutions du jour. Political parties have platforms. Politicians have visions for our future and legislative agendas. They all have pet projects they want us to accept and fund, goals they want to achieve with what we've earned, notions about what's best for us, the – too often, in their minds – ignorant and unwashed masses. Let's closely compare whatever they propose with the American ideas. There are only 13 of them. Surely someone who wants to govern us can understand the measuring stick we intend to use.

4) Rejecting the notion that "bigger is better." There are two opposing trends today. One is about decentralization. It supports individual freedom and initiative – the internet, electronic media, digital printing, mobile phones, a global marketplace. The other is about centralization. It crushes individual freedom and initiative – bigger government, higher up and further away; bigger foreign entanglements, dictating our direction and wasting our blood and treasure; bigger business, colossal in size and insatiable; bigger school systems, ever more remote from their true masters, the parents. How can individuality thrive in a world of such titans? Cut them down to size. Bigger isn't usually better. It's just…bigger.

5) Rejecting false equations. There are those who want us to believe incorrect notions like:

• Freedom = license and perversion

- Diversity = natural division and warfare of racial, ethnic, and gender groups
- Justice = favoritism and elevating the rights of some over others
- Equality = sameness
- Dignity = the ability to discard the "unwanted" and "useless"
- Opportunity = guaranteed outcome
- Business = big business, and labor = unions
- Responsibility = government intervention and scapegoating others while requiring those others to pay for our "rights"
- Generosity = redistribution
- Religion = loss of public voice because of "separation of church and state"
- Society = interest groups, and unity = no dissent
- Nation = government, and taxing = direction and control
- Society and the people = government
- Independence = isolation
- Peace = taking the war to them on the one hand or disarmament on the other

People will take good words and turn them to bad ends. Being aware is the first step to defeating them.

6) Abandon cheap commentary by labels and replace it with deep analysis by the American Ideas. Right-wing, left-wing, center-left, center-right, moderate, extremist – these identify others. They are useful to political pundits but to no one else, letting us do political cursing but not political thinking. Conservative and liberal aren't much better, with meanings changing over time. Even Democrat and Republic mean different things at different times and in different places at the same time. And who is the real "progressive"? We will do much better if we analyze everyone and everything by their relationship with – or distance from – the American Ideas.

7) Comparing all proposals and programs to the American Ideas. We have to have a baseline, something against which we can measure this continuous flow of spontaneous and expanding rule-making and society-breaking. We have to have a way to throw the opposing notions overboard and to reform the notions that can perhaps be fixed and aligned with something durable. What is that way? The American Ideas.

8) Proposing and supporting strong change when it's called for. In this book, we've suggested a number of major changes, some of which would require modifications to our Constitution and laws. We shouldn't shrink from that concept. Washington said, "The basis of our political systems is the right of the people to make and alter the constitutions of government."[25] Lincoln said, "Whenever [the people] shall grow weary of the existing Government, they can exercise their constitutional right of amending it, or their revolutionary right to dismember or overthrow it."[26] We shouldn't worry about negating the founders' work – they were the ones who included the right to amend it.

9) Building on hope rather than fear. Americans are a positive, optimistic people. But we've been battered for decades by fear-mongers of the left and right. What they tell us to fear differs, but fear-peddling is their common theme. In their world, hope means believing in them, and fear means believ-

ing in their opposition. Americans know that no one operates nearly as well under fear as they do under hope. If we've got a mess – even if we helped to make the mess – we can fix it. And as a matter of fact, we will fix it.

10) Believing that America can be the world's greatest exception. President Ulysses Grant said, "It is my firm conviction that the civilized world is tending toward republicanism, or government by the people through their chosen representatives, and that our own great Republic is destined to be the guiding star to all others."[27]

Maybe someone else will do this for us. But we can't wait for someone else. In one sense, there is no one else. If we won't do it, who will do it before the Ideas fade to black? But in another sense, even if we can't get it all done, the American story is that there will be others behind us, people who can once again see the Ideas shining after we have lovingly uncovered them.

In the World War II movie *To Have and Have Not,* based on a novel by Ernest Hemingway, one patriot sums up the problem faced by the enemies of human life and freedom: "That's what the Germans always forget: There will always be someone else."[28]

The good news is that we really are in control of our own destiny. The truth is that an American Renaissance begins with an individual renaissance. We can experience the titanic import of Emerson's thought: "The essence of greatness is the perception that virtue is enough."[29] And we can do something. As statesman Edmund Burke said,

> *Nobody makes a greater mistake than he who did nothing because he could do only a little.*[30]

We don't want to be content with the rights that we still have. We don't want to be satisfied because we still have more freedom than people in other countries. We don't want to muddle through or accept the bad with the good. We want the whole American buffet, prepared for us by thousands of Americans over centuries. And we want the food served hot.

President Calvin Coolidge was right when he said that "we have been, and propose to be, more and more American."[31] But he missed it when he said, "The business of America is business."[32] It isn't. Why not?

Because the business of America is – or at least ought to be – the American Ideas.

Building Anew on the American Ideas

The German philosopher Goethe exhorted us:

> *What you have inherited from your father, earn over again for yourselves, or it will not be yours.*[33]

Americans have a fabulous inheritance. It's so fabulous that we can take the path too often taken by people who inherit great wealth – we can party, spend away, and squander it all. Or we can take it as a wondrous gift to be enjoyed and work with all our might to preserve it and grow it for our own American descendants.

British philosopher Samuel Johnson noted, "The future is purchased by the present."[34] Now is the time. Waiting, negotiating with milquetoast leaders of all political persuasions, hoping that good consequences will grow out of bad ideas – none of this will buy a grand, or even decent, future.

We've inherited an amazing set of Ideas. They are the real treasure – not the national parks or the big economy. But they are being eroded by time and power and ambition, and – sadly – by us forgetting, by us not staying vigilant. These Ideas are our inheritance, and they're pure gold.

What are these incredible American Ideas that we have been relishing together?

Freedom for all as an unalienable human right. Acceptance and celebration of diversity. Legal, social, and economic justice as the norm. Equality of value based on shared humanity. Respect for the dignity of the individual, first and always.

Unlimited opportunity for success and happiness. Unflinching responsibility for yourself and your family and for others sharing your journey. Uncoerced and unsurpassed generosity. God as the foundation of rights, and religion and faith as the foundation of decency.

Civil society that brings out the best in human beings. Limited government that serves rather than rules. Independence from the lunacies of foreign affairs and entanglements. And peace stretching out far into the future and enjoyed by countless generations.

If we lose these Ideas, the many things that can divide us as human beings will be greater and more powerful than whatever is left to unite us.

We need a new revolution, peaceful but irresistible. It needs to begin as a revolution inside each of us, in what we think and feel, in what we know and believe. President John Adams, speaking about the American Revolution, said,

> The Revolution was effected before the war commenced. The Revolution was in the minds and hearts of the people.[35]

Not everyone will be glad about our efforts to restore the American Ideas. President Theodore Roosevelt said about a group that had accomplished great work against corrupt, powerful forces:

> I warned them not to expect any credit, or any satisfaction, except their own knowledge that they had done well a first-class job, for that probably the only attention Congress would ever pay to them would be to investigate them.[36]

Which is in fact what happened. We can't do this for the glory. We have to do it for ourselves and for our posterity and for the future of the American Ideas. President John Kennedy told a story about a French officer "who walked one morning through his garden with his gardener. He stopped at a certain point and asked the gardener to plant a tree there the next morning. The gardner said 'But the tree will not bloom for 100 years.' The marshal replied 'In that case, you had better plant it this afternoon.'"[37]

Today there's a lot of talk about "change." Americans, always progressive and forward-looking, can usually be seduced into going for change. But they're also wise and practical and want it to be change for the better – and, for them, that always means that the change will line up with the American Ideas.

If it doesn't line up, they know that it is just experimentation. They know that it's likely to lead to the very evils the Ideas were established to obliterate. Americans always want to soar, but they want a tether that connects them to four centuries of truly first-rate Ideas.

Even as life changes at an accelerating pace, can we identify and hold onto any enduring truths, truths that have been handed down to us? Can we hold onto Ideas that we shouldn't lose, give up, or allow to be taken away?

Yes. And only when we know who we are and what we believe are we able to have an intelligent and productive dialogue on how to make change that is both effective and principled.

And then we can and will make that change. Americans are pragmatic people capable of making principled change. Historian David McCullough said about us,

> *We will find out what's not working right and we will fix it, and then maybe it will work right. That's been our star, that's what we've guided on.*[38]

People may attribute progress to movements like the civil rights movement. But we can attribute all of those good movements to the American Ideas. Those movements were in opposition to perversions and opposites of the American Ideas, not to the Ideas themselves. And the best of those movements extended the power of the Ideas.

Americans – either citizens or "Americans in spirit" – have been given an extraordinary heritage. It grew out of a quest to find El Dorado, the city of gold, the America that breaks with the brutal message of history, a way of life based on Ideas rather than on power and coercion and manipulation.

Many along the way identified this better way. They crafted a philosophy and then a nation based on these Ideas. Together we can see what they knew, things that we may not have known or that we may have forgotten.

As an American, both in citizenship and in spirit, I love these Ideas. I am an American-American – American by heritage, American by birth, and American by choice. I was born in America, but I have become an enthusiastic immigrant to the American Dream – not money or houses or cars or boats, but 13 glorious Ideas.

I remember looking at pictures of the Statue of Liberty seen through smoke and ashes on September 11, 2001, when the American Ideas were under attack and in confusion. The duality of this amazing Lady, so forceful yet so inviting, made a statement so strong that only lunatics deafened by their own screaming could miss it.

America is like that Lady.

America is a defiant Statue of Liberty who throws her flame into the dark and smoldering sky and strides boldly forward to challenge the enemies of freedom. And America is a welcoming Statue of Liberty, who lights the way to safe harbor for the tired and poor and huddled masses yearning to breathe free, and who softly whispers "Peace." America is, indeed, a magnificent paradox.

God bless America.